RUSSIA IN PACIFIC WATERS

University of British Columbia Press Pacific Maritime Studies

Russia in Pacific Waters is the first in a continuing series dealing with naval history and related maritime subjects published by the University of British Columbia Press.

This series has been established as a result in part of the success of the following University of British Columbia Press books:

The Wind Commands: Sailors and Sailing Ships in the Pacific, by Harry Morton

The Royal Navy and the Northwest Coast of North America, 1810-1914, by Barry M. Gough

Ocean of Destiny: A Concise History of the North Pacific, 1500-1978, by J. Arthur Lower

Other volumes in this series are:

2. *Distant Dominion: Britain and the Northwest Coast of North America, 1579-1809*, by Barrry M. Gough

RUSSIA IN PACIFIC WATERS,
1715-1825

*A Survey of the Origins of Russia's Naval Presence
in the North and South Pacific*

Glynn Barratt

UNIVERSITY OF BRITISH COLUMBIA PRESS
VANCOUVER AND LONDON

RUSSIA IN PACIFIC WATERS, 1715-1825

*A Survey of the Origins of Russia's Naval Presence
in the North and South Pacific*

This book has been published with the assistance of a grant from the
Social Science Federation of Canada, using funds provided by the
Social Sciences and Humanities Research Council of Canada.

Canadian Cataloguing in Publication Data

Barratt, G. R. V., 1944
  Russia in Pacific waters, 1715-1825

(Pacific maritime studies; 1)
Bibliography: p.
Includes index.
ISBN 0-7748-0117-4

1. Russians in the North Pacific Ocean. 2. Russia—Exploring expeditions.
3. Northwest coast of North America—Discovery and exploration. 4. Rus-
sia—History. Naval.
 I. Title
II. Series.
F851.5.B37   979'.01   C80-091228-4

International Standard Book Number 0-7748-0117-4
Printed in Canada

For Nana B. and K. the W.

Contents

Photographic Credits

Plate 1 was contributed by the Provincial Archives of British Columbia, and Plates 6, 11, 15, and 22(inset) were provided by the Special Collections Division of the Library of the University of British Columbia. Plates 16, 17, 18, and 19 appear courtesy of the State Russian Museum, Moscow (R. 29277, R. 29047, R. 29136, and R. 29137), and Plate 22 appears with the permission of the Scott Polar Research Institute (P75/15/5). Richard A. Pierce and S. V. Glad kindly provided Plates 7 and 14. Plate 20 is courtesy of the Auckland Institute and Museum, and Plate 21 is from the State Archive of Hawaii. The *Alaska Journal* provided prints for Plates 8 and 13, and we are indebted to the Alaska Historical Society for Plates 3 and 4. Plates 12 and 21(inset) are reproduced from N. N. Baranskii et al., *Otechestvennye fiziko-geografy i puteshestvenniki* (Moscow, 1959).

Illustrations

Preface and Acknowledgements

This book concerns the earliest Russian naval ventures, as opposed to either mercantile or other service/cossack enterprise, in the remote North-East of Asia and beyond, in the Aleutian and the Kurile Island chains, and in America. It is a subject with insistent international implications. Vitus Bering, after all, was born in Denmark, Joseph Billings was an Englishman, the leaders of a half a dozen other expeditions to the far North-East of Asia and beyond had served abroad. On his final expedition Cook met Russian hunter-mariners on Unalaska Island off Alaska and alarmed the Russian court, while Spain insisted on regarding the Pacific as a Spanish *mare clausum.* Every step taken by Russia in the North Pacific region, in the later eighteenth century at least, produced an echo to be heard in foreign courts. It seemed appropriate, therefore, to treat the subject—which of course also has national and peculiarly Russian or "internal" aspects—in an international context and not only as a much-neglected chapter in the history of Russia's naval growth around the world. I have avoided detailed discussion of sub-Arctic exploration, of the early Russo-Japanese encounters, and, above all, of the "Coast-to-Canton" fur trade and the economic questions that relate to it, for all these topics have recently been dealt with in the West. By not attempting to repeat the work of others, I have hoped to find the breathing-space to emphasize what others have ignored: inherent tension between mercantile and naval interests within Kamchatka and in Russia's North Pacific outposts and the early signs of international rivalry and friction in the North Pacific area at large.

The choice of timespan needs a word of explanation. 1715 marked the beginning of a Russian naval presence at Okhotsk. That year, a naval party built an open boat, *Okhota,* for the purpose of "discovering the sea-route" to Kamchatka. The voyage from Okhotsk to the Tigil River mouth was duly made, and an important precedent thereby established. Several years before the launching of the first of Captain Bering's expeditions to those areas in 1726, the Navy was assisting with the hunting-trading venture in the far North-East and East. The economic thus preceded other motives for a modest naval presence on the far side of Eurasia. 1824-25 marked the collapse of hopes for Russian naval hegemony in the North Pacific Ocean and in Russian North America especially. As such, it marked the end of an expansionist and enterprising era for the Navy in the North Pacific colonies and the beginning of another, longer era of decline.

It is a striking fact that not one writer, either Soviet or Western, has deliberately focused on the rise and fall of Russian naval influence about the Coast and

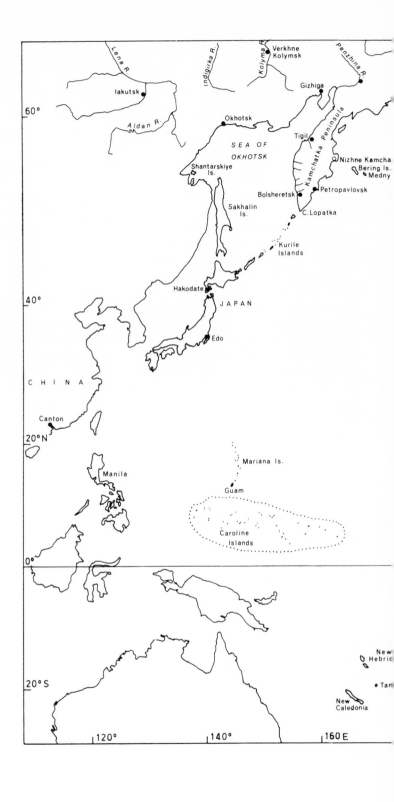

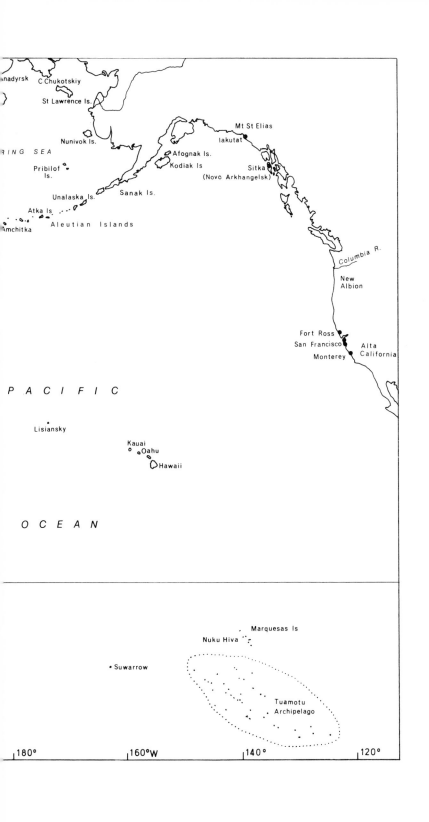

anadyrsk C.Chukotskiy

St Lawrence Is.

Nunivok Is.

RING SEA

Pribilof Is.

Unalaska Is.

Atka Is

Amchitka Aleutian Islands

Sanak Is.

Afognak Is.

Kodiak Is

Mt St Elias

Iakutat

Sitka (Novo Arkhangelsk)

Columbia R.

New Albion

Fort Ross

San Francisco

Monterey

Alta California

P A C I F I C

Lisiansky

Kauai

Oahu

Hawaii

O C E A N

Marquesas Is

Nuku Hiva

Suwarrow

Tuamotu Archipelago

180°   160°W   140°   120°

in the North Pacific Ocean in the early nineteenth century. It is a subject, on the other hand, that numerous historians have touched on incidentally, while concentrating on some facet of the drive eastward to empire. There are historians of the Pacific seaborne fur trade (Berkh and Khlebnikov, Polonskii, Okun' and Makarova, Golder and Gibson); of particular localities in which the Russians made their presence felt by 1825 (the North-west Coast, the Kurile Islands, the Hawaiian Islands, Upper California); of specific expeditions; and of early Russo-Japanese relations (Fainberg, Novakovskii, Lensen). Is it possibly because the maritime and naval are not readily discernible and promptly disentangled from the mercantile, political, and scientific threads that form the canvas of the Russian enterprise in the Pacific that they have never been examined? It is certainly impossible to *isolate* the naval thread from others that surround it and to study it to any good advantage; for to do so is to lose proper perspective. Yet the fact is not a reason for declining to examine what *was* naval in the early Russian ventures in the far North-East and East, in the Aleutians, and beyond.

My work in certain Soviet and British archives has, I hope, complemented an examination of the published literature on naval and Pacific history in languages that are accessible to me. I have attempted to reduce the inconvenience resulting from my ignorance of Japanese by placing confidence in Lensen and his sources. I may add that, in the case of certain main Soviet archives, it has always been my custom to seek access to such manuscript materials as have been published or, at least, described by Soviet historians. Because most documents are kept with other papers, in a single *delo* (file), it is a policy that has enabled me, at times, to wander slightly from the "academic tour." One need hardly add that matters, and in consequence procedures, are quite different in Tallin and in Riga. The decision to approach the work through Soviet, American, and British and not French or Spanish archives, was a simple one. Professor W. L. Cook is but the latest of a series of American researchers who, since C. E. Chapman's day, have published works, solidly grounded in original materials, that deal with Russo-Spanish counterfeint and friction on the North Pacific coast. The French involvement in events that I describe was marginal, and I rely on published narratives of voyages. I hope that the material employed will throw some light on the variety, as well as on the naval and political ramifications, of those international maritime connections for which Soviet historians have all too little time.

I am grateful to the staffs of many libraries and archives for assistance, and to many individuals for their constructive criticisms of the first draft of this survey. The archives and manuscript repositories include the Central State Archives of Ancient Acts and of the Navy of the USSR (TsGADA and TsGAVMF), each with their dependent library; the Central State Historical Archive in Leningrad (TsGIAL); the Archive of the Foreign Policy of Russia (AVPR); the Archive of the Geographical Society of the USSR (AGO); the Estonian State Museum of History, in Tallin; the Central State Historical Archive of the Estonian SSR, in

Tartu; the Lenin Library, Moscow and the Saltykov-Shchedrin Public Library, Leningrad; the Public Record Office, London; the British Library; the Public Archives of Canada and the Hudson's Bay Company Archives (microfilm), Ottawa; the Bancroft Library, Berkeley, California; and the Mitchell Library and Archives Authority of New South Wales, Sydney, Australia. I also acknowledge assistance, in the forms of microfilm, photocopies, or expert advice, from the State Naval Museum of Sweden, the National Maritime Museum, Greenwich, and the Alaska Historical Museum in Juneau. Individuals to whom I am indebted for help of one sort or another include, Captain Solov'ev, of TsGAVMF; the late S. B. Okun', of Leningrad State University; Dr. Y. Kakh, Director of the Historical Institute of the Estonian Academy of Sciences; Irina Grigor'eva, of the International Exchange Section of the Saltykov-Shchedrin Public Library; Eve Peets of the Estonian State Museum of History, Tallin; Mrs. Ann Shirley of the National Maritime Museum, Greenwich; Dr. Terence Armstrong, of the Scott Polar Institute, Cambridge; Dr. Anders Sandstrom and Dr. Bertil Broome, of Stockholm; Professor R. A. Pierce, of Queen's University, Kingston, Ontario; Mrs. M. McRae, of the Archives Office of Tasmania, Hobart; Mr. D. J. Cross and H. V. Evans, both of Sydney, Australia.

Finally, I am grateful to the Social Sciences and Humanities Research Council of Canada, for research grants, Carleton University for exchange grants and study leave, and Eesti NSV Riikliik Ajaloomuuseum, Tallin, and my friends in Leningrad, for help and hospitality above and beyond the call of academic duty.

Preliminary Notes

A modified form of the Library of Congress system for transliterating the Russian alphabet has been used in this survey. Thus: Andrei, Fedor, Iakutsk, Mulovskii. However, recognized anglicized forms are employed for certain proper names, e.g., Alexander, cossack, Moscow. Rouble values are expressed as silver units. Unless in an American or British colonial document, dates may be taken as given in the Russian, that is, Julian, calendar. To convert to New Style, add twelve days to eighteenth-century dates, thirteen to later ones. The following terms may not be familiar to all readers:

Baidarka	Aleut craft of skins stretched over a frame.
Iasak	Tax paid in furs by native peoples.
Kazachestvo	The cossacks, cossack authority.
Ostrog	Fort or blockhouse.
Prikazchik	Administrator of a fort, village, or district.
Promyshlennik	Private hunter-trader in Siberia and beyond.
Versta	Unit of length: 3,500 ft.
Voevoda	General, or military governor.

For the sake of convenience and brevity, I regard both the Bering Sea and the Sea of Okhotsk with its gulfs (Penzhinsk and Gizhiginsk) as portions of the North Pacific Ocean and not merely as extensions. By "the far North-East and East," I mean the countries of Chukotka, Kamchatka, and Okhotsk, each with their hinterland as well as with their littorals and coastal waters, and the islands to the east of Petropavlovsk to 180°.

But the very ice, which seems so awesome and so terrible,
Will offer *us* a path free of those fierce dangers . . .
Our dominion shall stretch into America.

Lomonosov, "Petr Velikii," Canto I, ll. 169-73.

And under the white foam of the waves,
The Golden Sea-otter,
Suddenly, like the glint of a sword,
Flashed above the breakers of the sea.

The Ainu Epic (Wakarpa-Kindaichi text),
Canto II, ll. 113-17.

One must not provoke the Japanese, a populous, intelligent, patient and imitative people. For if ever there ruled over that people a monarch like our own Peter the Great, it would not be many years before Japan was lording it over the whole Pacific Ocean.

V. M. Golovnin (1816)

1

The Sea-Route to Kamchatka and the Strait of Anian

At intervals throughout his life, Tsar Peter I showed active interest both in the China trade and in the "Strait of Anian," which was supposed by most geographers to separate the continents of Asia and America. The interests were linked, for Peter recognized that the discovery by Russians of a navigable sea-route to the Orient around Siberia and through the Strait of Anian would give them great trading advantages over the Western European states in China and, conceivably, Japan.[1] The modest volume of all Russo-Chinese trade and the impediments placed in the path of Russian merchants by the Chinese government[2] further suggested the importance and potential of a sea-route to the Orient. The charting and exploiting of the Strait of Anian would also, Peter recognized, have major scientific and Imperial significance.[3] It would, moreover, be a mission for the youthful Russian Navy, being maritime in essence.[4] Many times during his life, Peter was urged to send a major expedition to the region where the strait might be expected to be found, if it existed. Of the projects and petitions handed to him on the subject, some were scientific and/or geographical by nature. Others were commercial. Most were both in some degree. Explicitly or otherwise, all recognized the fundamental maritime and naval element, if not the basic international implications, of such an expedition. Peter's interest in "all things that relate to seafaring"[5] being far greater than his interests in China and the problem of the Strait of Anian itself, he merely brought about the probable when, in the last weeks of his life, he signed the orders that sent Bering to the far North-East of Asia. By then, however, military setbacks in Kamchatka and the consequent importance of developing a sea-route to Kamchatka from the south (Okhotsk), had led to the arrival in the East in 1714-17 of other servants of the Navy who were truly pioneers.

FOREIGN ENCOURAGEMENT: WITSEN AND LEIBNITZ

Nicolaes Witsen (1641-1717), a scientist, historian, and mayor of Amsterdam, had had connections with the Russians for some forty years when the young tsar called on him in August 1697, in the course of his Grand Embassy abroad.[6] His study, *Noord en oost Tartarye . . .,* of 1692 was an authoritative work, based upon Dutch and Russian primary material, on the remote North-East of Asia and Japan. Among its several allusions to the Strait of Anian was one connected with the death of sixty cossacks led by Tolstoukhov, an aristocrat's son, on their way via the Lena River from Iakutsk into the Eastern, that is, North Pacific Ocean.[7] News of the disaster had been sent to Amsterdam by Andrei Vinius of the Sibirskii Prikaz. Peter was acquainted with the work and had indeed made use of Witsen as his main Amsterdam agent for the purchasing of vessels and for other naval business in the 1690's.[8] Reaching Amsterdam in 1697, he greeted Witsen as a friend.[9]

In the course of their discussions, the subject of the Orient and of the Strait of Anian arose. Witsen himself had made a study of the 1643-45 maritime expedition of his countryman, Maerten Gerritszoon Vries, and had more recently incorporated Vries's cartographic data in a new map of Japan.[10] At the time of Peter's visit, he was working on a new draft of his 1687 map of the remote North-East of Asia.[11] The latter could be forwarded to Russia when completed; the former Witsen offered to his guest with the remark that Russian seamen might in due course find it useful.[12]

On another day during the Russian embassy's sojourn in Amsterdam, Witsen joined a group of Dutch savants in asking Peter more explicitly if he would not attempt to solve the ancient problem of the passage between Asia and America. Russia was more favourably placed than any European power to attempt it and could further solve the problem of the region north of Yezo (now, Hokkaido): such maps as could be had were contradictory, showing a jumble of perhaps fictional islands: "Gama Land," "Company Land," "Terra Esonis," "El Dorado." Russian mariners would gain great honour by discovering a navigable passage over Asia to the Orient, as Barents, Pet, and Borough had in other times all failed to do. Peter promised that the savants' hopes and wishes would, in due course, be fulfilled.[13] Orders went at once to Andrei Vinius in Moscow to investigate the possibility of sending a small cossack expedition from Iakutsk to find the strait, which was presumably beyond the River Anadyr'.[14]

Peter's presence in the northern German states, Holland, and England in itself provoked increased awareness, on the parts of learned men, both of the problem of the Strait of Anian and of their limited familiarity with the geography even of "Tartary." Gottfried Wilhelm von Leibnitz had been hoping for an audience with Peter when he arrived in Koppenbrugge on 27 July 1697 to be entertained by the Electress of Brandenburg. Disappointed, Leibnitz wrote to Huyssen and

Witsen, J.-C. Urbich, J.-G. Sparfvenfeld, and other European scientists about the destiny of Russia in the East.[15] Meanwhile, he formed a project that the tsar alone could implement.

No record has survived of the first meeting of Peter and Leibnitz, in 1711. It is evident, however, that Leibnitz spoke both of the need for a large programme of magnetic observations to be undertaken from the westernmost to easternmost extremities of Peter's realm and of the need to send a naval expedition to the waters which, supposedly, flowed between Asia and the western tip of North America.[16]

Leibnitz and Peter met again in 1716. This time Leibnitz had a well-developed project for the exploration of the Strait of Anian. It is regrettable that when, in 1946. A. V. Efimov searched the Leningrad and Moscow archives for a copy of this project, which V. S. Guerrier's (Ger'e's) work on Leibnitz and the tsar (1871) convinced him had existed then at least, he could not find it.[17]

As in Germany, so too in France, reminders of the far North-East of Asia followed Peter. Once again approached by scientists, this time from the Académie in Paris,[18] he again promised to see what could be done about discovering the Strait of Anian or disproving its existence. He declined to let French scientists participate in any expedition that he might ultimately send.[19]

OKHOTSK AND THE SEA-ROUTE TO KAMCHATKA

Events on the extreme north-eastern limits of the Empire, meanwhile, had led the tsar to order servants of the Navy to Okhotsk on the Pacific littoral without delay (1713-14). Ignorance of the position of the Strait of Anian cost Russia nothing in immediate political or economic terms. By contrast, cossack inability to reach Kamchatka from a fort or depot on the "Lama Sea," the Sea of Okhotsk, could cause the loss of that peninsula.[20]

Since 1695 the Koriaks, frequently aided by the no less warlike Chukchi of the northeast tip of Asia, had been struggling with notable success against the cossacks of the area. Fur-tribute (iasak) had been gathered in Kamchatka only intermittently and at great cost.[21] Since the murder of the cossack officer Volodimer Atlasov by a band of cossack mutineers in 1711, the position in Kamchatka had been grave. Led by Kozyrevskii and Antsyferov, the cossack rebels had defied outside authority, killing and plundering; parties of Koriaks and Iukagirs rose. The Chukchi had never been subdued. Russia's grip on the North-East right from the River Kolyma to the River Anadyr' and from Cape Bol'shoi Baranov to Kamchatka's southern tip grew tenuous.[22] To bring in forces from Okhotsk or Gizhiginsk was possible only in theory: at neither place was there a single solid vessel.[23]

Starting in 1706, the cossack authorities at Bol'sheretsk, Okhotsk, Iakutsk, and other eastern centres of *kazachestvo* had made attempts to face the problems: lacks of seamen, ships, and shipwrights.[24] All had failed. At length the *voevoda* at Iakutsk, Colonel Ia. El'chin, so impressed upon the governor, Prince Matvei Gagarin, the disasters in Kamchatka of the past several seasons, that the latter felt impelled to send reports of them to Peter.[25] Had he not, the sorry news would have arrived in all events, in blacker form. Peter sent orders to Gagarin to take steps to quash rebellion in the peninsula and to investigate the maritime potential of Okhotsk which, after all, stood by a sea.[26]

Peter wrote again to Prince Gagarin (26 July 1713) on the matter of the sea-route to Kamchatka. Colonel El'chin had reported that no seamen or shipwrights could be found where they were wanted in the East. It was obviously necessary to dispatch them from Tobol'sk or even European Russia. Peter ordered that twenty cossacks with a boyar should travel to Okhotsk and there investigate the problem of constructing solid vessels. In the interim, a naval party would be formed and also sent to the Pacific littoral. In fact, both parties left Iakutsk, after a briefing by the *voevoda,* on 3 July 1714. Together they were fifty strong.[27] Among their number were two carpenters trained in the Navy, Kirilo Ploskikh and Varfolomei Fedorov; a native of the town of Hoorn in Holland, Andrei Bush or Busch; several Russian-speaking Tungus; and a group of Russian sailors with experience of tidal waters, led by Iakov Neveitsin and Nikita Triaska or Treska.

Motley though it was, it was a naval party that in 1714 left for Okhotsk, there to perform a naval task. Its members wore no uniform, but neither did most sea-men in the Russian Baltic Fleet. It flew no special flags or ensigns at its winter quarters at Okhotsk; but that was immaterial. Pennants did not signify, as yet, in the remotest of all Russian ports and depots. With the party went 480 yards of sailcloth, three anchors, and a quantity of tackle, ropes, and tools.[28] Mindful of Peter's promised floggings for unwarranted delays, seamen immediately felled and quartered timber. Winter quarters were erected, and a keel was soon laid by the Okhota's sandy mouth.[29]

Okhota, as the party named their boat, was launched in April 1716. A 51-foot-long one-master, she was built both for stability at sea and for use in shallow waters. She drew no more than 40 inches laden, was 18 feet across the beam, and was a relatively safe but sluggish sailer. G. F. Müller, the historian, who spoke to Bush about this voyage after more than twenty years writes suggestively and in connection with the Dutchman of the boats used to take goods to Pustozersk from Arkhangel'sk in the White Sea. The allusion might be taken as a hint about the earlier activity of Bush or the pair of naval carpenters.[30]

With Triaska at the helm, *Okhota* made her maiden voyage in June 1716. The mariners followed the coastline north till they were driven briskly east towards Kamchatka from the River Ola's mouth. The first land sighted was a promontory near the River Tigil, where Triaska beat to windward and dropped anchor. The party landed. Not a soul was to be seen. They moved along the coast after a watchful night ashore, then headed out to the sea, bearing south-west. This time conditions were considerably rougher. All survived to see Okhotsk again, however, where they rendered thanks to God for His mercies.

Okhota was a primitive enough small craft by Baltic standards, though sufficiently well built to remain sound after five years of neglect.[31] But Okhotsk was not a Baltic port. No oak or elm grew by its shores, and there were neither wharves nor iron-works nearby. Iron was constantly in short supply.[32] Problems of transport were unsolved,[33] as were the still more urgent problems of provisioning. Located on a current-ridden, empty waste of water, enormously far from St. Petersburg, and lacking all marine and other stores, Okhotsk offered a challenge to the Navy. The Navy was required to accept it, for the stakes were high enough. The cost in human lives simply of gathering fur-tribute in Kamchatka and conveying it to the interior was in itself a reason for establishing a shipyard at Okhotsk, all other possible advantages apart.[34]

THE POSITION OF THE SERVANTS OF THE NAVY AT OKHOTSK

When Kuz'ma Sokolov, Triaska, Neveitsin and company arrived there, Okhotsk was in all senses a backwater *ostrog*—remote, damp, ill-provisioned. The chief official there was, as always, a *prikazchik*. Under him were serving men of two main classes: town (as opposed to freehold) cossacks and Tungus auxiliaries.[35] Both were few in number. There were also occasional "one-year men" *(godovalshchiki)* to assist in the maintaining of a garrison.[36] All classes were perforce jacks-of-all-trades as they had been since the arrival of the cossacks in the area. As a result, crude vessels sailed the Okhota, Aldan, and Maia rivers, bringing foodstuffs and supplies out from Iakutsk. Yet, paradoxically, no "boat duty" *(sudovoe delo)* was imposed on the *prikazchik* of Okhotsk beyond that necessary if the food to keep the whole *ostrog* alive was to be carried out by river.[37] At times, specific orders would be given at Iakutsk to the effect that other craft should be constructed at Okhotsk. Thus, vessels had been sent in 1711-13 to survey the Shantar Islands, which lay fairly close to the River Uda's mouth.[38] By and large, however, there was very little shipbuilding activity; nor were there specialists in shipbuilding at any other coastal fort in the North-East.

These realities had led to the importing of skilled carpenters and seamen. Bush, at least, came from the West; and there is some reason for associating others of the pioneer party with the northern coast of European Russia (Pomor'e). The ancient custom of obtaining extra serving men for the North-East and for Siberia at large by an enlistment in the main towns of Pomor'e[39] was thus adapted to a new, maritime context. Many of the pioneer party were Siberians by birth, no doubt, and may be viewed as serving men on special naval duty at Okhotsk. Even they, however, changed their status temporarily by virtue of the order of 3 July 1714. For one thing, they were now treated as specialists both by Iakutsk and by the government itself; for another, they maintained a group identity whilst at Okhotsk and were not subject to the arbitrary orders or whims of the *prikazchik*. He, indeed, had orders to co-operate with them and to assist in transporting their powder, lead, and foodstore to Okhotsk. Neither Moscow nor Iakutsk, of course, had means of guaranteeing the co-operation of officials in such areas. Much consequently rested on relations between any given leader of a special party and the individual *prikazchik*.

THE DEVELOPMENT OF THE NEW SEA-ROUTE

In 1714, as Triaska and his comrades were preparing for their journey to Okhotsk, the Iukagirs and the Koriaks launched separate attacks against the much-extended cossacks of the area of Anadyrsk. Chukchi later joined the Koriaks in an alliance of convenience, and more than ninety cossacks died in 1715 as well as many more native auxiliaries.[40] El'chin himself brought news of these disasters to the government in Moscow. Land communication with the fort on the Bol'shaia River in south-west Kamchatka (Bol'sheretsk), he stated, had been virtually severed. Its garrison was on its own.[41]

So great were the delays and difficulties in communication between Moscow and Okhotsk that at the close of 1715 nothing was known to the Sibirskii Prikaz about the Sokolov-Bush-Triaska band beyond the fact of their arrival at Okhotsk. If they had built and launched a vessel, it was timely. Even so, a single craft would not suffice to meet the worsening Kamchatkan crisis; and more seamen too would certainly be needed. For five years, the Sibirskii Prikaz had been receiving news of crisis, disappointment, and disaster from the far North-East and East. The Koriaks and Chukchi were as dangerous to Russia's far frontier as at any time. The Kurile Islands, one of which was said to have some silver,[42] were uncharted, while Kamchatka had itself not yet been competently mapped by a geodesist in government employ. Lastly, the sea-route to Kamchatka from Okhotsk needed immediate development, for which investments of materiel and personnel were vital. El'chin's presence and activity at Moscow in the early weeks of 1716 served as a catalyst for the establishment of a command—the Great Kamchatka Command (*Bol'shoi Kamchatskii Nariad*)—to cope with all these problems. The command was formed around him.

Wasting no time, El'chin proceeded to Tobol'sk, where he was joined by naval officers and seamen among others and provided with a set of detailed orders. They were formidable: he was to survey the Kurile Islands and investigate trade prospects with the Japanese; to undertake a study of Kamchatka; to discover unknown islands and annex them in the tsar's name; and to develop the sea-route to Kamchatka.[43] El'chin delegated some authority to recommended officers, giving them major and specific projects. The development of the sea-route to Kamchatka fell to Ambjorn Molyk, late lieutenant in the Royal Swedish Navy, now a prisoner-of-war. El'chin sent Molyk, whom he trusted, to Okhotsk with a detachment formed of seamen, serving men, and native carriers. He reached Okhotsk late in the June of the next year (1717) and, with exemplary speed, made a passage to Kamchatka.[44]

In 1718 a second vessel took Porotov, Kochanov, and Uvarovskii to the peninsula.[45] In 1719 Kochanov returned with *iasak* to Okhotsk, while Kharitonov went with foodstuffs, guns, and powder from Okhotsk to Bol'sheretsk. Year by year, the seaway to Kamchatka grew more familiar to Russian subjects, though not safer, as a result of poor cartography, currents, and summer fogs. Such familiarity had, in itself, both military and economic value. Southward from Kamchatka stretched the Kurile Islands and Japan. Kozyrevskii and Antsyferov had visited a number of the former in 1713. The latter beckoned.[46]

SALTYKOV'S AND SOIMONOV'S PROJECTS

Almost necessarily, in view of Peter's interests, various high Russian officials took an interest both in the problem of the Strait of Anian and in connected mercantile and naval matters. One of these was Fedor Stepanovich Saltykov (1682?-1715), another, Fedor Ivanovich Soimonov (1692-1780). Both had naval training. Both were energetic patriots, aware, like their sovereign, of Russia's splendid eastern opportunities.[47]

Fedor Saltykov was the embodiment of the new Petrine civil servant: loyal, versatile, and despite his noble birth, unfriendly towards Muscovite tradition. As a youth, he had acquired wide mechanical and diplomatic skills in Leyden, Amsterdam, and London. For a period, he was a guardsman, and for a year or two (1703-4), he supervised the dockyard at Olonets. Finally, in 1711, Peter sent him to acquire ships abroad, one of the earliest of Admiralty agents. He spent several years in Holland and in London, where he died. It was on maritime and economic questions that he chose to dwell in *Propozitsii (The Propositions)*, as in all the other extant writings of his final years. Here are three proposals *(punkty)* from that section of the *Propozitsii* sent to St. Petersburg from London on 23 April 1714 and headed, ''On Siberia'':

1. Order ships to be built at the mouth or on the shore of the Enisei, for the coast from the mouth of that river on the Arctic Sea across Siberia to China is all under Your Majesty's sovereignty.
2. With these ships, investigate wherever possible around the coasts of Si-

beria and ascertain if there are islands that might also be brought under Russian sovereignty.

3. Should such islands not exist, it would still be possible to trade with such ships to China and to other islands. Moreover, timber, masts, and resin and tar could be sent from that region to Europe, since there is abundance of timber there and here in Europe timber is in great demand and very costly. There might be considerable profit to the state in this.[48]

The ideas were decidedly not new. Saltykov could well have heard them recently expounded by John Perry (1670-1732), a naval officer who had been fourteen years (1698-1712) in mostly unpaid Russian service.[49] The two had met in London in 1713 when Perry was preparing his "Account of the Czar's Dominions, and of his Intentions to discover a Passage . . . to China by the Tartarian Sea." Perry had himself heard Peter toying with exactly such ideas, which indeed had been adopted by the Muscovy Company. Nevertheless, Saltykov's comments merit notice. For the first time, connections between Russian trade with China and Japan by sea, Russian control of all the shores of the North-East, and the discovery by Russians of a navigable passage over Asia and between it and America had been spelled out, in Russian, by a Russian.

Saltykov gave further thought in 1714 to naval aspects of the problem of establishing a Russian presence on the littoral between the estuary of the Enisei River and China. He had no idea of its length; but his childhood in Tobol'sk, subsequent journeys through Siberia, and, recently, experience of shipbuilding and commerce in the west of Europe gave him insights into the potential value of the far North-East to Russia. The result of his reflections, "On the Search for a Free Seaway from the Dvina River to the Amur River's Mouth and China," formed one section of a manuscript entitled *Natural Resources of the State.* There should be regular, seaborne communication, argued Saltykov, between the White Sea and the Amur River. To that end, small craft modeled on ice-boats should be built in twos and threes beside the Rivers Dvina, Ob', and Lena, and at Sviatoi Nos, as well as on another river nearer to the Amur, if not actually on it. Seamen, foreign-born and Russian, should proceed in these small craft, which would have shallow draughts, around Siberia, surveying as they went. River mouths and inlets should be thoroughly examined: the topography, timber, and climate should be noted, "also from which rivers landings can be made . . . and in what places there is good mooring."[50] There should be depots on the Arctic coast from Waygatz Island eastward and also in Kamchatka. Russia could ultimately plan to send her own Indiamen to trade in the East Indies and the Orient, and they would sail through Russian waters and not around the globe. Thereby, rigours of the "torrid zone" could be avoided. Dutch and English shipowners would gladly pay a tax to use the northern, Russian passage to the Orient.

What was significant in Saltykov's "Free Seaway" proposition was the way in which its parts were put together. It helped to crystallize in Peter's mind ideas that, for all the cares of state, he had been entertaining for at least ten years. "I have often heard the Czar say," noted Perry in connection with the period preceding 1711, "that . . . as soon as he has Peace and Leisure to apply his Mind to it, he will search out whether it be possible for ships to pass by way of Nova Zembla into the Tartarian Sea; or to find out some Port eastward of the River Oby, where he may build Ships and send them, if practicable, to the Coast of China & Japan."[51]

Ten years after Perry's departure, Peter had still not found the "leisure" to direct such an attempt; neither, however, had he ceased to listen patiently to those who urged him on. Most suitably, it was while F. I. Soimonov and the tsar were in a vessel on the Caspian together (28 July 1722) that the former "judged it proper" to remark that trading voyages from Europe to the Indies by way of the Cape of Good Hope were both gruelling and risky. (Russians' unfamiliarity with tropical and sub-tropical waters caused them often to exaggerate their horrors. The tendency would last into the nineteenth century.)[52]

> But as Your Majesty knows, said I, the Eastern Siberian region and Kamchatka especially cannot be far distant from the western coast of the island of California and America itself, or from the Japanese and Philippine Islands. So it would be more possible and more profitable for Russian seamen to reach those parts than for Europeans, who are now obliged to sail practically halfway round the globe.[53]

THE ECONOMIC FACTOR

Judging from the tenor of his observations, F. I. Soimonov did not know that as he spoke reports were being written on the failure of a two-ship expedition sent from Arkhangel'sk the year before (1721) with the object of discovering a sea-route from the White Sea to the Ob' and thence, "between America and Tartary," to the East Indies.[54] The failure had at least shown that a passage could be made around Kamchatka to the Orient, assuming that the Strait of Anian was not a myth, only from the Lena River mouth or from a spot still further east.[55] But Soimonov was correct in thinking Peter highly conscious of the strait and of the several implications of its future charting by a Russian expedition.

Soviet historians have long engaged in controversy as to whether economic, scientific, or Imperial considerations weighed most heavily with Peter when, near his death, he launched the first of Vitus Bering's expeditions to the East.[56] The recent tendency has been to follow Efimov in proposing that, while neither scientific nor commercial factors should be overlooked, it is most properly in its political (Imperial and territorial) perspective that the launching of the Bering Expedition should be viewed.[57] The tsar, it is contended, recognized that other powers were about to fill the vacuum that then existed between Asia and America and in the North Pacific area at large and rightly hastened to forestall them.[58] It is certainly provocative to argue, as have various historians,[59] that Bering's Expedition was a venture either totally or almost lacking in Imperial-political significance. (It would have been remarkable had Peter not been conscious of the misty international implications of the enterprise.) But what perhaps is most regrettable is that historians have in the main chosen to focus on the final months and weeks of Peter's life as they consider what it was, essentially, that he expected of the venture. Not only have they failed to stress its purely naval element; they have also not recognized that Peter sometimes thought about the Strait of Anian in economic, rather than Imperial-expansionist or scientific, terms—and quite the opposite at other times. Never did he lose from *sight* either the naval or the economic elements and implications of finding a sea-route between Asia and America to the Pacific Ocean.

From the first, it was the function of the servants of the Navy in the far North-East and East to lend support to Russian economic interests, by strengthening security throughout Kamchatka, gathering *iasak,* discovering and charting islands that contained, perhaps, new subjects for the Empire and valuable fur resources, and maintaining sea-communication with Kamchatka. That function did not change. So much is evident from an assessment of the origins and nature of the Luzhin-Evreinov surveying expedition of 1719-21. The origins go back at least to 1716.

In that year, while Peter was abroad, a group of merchants in St. Petersburg proposed to form a trade-link with Japan. A good deal had been learned about Japan since the beginning of the century from castaways taken to Moscow from Kamchatka. The first of these, Dembei, an Osaka merchant's clerk, had been granted a long audience by Peter on 8 January 1702.[60] There had been other castaways in 1708 and 1710.[61] More recently, in 1713, the cossack Kozyrevskii had returned from an obligatory voyage to Shumshu and Paramushir, most northerly of the Kurile Islands, with much information about islands to the south and with lacquered wooden ware, swords, silken stuffs, and paper of Japanese production.[62] Kozyrevskii and his men echoed the rumours that had earlier been gathered from the castaways that not far from Japan there lay the "Islands of Silver and of Gold."[63] Lastly, Dutch merchants long established in Moscow offered certain information about Japan which, in conjunction with the rumours of adjacent islands filled with precious minerals, made Russians wish to form a trade-link with that empire at once.

The merchants approached the Russo-Scottish courtier and functionary Jacob Bruce, an able man whom they knew Peter respected, with their trading proposition, and Bruce supported them in Senate. They proposed to send their goods along the Arctic coast by vessel to the River Ob' and thence, by way of Lake Baikal, using the Rivers Selenga, Ingoda, Shilka, and Amur, and a number of their larger tributaries. The plan was not realistic. The country over which the goods were to be sent remained unmapped; nor was it practical to send them either over or around the Saian Mountains to Baikal.[64] There were also diplomatic complications over the use of the River Amur for such purposes.

But Bruce was irritated by such ignorance of Russian territory. Furthermore, he thought the need to foster trade with China quite as obvious as that for a correct and detailed survey of the whole north-eastern coastline of Siberia. Then came the news that Ia. A. El'chin had done nothing about coastal survey work.[65] Within six months, El'chin was summoned to St. Petersburg to answer charges. His second-in-command died shortly afterwards. And so the Great Kamchatka Command was, in effect, brought to an end in June 1718.[66]

Together, Bruce's memoranda on the matter of Oriental trade and El'chin's inability to organize a survey of the seas between Kamchatka and Japan led Peter to send Fedor Luzhin and Ivan Evreinov to the Far East. Both were graduates of the new Naval Academy and had been taught by Henry Farquarson, the founder of the School of Mathematics and Navigation, which, in 1714, had formed the basis for the new Academy. Both had been recommended as geodesists.[67] Peter himself gave them their orders: ''You will proceed to Kamchatka and thence as instructed, and will ascertain . . . whether or not Asia and America are joined by land; and you will go not only north and south, but also east and west, and will place on a map all that you see.''[68] The pair left for Kamchatka in July 1719.[69]

As a study of their movements shows, Luzhin and Evreinov also had secret orders from the tsar. Apparently one such instruction, if not the major one, was to investigate the Kurile Island chain and to determine its precise relationship to Sakhalin and to the main Japanese islands. Reaching Okhotsk and there repairing the *Okhota,* the two arrived at Bol'sheretsk in September 1720. They sailed from the Icha River mouth on 2 June 1721 with Kondratii Moshkov as pilot. Bearing south-west, they visited and charted the first five Kurile Islands. *Okhota* was then caught in a storm which ripped her sail. Luzhin and Evreinov were tossed about for seven days, then driven onto Paramushir Island. They lowered a cannon and anvil as a clumsy makeshift anchor, but the cable snapped. Again they drifted helplessly. At last, by dint of ceaseless effort and a scrap of sail, they reached the mouth of the Bol'shaia River whence, with wooden anchors and a prayer, they limped to the Okhota. Logbook, map, and commentary all intact, they hastened off to Moscow as instructed. Peter was in Kazan' when they arrived there on the journey west. He received them, and they handed him a map.[70] It showed their progress eastward from Tobol'sk, on to Kamchatka, and to fourteen of the Kurile Islands.[71] Because they had used an astronomical quadrant, as they had been taught at the Naval Academy, Luzhin and Evreinov made tolerably accurate reckonings of latitude: those of the Kurile Islands, for example, were accurate to within one and a half degrees. Longitudinal reckonings, by contrast, were inaccurate.[72] Little if anything was learned about Japan itself from the voyage in *Okhota;* on the other hand, the geographical relationship of Japan to the Kurile Islands and Kamchatka had been clarified. Peter was satisfied with their work.[73]

Scarcely four years had passed since the establishment of the Academy at which the pair had done so well when Peter gave them orders for Kamchatka and the Kurile Island chain. Thus did he forge a link between it and hydrography in the remote North-East and East and make it likely that for many years to come, if not indefinitely, servants of the Navy would lend weight to Russia's economic interests in the Pacific area. Patterns of Imperial activity beyond Kamchatka were established with aid of naval specialists some years before the start of the First Bering Expedition.

THE BIRTH OF THE FIRST BERING EXPEDITION

In a sense, it was Peter's passion for the sea that finally led to the launching of an expedition to the Strait of Anian: the necessary orders were extracted by an illness brought about by Peter's wading waist-deep in the chilly Gulf of Finland in an effort to retrieve a grounded boat.[74] A. K. Nartov, a former serf who had won Peter's favour through his brilliance as a mechanic and was sometimes in his company, was present as his master strove to concentrate on state affairs despite his bouts of strangury and fever. In his *Tales (Rasskazy),* Nartov gave his version of the circumstances in which Peter, close to death, issued the orders that sent Bering and the Navy to the far North-East. Peter, says Nartov,[75] was aware of his condition and anxious to launch the expedition that might find a northern seaway to the Orient and Indies. Russians might succeed where both the English and the Dutch had failed and bring glory to the state, as well as profit. Nartov himself does not elaborate on Peter's choice of agent or executor for the new enterprise, General-Admiral F. M. Apraksin. And yet the choice was crucial. Apraksin headed the Navy. The charting of the Strait of Anian was not to fall to serving men in the North-East; nor were Siberian officials to control the expedition.

Nartov witnessed the confirmation of this fact, for on 23 December 1724 Peter instructed that an expedition should be sent to find the strait, and while one copy of the edict was delivered to the Senate, a second was delivered to the Admiralty College. It was naval in its essence. Officers, shipwrights, geodesists, and seamen should be found to man an expedition from Kamchatka.[76] Here are Peter's orders, in the (1914) Golder text:

Orders For the Selection of Officers . . .

(Imperial Instruction)	(Senate and College Responses)
1. To find geodesists who have been in Siberia and have returned.	The Senate learns that the following named geodesists have been in Siberia: Ivan Zakharov, Peter Chichagov, Ivan Evreinov, who died, Fedor Luzhin, Peter Skobeltsyn, Ivan Svistunov, Dmitri Baskakov, Vasili Shetilov, Grigori Putilov.
2. To find among deserving naval lieutenants or sub-lieutenants such as could be sent to Siberia and Kamchatka.	Admiral Sievers and Rear-Admiral Senyavin recommend among the naval lieutenants, Stanberg, Zverev, or Posenkov; among the sub-lieutenants, Chirikov or Laptev. It would be advisable to have over them as commander Captain Bering or Fonverd. Bering has been in the East Indies and knows conditions, and Fonverd has had experience as navigator.
3. To find among the apprentices or assistant master-builders one who could build there a deck ship along the lines of the big ships here. For that purpose, there should be sent with him young ship's carpenters, such instruments as may be needed, one quarter-master and 8 sailors.	The student of shipbuilding, Fedor Koslov, is able to build either deck or open ships, if he is furnished with a plan. *It is very necessary to have as navigator or assistant navigator one who has been in North America* [in Peter's hand]
4. Likewise to forward from here one and a half sets of sails*; blocks, cables and such like; four falconets with the necessary ammunition; and one or two sail-makers.	Rigging is being sent. *Two sets** *The rest is all right.* [in Peter's hand]

5. If there are no such navigators in our Navy, a letter should be dispatched at once to Holland that two men who know the sea in the north and as far as Japan be sent. These men should come by the Admiralty post.

Vice-Admiral Sievers has written that he has among our men navigators who know the sea and that he will send them without delay.

December 23rd 1724

From the names proposed by Sievers, who thus played an important role in the selection of personnel for the new venture, Peter selected Bering as commander, "Stanberg," who emerged as Morten Spangenberg or Spanberg, as his second-in-command. They and Aleksei Ivanovich Chirikov, who was also to go, were informed of their selection, offered double-pay, and ordered to respond without delay. All three accepted the positions: they could hardly have refused without an excellent excuse. Bering hastened to the capital from Vyborg, where he had a small estate. Partly because his strangury made it increasingly more difficult for him to write, but also partly because to the last he remained open to the possibility of modifying and improving them, Peter delayed signing the new commander's orders. Finally, he did so on 26 January 1725. On the same day, he scrawled on terse instructions for Prince V. V. Dolgorukii in Tobol'sk.

To Prince Dolgorukii, Governor of Siberia.

January 1725

We are sending to Siberia Fleet-Captain Vitus Bering with assistants, to undertake a naval expedition and carry out such instructions as he has from us. When he comes to you and asks for help of one kind and another for the expedition, you are to give it.

To Fleet-Captain V. I. Bering. Orders.

January 26 1725

1. Build in Kamchatka, or in some other place in that region, one or two decked vessels.
2. Sail in those same vessels, north up the coast which, since its limit is unknown, appears to be a part of America.
3. Ascertain where it joins with America and go to a settlement under European authority. If you encounter a European ship, learn from her the name of the coast off which you stand, and record it. Make a landing and so obtain more detailed information, prepare a chart, and return here.[77]

Shortly after signing Bering's orders and entrusting supervision of the expedition to F. M. Apraksin, Peter suffered a collapse. It was the Empress Catherine who handed Bering the signed orders. Three days later, Peter died. Apraksin drafted instructions that related to enlistment of mechanics in Siberia, to transport overland, and to provisioning.[78] Bering was ordered to report at least once monthly to the Admiralty College until further notice. He was also asked to leave without delay.

2

The Bering Expeditions

BERING'S EARLIER CAREER AND APPOINTMENT

Bering's appointment influenced both the direction and the results of the first expedition to the Strait of Anian in which the Russian Navy played a part. That being so, his character, his earlier career, and the circumstances that surrounded his appointment in preference to Karl van Werden may be summarized.

Bering was a cautious man. He neither rushed into decisions nor embraced unnecessary risk. Brought into danger by events, or by the naval service, he did not lack courage or ability; but by temperament and early training, he preferred to bear away from danger signs. His temperament no doubt derived in part from the two Jutland families from which he was descended, the Berings and the Svendsens: neither was a military or naval family.[1] He was trained in adolescence in the service of the Dutch East India Company, then barely entering its long decline.[2] Bering sailed to the East Indies and back to Amsterdam in a Dutch Indiaman. As an apprenticeship in ocean voyaging, his trip was calculated to encourage carefulness in dealings with superiors, subordinates, and foreigners; in hygiene and avoidance of disease; in attitude towards originality.[3] With their established routes and timetables, company ships encouraged order.

Bering was offered a lieutenancy in Peter's youthful navy in 1704 when he was twenty-three on the joint recommendation to two fellow Danes, Peter Sievers and Cornelius Cruys.[4] Both men were in due course to attain the highest ranks in Russian service, as vice-presidents of the new Admiralty College. Bering's first known contacts with the Russian Baltic Fleet were thus potentially extremely influential ones—indeed, as one who had the tsar's friendship and trust, Cruys was already powerful.[5] Bering accepted the commission, left for Russia, and strove to satisfy his new employer. He was steadily promoted, to captain of the fourth (1715), third (1717), and ultimately second (1720) rank, and was regarded as a competent sea-officer.[6] As such, he had command of a new frigate while still relatively young.[7]

At the conclusion of the Russo-Swedish or Great Northern War, and with the signing of the Peace of Nystadt, many Russian naval officers received promotions and rewards. For Bering, there was nothing. While others were surpassing him in rank, he was kept occupied with routine training duties. Moreover, peace reduced the likelihood of prompt advancement. Bering's disappointment was keener because he recognized what had caused it: twelve months earlier, he had been caught between two factions of mutually hostile naval officers, headed by Sievers and a Scot named Thomas Gordon. As a Dane and as the brother-in-law of Siever's colleague Thomas Saunders, Bering had been linked to Sievers's group. The tsar had taken Thomas Gordon's side, and Gordon used his interest against "the Danes" in June 1722. Within two years, Gordon's star was waning, and as Sievers rose in Peter's estimation, so did Bering's further prospects. Admiral Apraksin, too, favoured Bering, Saunders, Sievers, and their friends rather than Gordon. But Bering had already had enough of naval politics. Complaining of discriminatory treatment over matters of advancement and pay, he sought an honourable discharge from the Navy in the spring of 1724. After some difficulty, he obtained it on 3 June. Frustrated, tired, and convinced that rank and fame had passed him by, he left St. Petersburg for Vyborg. He was forty-three.

Within eight weeks, when the tsar had found the time to hear the outline of the case from Apraksin, Bering was ordered to rejoin the fleet as captain of the first rank. Not long after, he was given his essential role in Russian and Pacific history.

Captain van Werden's candidacy for the leadership of the new expedition was, in one respect at least, stronger than Bering's. For three years (1717-18, 1722), he had been charting in the Caspian Sea and had demonstrated competence both as a navigator and, especially, as a hydrographer. His courage too was recognized: after a savage small-boat action fought near Schlüsselberg on the Neva, at the beginning of the Russo-Swedish War, he had been brought before the tsar as an aggressive prisoner-of-war. Invited to join the Russian Fleet, he had at once agreed to fight against the Swedes, his own recent employers. Though subsequently treated as a Swede by Russian writers, van Werden was in fact of Dutch and Danish origin; King Charles XII of Sweden had hired his professional services.[8] Two factors told against him: his having switched allegiance twice already and Bering's greater intimacy with the influential Sievers. Relevant though it doubtless was to the new expedition, van Werden's experience of survey work did not outweigh Bering's long service and known steadiness of temper. Also in the latter's favour was his visit to Batavia as a young man and Apraksin's support.[9] As was so frequently the case in Peter's navy, a reward—for loyal service, in this case—assumed the aspect of a challenge.

THE JOURNEY TO OKHOTSK (1725-27)

On 24 January 1725, Lieutenant Aleksei Ivanovich Chirikov and two dozen men left for the Urals, with twenty-five large wagon-loads of foodstuffs and equipment.[10] A second party followed slightly later, led by Bering. It too comprised a veritable caravan of wagons, though, to keep its size in perspective, it should be noted that since 1678 new *voevodas* of Iakutsk had been entitled to a train of thirty wagons to convey their private goods.[11] Both parties picked up men as they went east, finally joining forces.

The difficulties met even on early stages of the journey showed that the land portion of the expedition was itself to form a challenge. There were arguments with the officials of minor posting stations, even west of Verkhoturie, who had not been notified of the arrival of large parties or who were unco-operative anyway. There were repeated problems over horses, bogs, and streams. Spanberg and Chirikov were tested by these early months far from the Navy's proper element, the sea. The differences in their characters grew evident.[12]

Russian and Soviet historians have tended to magnify the merits of the Russian-born Chirikov in about the same proportion as Bering's failings.[13] Nonetheless, it is apparent that Chirikov was courageous and extremely commonsensical. When recommended to the Admiralty College by Saunders, he was serving as instructor of cadets at the Naval Academy in which he had himself been taught. Such was his competence that news of his selection gave his chief at the Academy a lively sense of loss.[14] In contrast, Morten Spanberg, the second-in-command and a compatriot of Bering, was a surly officer and little liked. That he was cruel, avaricious, and semi-literate at best in Russian is attested by contemporary documents.[15] While both Bering and Chirikov were resented by the numerous Siberians who were instructed to assist them, Spanberg was hated.[16] However, he was also an experienced and hard sea-officer.

Week after week the expedition pressed on east, using the Rivers Irtysh, Ob', Ket', and Verkhniaia Tunguska, among others. Portages were often gruelling, but they were at least safer than rapids. "On the Tunguska," comments Bering, "there are three sets of rapids and numerous shoals besides. There are large concealed rocks in the rapids."[17] More men and other horses were added to the expedition, at Tobol'sk, Eniseisk, Iakutsk, and several other places; but size itself brought problems of provisioning. More than six hundred horses needed to be fed, and like the members of the growing expedition, they were widely spread. The main group wintered at Ilimsk, proceeding down the Lena from Ust-Kut on little barges to Iakutsk. Here, preparations had been made by the *voevoda*, Poluektov, and by Midshipman Petr Avraamovich Chaplin, whom Bering had dispatched ahead, to receive the weary travelers and to facilitate the last part of their journey to Okhotsk. Chaplin had reached Iakutsk as early as 5 September 1725, and done extremely well. Having decided that the expedition's foodstuffs and equipment must travel to Okhotsk partly by cart or sled and partly by water, he had taken many actions. Half-tame cattle had been sent off to Okhotsk with several carpenters. More stores had been acquired, packed, and sent. From Iakutsk, a group headed by Spanberg went ahead to the Aldan and Maia Rivers. After resting, the main group followed.

Progress was slower now, in wilder country. Bering split his force into three groups. As before, his own group travelled fastest. By 1 October 1726, it had reached Okhotsk. The other parties under Spanberg and Chirikov were less fortunate. Spanberg had fallen victim to an early freezing spell. His little boats stuck fast in the Gorbeia River far from any settlement. His men dragged makeshift sleds through mounting snowdrifts; then the food supply gave out. "They had been marching since November 4, and had suffered greatly from hunger, being compelled to eat dead horses that had fallen by the wayside, and their harnesses, and leather clothing and boots."[18] Among the men who died as a result of this grim march was Luzhin, the geodesist. Not until April did the rescuers and rescued drag themselves and a small portion of the stores that had been loaded at Iakutsk into Okhotsk. Men and material brought from St. Petersburg at huge expense had been lost within a few days' summer march of the Pacific littoral.[19]

NEW APPROACHES AND THEIR IMPLICATIONS

The Admiralty College's attempts to make provision for the difficulties that it foresaw for Bering's people as they travelled to Okhotsk, may seem amateurish. In fact, the College did not lack either imagination or intelligence: Apraksin's orders to V. V. Dolgorukii, among others,[20] demonstrate that he, at least, had grasped the full complexity of the new venture. By its nature, nonetheless, the Admiralty College was ill-fitted to direct an undertaking in Siberia. It had no offices east of the Urals, no couriers, no ships.

Just as the College and the Navy were ill-fitted to be dealing with a landmass, however, the colonial administration of Siberia had shown itself lacking in competence and confidence where open-water navigation was concerned. Indeed it was familiar with inland navigation, and several great rivers of Siberia were many miles in width. For decades, many towns had been obliged to build a fixed number of river-craft and to provide the wanted carpenters or shipwrights to repair them.[21] During the summer months, most traffic in Siberia moved along rivers and across portages. At Verkhoturie, in particular, boatbuilding had long been undertaken on a major scale; and other centres too built little craft in quantity.[22] Okhotsk was not among them. Certainly some local craft were built to carry grain and other foodstuffs and supplies to the *ostrog*. Only recently, however, had the regional authorities begun to look due east. Vessels were built for the Kamchatka run, but only periodically, one at a time. Investigation of the

Shantar Islands had been poorly carried out,[23] and the lack of shipwrights had not been overcome.

When the Navy arrived, in the form of the First Bering Expedition, it brought skills to the remote North-East and East that made some deep-sea sailing possible for local serving men and more particularly for the private hunter-traders or *promyshlenniki* with a greater expectation of arrival and return than heretofore. The cossacks had been bold enough indeed before to venture out from shore. But now the Navy brought the means whereby the fundamental maritime and economic problems of the region might be tackled and altered attitudes towards the sea. It brought in shipwrights and examples of the European shipwright's art to add to that of the *Okhota*. It brought pilots and led to the creating of a School of Navigation at Okhotsk.[24] The Admiralty Office at Okhotsk, which was soon founded, served as a reminder of new attitudes. Needless to say, local serving men, specifically the *prikaznye liudi,* had to sustain those attitudes.[25]

In other ways, too, the beginnings of the Bering expedition set a pattern in the far North-East and East. For instance, Bering's orders did not spell out how far he could exert authority over the cossacks and those officers who had no orders to assist the expedition, more specifically, those at Okhotsk and in Kamchatka. In his orders, it was understood that the Siberian administration would assist as and when possible; but should officials be recalcitrant for any reason, how did naval ranks compare with those of *voevoda, golova, pod'iachei,* and *prikazchik*? The question had been raised but not yet answered in the detail that prudence might dictate.

Again, the orders recognized that the new enterprise had diplomatic, as well as economic, implications. If a European vessel were encountered off the coast of North America, or if a European settlement were visited, it would be necessary to explain the Russian presence. From the moment of the Russian Navy's presence in the seas east of Kamchatka, the government was conscious of the possible political and other implications. From the outset, naval officers were not to claim or annex new territory, but to study, to investigate, to further Russian interests in quiet ways. Thus were the outlines of the Russian Navy's role east of Kamchatka for the next half-century established by documents exemplary in their brevity and comprehensiveness.

PREPARATIONS IN OKHOTSK AND KAMCHATKA (1726-28)

When Bering reached Okhotsk, his carpenters had been at work for months on the decked vessel that would take the expedition to Kamchatka. Even so, it was by no means ready. Then came news of Spanberg's troubles with the ice-bound boats and stores, ''which he had left scattered in four different places on an un-inhabited trail.''[26] There could be no thought of leaving for Kamchatka for the present. Okhotsk did not have even rough accommodation for as many men as Bering had brought: stores and barrack huts had to be built immediately. While a party went to Spanberg's aid with dog-teams, another therefore set to felling trees and squaring timber. Some men fished and salted down their catches, while others butchered cattle and preserved the meat, all with the aid of local serving men. The work proceeded on the *Fortuna,* the vessel that would take the expedition on its way.[27]

Matters did not look promising for Bering in the early months of the new year. Only through success could he obtain advancement in the service; but already he had lost some men, others were weak, and all were restless. Many stores were lost, too, and the memory of hunger cast a pall over the reunited companies. Bering had failed to gain the friendship and support of the *prikazchik* at Okhotsk, and he was increasingly entangled in a web of petty personal intrigues. At last, on 8 June the new vessel was launched. They spent three weeks rigging her, lading, and making final preparations for the voyage to Kamchatka. Spanberg sailed for the Bol'shaia River mouth on 30 June with orders to discharge the cargo of equipment and supplies, leave a shore-party to "prepare ship timber," and return without delay.[28] On her return, *Fortuna* was reladen with flour from Iakutsk. Bering and the main party proceeded from Okhotsk to Bol'sheretsk on 21 August.

The passage proved relatively easy. Thus far, the expedition's problems had been less of navigation than of transport and supply. But now, by choosing not to risk a voyage round Kamchatka to its eastern shore, Bering himself worsened those problems. Foodstuffs were soon in short supply. There was little to be bartered, bought, or stolen once the summer season ended in the area of Bol'sheretsk. The Kamchadals, whose services were soon impressed to bring the expedition's baggage and equipment to the east coast of Kamchatka, with enormous loss and hardship,[29] were a backward people who did not engage in agriculture. They had neither sheep nor cattle. The authorities at Bol'sheretsk had sown no grain. If servants of the Navy were to spend long periods on the peninsula, they must concern themselves with their own diet. Bering had a patch of barley sown and a larger patch of rye.[30]

Exploiting native labour and the Bystraia and the Kamchatka rivers, Bering's expedition reached the east coast where, eventually, work was started on another vessel. Till the summer of 1728 came, however, there was much hardship from blizzards, cold, and hunger.

Timber we hauled by dog-team. Tar we manufactured from a tree known there as larch. . . . For lack of anything better to take on the coming voyage, we then distilled a liquor from grass, by a process known in that country. Salt we boiled out of sea-water; fish-oil gave us our butter; and instead of meat, we took salt-fish.[31]

On 6 July, *Fortuna* reached Nizhnekamchatsk with pilot K. Moshkov aboard. By then, the *Sviatoi Gavriil,* a vessel 60 feet in length, was ready to make sail. Within ten days, she had been laden. The expedition put to sea on 14 July.[32]

Bering and his company soon rounded Cape Urinskii, crossed Oliutorskaia Bay, and pressed north-east. On 29 July they crossed the mouth of the River Anadyr'. After a pause, they turned north, then east again, following nameless rocky shores. They had no chart to keep them safe—only their eyesight and the hope that hidden rocks were well submerged. By 10 August, they had discovered and named St. Lawrence (Sv. Lavrentii) Island, where they encountered Chukchi and questioned them with the aid of two interpreters about the ''strait'' between their country and a country to the east. The answers were inconclusive. *Sv. Gavriil* rounded Chukotskii Nos and stood in latitude 65° 30'N. No land was to be seen.[33]

Bering now believed that they had passed the eastern tip of Asia and left it to the south. Summer was drawing to its close; it was essential to decide where they would winter. Spanberg suggested sailing north for three more days, until the sixteenth, then returning to the mouth of the Kamchatka River, which they knew. Chirikov spoke for sailing round the coast, then out of sight and on their port side, to the estuary of the River Kolyma: only by doing so could they prove that North America was separated from Asia. At the least, Chirikov argued, they should press on north till they met ice. Bering agreed with Spanberg, putting certainty beyond his grasp. On 16 August, from latitude 67° 18'N., he turned back towards Kamchatka. Next day the islands of St. Diomede grew visible; but fog concealed the coastline of America. After a second encounter with the Chukchi, Bering returned to the Kamchatka River by the route that he had taken north.[34] *Sv. Gavriil* arrived off the Kamchatka on 1 September 1728. The company prepared to winter at Nizhnekamchatsk. Bering at least firmly believed that he had carried out his orders and was certain that he had discovered a strait. So he had; but he had failed to demonstrate the fact. Chirikov understood the nature of proof as he, apparently, had not.[35]

Bering sailed again the following season on 5 June 1729, having deposited a cache of flour, salted meat, and other foods by the Kamchatka River. This time he went due east. *Sv. Gavriil* covered two hundred versts by his own reckoning, but still no land was sighted to the east. Bering turned back, charted the southern coast of the Kamchatka peninsula, sailed on to the Bol'shaia River post and thence returned as soon as practicable to Okhotsk.[36] From there he travelled light, reaching St. Petersburg on 1 March 1730.

Aleksei Chirikov's reason for declining to believe that the return to Kamchatka in 1728 was necessary did him credit as a maritime explorer. He had heard of, or had read, a brief account by the cossack Tatarinov, whom D. M. Lebedev identifies as the same man as Petr Popov, about ''the land facing Chukotskii Nos . . . on which there is timber.'' The account, which only he of Bering's people would appear to have thought important and deserving of credence, was of Chukchi provenance. It was not published until 1736.[37] Chirikov afterwards received some credit for his attitude and knowledge from the Admiralty College.[38]

THE POST-PETRINE CAPITAL: BERING AND J.-N. DELISLE (1730)

Bering returned to the St. Petersburg of Anna, formerly Duchess of Courland, and of her petty Baltic German favourites. For naval officers imbued with the ideas of the Petrine age, Kronstadt presented a sad spectacle. The Baltic Fleet was in decline. In the capital itself there was confusion; barely thirty days before Bering's arrival, the Supreme State Council had dissolved. The first of many members of the ancient Russian families, most notably the Dolgorukiis and the Golitsyns, had lately been condemned to exile in Siberia. Within the Admiralty College, chaos reigned. Bering's return did not increase it; for the moment, his professional superiors were little interested in Kamchatka, and in all events they were unwilling to evince a public interest in any distant project. It was not that the whole College had in fact lost interest in the remote North-East and East or in the Bering Expedition; it was merely that at court, only the aging Golovkin had any interest in maritime discovery. The empress and her favourites knew little of the Navy and did not wish to know more. Long absent from St. Petersburg, Bering had to adjust swiftly to new realities. One of these was the new, select Academy of Sciences. Bering had to assess accurately how the Academy, the Admiralty College, and the Senate all stood *vis-à-vis* the court—and his own enterprise.

From the time of its establishment, he gathered, the Academy had welcomed foreign, and particularly French and German, scientists. A number of them had been men of more pretension than distinction. In a capital kindly disposed towards them, German immigrants were in effect discriminating against Russians, whom they generally scorned. While Germans had inaugurated a teutonic reign at the Academy, however, other foreigners and Russians maintained their former influence in the diminished and declining Navy. It was not to be expected that the Admiralty College and Academy would work in harmony on many issues, or that senators would not, in this new era, treat the Navy in accordance with their reading of the mood at court.[39]

Within a week of his arrival, Bering submitted to the Admiralty College three maps drawn up by Chaplin: one of the whole Empire; one showing Chaplin's and Bering's routes to the Pacific from Tobol'sk; and a summary map showing the coastline of Kamchatka in some detail, with waters to the south and east. At the same time, Bering presented his own logbook and prepared himself for interview. When it was held, he spoke emphatically in favour of continuing activity by Navy men and ships about Kamchatka. The College thanked him for the maps, papers, and comments and dismissed him. There was no second interview. A little later, he was told that since the empress alone possessed authority to launch new ventures of the sort that he had mentioned, he should send her a petition through the Senate, then in Moscow.[40]

The College, in short, made Bering understand that he would get no favoured treatment in the capital, however well he might believe his work to have been done. Yet the worth of his achievements in the *Sv. Gavriil* had already been acknowledged publicly. Several days earlier the newspaper *Sankt-Peterburgskie Vedomosti* had printed a formal statement that he had indeed "discovered that there is a North-East Passage such that, if ice did not hinder in the northern regions, a passage could be made by sea from the River Lena to Kamchatka and so to China, Japan, and the East Indies" (16 March). The statement was translated into Danish for the benefit of readers of *Nye tidender om laerde sager* and produced a little stir in Copenhagen. Certain pressures, Bering gathered, were at work to counteract the fair impression that the notice might already have produced. That feeling was confirmed on 30 March, when he received a reaction to his own written report from the Admiralty College. The College voiced its doubts about the accuracy of his maps. It was, he read, likely that many of the readings taken from *Fortuna* and *Sv. Gavriil* were faulty. "L'Amirauté," as J. G. Gmelin put it later, "crut avoir des raisons importantes pour regarder la decision comme en quelque façon douteuse."[41] Bering set out to learn what these "important reasons" were. The trail led him straight to the Academy of Sciences and the desk of Joseph-Nicolas Delisle.

Delisle (1688-1768), a younger brother of the eminent geographer Guillaume Delisle, had studied with Maraldi before coming to St. Petersburg to occupy a post at the Academy in June 1727. Regrettably, he was a poor cartographer. Family pride and vanity induced him to append his name to maplike but essentially imaginative reconstructions of remote parts of the globe and to defend his brother's errors to the hilt. Ironically, he had dismissed the Chaplin maps as unreliable and as the work of men unable to depict on paper what they saw. He was moreover highly sceptical of Bering's scientific competence. Delisle had faith in a composite of earlier representations of the area where the *Sv. Gavriil* had been—those of his brother, Texeira, and Homann. According to the Chaplin map, there were no islands off Kamchatka but the Kuriles—not a sign of Staaten Eyland, or Gama Land, or Yezo. Chaplin's work did not accord even with that of the cossack Shestakov; still less did it agree with the Kamchatka and Chukotka drawn by the returning Swedish prisoner-of-war, Philip von Strahlenberg, alias Tabbert, and published in 1726.[42] In sum, the Bering-Chaplin map clashed inadmissably with Homann's, which was based on that of Tabbert-Strahlenberg, and Delisle's, which was worthy of acceptance as the work of his brother Guillaume.[43]

However, Joseph-Nicolas Delisle dispatched a copy of the large summary map drawn up by Chaplin to the French geographer, J.-B. d'Anville in March 1732. Far from scorning Chaplin's work, or questioning his competence as a cartographer, d'Anville accepted it as sound. It was incorporated in his own, seminal *Atlas de la Chine* (1737).

I. K. KIRILLOV AND THE ORIGINS OF THE GREAT NORTHERN EXPEDITION

Being undermined by certain individuals in the St. Petersburg of Anna and the new, germanophile Academy brought the support of other men. Among Bering's most influential allies and supporters in his hope to lead another expedition from Kamchatka was Ivan Kirillov, chief secretary of the Senate and an indefatigable statistician and geographer.[44] Since 1726, Kirillov had been working on the *Atlas of the Russian Empire* that he was never to complete. And since June 1720, he had laboured on his other major project, which in itself might have occupied a team of writers all their lives: *The Flourishing Condition of the Russian State*.[45] In neither task had he received the least assistance from Delisle. He took an interest in Bering and his shelved reports and charts as a geographer, as an admirer and protégé of Peter, as a high Senate official, and as one with a particular dislike of Joseph-Nicolas Delisle.

By May 1731, Kirillov was exerting all his influence to see that Captain Bering's projects for the far North-East and East were not "mislaid." Prompted by Kirillov, the vice-chancellor, Count A. I. Ostermann,[46] added his weight to a petition which, belatedly, the Admiralty College now submitted to the Crown on Bering's behalf. It sought for him the rank of *kapitan-komandor* and 1,000 silver roubles. The former was in due course granted. In the interim, Kirillov gathered more support, as and where possible, for a new venture in the far North-East.

Bering submitted two projects to Anna through the Senate.[47] In the first, he emphasized the need for the development of natural resources in Siberia at large and for extensive missionary work among the Iakuts, Iukagirs, and other native peoples. The second had to do with exploration from Kamchatka and especially with an attempt to reach America by sea. Again the theme of trade was struck; and, as in Peter's day, Okhotsk was viewed as a potential base for the preliminary maritime activity. Bering proposed the prompt development of the *ostrog* into a settlement or township with facilities for shipbuilding, an element of local agriculture, and a school of navigation.[48] What Bering envisaged for Okhotsk, however, had to be adjusted to political realities.

One of these was that I. Kirillov and the Senate had considerably greater interest in the development of trade and agriculture in Siberia and the North-East than in the strictly naval parts of Bering's earlier proposals *(Predlozheniia)*. Bering therefore emphasized the "inland" and the "coastal" elements of his proposals: the establishment of iron-works close to Iakutsk or on the River Angara;[49] the introduction of horned cattle to the River Urak valley and some other regions and of pigs to Bol'sheretsk; the growing of such crops as hemp, barley, and turnips in Kamchatka; and the settling of carpenters, spinners, and smiths in the peninsula. Kirillov tended Bering's projects in the Senate. Finally, there were developments: on 10 May 1731, an exiled former favourite of Peter and sometime director of the Naval Academy, Grigorii Skorniakov-Pisarev, was ordered to proceed from Iakutsk to Okhotsk as commandant.[50] He was to implement large parts of Bering's project for Okhotsk: to supervise grain-growing and cattle-herding; to construct a little quay and dockyard at Okhotsk itself; and to encourage merchants to proceed to Bol'sheretsk.[51] By June, Kirillov had so dexterously handled Bering's cause that a new expedition to Kamchatka was already certain.[52] It was certain thanks in part to the Koriaks' great turbulence, which had resulted in the deaths of many members of the recent expedition to Chukotka under Afanasii Shestakov, a cossack officer who had been working independently of Bering's company.[53] Also a factor, it appears, was the sympathetic attitude adopted towards plans for a new venture in the East by the vice-chancellor, Count Ostermann. Ostermann had gained an early footing in St. Petersburg as a result of the patronage of Cruys, whose secretary he had been. He had not wholly forgotten his indebtedness to Cruys.[54]

Further orders went to Skorniakov-Pisarev on 30 July. From Iakutsk he was to take three hundred men, debtors and prisoners if possible, and set them all to breaking land and sowing seed around Okhotsk. Tungus were also to be ordered to Okhotsk to herd cattle and tend sheep.[55] Many months before the order for the Second Bering or Great Northern Expedition was officially announced on 17 April 1732,[56] Kirillov and the Senate had essential preparations under way.

THE SAUNDERS AND GOLOVIN PROPOSALS (1732)

Even in this period of general decline for the whole Navy, there were officers who took as genuine an interest in Bering's half-success and further plans as Peter I would have done. Two such officers were Captain Nikolai Fedorovich Golovin and Vice-Admiral Thomas Saunders. Both were able men who well recalled the naval glory of the days of Hangö (Gangut), when the Russian Baltic Fleet had overcome the strength of Sweden. Both deplored Russia's continuing decline as a sea power and had private reasons for an interest in Bering and in Russia's naval prospects in the East. Count Golovin's father, F. A. Golovin, had in 1686 dispatched the earliest of Russian expeditions to seek out a North-East Passage to the Indies from the River Lena's mouth, and in 1689, he had signed the Treaty of Nerchinsk on Russia's part.[57] Bering and Saunders were related through their wives, the Godwig sisters. Their professional connection would in all events have been inevitable.[58]

Saunders and Golovin had both had sight of Bering's written report of 1730 on his first expedition and had subsequently met him in St. Petersburg on numerous occasions. They were struck by his remarks about the painful difficulty of the journey to Okhotsk. They were aware that another venture was afoot in the remote North-East and East under the cossack Shestakov and that Kirillov was developing another. Anxious that the Navy play its part in the new Bering enterprise, at least, and thereby satisfy the Imperial demands of 31 January 1732 that it look to the condition of its ships and give more and better training to the Russian-born,[59] both drafted papers on the matter.[60]

Bering's experience, they argued, showed the folly and expense of sending seamen and equipment from the capital, or even from Tobol'sk, to the Pacific littoral. Perhaps it was imprudent to send everything for a new enterprise by sea; but the Navy might take much heavy equipment to Kamchatka by way of South America. It might be stormy, but the Cape Horn passage was well known; nor was the "tropic zone" inevitably dangerous for northern mariners. En route, a Russian cargo might be sold, perhaps in China. On 12 September 1732, the Admiralty College's representation on these matters, that is, Golovin's and Saunders' complementary proposals, were considered by the Senate. "Members of the Admiralty College," reads the Senate record for that day, "were summoned to this Senate and declared that it is possible to send ships to Kamchatka from St. Petersburg. The ships could be repaired there, as it is proposed that they should be, and naval officers would gain in practical experience."[61] In turn, the Senate sent a paper to the College with instructions that the sending of vessels to Kamchatka from the Baltic Sea be further studied.[62] Golovin and Saunders now developed and refined their own proposals, stressing the time that could be saved by sending seamen and equipment by the southern route. Bering's experience, they noted, had shown that it took two years to convey all the supplies for a North-Eastern expedition to its starting point. Two more years were needed to construct an ocean-going craft or two, and yet two more to make a voyage from Kamchatka, to return, and to report back to St. Petersburg. A vessel, on the other hand, might reach Kamchatka from the Baltic in ten months. In its entirety, an expedition need not last more than three seasons if it sailed around Cape Horn to the peninsula. There were other either probable or certain benefits from the approach. Denmark and Sweden were methodically developing their commerce overseas. Russia could also have a mercantile marine, for which an annual voyage round the world by one or two ships would prepare the needed officers and men. Too many naval vessels were inactive, even rotting at their moorings. Yet ships were wanted in the North Pacific region to defend the Russian interest from the inevitable jealousy of other naval powers and from native depredations and attacks. Their presence would moreover give unruly native peoples an impression of the might of Russia. Those same natives could conceivably be trained in naval arts. "By the time vessels return to St. Petersburg, they may indeed be splendid seamen, like the men who brought the vessels out. Natives might also be employed in little boats, according to the need."[63]

Saunders's and Golovin's proposals were completed and submitted to the Senate on 1 October 1732. Golovin was actually working on "Instructions For the Sending of Two Frigates to Kamchatka,"[64] confident that they would sail, when he learned of his defeat by the proponents of a different approach towards Kamchatka and the imminent Great Northern Expedition, as the second Bering venture was later to be known (28 December 1732).[65] Nonetheless, his views and those of Saunders marked the dawn of a new age and attitude in Russian naval circles where the North Pacific Ocean was concerned. Despite those officers' opinion on the subject, the Russian Navy was in fact to expend enormous energy on Arctic exploration in the effort to determine once and for all whether a ship could reach Kamchatka and the Orient from northern Russian ports or river mouths. But Golovin and Saunders, though frustrated at the time, had sown a seed that would fare better in the long term than the seed planted by Fedor Saltykov.

Kirillov was a man of sweeping intellect; yet he was little interested in the strictly maritime. He had never been to sea for any period nor laboured in a shipyard. Of the 14 local maps that he completed for his *Atlas* (360 were projected), not one was of a coastline. Ever conscious of the need for better surveys of the northern parts of Russia and Siberia and of the need to foster industry and trade in their immense interiors, he was unmoved by the oceanic projects that he read. There was, he said, "no cause for Russian mariners to pass through the equator and to suffer from the sun." Nor, by exploiting northern waters and perhaps finding a navigable passage to Kamchatka, need they ever "brave Algerians or other ocean pirates."[66] In the North, new wealth and trade might be developed for the exclusive benefit of Russia; overseas, wealth would be lost to foreign merchants.

PREPARATIONS FOR ANOTHER EXPEDITION (1731-33)

Here in extract are the first three points or articles of Bering's *Propositions (Predlozheniia)* relating to discovery and maritime activity beyond Kamchatka:

1. According to my observations, waves off Eastern Kamchatka are smaller than in other seas; moreover, I found on Karaginskii Island large firs that do not grow on Kamchatka. These are both indications that America, or some land to the west of it, is not far from Kam-

chatka—between 100 and 250 miles, perhaps. One might easily ascertain this by constructing a vessel of 40 or 50 tons and sending it to explore. If such land is, in fact, close, a trade might be established between its natives and the Russian Empire.

2. Such a vessel could be built in Kamchatka: the necessary timber can be obtained there more easily [than in Okhotsk]. The same is true of foodstuffs: fish and game are very cheap there. Also, more assistance may be had from the Kamchatkan natives than from those at Okhotsk. One final factor should not be overlooked: the Kamchatka River mouth is deeper than the Okhota's, and offers better shelter for craft.

3. It would be beneficial to discover a sea-route from the Okhota or Kamchatka Rivers to the Amur River and Japan. Those parts are known to be inhabited, and it would be very profitable to trade with the people in question, the Japanese especially. Since we ourselves have no boats in those parts, we might so arrange matters with the Japanese that they meet us halfway in their own vessels.[67]

Bering's proposals were discussed first at the Admiralty College and Academy of Sciences, then in committee in the Senate; and, in principle, they were approved by May 1731. Kirillov now established a rapport with the Academy by dealing, not with Joseph-Nicolas Delisle, but with such younger German scientists as Johann-Georg Gmelin and Georg-Wilhelm Steller.[68] At the same time, he drew Ostermann into discussion of the international facets of the expedition's work and made a study of despatches that had lately been received, via Tobol'sk, from members of the Shestakov-Pavlutskii expedition to Chukotka.[69] Not only had that expedition taken over Bering's *Sv. Gavriil* and *Fortuna*; it had also built two other vessels at Okhotsk and made (in general disastrous) voyages towards Penzhina Bay, the Shantar Island group, and Bol'sheretsk.[70] Again the Koriaks had shown their hatred of their conquerors.

Not without some tension between members of the Admiralty College and the Senate, then, but nonetheless with an increasing sense of purpose, a committee met to organize the details of the coming expedition. It continued to meet often until March 1733 and soon began to stretch the scope and objects of the latest expedition, thereby rendering its overall administration difficult even for ten or fifteen men, let alone one. In due course, it was agreed that the Great Northern Expedition should be treated for logistic and administrative purposes as several, distinctive undertakings, but that Bering should direct the complex whole as best he could. Slowly, the nature of the planned "sub-expeditions," each of which was to require its particular equipment and supplies, became apparent. There were geological, meteorological, botanical, and ethnographic surveys to be carried out by land and sea, regardless of conditions, over periods of months.[71]

There was charting of the northern shore of Russia and Siberia, a voyage to America, a voyage to Japan. Bering himself should make the voyage to America; Spanberg should proceed via the Kurile Islands to Japan, while in the Arctic, other groups moved in the opposite direction.[72] As an order for an enterprise to be directed by one man, the edict of 28 December 1732 was quixotic.

Years had already passed since Bering had submitted his original report to his superiors. At least the preparation for departure had accelerated when, in May 1732, an outline of the expedition's objects had been published by the government.[73] Since June 1732, College, Academy, and Senate had been scanning lists of possible participants. J.-N. Delisle's half-brother, Louis Delisle de la Croyère, and Gmelin both expressed the wish to go themselves. So did Steller (1709-46) and Gerhard Friedrich Müller (1705-83), the historian. All were accepted and required to engage in astronomical, botanical, or geographic work, both in the far North-East and East and on the way. Attempts were made, however, to take Russian-born rather than foreign naval officers—with only moderate success.[74] Vanguards were selected and their march routes fixed; instructions went ahead to Turukhansk, Tobol'sk, Iakutsk, Okhotsk, and other places. Altogether, seven parties were to work in seven interlocking areas of coast. The first four were to chart the northern littoral of Russia and Siberia between the mouths of the Pechora and the Enisei. The fifth was to survey the shore between the Enisei's mouth and that of the Kamchatka, the sixth, to make a voyage from Kamchatka to America, the seventh, to sail to Japan. All parties were to study watercurrents on their areas of coast as well as air and water temperatures, changing ice conditions, and local timber types.[75] If either the sixth or seventh party happened to encounter a European vessel, the officer in charge should state that scientific motives, and no others, had resulted in his temporary presence.[76]

Here are extracts from those parts of Bering's orders that relate to naval matters. Taken from Sections V and XIV, they are illustrative of the government's acceptance of the Navy's growing function as an instrument of further exploration in the far North-East:

> With regard to the voyage to America: it was ordered earlier, in 1731, that ships for this purpose should be built at Okhotsk. If they are ready, Bering should take two and proceed; if not, he should have them brought to readiness. If they have not yet been started on or have proved unseaworthy, the Admiralty College is of opinion that the vessels should not be constructed at Okhotsk. Bering recommends that, because it offers more building timber and a better harbour, Kamchatka should be the building place. He wishes to have two vessels for the voyage, one to stand by in case of misfortune. If one vessel has been completed at Okhotsk, it would be well to take her to Kamchatka and there build the second. Bering will command

one of these vessels, Chirikov the other. They will keep company on the voyage, work together, and do all that they can to advance the naval sciences.

To prevent the expedition from being delayed as a result of the slowness of transporting supplies and provisions of various kinds, the Admiralty College will immediately send special officers to Iakutsk to build boats there and so expedite the transporting of materials.[77]

Lessons had been learned both from the former expedition led by Bering and from Shestakov's more recent and more terrible experiences in Kamchatka and Chukotka. Still the Kamchadals, the Koriaks, and most of all the Chukchi posed a threat to cossack rule in their respective areas of the North-East. Coincidentally, the fact lent weight to Bering's argument that it was time to pay attention to Okhotsk. "Convinced that the remoteness of Iakutsk made it difficult for the officials there to follow the deeds of persons sent to such remote places for *iasak*, St. Petersburg [now] made Okhotsk the administrative centre for the whole northeastern region of Siberia."[78] Bering was given greater latitude of action than before; and it was recognized, at last, that special officers were indispensable, unless a period of years was to elapse before the sixth and seventh parties reached their foreign destinations. Also, the Senate sensibly recommended that the expedition's officers at least should receive a full year's payment in advance and, if they wished, one more year's pay upon arrival in Siberia. There should, moreover, be promotions at an early stage of the new expedition and not only, as before, at the conclusion.[79]

FOREIGN INTEREST (1730-33)

Again, for lack of strength in the remote North-East and East, the Russian government was trusting that no meeting would occur between the members of a Russian expedition in the North Pacific Ocean and a Spanish company. Again its servants were obliged to act with constant circumspection; for if Russia's dignity could not be bolstered militarily in waters or countries claimed by Spain, then policy dictated that the very possibility of a humiliation be avoided. The dilemma was to grow familiar to Russian naval officers in the Pacific.

In fact, Madrid was not on guard against incursions by the Russians or their agents into Spain's Pacific empire. The Duque de Berwick y de Liria, as Spanish minister, had more than once mentioned the Strait of Anian and Captain Bering in despatches from St. Petersburg or Moscow,[80] but he had had no orders to protest against such ventures and, in any case, had been recalled in November 1730.[81] The Spanish interest remained unrepresented in St. Petersburg, and

Spain was consequently ignorant of cossack enterprise and naval ventures off Kamchatka. She had neither books nor contacts to provide her with alarming information. Elsewhere in Europe, there were pockets of awareness of the Russian enterprise. As well as in the newspaper accounts noted earlier, it was dealt with, for example, in Strahlenberg's *L'Empire de la Russie* (Stockholm, 1730) and was reflected in the maps of Johann Baptiste Homann, to whom Jacob Bruce had forwarded a map of the North-East by I. K. L'vov, late of Iakutsk,[82] and of J.-B. d'Anville.

In London, both scientists and speculative merchants took an interest in Bering's half-success. The British had no vested interest, no claim to the "Great Land," as did the Spanish Crown. But, on the other hand, the British interest in navigable passages to China over Russia was traditional, dating from the early sixteenth century. There had, moreover, been an English element in the First Bering Expedition (Richard Ensel, George Morison). In offering the Russian minister, Prince A. D. Kantemir, a "Project for Discovering a Navigable Passage from the Town of Arkhangel'sk round Nova Zembla to Japan, China, the Indies and America," the merchant and adventurer John Elton merely followed ancient precedent.[83]

Elton, whose origins remain obscure, spoke to Kantemir of profits to be made if only Russia used a seaway to Kamchatka. Quite apart from other trade that might result, a whaling industry might be established in the North. Use of the passage to Kamchatka and beyond would in itself constitute valuable training for whole naval companies. And for an outlay of £1,200, he would undertake to discover such a passage with his own two ships. He sought only a small share of the profit from a new trade with the East.[84] Kantemir engaged his services; dispatched a copy of his project to St. Petersburg on 29 December 1732; gave him a passport; and expressed his great displeasure when, some five weeks later, Captain Elton was arrested for a criminal offence in Middlesex.[85] Elton did ultimately join the Russian service (and for good measure, the Persian service too).[86] By then, however, his involvement in the Russian North Pacific enterprise was at an end. His service to the Admiralty College showed that advocates of naval expeditions to the far North-East and Orient might hope to justify such costly undertakings by referring to valuable products (oil, whalebone) to be gathered on the way.

THE SECOND BERING EXPEDITION: ST. PETERSBURG TO OKHOTSK (1733-39)

The first detachments of the Second Bering Expedition left St. Petersburg in March 1733. Bering himself left in mid-April.[87] His route, and that of the fourth, fifth, sixth, and seventh parties, lay through Vologda, Solikamsk, Turinsk, Tiumen', Tobol'sk, and Iakutsk. Spanberg went ahead to the Pacific to direct the fitting out of vessels which, it was imagined very wrongly, Pisarev had on the slipway in Okhotsk. What he found on his arrival angered him. The commandant had not established quarters in Okhotsk until May 1733 and had immediately quarrelled with the cossack officers. Made furious by an attempt to jail and try him, the cossack captain seized equipment and supplies that Pisarev had had transported from Iakutsk, whereupon Pisarev departed for Iakutsk once more, intending to make trouble for his enemy. Denunciations flew. It was in Iakutsk, at the beginning of another year, that he and Bering clashed for the first time. By then, relations between Pisarev and Spanberg, who was also in the region, had deteriorated to the level first of slander, then of threatened violence. The man who claimed to be the local commandant, Spanberg wrote to the Admiralty College, was a drunkard and a villain, tortured natives, and was known to keep a harem. Captain Spanberg, answered Pisarev, was morally, politically, and professionally dangerous, a friend of common criminals, a bandit. At this juncture, Bering reached Okhotsk. The air was thick with malice and mutual contempt.[88]

An unhappy series of deliberate or unavoidable delays, slanders, and outbreaks of envenomed bickering marked the expedition's progress—or, more accurately, lack of it—in 1735-37, but they do not directly bear on naval matters. Suffice it to note that, six full years having elapsed since Bering's venture had been formally approved in Senate, neither the sixth nor seventh party had yet sailed from Okhotsk; and constant bickering continued between regional officials and the expedition's officers. Despite his rank, Bering himself performed the work of petty officers, recruiting, requisitioning, examining minutiae, investigating losses and delays. At one time, he had publicly maintained that the whole set of expeditions in the North, North-East, and East could be financed for 12,000 or 13,000 roubles. Already, their cost had passed 300,000. Understandably, the time came when the Senate felt obliged to tell the Admiralty College to control its servants' spending in Siberia. The College acted in November 1737: Bering's pay was halved "as a result of failures to send wanted information and to undertake the work assigned to him."[89] To cancel the sixth and seventh parties was a possible response to such delays and mounting costs; but this solution was quickly put aside. Its adoption would confirm the loss of 520,000 roubles.[90] Instead, it was decided to send special officers holding extraordinary powers to investigate and hasten progress in the East.[91] Lieutenants Larionov and Tolbukhin were accordingly dispatched in March 1739. Their arrival brought results: within six months, all but a fraction of the necessary stores had reached Okhotsk; work speeded up on the construction of two vessels, the *Sv. Petr* and *Sv. Pavel*; and relations between Bering and Chirikov, who now found himself expected to report on his commander to the Admiralty College, became tense.[92]

Brig-rigged, 80 feet in length, and mounting fourteen cannon (two to three pounders), the *Sv. Petr* and *Sv. Pavel* were both ready to be loaded by mid-June 1740. Lading went ahead under Chirikov's supervision.[93]

THE POSITION OF THE NAVY IN SIBERIA

Again the Navy, and the Admiralty College in particular, had shown themselves ill-fitted to solve problems in Siberia. Those problems were of two connected sorts: communication and liaison. The former were perhaps inevitable, inasmuch as they arose from the location of the College on the Baltic and the Navy's former areas of operation. The College had no branch beyond the Urals, save that newly established at Okhotsk, no couriers, no local officers. The latter might have been much eased, if not removed, by timely administrative measures in the Senate.

All communications between European Russia and the far North-East and East were slow and difficult. Having control of neither drivers nor horses in Siberia or inland Russia[94] and depending in an urgent case on services of special officers like Larionov, the Admiralty College had to view delays in all responses to its orders as inevitable. Expectation of delay led to deliberate delay.[95] Siberian officials, for their part, did not propose to change a venerable, profitable transportation system for the benefit of servants of the Navy.[96] Coupled with the unco-operative attitude of a man like Pisarev and with resentment towards Bering and his men on the part of certain high-ranking Siberian officials,[97] such factors aggravated the communications problem.

A celebrated instance of delay in the reception of a piece of information from Siberia occurred after July 1732, when the *Sv. Gavriil*, with M. P. Gvozdev, I. I. Fedorov and other men aboard, stood in the shadow of the Chukchis' ''Great Land'' near modern Cape Prince of Wales. Some ten months later, Gvozdev sent his logbook and a brief report to Pisarev. They failed to reach the capital, even in extract.[98] Four years later, a seaman who had been with Gvozdev was suspected of a crime, interrogated, and alluded to the ''Great Land'' he had seen. News of this did reach St. Petersburg. By 1741, orders reached Okhotsk for Gvozdev and Skurikhin, who had also been aboard *Sv. Gavriil* nine years before, to make a full report about their voyage. Extracts only were dispatched, via Irkutsk. Spanberg now asked Gvozdev to compose another copy. Returning to Okhotsk a little later, he did so in September 1743. This copy went by courier to the Admiralty College, arriving a dozen years after the voyage.[99] The case was an extraordinary one, but it illustrated a perennial dilemma which, till solved, would necessarily affect the Navy's efforts in the East. Spanberg's experience was further proof of this. Returning to the capital after a voyage to Japan in 1740, he was halted by instructions in Iakutsk. The College wished him to remain there for a period. He then received a message from the Senate, telling him to hasten to St. Petersburg. He left. Within the week, he had an order from the Admiralty College, instructing him to go back to Okhotsk.[100] What could be done about the problem? To delegate more power to the officers in the remote North-East and East was possible, but it was hardly palatable as a policy.

It was unfortunate that such a policy was not, in fact, adopted, for the matter of professional relations between naval and cossack officers would thereby have been clarified to mutual advantage. As it was, the question remained cloudy; and beyond it lay the question of appropriate relations between naval officers and other social elements in the remote North-East and East—*promyshlenniki* (private hunter-traders), for example. As the naval presence grew more prominent, these questions were bound to grow more troublesome, unless resolved by definitions or, at least, delimitations, of the several parties' roles.

SPANBERG AND WALTON IN JAPAN (1738-40)

Spanberg was entrusted with the survey of the Kurile Island chain south to Japan (Hokkaido) and with the study of Japan itself. If any Kurile Islanders would pay him *iasak* and acknowledge Russian sovereignty, that was excellent; however, he was not to pass his time extorting *iasak* from the hostile or independent-minded, but to chart the sea approaches to Japan with some precision.[101] For lack of foodstuffs, he and his second-in-command, Lieutenant William Walton, were obliged to postpone their sailing from Okhotsk until mid-June 1738. It was from Bol'sheretsk, and not Okhotsk that they proposed to make their pass along the Kuriles. Their vessels were a new, one-masted brigantine, *Arkhangel Mikhail*, and a double-sloop, *Nadezhda*. Spanberg was to captain the former: she was 60 feet in length and had a crew of sixty-three; Walton took the latter and her crew of forty-four. Ensign A. E. Schelting commanded the *Sv. Gavriil*. Spanberg's navigator was Petrov, Lt. Walton's, Kazimirov. Both were able men.[102]

Passing Paramushir Island on their first voyage due south, they were surprised not to discover "Gama Land." Less surprising was the squadron's inability to move in station: *Nadezhda* was too fast, and *Sv. Gavriil* too sluggish under light or fickle winds. The sea was tranquil, the air grew warmer as they went; but summer fogs soon swallowed everything, splitting the squadron. Spanberg saw an island or cape beyond Uruppu, but he did not proceed. The jagged rocky shores, erratic currents, fogs, and other dangers became more alarming as autumn days grew briefer. Spanberg rounded Uruppu, and on 14 August 1738, in estimated latitude 45° 30'N., turned back to Bol'sheretsk, where he dropped anchor two weeks later. The *Nadezhda* had preceded him. When Walton finally arrived, now in the *Sv. Gavriil*, he reported having seen Hokkaido from 43° 20'.

Spanberg resolved to set out earlier the following summer. Accordingly, the squadron, which had lately been augmented by the launching of a small, eighteen-oar sloop, the *Bol'sheretsk*, left the peninsula at dawn on 1 June 1739. Again there was no sight of Gama Land. After a week, Schelting transferred into the *Nadezhda*, Walton again into the *Sv. Gavriil*: the transfer, for which Spanberg was later severely criticized, was symptomatic of increasing strain in his relationship with Walton.[103]

The squadron laid a course south-west, away from the Kurile Island chain.

Two weeks later, Spanberg's crew saw the north-east shores of Honshu, largest of the islands that comprise Japan, in lat. 39° 31'N. They followed them due south in drifting fog. Then Spanberg and Walton lost each other. Two days later, Spanberg and Quartermaster Ert, in *Bol'sheretsk*, which had remained in contact, stood at anchor off the east coast of Iwate Prefecture (lat. 38° 41'N.). The area is now part of Rikuchu National Coastal Park and recognized as being of especial beauty. Spanberg and his men were impressed by the luxuriance and freshness of the country that they saw. Later, the Russians landed and were met with cautious friendliness. A little trade ensued, and Spanberg made a careful study of the money, dress, and products of the Japanese whom he had chanced to meet.[104] The squadron then turned back, discovering three unknown Kurile Islands in latitude 44° 24'N. and landing on Figurnyi. Collecting shells, the shore party found pearls; but there was neither gold nor silver to be seen. The squadron, minus the *Bol'sheretsk*, now made for Nutsiam and the surrounding group, and thence for Matsumae. Here they met and studied a flotilla of small Japanese craft, "between seven and nine *sazhen*" in length, with "blunt bows, one mast, sloping decks . . . a cabin, and one fixed sail apiece."[105] The weather was becoming threatening; there was a swell, and crew members were growing sick from scurvy. Spanberg headed north for Bol'sheretsk, and not a day too soon. The company with Schelting in *Nadezhda* were enfeebled. Eleven seamen died before the voyage ended in Kamchatka.

Walton, meanwhile, had landed further south on Honshu (lat. approximately 35° 10'N.), by Amatsu Village in Nagasa County on the modern Boso Peninsula. From his anchorage in the open sea, he had sent a boat ashore for water. In the boat were Navigator Kazimirov, two assistant navigators, and six seamen. Many small Japanese craft came out to meet the Russian boat and soon surrounded it so closely that the visitors could hardly row. Since they persisted, however, the Japanese did not attempt to keep them from the shore. On landing, it seems they were civilly received. Kazimirov was apparently invited into several village houses, and the Russians, so they afterwards asserted, were regaled with wine, rice, fruit, and other foods. They looked around with open curiosity and were themselves objects of wonder.[106]

Once the Russians had departed, local Japanese officials drafted suitable reports. In fact, it seems, the strangers had been treated with politeness, even friendliness; but the reports avoided reference to local hospitality and curiosity. Instead, the Russians were portrayed as having entered certain buildings uninvited and moreover as having grabbed all that they wanted.[107] All question of the relative trustworthiness of Japanese and Russian versions of these incidents apart, it must be kept in mind that, being totally committed to a policy of national isolation, [108] the Japanese at least were not at liberty to give a full and honest picture of events.

Such were the earliest encounters between Japanese and servants of the Russian Navy. By their ambivalent though courteous reception of the Russians, the inhabitants of Awa Province struck a note that was to sound through Russo-Japanese relations for a century to come. To the Japanese official mind, a Russian naval squadron was a spearhead of foreign interference or aggression. On the other hand, the Japanese had individually not been hostile and had even welcomed unexpected trade with Russian seamen—a fact that Spanberg noted in his subsequent reports.

The Admiralty College was well satisfied with Spanberg's execution of his mission to Japan. He was rewarded and promised the command of the whole Northern Expedition in due course, in place of Bering.[109] Then, as a result of conflicting orders, he set off for St. Petersburg, returned to Iakutsk, and finally rejoined his squadron at Okhotsk. Instructions followed to return even to Matsumae and Japan, to continue charting of the northern sea approaches to Honshu, and to develop good relations with the government and merchants of Japan.[110] There were, in fact, more Russian visits to Japan in 1742—by the *Sv. Ioann* (Spanberg), *Arkhangel Mikhail* (Schelting), and *Nadezhda* (Kozin); but they were tentative and hurried and did not represent any commercial or scientific advance on the visits of June-July 1739.[111] Hydrographically, indeed, the work of 1741-42 was disappointing. Schelting visited the Shantar Islands and the mouth of the Uda but did little charting; nor, after several Russian voyages to Matsumae from the north, had the relative position of the southern Kurile Islands, Hokkaido, and Sakhalin been ascertained. If anything, an ancient muddle had been worsened by Schelting, who mistook the coast of Sakhalin for that of Hokkaido.[112]

News of the Spanberg-Walton visits to Honshu of 1739 reached Amsterdam within six months of their conclusion. A report sent from St. Petersburg by the Dutch resident, J. Schwartz, was published in the *Amsterdam Gazette* on 13 January 1740. It noted that Admiral N. F. Golovin expected a circumstantial narrative from Spanberg on the subject of his visit and a chart.[113] On 27 July, the *Gazette de France* offered its readers information about Walton's and Spanberg's later dealings with the Kurile Islanders. It was ironic, in view of foreign confidence that Russians had indeed been in Japan, that in St. Petersburg the fact was to be questioned and debated in committee for five years (1741-46).[114] Again the hand of Pisarev may be discerned.[115]

In summary: the Spanberg expeditions from Kamchatka to Japan disproved the existence of Gama Land, established that Company Land, or Uruppu, was only one of the Kuriles, and fixed the geographical positions of Matsumae and the east coasts of Hokkaido and Honshu. They also brought a company of Russians to Japan for the first time, greatly augmented Russian knowledge of the government, society, and natural resources of the Japanese and Ainu, and, finally, made it apparent that the forming of official trade links between Russia and Japan would not be easy.

BERING'S AND CHIRIKOV'S VOYAGES TO NORTH AMERICA

By 1740, the several northern parties had been working, for the most part with remarkable success, for five whole years. The courage and endurance of the Laptev brothers is commemorated in the modern atlas by the Laptev Sea. Lassenius, Malygin, Pronshchikov, and others had also already earned their places in the annals of both Arctic exploration and naval history. Their work is a reminder of the extent to which sub-Arctic latitudes were involved in the early Russian presence in the North Pacific Ocean. Yet still the Bering party had not left Okhotsk. Only in June 1740 did the last of its equipment and supplies arrive, in poor enough condition, from Iakutsk. Delisle de la Croyère alone was to be given in Kamchatka five assorted telescopes, five astrolabes, twenty thermometers, and twenty-seven large barometers, as well as bulky copper spheres, chains, magnets and clocks enough to fill three carts.[116] By now, almost two hundred men were working on the *Sv. Pavel* and *Sv. Petr*. Bering was no longer young, and seven years had passed since his departure from St. Petersburg, when he set sail for Bol'sheretsk on 4 September 1740. A party had been working at Avacha Bay for months, charting and building. The new settlement was known as Petropavlovsk in honour of the expedition's vessels and the light "traveling church" that Bering brought to the peninsula and raised beside his modest winter quarters.[117] For a final nine-month period, the scientists, seamen, and officers all prepared for the voyage east. A warehouse, a powder-house, and a smithy were completed. All was readied on the ships, which stood on blocks above the ice. On 23 April 1741, Master Sofron Khitrov of *Sv. Petr* opened his log. That log and Iushin's are the basic records of the final Bering voyage.

In the Harbour of the Holy Apostles Peter and Paul.

> April 23 1741.   Today with the help of God, we began to load the ship *Sv. Petr*, on which worked eighteen men. The main shrouds were made fast to the mainmast, the preventer stay was also loosely secured; caulked inside the ship, and near the mainmast hole nailed blocks for opening the cannon portholes; cleaned the hold, and in the afternoon took on ballast.[118]

Once at least, Bering discussed the best course to be steered with his officers at large and with Delisle de la Croyère. They resolved to make for Gama Land, which Joseph-Nicolas Delisle's map showed lying between 45° and 47°N. At the close of May, Bering examined *Sv. Petr* and *Sv. Pavel* and was satisfied. Water was stowed. Both vessels headed out across Avacha Bay and thence south-east.

It was arranged that, if no land was sighted before they came to 45°N., they would then change their course to north by east—a course which Bering felt must bring them up to North America, the coast of which they would then follow north to 64° or 66°.

Bering and Chirikov sailed to 46°, changed course without having spotted Gama Land, and parted company in wretched conditions in mid-June. They never met again. Despite the need to change his course repeatedly to cope with veering winds, Bering kept generally east and sighted land on 16 July. There were snow-enveloped mountains in latitude approximately 58° 28'N. After tacking north-west, he dropped anchor with a prayer in the lee of Kayak Island (lat. 59° 48'N., long. 144° 3'W. by his own reckoning) and named the highest peak after St. Elias, whose day it was. Here, they obtained fresh water and Steller was allowed ashore for a few hours to explore and botanize. No one set foot on the mainland to the east. Within a day, in an increasing state of worry, Bering ordered the return to Petropavlovsk.[119]

The *Sv. Pavel*, too, had reached the coast of North America. Chirikov had in fact preceded Bering there by two days, to the satisfaction of all later Russian patriots, but he had encountered an immediate misfortune. A boat sent to the mainland with eleven men on board did not return. Fearing an accident or an attack, Chirikov had a second boat put off with four more men. It too failed to return, either having been attacked by local Indians or, what appears more probable, having foundered in the swell formed by the heavy tidal stream at L'tua Bay.[120] Chirikov had no other boat to send, either to aid his countrymen or to collect supplies and water from a mainland that had proved inimical. He therefore ordered the return against the wind to Petropavlovsk, where he finally dropped anchor nine weeks later. Six men died of scurvy on the weary voyage back including Louis Delisle de la Croyère.

The men of the *Sv. Pavel*, however, were fortunate compared with those in the *Sv. Petr*, for the latter's homeward voyage was dreadful. They were quickly lost in fogs and storms. Many were drawing close to death when, on 6 November, the *Sv. Petr* was thrown up on a barren, rocky shore which Bering wrongly took to be Kamchatka. It was actually Bering Island, more than a hundred miles from the peninsula. At sea or on this island, thirty perished, including Vitus Bering. Wracked by fever, thirst, and scurvy, the survivors of the shipwreck settled in for an appalling winter. Here and there along the shore lay corpses, dying men, and helpless sick. Blue foxes scattered the provisions, which the strongest men had carried from the *Sv. Petr* and piled in a heap, and nibbled corpses. Spring revived their hopes. There were fish and seals to be caught and there was water. The survivors started work on a crude, 40-foot boat, using timber salvaged from the *Sv. Petr*. They left the island, and many sandy graves, on 16 August, reaching Kamchatka three weeks later. They recuperated for eleven months before proceeding to Okhotsk.[121]

So perished Bering, whom it is customary to regard as a great mariner and eminent explorer. Certainly, it was a large achievement to have turned a fabled strait into a charted one. As an achievement, moreover, it was pregnant with political and economic consequences, for the Russians in particular but not exclusively. But what if Bering is detached from his voyage, with its worldwide implications for geographers and mariners alike? Was he a great commander? Hardly. On his first expedition he had shown great caution. On the second, he could hardly overcome the thought of failure in the hour of achievement. As a consequence, he placed success itself in jeopardy, staying at Kayak Island only long enough to water and provoking Steller's biting comment that the expedition had been planned "merely to carry some water from America to Asia, while ten years of preparation led to ten hours' exploration."[122] A study of Bering's actions of 1740-41 reveals how greatly his responsibility and age had worn him down.

Yet in his caution as in other ways, Bering established precedents for future naval officers in the Pacific area. Indeed his ventures set a pattern for the Navy's future expeditions in several respects: first, by the air of secrecy surrounding them, and seen as proper to them; second, in their prominent non-Slavic element; and third, in their attracting and sustaining the attention of the government with promises of great rewards in the event of success.

The very objects of the Bering expeditions were concealed from foreign governments, or at the least misrepresented and considerably simplified, for fear of diplomatic repercussions in which Russia might lose face. The Russian government did not and could not know the sites of Spanish settlements along the coast of North America. Hence they issued secret orders, which gave rise to that tone of hypercaution that pervaded even Bering's and Chirikov's own instructions to subordinates. Hence, also, there were several years of wholly inconclusive argument among geographers in Russia and abroad over the details of Russian sightings, landings, and activities in North America and the Aleutians. In itself, the failure of the government to publish what were obviously major geographical discoveries was partly the result of its attitude towards landings and activities in regions to which Spain had vague, but grandiose, pretensions. Possibly the Russian court rejected those pretensions, in fact if not in principle; nevertheless, it saw no reason to seek trouble far away and on another continent. Ignorant perforce of the facts of the *Sv. Petr*'s voyage, since the Russians had as yet to publish detailed information on it even after seven years, J.-N. Delisle provoked an international argument by stating in July 1748 that his half-brother had indeed set foot on North America, while Bering and his men had not. Delisle had gained his faulty information from reports recently printed in *Gazette de France*.[123] (Even the Admiralty College was not sure of the position of Bering Island; but the reason here was not political.)

Politically, all these uncertainties and controversies were of little moment.

Bering's and Chirikov's vessels had, no doubt, been fragile, noisome little craft; many had died as a result of their experiences in them. The mainland of America had yet to be examined by a Russian naval company. Even the charts that had been offered to the Admiralty College by Lt. Waxell, Bering's successor as the leader of the "sixth detachment," were not altogether satisfactory.[124] But these realities did not affect one basic and strategic consequence of those misfortunes and successes that are still, after three centuries, linked with Bering's name. Whatever foreign vessels might arrive in them in later years, seas between Kamchatka and America were understood to be under Russian influence. So they are today.

Effectively, all members of the Bering expeditions who were servants of the Navy were on special naval service. Naval service in the far North-East and East was thus viewed differently from service in the other, more traditional arenas of the Navy. Bering's people were on double pay. His officers were promised much if they did well, and the survivors did in fact reap major benefits. Lieutenants Ovtsyn, Schelting, Laptev senior, and others later reached flag rank. When Waxell died, as captain of the second rank, his widow had the handsome pension of 2,000 roubles annually. Aleksei Chirikov was promoted *kapitan-komandor* and presented to the empress. He died shortly thereafter of consumption. The demands and the rewards of naval service in the far North-East and East were, from the outset, very high. If the latter barely recompensed the sick man for the former, that too was in the pattern of the future.

The Bering expeditions left one other eastern legacy to Russia and her Navy: the establishment of Petropavlovsk as an embryonic port and of Okhotsk as an administrative centre with a wharf or two attached. Neither was altogether satisfactory. For all its deep and sheltered water, Petropavlovsk stood in desolate terrain; its latitude made agriculture difficult and shortened the ice-free period within Avacha Bay. As for Okhotsk, it was made dangerous by sandbars, fogs, and currents. The bar of the Okhota was not constant. The tidal stream was strong and, on the bar itself, too shallow to be safe except at high tide or within an hour of it. Even rye refused to ripen on its damp and windy shores.[125] Still, it was better to have ports with major shortcomings than to have none. And for three-quarters of a century, till 1812, Okhotsk remained the Russian Navy's base of operations and administrative centre in the East. For a period, the School of Navigation founded there at Bering's instance demanded little more than literacy of its pupils, who were children of the serving men and natives of the area. In 1755, classes were added in the technical and scientific skills of navigation.[126] It was more than a beginning.

3

Furs and Spaniards: Sindt and Krenitsyn

For twenty years and more after the death of Peter I, the naval strength of Russia declined. So also, by extension, did the prospect of officially avowed Russian activity in countries claimed by Spain. In the course of the Great Northern War with Sweden, Russia had become a significant naval power, with a Baltic Fleet of thirty-four ships-of-the-line, fifteen frigates, almost eighty galleys, and two dozen other vessels. Twenty-seven thousand seamen manned these vessels.[1] The establishment of a fresh Naval Commission—a delayed, grudging reaction to decay of the whole Baltic Fleet in January 1732—failed to arrest the slide, for its members all lacked influence at court. To the extent that it was conscious of defences and of Russian national interests, that German-speaking court was army-oriented.[2] The commission recommended that the strength of Russia's Navy remain steady for the next five years at twenty-seven ships-of-the line, six frigates, and a dozen other craft.[3] In fact, even these numbers were not reached. When Bering died, the Russian Navy had become incapable of actively exploiting his or any other distant findings or of waging a successful naval war even with Sweden. Nonetheless, war was declared against the Swedes in 1741. Russian relations with both Britain and France grew very strained. There was no need for Skorniakov-Pisarev to have denigrated Bering and belittled the achievements of his people in a "Short Account" of the report sent to the Admiralty College by Chirikov (August 1741)[4] in an effort to persuade the government that the Great Northern Expedition should be ended. Political developments closer to home had drawn the government's attention, and would soon draw its resources, from the east to the west.[5] The Senate urged the termination of the expedition on 23 September 1743, and the Crown consented.

All thought of complications with Spain over activities by Russians on the shores of North America was over for a period. Now was the time for wars with Frederick of Prussia; Russian victories at Kunersdorf and Zorndorf were the victories of soldiers, not seamen. Count Shuvalov, the minister responsible under Elizabeth Petrovna for economic matters, which reduced themselves in time to raising money for his mistress, was a grandee with an interest in maritime affairs. He was also the new empress's trusted adviser. Even he, however, was not able to do more than stop the Admiralty shipyards on the Baltic and at Arkhangel'sk, the latter under English supervision at this time, from falling altogether idle. As minister responsible for national solvency, his wings were clipped by his own policies.[6] One year after acceding to the throne, Elizabeth had made symbolic gestures of support for the navy that her father had founded, but still it had less than twenty men-of-war and fourteen frigates available. The rest were judged unfit to put to sea.[7]

SLACKENING OF NAVAL ACTIVITY ON THE PACIFIC LITTORAL

Neglected by the Admiralty College and forgotten by the court, the Navy's few remaining officers and seamen in the far North-East and East were by and large left to their own devices. Other State officials judged that heavy State investments in remote north-eastern regions had produced a poor return.[8] The judgment was too harsh. Politically, the Bering and Chirikov voyages to North America were of immense significance.[9] Four thousand miles of Arctic or sub-Arctic coastline had been charted, and a sea-route to Japan had been discovered. As a scientific venture, Bering's Second Expedition had been fruitful far beyond the expectation of Delisle. Suffice it to mention the ethnography of Jacob Lindenau, the botany of Steller, and the work of founding fathers of Siberian historiography, Müller and Krasheninnikov.[10] As to the venture's cartographic benefits, they were apparent from a glance at the Academy of Sciences' *Atlas Rossiiskii (Russian Atlas, 1745).*[11] All this, however, failed to counteract a loss of interest in the remote North-East of Asia on the part of many senators.

In their view the expedition had assuredly underlined problems for development of the remote North-East and East, but had suggested few solutions. Agriculture, it emerged, was difficult in many areas, if not impractical;[12] nor was it evident that iron could be worked in Transbaikalia—much of the expedition's iron had been brought from the Tamginskii foundry in the Urals.[13] There were insufficient colonists in Eastern Siberia to foster rapid economic growth. The Senate's mood, in short, no longer favoured the continuation of Chirikov's work in the North-East; and his suggestion that at least two of the expedition's

ships be kept employed about Kamchatka and the islands on defence and training duties and "in finding a suitable island, sea-girt but adjacent to the mainland, where a fortress might be built that could withstand even an onslaught,"[14] though accepted by the Admiralty College, was rejected by the
Senate, which reflected the prevailing mood at court. From the government's
altered perspective of mid-century, even Okhotsk seemed a distinctly less attractive and important proposition than it had a few years earlier. It seemed, in
fact, to be a place that both the Admiralty College and the Senate could allow
to lie in peace, always provided that a few vessels were built and a few navigators trained there, while occasional hydrography proceeded.

Only at Okhotsk, as a result of this official attitude, was there professional
marine activity on Russia's eastern shore in the mid-1740's. There, at least, the
very frequency with which the products of its yard foundered in storms, as a result of leaking hulls or of a pilot's inefficiency, made periodic building and repair of little vessels a necessity. Ten craft had been constructed there by the
mid-1730's, after which the following were built and launched: the brigantine
Arkhangel Mikhail, 1735-37, finally wrecked in 1753; the double-sloop *Nadezhda,* lost in the same year; the galiot *Okhotsk,* 1737, lost in 1748; the vessels linked with Bering, *Sv. Petr* and *Sv. Pavel;* and Spanberg's *Ioann Kresti-
tel',* wrecked in 1743.[15] There is no reason to believe that the two Admiralty
shipwrights at Okhotsk during the 1740's, Kozmin and Rogachev, were not
competent. A number of their vessels, after all, saw ten years' service, and the
builder bears no blame if ships are lost through the incompetence or drunkenness of pilots. But about Okhotsk, in the mid-eighteenth century, carelessness
was normal. Remoteness from all other centres and neglect by central government officials were reflected in the fact that, at the centre of the Navy's eastern
presence, less than twenty craft were built in thirty years (1716-46). Nor could
many of those galiots that sailed out to Kamchatka from Okhotsk have safely
ventured on a voyage to the ports and towns of China or Japan.[16] Enormous
trading opportunities were lost for want of Baltic-standard vessels, seamen, and
pilots. If the Admiralty Office at Okhotsk was growing conscious of the fact by
the mid-century, it was because its own involvement in fostering local trade
and commerce was already far more open and substantial than analagous activity by any other Admiralty Office.[17]

During the 1740's, local survey work was carried out intermittently under its
aegis. Lieutenant A. Khmet'evskii drew a chart that covered the whole Sea of
Okhotsk in a broad, undetailed way, while a cartographer in Admiralty pay, F.
Ushakov, drew up a map of the Kamchatkan coast between the mouths of the
Bol'shaia and the Tigil rivers which was forwarded, via the Admiralty Office at
Okhotsk, to the Academy of Sciences. Khmet'evskii took the coastal survey on
from Gizhiginsk to Okhotsk. Neither he nor Ushakov obtained promotion for
this work. Like the School of Navigation at Okhotsk, the school founded at

Bol'sheretsk by Skorniakov-Pisarev's successor as commandant, the exile Antoine Devière, had been neglected altogether by Tobol'sk since his recall to fame and favour in the capital in 1742.[18] The local school at Bol'sheretsk collapsed. The School of Navigation was enabled to survive by high mortality among the region's pilots: some at least had necessarily to be replaced.

THE COSSACK ADVANCE THROUGH THE ALEUTIAN ISLAND CHAIN

By comparison, contemporaneous activity by groups of serving men based in Kamchatka and, especially, by *promyshlenniki* was intense.[19] Encouraged by the voyages of Bering and Chirikov to the "Great Land" and by those of Spanberg, Walton, and their squadron down the Kuriles to Japan, they did not hesitate before embarking upon long and risky hunting ventures, most particularly in the east. Without the aid of Navy men, except for men like Sannikov, pilot of the *Kapiton* (1743-46), who had received his training at Okhotsk, local furhunters were already reaching out by way of Bering Island and the Mednyi (Copper) Islands, to the "Near," that is, more westerly, of the Aleutians (Attu, Agattu). The cossack wave[20] soon rolled on east, over the Andreianov Group (Adakh, Atka, Kanaga). There were forty-two hunting or trading expeditions from Kamchatka to the Aleutian Islands in the twenty-one-year period 1743-64. Of these, a third were over by 1752.[21] Some vessels were commanded by their owners. Most were owned by groups of traders, some of whom were absent partners. Three or four had serving men from Bol'sheretsk or other strongpoints in Kamchatka as their captains. Most of the crews were comprised to some extent of volunteers on short contract, that is, of *promyshlenniki*. Many were manned entirely by such men; and an illiterate and lawless band they were. Barely controlled by their own leaders, prone to violence, courageous in adversity, which often came, they spread the influence of Russia ever eastwards.[22]

Initially, and in decreasing numbers till the last years of the century, "sewn vessels" (*shitiki*) were used on the long run between peninsula and islands. The *shitik* was a makeshift craft of green, slender, unseasoned timbers lashed, or "sewn," together by an inner and an outer row of perishable thongs, often of leather but not always; in the North-East any material at hand was put to use. It was a rough, eastern descendant of the inland river vessels used by cossacks for centuries, but adapted by a higher bow, raised side, deep waist, and little deck for ocean-voyaging. As time progressed, the deck grew larger, but the bottom remained rather flat and heavily constructed, like that of a Dutch dogger of the period.[23] It was the lineal descendant of the single-masted *koch,* or wooden vessel of North Russia, strongly influenced, however, by the ancient Volga *strug.*[24] Surviving features of the inland river *strug* were disadvantages in the open and current-ridden waters of the Aleutians, where the "Current of Japan" met and did battle with the failing Arctic current from the north.

The Aleuts had a better craft for use about the islands. The *baidarka* was a practically unsinkable light frame of driftwood, over which were stretched taut skins. The Aleuts used a double-bladed paddle and a one-piece seal-gut jacket (the *kamleika*) and confidently took their little kayaks far from sight of any land. For the *promyshlennik,* co-operation from the Aleuts was essential. Therefore, if he could not gain rapid assistance from them peaceably, he soon extorted it.[25] The tale of the *promyshlennik* advance through the Aleutian Island chain is one of outrage and oppression. It is also one of daring that occasionally verges on the fabulous. With their teeming seal and otter colonies, green grassy precipices, and persistent fog, the islands initially seemed wonderful to the seamen from Kamchatka. Returning with a cargo of three thousand fresh sea-otter skins, many from Kanaga and Adakh, Andreian Tolstykh, owner and master of the vessel *Andreian i Natal'ia,* overcame disaster in the form of storm and shipwreck, saved his furs, and so became a wealthy man.[26] He was quickly followed east by other captains, some of whom found islands of their own between Kamchatka and America. Self-interest dictated that reports of such discoveries be neither too precise nor too elaborate. Profitability could, after all, only decline with the demise of secrecy.

GOVERNMENT CONTROL AND INTERVENTION

> The Kamchatkan and Siberian *promyshlenniks* were a kind of fur-hunting and trading privateer, under Government control only in being required to pay tribute on the products of their enterprise.[27]

So wrote H. H. Bancroft more than ninety years ago. Since then, there has been almost ceaseless controversy over the extent to which the central, or even the Siberian, administration was able to direct or control the flow of serving men and private hunter-traders to the Kurile and Aleutian islands. Some scholars have contended that the central government played only the most marginal role in the expansion of the cossacks' enterprise in 1743-53. "Infected by a passion for great voyages,"[28] these scholars have suggested, the cossacks and *promyshlenniki* were themselves the driving force behind the movement to the east.[29] Other writers have insisted that the enterprise was given its direction, even shaped to some extent, by high Siberian officialdom and that far from representing a departure from preceding economic processes in the remote North-East and East,[30] the cossack enterprise on the Aleutian Island chain was a controlled continuation of those processes.[31] The argument continues; the truth appears to lie between the two positions. Certainly, there was some government involvement in the seaborne hunting enterprise during the 1740's. Reports of Basov's voyages, for instance, were submitted to St. Petersburg, via Tobol'sk, and two years later long instructions on the subject of such voyages by other serving men based in Kamchatka reached Okhotsk. Again, samples of copper from the island of that name were sent to the Academy of Sciences in 1748, where Lomonosov and Christian Leyman analysed them and pronounced them almost pure. As a result, a mineralogist, Iakovlev, was dispatched to the Pacific to survey, mine, and report. Peltry too went to St. Petersburg from several island groups; and so did charts such as Mikhailo Nevodchikov's of Agattu and Attu. Again, long orders were remitted to Okhotsk. Yet it is true that in the 1740's St. Petersburg's involvement in developments in the Aleutians was extremely tenuous. The physical remoteness of the islands, and even the remoteness of Okhotsk and the slowness of communications with it, made it difficult for any central organ to administer, let alone govern, the activities and movements of the hunters.[32]

Government and naval involvement in the eastern and Pacific (hunting) enterprise greatly increased during the 1750's. Awareness of Kamchatka and its natural resources also grew within a Senate now prepared to face two questions earlier raised by the Great Northern Expedition: how to foster trade and industry in Transbaikalia and the North-East and how to stimulate the growth of farming settlements, whose produce might support the populations of Iakutsk, Okhotsk, and other grainless places.[33] In July 1752, a new governor-general of Siberia was named: Rear-Admiral V. Miatlev. Nine months later the Great Northern Expedition was revived with Miatlev as its overall director. With his energy and his awareness of both river and seaborne navigation as the key to the development and settlement of Transbaikalia, Admiral Miatlev brought a new, urgent approach to the great problem that the final Bering venture had made obvious to *him:* that of mastering the spaces and resources of Siberia to the advantage of the Russian state at large.[34]

Miatlev soon submitted a memorial on the enormous subject of Siberia's commercial, agricultural, and maritime development to the Senate. In it, he argued that Kamchatka and the coasts north of Okhotsk should be provisioned less from Iakutsk and the higher Lena Valley and more from countries to the south, for example, the valleys of the River Amur and its tributaries. He suggested that a shipyard should be built without delay close to the Amur's mouth or estuary. Naval strength could never come amiss.[35] But Russia's whole position in Kamchatka and the islands must depend upon the economic base and on the food base in Siberia no less than on the number of her vessels. Nerchinsk should be a point of rapid growth in agriculture as in mining. Very possibly, the sight of new prosperity and wealth in Russia's East would not be pleasing to some powers and would offer a temptation to some others. Russian interests should therefore be defended from the outset: the new shipyard and supply post on the Amur should be strongly fortified.

It should be a dockyard for the construction of regular warships; and there should be built there a minimum of three frigates, of 26 to 34 guns, equipped in all respects in accordance with naval regulations, if not better . . . and also three or four brigantines or other such naval craft of shallow draught. The latter could sail more easily than frigates in the shallow waters which surround the lately discovered [Aleutian] islands, and more easily enter river-mouths.[36]

Miatlev asked the Senate to send seamen, shipwrights, and above all colonists; meanwhile, he placed responsibility for a new ship-building programme in the East, and in Siberia at large, on an official who had, like himself, served with the fleet: Fedor Ivanovich Soimonov. To Soimonov he sent sensible, albeit over-detailed, orders (4 May 1754): for a beginning, he should see if building timber could be floated down the River Ingoda; describe the River Shilka and determine its depth at many points; and find adjacent, fertile land that could be sown with rye and barley for the mariners' and settlers' common use. Soimonov did his best, but the results were disappointing. Even small-boat navigation was not easy on the Ingoda; nor was much acreage beside the Shilka planted. But at least the central government's ambitions for the East had been spelled out by an official in Siberia.[37]

Admiral Miatlev likewise strove to study, harness, and direct all such development and enterprise in the remote North-East as came to his attention. It was a difficult task. Reports from Okhotsk were out of date when he received them, and yet more out of date if they related to events in the Aleutian Islands. He himself lacked the resources to control or aid the merchants, some of whom were now arriving in Kamchatka from North Russia, or to supervise their motley hired crews. Indeed, the knowledge that they would be free of strict government supervision, combined with news of profits such as that made by Tolstykh, lured merchants to Kamchatka from as far afield as Beloozero, Velikii Ustiug, and Arkhangel'sk.[38] In the Aleutian fur trade, private traders large and small planned to relive remembered days of almost unrestricted hunting in Siberia itself—the days before the issuing of licences that gave the merchant or the hunter certain rights in certain areas.[39] Despite all difficulties, Miatlev did assist and gain some measure of control over a few Kamchatka traders of the 1750's: Bechevin, for instance, and Shalaurov and his partner Bakhov. In return for his assistance or, more properly perhaps, non-interference in their ventures, all three found it expedient to make an effort to fulfil his known and stated expectations of their voyages.[40] Bakhov and Shalaurov were to look for new varieties of animals "while sailing through the Northern Sea from the mouth of the River Lena to the Kolyma and thence, around Chukotskii Nos, to Kamchatka . . . for the benefit of Russia's navigation."[41] The animals might have commercial value or be edible. The merchant Ivan Bechevin was aided on a rather larger scale by Miatlev and by Soimonov, who succeeded him as governor, and was accordingly beholden to Siberian officialdom.[42]

By their success in the sea-otter hunt, by their attempts to operate in semi-secrecy, and by their violence and lawlessness, the cossack hunting parties made it likely that the government would take new measures to control them. If the privateers' efforts to avoid even the payment of the regulation tithe by concealing furs in caches on out-islands or by giving false returns or estimates upon returning to Kamchatka was an irritation, their attempts to keep their very hunting areas a secret from the government were an affront. Too often, information about islands was sketchy or contradictory: one island would be variously named and its position differently fixed in the reports of different traders, while the same name and position was applied to several islands. As to solid information on the size and elevation, population, anchorages, and resources of such islands, they left much to be desired. So, too, did the treatment of the natives by *promyshlenniki:* slavery, extortion, murder, liquor, and venereal disease—such were their gifts to them. Soimonov struggled ineffectually to protect the Aleuts. Regulations were enacted to prohibit stills in the Aleutians and to make it possible for *iasak*-collectors who were known to have committed outrages to be punished. But the fear of retribution from Irkutsk did not contain the brutal tendencies of many; and *promyshlenniki* brazenly continued to exploit the Aleut people to the limits of endurance and beyond. Rebellion was quashed in blood. Abuse of native women was the norm.[43] Concerned about the loss of revenue through tax-evasion, the government appointed special officers to larger hunting vessels.

At the Admiralty Office in Okhotsk, meanwhile, reports built up on shipmasters and traders who had found prosperity in the new island enterprise. Year after year, moreover, these reports went to Irkutsk and thence, often in extract, to St. Petersburg. It was appropriate that members of the Admiralty College and the Senate, among other central organs of the government, should know of such developments nine thousand miles away. The value of the seaborne trade was swelling. Bechevin and others had their galiots, now 80 feet in length and weighing sixty tons or more, off North America itself. Protasov Bay was visited at shrinking intervals; plans were afoot to press on east in search of the lucrative sea-otter.

Yet the government continued to restrict its involvement in this fast-expanding trade to the gathering of *iasak* and taxes. In the mid-1760's, the main functions of the Admiralty Office at Okhotsk were still assistance and surveillance of such shipping as there was. All suggestions that a warship might be useful by the eastern shores and undefended islands of the Empire remained unheeded.[45] It was paradoxical: the central government encouraged men like Andreian Tolstykh and Bechevin to find new islands off America and to exploit their fur resources.[46] It was ready to accept the fealty of Aleut chiefs and to regard Aleutian Islands as a province, or at least as an appendage of a province. Serving men were to regard Aleuts as fellow-subjects of the Russian Crown. And yet, no sign of sovereignty has been made outside the islands for the benefit of other powers. Not one warship was on station. Not one signal of Imperial intention was transmitted, for the Navy had no mandate from the autocrat to interest itself in the Aleutians or the Kuriles or the fur trade. It was, first and last, an instrument of the autocracy. If it so happened that the autocrat was willing to neglect it and to leave the spread of Russian arms and influence beyond Kamchatka to *promyshlenniki,* there was nothing to be done.

CATHERINE II AND NAVAL RENOVATION

Catherine II's accession to the Russian throne in 1762 marked the beginning of another naval age after a night of deep neglect of naval matters by the Crown, or, in the case of her late husband, Peter III, of impetuous mismanagement.[47] It soon became apparent that Catherine intended that the Russian Navy should again be strong.[48] Coming to Russia from a land-locked German duchy, she had very little knowledge of the sea. Not only was she willing to be seen to further Peter I's naval work, however; she grew genuinely interested in the problems of naval renovation, thus distinguishing herself both from Elizabeth I, for whom such interests had always been essentially symbolic, and from her German predecessors in St. Petersburg. Both her administrative innovations and her hiring of well-trained but impecunious or disillusioned foreign naval officers were to have visible effects upon the growth of Russian policy and strength in the Far East.

Catherine II was pragmatic, and flexible therefore, about the means to be employed to gain her ends. Some steps that had been taken by her unlamented husband, she pursued. Thus, work continued to strengthen Kronstadt and to form a library of foreign ocean charts and works on naval and related sciences, the latter with the aid of Russian diplomats and Admiralty agents overseas.[49] But Catherine also adopted certain measures of her own: within six months of acceding to the throne, she had established a "Commission on the Russian Fleet and Admiralty Governance, Whereby that Noble Arm, the Navy, May Defend the State in Constant, Perfect Order." Chaired by Admiral S. I. Mordvinov, the commission proved efficient. In keeping with its main recommendations, the Baltic Fleet and Admiralty College were reorganized without delay. "It was resolved that Russia should maintain a navy equal in operational strength to that of both neighbouring Powers, Denmark and Sweden."[50] In the Baltic, there should be a minimum of thirty-two ships-of-the-line, carrying sixty-six to eighty guns, eight frigates, and some thirty smaller craft. More foreign officers might be employed. Since the conclusion of the Seven Years' War, the Royal Navy list had been dramatically reduced by two successive British cabinets. In consequence, many young officers were now on half-pay or were unemployed.[51] At least a dozen of them joined the Russian naval service in the early years of the new reign.[52] Efforts intensified, meanwhile, to purchase charts and surveys, harbour notes, and other such materials abroad. Even as the French and British struggled for control of distant colonies and waters, Russian Admiralty agents were acquiring charts in London and Paris; and dozens of charts of the North Sea and the Baltic, of the West Mediterranean approaches, and of the North and South Atlantic Oceans went to Russia. Under Catherine, such purchasing continued.

But the market was a tighter one where the Pacific Ocean was concerned. No government, in fact, was able to oblige the would-be buyers, least of all the Spanish government, which was annoyed by the approaches of the Russian minister then in Madrid on the topic.[53] Even the remotest northern reaches of the North Pacific Ocean, Russian subjects were reminded, were the patrimony of the kings of Spain and had been recognized as such by Rome since 1493.[54] Less complacent in her grandiose Imperial pretensions now under the ablest of the Spanish Bourbon kings, Carlos III, Madrid reacted promptly to suggestions that the Russians had pretensions on the fringes of that ocean. In June 1760, Carlos III named the marques de Almodovar as his minister in Russia in response to news and rumours of the cossack enterprise about the North Pacific rim,[55] which had filtered to Madrid via the Netherlands.

RUSSO-SPANISH TENSIONS (1761-64)

Russia and Spain still had to pay in apprehension and alarums on the North Pacific "front," for the neglect of formal diplomatic links since the departure of the duque de Liria from Moscow in 1730 and for policies of unabating secrecy. As a result of that neglect, the Russian government relied wholly on published books and journals for news of Spanish moves and plans in the Pacific. One such work was the third volume of *Noticia de la California, y de su conquista temporal* by padre Miguel Venegas, prepared for publication by padre Andres Burriel (1757). Venegas's *Noticia,* which was translated into English, French, and Dutch, caught the attention of the Admiralty College in St. Petersburg. It rested principally on manuscripts by Venegas himself or by his colleague Tarabal, which had been written in New Spain before the start of the Great Northern Expedition under Bering; but the Russians did not know this. Burriel had not spelled out the dates and provenance of all the manuscripts that he had lately edited. The College therefore pondered on appeals written fifty years before for an accelerated Jesuit expansion to the north-west of Sonora to the areas of Monterey and Cabo Mendocino, if not further to the north, where threats of foreign interference were most obvious.[56] The English had already paid a visit, under Drake, and could return to their "New Albion," as they referred to part of Alta California; and to the north, there were the Russians.

Padre Venegas's worries on these matters gained in substance as he aged; he had been born in 1680 and was thus Bering's contemporary. First arrived the trying news of Bering's and Chirikov's rapid visits to America. That Bering had discovered a strategically important strait between America and Asia, through which foreigners might possibly descend on California, had been known for many years. Then came J.-N. Delisle's volume, *Nouvelles cartes de découvertes de l'amiral de Fonte et autres navigateurs* (1753), with its map showing the "Great Land" or the north-west part of North America. Such articles and maps made it apparent to another generation that Venegas had some reason for concern about the territorial integrity of Alta California, the shores and the interior of which remained unmapped. The Californias, the Jesuits observed through Burriel, extended north to an unspecified degree of latitude. That being so, it was apparent that the interests of Spain and of the church in the New World would be promoted by significant northward expansion up the Coast. An early warning of advances by the Russians from the opposite direction could be sent to the authorities in Mexico.[57]

Then came the publication of Fray José Torrubia's *I Moscoviti nella California* (Rome, 1759). The Franciscan Torrubia, who had lived in Mexico and the Philippines, was worried lest the ancient Spanish claim to the Pacific and its riches not be backed by strength of arms in a new age. He was intent upon alerting Spain to the increasing threat of "Muscovite" expansion from the north.[58] But just as Russia was ignorant of Spanish moves and objects in America as a result of Spanish secrecy and diplomatic lethargy, so were such men as Torrubia short of facts with which to buttress any anti-Russian warnings. This, in turn, lent some importance to the third volume of Gerhard Friedrich Müller's *Sammlung russischer Geschichten* (1758) with its map showing large portions of the North-west of America and its accounts of the Chirikov and Bering landfalls.[59] Venegas, Torrubia, Müller: three warnings in as many years sufficed to draw attention to the threat, and Almodovar left for Russia.

He departed with a double mission: first, to seal a non-aggression pact between the courts of Spain and Russia, to last until the European struggle with its echoes and extensions in America and India might end; second, to pierce the veil of secrecy behind which Russian ventures in the North Pacific area were hidden. That Russia was advancing south and east towards America, using small islands as her stepping-stones, was readily accepted in Madrid. The question was, had Russian influence spread to the mainland? If so, where were the southernmost positions of the cossacks? To answer both questions, which were put to him directly in March 1761,[60] Almodovar set about making contacts in the Admiralty College, the Academy of Sciences, and, most especially, at court.

For seven months, he scented out both unofficial and official information about Bering's expedition, cossack navigation from Kamchatka, and the latest hunting-trading voyages to the Aleutian Islands. On 6 October 1761, he sent his first despatch concerned specifically with Russian moves and plans in the remote North-East and East. It showed the soundness of his sources and his own sense of proportion. The Russians, he reported, had not yet taken possession of a portion of the mainland of America, but they could well do so in future. However, Chirikov had observed the Coast and lost some men 13° north of the point called Cabo Blanco. Bering's landfall had been even further north. As to the danger of an unannounced descent on Alta California by a squadron that had entered the Pacific through a northern passage, more specifically, from Northern Russia or Siberia, it was remote. Russian experience had shown convincingly that, "even if a passage through the Arctic Sea into Pacific waters were a possibility, it would be economically impractical."[61] A ship could take four seasons to proceed from a northern town or port or river-mouth to Bering's Strait; en route, her men would face "a million dangers."

For Ricardo Wall, to whom the marquis wrote, such news was comforting, and he took no further steps. He did not know, as Almodovar did, how energetically the question of a navigable passage to the Orient was still being discussed in academic and Admiralty circles in St. Petersburg.[62]

LOMONOSOV, SHILOV, CHICHAGOV: THE NORTHERN ROUTE TO THE PACIFIC (1763-65)

The question of a navigable passage to the Orient, which English, Dutch, and Russian mariners had sought in vain and for so long, continued to engage far-sighted persons in the middle of the eighteenth century as at its start. The value of the China trade had always been acknowledged; and its market was sufficiently extensive to accommodate new Arctic and, indeed, Pacific products. Possibly the passage from the White Sea was impractical, even impossible; presumably, however, a passage to Canton would be both easier and speedier from a more easterly departure point. Even a route between the Lena River and the Orient would be of evident commercial value to the state. Laptev's experience, admittedly, was not encouraging, but it had not disproved the possibility of northern passages.[63]

Born by the White Sea and acquainted with conditions in the North, the poet-scientist Mikhail Vasil'evich Lomonosov was among the many Russians of his own and preceding generations who reflected on the matter of the navigable sea-route to the Orient and Indies over Russia and Siberia. In early life, he wrote a "Letter on the Northern Route to the East Indies, by Way of the Siberian Sea."

Regrettably, it has been lost. His ode ''Peter the Great'' survives. Many a famous mariner, observes the poet, suffered hardships in the tropics on a voyage to the far side of the globe; ''But the very ice, which seems so awesome and so terrible, will offer *us* a path free of those fierce dangers, . . . Our dominion shall stretch into America.''[64] Some four years later and within eight weeks of Catherine II's accession to the throne, which encouraged him to do so, Lomonosov placed a prose work in the Senate's hands. It was entitled, ''A Concise Account of Divers Journeys through the Northern Seas and an Indication of a Possible Sea-Route through to the East Indies' (20 September 1763). There is reason to believe that he had written it considerably earlier and now merely revised and submitted it, its moment having come.

Russia and the Russian Navy, Lomonosov argued, would win glory and, besides, open a highly profitable trade with other powers were a navigable passage to be found. During the months of northern summer, the seas by Novaia Zemlia and off the mouths of all main rivers of Siberia were navigable: ice was thin or broken up, and there was no reason to suppose that it was always packed and solid round the Chukchi country, that is, east of Cape Shelagskii. Nonetheless, it was better that the next Russian attempt to reach Pacific waters from the North be made not to the east but to the west. He would recommend Spitzbergen as the starting place. The Arctic ocean-drift was to the west. The voyage west from Spitzbergen, though longer than around the Chukchi country, would in every probability be safer. He was wrong on both counts; but his influence, together with the timely arrival in St. Petersburg of precious black fox skins from the Aleutians, proved sufficient in a time of new beginnings and infectious optimism to conclude the matter.[65]

Catherine herself spoke to Count I. G. Chernyshev of the Admiralty College on the question of a navigable sea-route from Kamchatka to a Northern Russian depot. Apparently, the College planned no measures to facilitate the hunters' island enterprise. Provisioning Kamchatka by sea, as recommended by John Elton more than thirty years before, remained no more than an idea. Orders were issued on 14 May 1764, at the empress's behest, that Admiralty College and Academy of Sciences co-operate once more in preparing a naval expedition to attempt to find a navigable passage to the North Pacific Ocean's fur-rich islands and beyond them to the Orient and Indies. Lomonosov and officials of the Admiralty College received copies of reports and memoranda on the subject by the present and the past governors-general of Siberia, D. I. Chicherin and F. I. Soimonov. A committee was established to draft orders for the leader of the venture. Lomonosov was its moving force and chairman.[66] The officer selected was a naval captain, V. Ia. Chichagov (1726-1809). ''A loyal and proficient seaman,'' Chicagov was to be aided by ''two other officers of similar experience'' and by ''efficient navigators who have been to Spitzbergen and Novaia Zemlia, placing as many in each vessel as the College may think best.''[67] Three vessels should be fitted out at once, in secrecy. They should be readied for their voyage west from

Bellsund to the north of North America and so "across the Northern Ocean to Kamchatka and beyond."

The enterprise was a quixotic one. Though reinforced internally, the vessels that were chosen—the *Chichagov, Babaev,* and *Panov,* all named after their captains—were not suitable for work in heavy ice. Their crews were competent and physically resilient, but they had received no special training for the Arctic. Neither victuals nor clothing had been issued with prolonged exposure to such latitudes in mind; or, at least, the proper stores were not available when wanted and in proper quantity.[68] Lastly, the very preparations were unfortunately hurried. Chichagov had orders to proceed without delay that very season. Rightly, he protested. Memoranda flew. After eleven hectic days, on 25 May 1764, the Senate sent quite different instructions from those he was following, postponing the departure of the expedition by a year. The delay barely sufficed to bring the squadron into readiness. Of the misfortunes that beset the expedition when at length it did leave Bellsund for the trackless wastes of ice to the north-west, scurvy and leaks were the most notable. The ships met solid ice in latitude 80° 26′N.(23 July 1765). Making a fresh attempt the following summer, they did little better, being stopped by ice four minutes higher, five days earlier. Much had occurred in the North-East and in the Bering Sea before the luckless Chichagov brought all three companies and vessels safely home.

Recognizing that it must depend on Russian efforts for its charts of Russian waters in the far North-East and East, the Russian government turned its attention to the matter once again in the mid-1760's. The most senior hydrographer then serving in the Navy was Aleksei Ivanovich Nagaev (1704-81). The matter was accordingly placed in his hands. Earlier, on the basis of the logs, journals, and maps of Bering, Chirikov, and their officers, he and Lieutenant Afrosimov had prepared detailed charts of the "Kamchatkan waters."[69] Now, as doyen of his section of the service, he was ordered to direct the preparation of a set of new and detailed coastal surveys. Hydrographers were to be issued with the latest instruments, purchased abroad, and well instructed in their use, as well as in the astronomical techniques and "solid hammock" recently devised by Lomonosov.[70]

Nagaev saw to it that the North-East was not neglected by a Baltic-oriented corps of officers or by the Admiralty College. He had practical assistance from Siberian officialdom as Bering and his officers had not, for Catherine had named the able Denis Ivanovich Chicherin (1720-85) as Soimonov's successor in Irkutsk. Governor-general for eighteen years, Chicherin won some popularity among Siberians. Until at length he lost her trust, he corresponded steadily with Catherine. On Admiral Nagaev's instances, but on instructions from the Senate and Chicherin, survey teams set out for the remote North-East again. From modern East Cape, they made their way along the coast to Cape Shelagskii and, skirting the Aniui Mountains, to the River Kolyma. Also on orders from Chicherin, meanwhile, Nikolai Daurkin, a Chukchi long employed as an interpreter and guide by the Iakutsk authorities, proceeded with his own regional surveys in the far North-East and East.[71]

In the opinions of certain of the Admiralty College's more active members and of various Siberian officials, among them Major Friedrich Christian Plenisner or Plenstner, a Baltic German officer who until lately had been building (or rebuilding) Anadyrsk, it was time that the government assumed a larger role in seas and islands off America. Unruly elements continued to be troublesome, though kept in check to some extent by Major Plenisner.[72] *Promyshlennik* activity had grown so widespread that Siberian officialdom could not keep pace with it. Rumors of crimes against the Aleuts found their way to him repeatedly. And even on the rare occasions when they strove to do so, private hunters lacked the skill to draw maps of their discoveries and movements that would satisfy the Admiralty College. Plenisner's own interest in mainland North America was of long standing: he had sailed in the *Sv. Petr* under Bering. More recently, he had dispatched Daurkin to the Diomede Islands to obtain more information about natives and resources of the "Great Land" to the east. Daurkin had only just returned (July 1764) with news of sable-skins worn by the natives of America and of intermittent trade between the natives of the "Great Land" and the Chukchi.[73] For different reasons, Plenisner, Chicherin, and the Admiralty College all agreed that a naval expedition was required: first, to bring some order to the swelling, seaborne fur trade; second, to examine all the islands that were known between Kamchatka and America; and, finally, to estimate their natural resources. Catherine concurred. Her latent interest in peltry from the North Pacific islands, which a half a dozen merchants were so soon to reinforce by precious gifts of black fox skins, had only recently been sparked by a memorial from F. I. Soimonov on the subject.[74] On 4 May 1764, she signed the orders for a naval expedition to those seas. Within the week she was examining instructions very carefully drawn up by Lomonosov for the leader of another expedition to the East from Spitzbergen. By 14 May, she had already signed the relevant ukases.[75] The former expedition was entrusted to a naval captain, P. K. Krenitsyn, the latter, the results of which have been surveyed, to Chichagov.

The empress was correct in her insistence upon speedy action in the new Pacific venture. Soon enough, it was reported that the British government proposed to send an expedition to the North Pacific Ocean which would call at Drake's New Albion and thence attempt to find a passage linking Hudson's Bay or Baffin's Bay with Bering's Strait or an adjacent northern inlet.[76] If its leader was successful, he would win a prize of £20,000. By mid-July 1764, the *Dolphin*

(Commodore Byron) and *Tamar* (Captain Mouat) had already left the Downs. The news went to St. Petersburg by courier.[77] In the event, Byron paid minimal attention to his orders and was never in the same part of the world as the Kamchatka hunter-traders. Merely by sending him to seek a northern passage, even so, the British government had strengthened Catherine's increasing inclination to assert the Russian presence off America, always provided that her doing so would not result in confrontation between Russia and a European power.

Catherine's orders launching these new Pacific ventures were developed in May 1764 on the basis of reports by Soimonov and Chicherin. Since it was obviously necessary, wrote the latter, that discoveries of distant, fur-rich islands all be verified and since the verifying could be undertaken most efficiently by servants of the Navy, commonsense argued that naval officers participate in voyages to the Aleutian Islands from Kamchatka. Such men would keep full, serviceable journals and take bearings day by day; they would be eyes, not for the regional authorities or even for Irkutsk, but for the central government. Catherine endorsed his reasoning.[78] The Senate issued orders for a group of naval officers and men to "aid" the cossack hunting parties on their voyages to islands found by Russians in the past. The Admiralty Office at Okhotsk would at the same time lend assistance to all traders insofar as it could as before. But naval vessels, as such, were not to cruise among the islands; nor at any time would ensigns fly on vessels in which Navy men took passage for the purposes of gaining information about furs, harbours, and tides and helping with the peaceable collection of the Aleuts' *iasak*. As a function for a navy, it was hardly glorious.

THE SINDT EXPEDITION

Chicherin sent these orders and accompanying documents to Major Plenisner, who was commanding at Okhotsk. Chicherin had decided that Plenisner should direct their execution, being better placed to name suitable officers and men to trading vessels than his seniors. He was acquainted with the fur trade, with Okhotsk, and with local navigation. Governor-General Chicherin had no knowledge of the latter and recognized it.

An able officer, Plenisner responded promptly to his orders.[79] At Okhotsk, there were no Navy-trained hydrographers who could take passage in private trading craft. There was, however, a Lieutenant Ivan Sindt, or Sind, who had like Plenisner participated in the Second Bering Expedition. For the past several years, he had been making voyages between Okhotsk, Avacha Bay, and the Aleutians.[80] He was competent by local standards, and he knew the basics of cartography. So, in an atmosphere of haste and "second best," originated the so-called Sindt Expedition (1764-67).

Sindt sailed from Okhotsk with two small galiots, making directly for the mouth of the Bol'shaia River. After a brief pause, he pressed on round Cape Lopatka and continued up the rocky eastern coast of the peninsula to Petropavlovsk, where he wintered. Having watered and revictualled, he set sail after the breakup of the ice in May 1765, again steering north-east. After a while, he went due east. No full account of either this or his second voyage, from Avacha Bay in 1766, was subsequently published.[81] It is difficult, therefore, to know his routes. From the reports and map that Sindt later submitted to the Admiralty Office at Okhotsk, however, it is evident that he exaggerated both the size and number of the islands he had seen. "By degrees," the German secretary of the Academy of Sciences, Stählin von Storksburg, could declare in 1771, "Lt. Syndo [*sic*] discovered a whole archipelago of islands of different sizes, which increased upon him the further he went between the 56th and 67th degrees of northern latitude."[82] Count A. R. Vorontsov had the impression in 1786-88 that Lt. Sindt had found his islands between 60° and 65°N.[83] One thing, however, was apparent to all writers of the time. Sindt's map and journal made, in Stählin's words, "a considerable alteration" to contemporary estimates both of the Gulf of Anadyr "and of the situation of the opposite coast of America." It gave no support to G. F. Müller's map of the same region. Indeed, the Stählin map, based upon Sindt's report and map, suggested that a fist had smashed the north-western extension of America, reducing parts of it into small islands, "and sending some of it into thin air."[84] Far from dispelling doubt about the actual positions of the islands in the Bering Sea, Sindt had redoubled it. He had by no means justified Plenisner's trust, and the price was to be paid by later mariners, including Cook.

The fact that Sindt had been named as a "surveyor" on a private hunting vessel belonging to the Shilov-Lapin company further confused and obfuscated the relationships between the Navy and the merchants of Kamchatka and Irkutsk.[85] For its part, the Russian government had chosen to allow open confusion to persist as to the Navy's future role in the Pacific.

THE KRENITSYN-LEVASHEV EXPEDITION: ORIGINS AND PREPARATIONS

Chicherin's argument that steps should be taken to consolidate Russian authority over the whole Aleutian chain without delay and to check the information and cartography of private hunter-traders echoed that of F. I. Soimonov. It was merely reinforced by news from London of the Byron expedition. To avoid the necessity of offering accounts of Russian moves off North America, to the new Spanish ambassador, Conde de Herreria and to others, the empress made her moves in secrecy.

Treating the venture in the North Pacific Ocean as a naval one was logical: the Navy was to man it, and charts would be a principal result. The Admiralty College received orders from the Senate "to dispatch as many officers and pilots" to Okhotsk as it judged proper, and "to place over them a senior officer whose knowledge of the naval science and whose zeal for it are recognized."[86] That there should be a cloak of secrecy was, on the other hand, a consequence of Catherine's own character and policy. She swore to silence a committee, formed of members of the College and the Senate, that had supervised arrangements for another expedition to the East and then announced that a minor expedition would be launched to look at forests in the Belaia and Kama River valleys.[87] The Senate was never officially informed of the true object of the coming expedition under Captain Krenitsyn. And the Admiralty College was never given liberty to write about the expedition's aims. Ostensibly, it too was satisfied by the ukase giving an outline of the venture, and of generous allowances for all involved in it: promotion at its end, life pensions, double pay and various allowances over a two-year period with possible extension.[88]

The leader of this tree-inspecting tour was only to build craft if it was unavoidable; his presence at Okhotsk should not be advertised. He and his men would "board a hunting ship or merchant vessel, and then only in the general capacity of passengers." He and one pilot would take passage in one vessel; his second-in-command and one more pilot, in another.[89] Other expedition members would travel to the islands individually in as many "local craft" as were available. All would be done with circumspection. Chicherin thought they would have little trouble in persuading the owners and masters of whatever hunting vessels they encountered at Okhotsk that it was much to their advantage that the whole Aleutian chain be charted competently. "The *promyshlenniki* cannot well oppose this . . . for it might be their salvation from a possible disaster."[90] Here, Chicherin was mistaken: even at so late a date, many *promyshlenniki* would have risked disaster on a falsely charted reef rather than work under the eyes of naval officers sent from the capital.

Petr Kuz'mich Krenitsyn was able to select his own subordinates. As second-in-command, he chose Midshipman Mikhail Dmitrievich Levashev, whom he had met at Arkhangel'sk.[91] Krenitsyn himself had spent ten years on Baltic duty before undertaking survey work in the White Sea. At the time of his appointment as commander, he was serving with the frigate *Ul'riksdal'*. His record was reasonable for the leader of a North Pacific enterprise: at least he had experience of survey work and Arctic navigation, and, moreover, he had shown great courage in the Kolberg operation as the acting commander of a bombship.

To Krenitsyn and Levashev, the scope and true objectives of their expedition were, of course, explained in full. They were instructed to regard themselves neither as agents of Imperial expansion nor as partners of expansion-minded traders, but as visiting cartographers, observers, and recorders.[92] In particular, they should survey one fur-rich island, Umnak, and from there sail to Kodiak or Kad'iak, whose climate and soil both apparently favoured husbandry. They should determine the dimensions and topography of Kodiak, and its distance from the mainland of America. While on the islands, they were to gather specimens of rock, flora, and seeds and carefully describe the local timber. Seven petty officers were put at their disposal for those and other purposes en route to the Pacific.[93] Above all, they were to chart accurately the courses of the craft in which they sailed; keep full daily records, noting incidents of every kind; and generally "rectify the errors" and improve the "seaborne practice" of their scientifically untrained associates. Krenitsyn was told that the empress had herself evinced an interest in maps of the Pacific area prepared by Soimonov and Nagaev. Only recently, she had been studying them. "Mr. Kropotov," she had written on 24 May 1764 to Soimonov, "has just brought me the map prepared by you and showing American islands visited by our *promyshlenniki*. I am grateful for it. Knowing how great your interest is in that continent, I send you the secret map prepared by Mr. Lomonosov, with which Mr. Nagaev's is almost in accord."[94] Thinking it possible that Krenitsyn might come on members of the Chichagov-Panov-Babaev expedition in the region of Kamchatka, the Admiralty College spent some time preparing instructions on the matter of approaching, recognizing, and addressing fellow-countrymen.

Catherine's caution was rewarded: the departure of the expedition's members for Okhotsk raised not a ripple on the diplomatic pond. Chicherin, meanwhile, the nominal head of the whole venture, was corresponding with Chernyshev of the Admiralty College on its prospects and dispatching more instructions to Okhotsk, for Krenitsyn on his arrival. The expedition reached Tobol'sk in mid-September and was swollen by ten students from the School of Navigation and a band of serving men. After a short, comfortable winter, it pressed on east with all its gear in March 1765. It reached Okhotsk late in October.

Chicherin sent more orders from the capital and on his own account. As a result, Krenitsyn found quite a bundle of instructions in Iakutsk, where he prepared for the last stage of the land journey, and others in Okhotsk.[95] In a typical despatch, Chicherin told him to obtain descriptions of as many of the islands to be visited as possible from private hunters. S. T. Ponomarev, the cossack navigator, and five others who had visited the Andreianov and the Fox groups, were to go with him to Kodiak. He might solve the growing problem of provisioning the fur trade in that region by suggesting where a farm could be established and where vegetables and grains would grow and ripen. Before the cossacks from Kamchatka made a major effort there, he was to confirm its insularity, that is, its separateness from the "Spanish" countries to the east.[96] The Russian government was taking the position that whatever rights the kings of Spain might arguably claim along the mainland of America, they had none to off-shore islands of which they were completely ignorant.[97]

For Krenitsyn, Levashev, and their men, matters were easier within Siberia itself than they had been for Bering, Spanberg, and their larger companies. As earlier, the Iakutsk-Okhotsk Tract offered transport problems to exhausted men; but now, the Admiralty College understood distant supply and transport problems, and allowances were made for misadventure and delay. Thus, the news that there was practically no rigging in Kamchatka that could serve the expedition's purpose was digested promptly in Tobol'sk. Fresh rope was woven there at once, and there was only slight disruption of the expedition's schedule.[98]

Yet in some respects nothing had altered at Okhotsk: sluggish shipbuilding, for instance, and the tendency for men to waste their energy on feuds continued. There were no private hunting vessels at Okhotsk to take the naval "passengers" to the Aleutians, and no vessels were expected before winter. Also reminiscent of the times of Pisarev was a "misunderstanding" that arose between Krenitsyn and Plenisner. Plenisner took offense when Krenitsyn, who could know nothing of the local situation, promptly superseded Captain Rtishchev as his deputy where regional administrative questions were concerned. Frustrated by the absence of expected galiots, Krenitsyn insisted on his rank and on his rights and was supported by "his" people. "It seems to me," commented Chicherin in an irritated tone to Krenitsyn, "that there is *something in the air* down at Okhotsk that makes all officers posted there quarrel."[99] Now postponing his replies to Plenisner, now acting as a channel between Krenitsyn and Plenisner, though the two men were quartered within yards of one another, Chicherin strove to soothe the "cossack party's" feelings, while dissuading Krenitsyn from sending messages which would impede the expedition's further progress.[100] Chicherin had scant knowledge of the sea and navigation. On the other hand, he had a lively interest in the Aleutian Islands, peltry, and the "Great Land" to the east, and he was anxious that the enterprise proceed.

Since it was evident that vessels would have to be constructed at Okhotsk, the necessary building timber was transported a considerable distance to the yard, and shipwrights laboured through the winter months. At length in August 1766 a brigantine, named *Sv. Ekaterina* in honour of the empress, and a hooker, named *Sv. Pavel,* were launched and fully rigged. Two local galiots, *Sv. Gavriil* and, most confusingly, another *Sv. Pavel,* were extensively repaired, outside and in. They too were readied for an ocean voyage and re-rigged. The squadron sailed at midday on 10 October 1766. Aboard *Sv. Ekaterina* under Krenitsyn was a crew of seventy-two. The hooker *Sv. Pavel,* with Levashev, took a crew of fifty-two. The smaller local craft, commanded by the Dudin brothers, carried crews of forty-three and twenty-one, both disproportionately large. Twelve quadrants were shared among the captains. Krenitsyn had charts by Bering, Chaplin, Shishkin, and Ponomarev and Bering's, Waxell's, and Chirikov's journals of 1740-41.[101] The expedition had already cost the Treasury more than 100,000 roubles.[102]

THE KRENITSYN-LEVASHEV EXPEDITION (1766-69)

Krenitsyn and Levashev were separated by a storm within three days of their departure from Okhotsk. Sea fogs made it impossible for the squadron to reform. All contact was then lost. Matters went from bad to worse when the *Sv. Ekaterina* was discovered to be leaking on 18 October. Kamchatka was in sight, in 53° 46′N., and Krenitsyn made for the nearest stretch of coast. Just then, a second storm blew up. The brigantine was close to the Bol'shaia River mouth. Two anchors failed to hold, and the crew could not control the rising water in the bilges. Boats put off. The rising wind and current carried the *Sv. Ekaterina* to the north of Bol'sheretsk, where she broke on a sandbank.

Levashev, meanwhile, was also approaching the Bol'shaia River mouth. He waited to take full advantage of a spring tide before venturing to cross the bar. Next day, he too fell victim to the storms, and the *Sv. Pavel* broke her anchor-cables. He tried to put to sea but, failing, ran the vessel carefully onto a sandy spit. Crew, equipment, and three-quarters of the stores aboard were saved. Dudin senior brought *Sv. Gavriil* to anchor hard by the Bol'shaia River mouth, but the small galiot was overcome by the same storm that caught Levashev and was lifted bodily onto the shore. The galiot *Sv. Pavel* drifted south a hundred versts. After nine weeks of suffering, thirteen survivors arrived on the seventh Kurile Island, their vessel smashed to pieces, without supplies or strength to ward off tragedy. By chance, they were found by Ainu hunters, who befriended and saved them.[103] Such was the beginning of a costly, state-supported expedition.

The shipwrecked crews of the hooker *St. Pavel,* the *Sv. Gavriil,* and the *Sv. Ekaterina* spent a miserable winter at the settlement of Bol'sheretsk, straining the local food resources to their limit. However, the men repaired the *Sv. Pavel* and *Sv. Gavriil* and on 17 August 1767, the mariners once more put out to sea. On board the *Sv. Pavel* with Levashev were now fifty-eight men; in *Sv. Gavriil* with Krenitsyn, no less than sixty-six. All rounded Cape Lopatka and reached Nizhne-kamchatsk by mid-September. Once again the expedition settled in for an unpleasant winter. For weeks they boiled sea-water for salt, extracting tar from local spruce. More time and energy were spent building a pair of crude *baidars* and several water casks. Lt. Sindt arrived in the galiot *Sv. Ekaterina* in April 1768. Krenitsyn transferred him into the *Sv. Gavriil* and had the ship refitted insofar as it was possible to do so. The expedition sailed again on 21 July, this time in Sindt's *Sv. Ekaterina* (Krenitsyn and seventy-two men) and the hooker *Sv. Pavel* (Levashev and sixty-five men.) Again both vessels in the squadron were conspicuously overmanned. A course was set for Bering Island, where they anchored and watered uneventfully.[104]

But the conditions soon deteriorated. Strong contrary winds slowed progress eastward, at length, and on 11 August, in lat. 54° 33′N., Krenitsyn and Levashev

Plate 1. Vitus Bering (1681-1741). A Dane by birth, Bering
rved in the Russian Navy more than twenty years before
ceiving his orders for the far North-East in 1725. On his first
pedition, he and his men failed to sight North America; on
s second (1733-41), he coasted in the shadow of Alaska and
ndfall was made on Kayak Island in the Aleutians. Bering
ed on the return voyage to Kamchatka.

Plate 2. Peter the Great, tsar of Russia and founder of the
modern Russian Navy, had a lifelong interest in maritime
affairs. He signed the order launching Bering's first expedition
only days before his death.

Plate 3. Iakutsk in the late seventeenth century. Though the town was the administrative centre for north-eastern Siberia, its
communications with both Irkutsk and Okhotsk remained tenuous even in 1800.

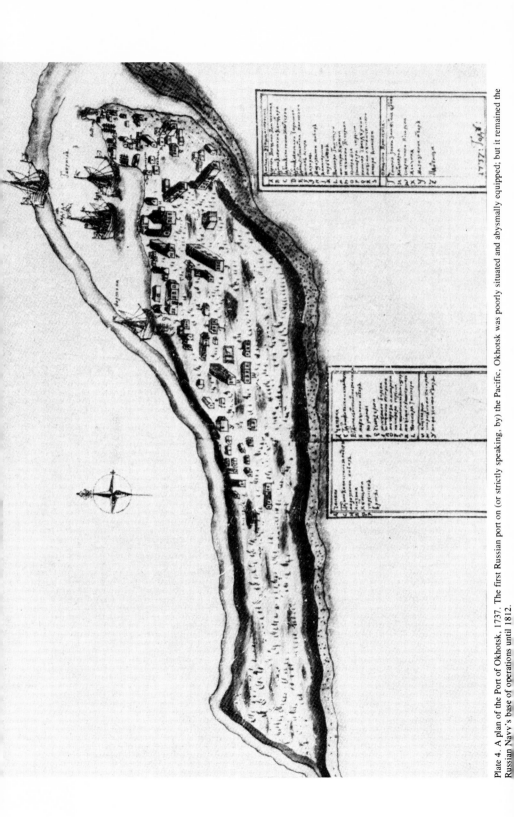

Plate 4. A plan of the Port of Okhotsk, 1737. The first Russian port on (or strictly speaking, by) the Pacific, Okhotsk was poorly situated and abysmally equipped; but it remained the Russian Navy's base of operations until 1812.

Plate 3. Petropavlovsk, on Avacha Bay, Kamchatka. Its deep and sheltered waters could have held the Russian Navy of the early nineteenth century, but agriculture did not prosper and provisionment was difficult on its remote and desolate peninsula.

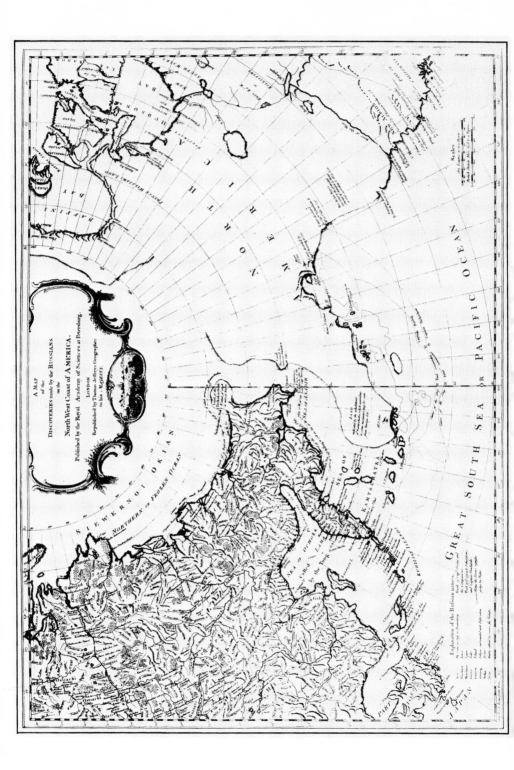

became separated. Three days later, Krenitsyn sighted the island of Siguam, easternmost of the Andreianov Group. On 20 August, he passed between Umnak and Unalaska Islands. *Sv. Pavel* arrived two days later. Both vessels watered on Unalaska before pressing on to Unimak and Alaska, where they surveyed for two days before seeking a winter anchorage. Then, on 5 September, they again lost sight of one another.

Krenitsyn resolved to winter on Unimak, in modern St. Catherine Bay. A rough shore-camp was built. The temperature fell. The Russians received a party of "American natives," who went off apparently satisfied with their gifts of beads and mittens; but they soon returned in force and shot arrows at the driftwood camp. The Russians replied with bullets. There were neither deaths nor injuries; but hopes for a peaceful winter had been shattered. In the absence of the *Sv. Pavel,* the strength of *Sv. Ekaterina*'s company was by no means overwhelming. Week after week, the Russians' nerves were strained by the prospect of sudden night attack by the "Americans." In December, signs of scurvy were quite plain. Slowly at first, then faster, the whole company was losing strength. Spirits fell dangerously low. There were burials each day. Occasionally, the tormenting "Americans" brought whale-meat, seal-meat, and whale-oil to barter with the now enfeebled Russians. By April, only twelve men were not suffering from scurvy. Still the natives had the Russian camp surrounded, but they did not attack it or the ship. The situation was already desperate when news arrived on 10 May that Levashev was safe and fairly near. The *Sv. Pavel* arrived at Unimak on 6 June. There was rejoicing on both sides.

On Unalaska, Levashev reported, he had not been actively harrassed by Aleuts or "Americans": a party of *promyshlenniki* had handed several Aleut hostages to him when he left for Kamchatka. Nonetheless, they had grown weary from the need for ceaseless vigilance, from an unbalanced diet, and from ignorance about their comrades' fate. They had surveyed and charted Unalaska Island, however, and had found that it had better anchorages than the spot where Krenitsyn had watered three months earlier. Its geographical position had been fixed by means of lunar and solar observations, and the Aleuts of the region had been carefully described.[105]

Krenitsyn was hesitant to carry out his further order to circumnavigate Kodiak Island with so many of his seamen sick and feeble. Summer storms blew up repeatedly and died away within the day. What would the autumn have to offer any poorly manned craft caught at sea? Prudence dictated that he make for a known harbour in Kamchatka before long. The vessels left for the peninsula on 23 June 1769. Again they met bad weather and were separated, but they reached Nizhnekamchatsk after long, gruelling voyages.

Again the expedition settled in to winter. Krenitsyn had lost some forty men. The whole of Levashev's crew were sick, some more than others. But the deaths that soon occurred on the peninsula at least had the effect of easing pressure on the main food source—dried fish.[106] Two hundred pounds of flour were sent overland from Bol'sheretsk for the relief of the ailing expedition. When it arrived, it was spoiled. Then, on 28-29 September, earthquakes alarmed the wretched settlement where Krenitsyn, Levashev, and their seamen were attempting to recuperate from scurvy, notwithstanding the lack of food and medicine. More major tremors shook Kamchatka in May 1770, and seamen continued to collapse. But by June 1770, there was no storm, earthquake, or tragedy that could alarm the hapless expedition's leader. Captain Krenitsyn had drowned crossing a river in a native dug-out.[107]

Krenitsyn's and Levashev's cartography was adequate. Because they lacked the means of fixing longitude precisely, their charts showed Unimak as lying closer to Kamchatka than it actually does, but the relations of Aleutian Islands to each other had been fixed with tolerable accuracy. On the basis of the expedition's work, new maps of the North Pacific Ocean were prepared by Admiral Nagaev (1772) and by V. Krasil'nikov (1777).[108] The expedition also benefitted the geologists and mineralogists of the Academy of Sciences: using Levashev's data, Peter Simon Pallas ventured to prepare a geological map of the North Pacific littorals of Asia and America.[109] Levashev's main achievement, however, unquestionably lay in his descriptions of the physical conditions and natives of Unimak and Unalaska Islands.[110]

CAPTAIN LEVASHEV IN ST. PETERSBURG (1771-72)

As command of the Great Northern Expedition had devolved upon Chirikov, who had brought a fair proportion of its maps and journals home, so Levashev took command of Krenitsyn's, and left Kamchatka for the Baltic with the record of the expedition's work. He reached Okhotsk from Nizhnekamchatsk on 3 August 1770 and St. Petersburg almost exactly one year later. More than seven years had passed since he had left.

Under questioning by members of the Commerce and Admiralty Colleges and the Academy, Levashev did his best to stress the benefits—commercial, scientific, and political—that might accrue from the recent expedition. By extension, he insisted on the wealth already won in the Aleutians by a group of Russian merchants and their agents and on cossacks' and the private hunter-traders' inability to represent the Russian state justly. As a result of his emphatic criticism, the collection of *iasak* from the Aleuts by conveniently passing bands of hunters from Kamchatka was condemned.[111] The empress, after all, had been explicit on the subject of brutality towards the Aleuts and the Ainu—for example, when she ennobled the cossacks Vasiutinskii and Lazarev in March 1766 ("Impress upon our hunters for fur that they shall treat their brothers and countrymen, the natives of our lately acquired isles, with the greatest kindness").[112] It was significant that, once again, a naval officer was drawing the attention of the central government to human suffering in the Aleutians and to cossack violence. Implicit in Levashev's attitude was the suggestion that a government-appointed force or agency should represent the Crown in its Pacific territories.

Like Chirikov a generation earlier, Levashev found himself an ingenu among the bureaucrats in 1771. He took some time to fix his bearings between College, Academy, and Senate. Having done so, he was able to appreciate how faithfully the Senate echoed Catherine's own attitudes towards the Kurile and Aleutian islands and their peoples and resources. The empress's position was, in essence, that discoveries of islands off America and visits by her subjects to America were not to be discussed with any foreigner unless, as when Krenitsyn's journal and chart were made available to William Robertson, she had herself decided otherwise[113] and that officials of the government should not discuss such matters openly. In the Academy of Sciences, he found, there was both sympathy with the idea of extending an official naval presence in the North Pacific area and disappointment with the sum of Krenitsyn's and Levashev's scientific and exploratory work.[114] As to the Admiralty College, it received Levashev well. The logs, journals, and charts, especially of Unimak and Unalaska Islands,[115] had made a generally favourable impression. Therefore, he emphasized the wealth of private merchants and the treatment meted out to native peoples by adventurers to officials of the College. Shilov, Lapin, and their partners, he observed, had made profits of approximately 30,000 silver roubles each since forming their company in June 1765. Since he had been in the Pacific region, galiots had been dispatched by Russian merchants to at least a dozen islands and, in recent months, to North America itself. Fortunes were being made. It was, Levashev said, growing imperative that the collection and delivery of valuable peltry from the islands be directed by reliable, trustworthy agents of the Crown. The volume of the seaborne fur trade was increasing. And the Shilov-Lapin company was even hiring the services of former Navy men like Potap Zaikov, who was now master of their galiot, *Sv. Vladimir*.[116] In its own interest, Levashev urged, the Crown should take more action to control the island fur trade and its agents.

The government did not respond, for Catherine was not disposed to alter what was now well-tried policy of secrecy and caution. Senate, College, and Academy all understood that the activities of "passengers," "surveyors," and "observers" on the coasts of North America were pregnant with political significance. Indeed the government itself was ignorant of the positions of the European colonies and forts from which withdrawal might become expedient. Catherine was dealing with policy, however, not minutiae. To make full use of private vessels on the fringes of America was a convenient and highly economical approach which, most importantly, shielded the dignity of Russia from possible embarrassment as a result of lack of military strength where it was needed. Even by 1771, Spanish suspicions of expansionist ambitions on the part of naval officers like Levashev were becoming justified.

But like Chirikov and Bering, Levashev had returned from the remote North-East to European Russia to discover that political events had overtaken his designs. He had been travelling across Siberia when Russia won her crushing naval victory over the Turks in Chesme Bay in Asia Minor. The Aleutians and the sea-borne fur trade were no longer on the sovereign's mind by 1771 as they had been at certain intervals six years before. Levashev rejoiced at Greig's and Aleksei Orlov's success against the Porte, while lamenting for the North Pacific cause. In the St. Petersburg of 1771-72, there was scant interest in islands on the far side of the world. Most of such interest as did exist was generated by those few persons of rank who, like himself, had seen their promise.

SPAIN AND THE RUSSIAN THREAT IN THE PACIFIC (1765-75)

By contrast with the Admiralty Office at Okhotsk, the office of the viceroy of New Spain was very active from 1765 to 1775. Soon after the reception in Madrid of Herreria's first despatches from St. Petersburg, an able officer named Galvez was appointed as the king's own representative (visitador) in Mexico (Nueva Espana). José de Galvez's arrival marked a turning point in the history of Spanish penetration north and west of the Sierra Madre.[117]

Visitador Galvez was an energetic man. For eighty years, memorials had been submitted in the Old World and the New on the desirability of widening New Spain to the north-west; yet very little had been done.Galvez's presence and the politic co-operation of the viceroys, first de Croix then Bucareli y Ursua, led to action on three fronts: the ousting of the Jesuits, the saving of Sonora from the Seri Indians, and the advance through Alta California towards the Russians.[118] Galvez was briefed by Arriaga, the minister responsible, about the Russian menace from the North Pacific; he consulted Torrubia's and Müller's books. But he regarded the supposed advances calmly. For his part, Arriaga kept Russia in the visitador's thoughts by frequent references in the next three years both to alleged cossack activities in North America and to Ambassador de Herreria's fears. Galvez received copies of Herreria's missives to Grimaldi, then prime minister. The first occasion was on 5 May 1768. The Russian empress, the ambassador had written six months earlier, meant to improve communications and to strengthen trade between Kamchatka and America. Another expedition was envisaged for those purposes. Arriaga wrote to de Croix and Galvez on the subject twice. He bade the viceroy to take measures to frustrate all Russian colonizing efforts in America and to discover the sites of any Russian settlements that had already been established. In turn, de Croix pondered on places where a Russian force might land. He thought of Monterey and wrote to Galvez. Galvez authorized the sending of two expeditions, one by land and one by sea. By now, Galvez himself was growing very conscious of the Russians. "It is known to our Court," he wrote in January 1768, "that the Russians have familiarized themselves with the Sea of Tartary . . . It would be neither impossible nor indeed very difficult for the Muscovites to establish a colony at the port of Monterey, and when least expected."[119]

Other high officials of the king in other parts of the Pacific were equally alive to Russian menace from the North, though it had yet to show itself. Hardly had Galvez made the above comment, before the russophobic Pedro Calderon y Henriquez of Manila was composing a memorial on the importance of dispatching the Manila galleon to a well-armed and populated Monterey, thereby dissuading Russian colonists and hunters from encroaching into Spanish California.[120] Russian naval officers would have felt flattered, had they known how far the ripples of their tentative and limited activities off North America had spread. In 1769, five Spanish parties made their ways from Mexico to Alta California, two by land and three by sea. Portola pressed north to San Francisco Bay. The Russian menace was no greater now than earlier. But the mounting fear of "Muscovite" encroachment was nevertheless the catalyst in this new process of advance and occupation, lending urgency to Galvez's designs for Monterey and San Francisco.

At this juncture, Herreria was succeeded as ambassador in Russia by Francisco Antonio, Conde de Lacy (1731-92). A soldier by both training and temperament, de Lacy was eventually to distinguish himself as an aggressive general. He was ill-suited to the diplomatic life, being contemptuous of court intrigue and gossip and intolerant of Russia and the Russians. In 1772, the conde did his best to penetrate the secrecy surrounding Russian enterprise on the Pacific shores of Asia and America. By mid-October, he could at least assure Grimaldi that the cossacks' unacknowledged exploitation of a Spanish patrimony was proceeding unabated. Even better, from the xenophobic standpoint, he could send a "royal order" dated two years earlier (5 September 1770), well calculated to inspire apprehension in Madrid. It recorded that the Russian government had had a warning that a foreign naval power had designs on Petropavlovsk in Kamchatka and called for preparations to be made in the peninsula, including stockpiling of powder, guns, and flour and strengthening the garrisons.[121] Grimaldi did not know the true position but he had sense enough to see the conde's message in its proper light: he did not panic.

But de Lacy grew determined to impress Madrid with the full gravity of the Pacific situation. He had recently discovered, he reported on 7 February 1773, that one Chirikov of the Russian Navy had been secretly exploring on the coasts of North America. Together with his secretary, this Chirikov had in 1772 reported on his probings to St. Petersburg; he had been sworn to secrecy and given further duties on the North Pacific littoral. Again Grimaldi was suspicious of the value of de Lacy's information, but he sent a note of it to Arriaga, who contacted

Bucareli in New Spain. Further precautionary measures were in order. Six more naval officers would be transferred to San Blas. Conde de Lacy continued to report in an increasingly alarmist vein. An informant who had access to the Admiralty archive had given him a report on Russian voyages to North America itself. Nine years before two Russian ships had sailed for North America from Arkhangel'sk, under two officers named "Estehacowy" and "Panowbafew," while a third had sailed under a Captain Krenitsyn from Kamchatka. The three had kept their rendezvous, then explored the coasts of North America from approximately 40° to 75°N. Madrid was thus presented with an oddly jumbled record of the first of Chichagov's and of the Krenitsyn-Levashev expeditions, several years too late to be of practical significance. De Lacy had more to keep Grimaldi from his sleep: Catherine proposed "to force the Great Wall of China" and, in due course, to attack Japan. A naval force would sail from Petropavlovsk under an Englishman, General Lloyd. For the third time in as many months, Grimaldi saw no need to chase such wild northern geese. Arriaga too was skeptical. He was, he wrote a little afterwards, "well satisfied" with all the preparations on the coast of Alta California, the more especially as anti-Russian measures "could well serve other purposes."[122]

The Russian threat did not simply evaporate, however, in the 1770's, and the exploratory voyages of Perez (1774-75) and of Heceta and Bodega y Quadra (1775) may be attributed to Spanish nervousness of the activities of Russians off the shores of North America. Russian activity along and near the North-west Coast also accelerated Spanish missionary work and occupation of the littoral of Alta California north of San Diego.

Shortly after the report on its results had reached Madrid, the Russian government learned of the expeditions led by Portola in 1769-70. From the resultant apprehension of attacks on Petropavlovsk by the irritated Spaniards, there sprang the order of 5 September 1770, reported by de Lacy. In the Admiralty College, there were serious suggestions that an Anglo-Russian North Pacific pact might be concluded with a view to halting Spanish advances on Kamchatka and the islands ruled by Russia. The idea was abandoned when the news arrived that Portola had reached a latitude of only 48°N. (He had in fact sailed to 38°. So much for secret diplomatic reportage.)[123] News of the Perez voyage similarly raised anxiety about the strength of Russia's position in the North Pacific islands in March 1775.[124] But this, too, quickly ebbed.

When, amidst her Turkish wars and Polish "problems" of 1771-75, Catherine II had spared any thought for the Pacific and American extremities of her domains, she had not wavered from her policy of lending State assistance to the backers and agents of the new Pacific fur trade, but not openly. The news of Heceta's and Bodega y Quadra's voyage of surveillance confirmed her views. And her policy was not entirely negative or unaggressive, for Catherine continued to aid those who were spreading Russian influence along the fringe of North

America. Spain failed to exert similar pressure on the people and resources of "the Coast" over the coming fifteen years. Not until 1779 did Bodega and Arteaga in *Favorita* and *Princesa* make a careful exploration of the coast of southwestern Alaska. Shortly after their return, orders were issued in Madrid on 10 May 1780 putting a stop to such defensive-cum-exploratory voyages.[125] Unwittingly, the king of Spain set the scenario for that eventual collision of Imperial and economic interests on the Coast known as the Nootka Controversy.

EULER'S MEMORIAL OF 1773

Since de Lacy's despatch dated St. Petersburg, 11 May 1773 is perhaps the most unconsciously prophetic of all papers of the period where Russia's naval presence in the North Pacific Ocean is concerned, it is quoted here in extract. "The Russian empress," read Grimaldi, "having told the famous Haller, professor at the Academy here, of the discoveries made in America, the latter has presented a detailed memorial."[126] When peace had been concluded with the Porte, Haller argued,

> part of the Russian squadron from the [Greek] Archipelago should be sent around the Cape of Good Hope to Kamchatka, in the ports of which it could refit after its long voyage and afterwards continue conquests advantageous to the Empire. According to Haller, this Empire has more right than any other Power to America, because America was formerly colonized by inhabitants of Siberia.

Conde de Lacy's despatch, with its confusing reference to pre-historical events or, possibly, to the legend of a mediaeval Russian settlement in North America,[127] is of great interest in the Pacific-naval context. There had certainly been earlier suggestions that a Russian squadron should sail to Okhotsk or Petropavlovsk by a southern route. There had quite possibly been similar proposals made in Catherine's own reign. None of these, however, sent ripples through St. Petersburg or chanceries abroad. Now, for the first time, such proposals caused disturbance outside Russia. It was well for Spain that "Haller," that is, Leonhard Euler (1707-83) was unversed in naval matters, though indeed he had at one time been proposed as a lieutenant in the Russian Baltic Fleet by Peter Sievers.[128]

Euler had long worked at the Academy of Sciences with Nicolas and Daniel Bernoulli and with Joseph-Nicolas Delisle. He had maintained his links with such members of Bering's expeditions as Steller and Gmelin.[129] His correspondence offered ample evidence of his deep interest in the search for northern passages to the Pacific. As it happened, he had incorrect, exaggerated notions of Russia's naval capabilities which were perhaps excusable in the afterglow of victory at Chesme Bay. But Euler was correct in his perception of the meaning and importance that would necessarily attach to the arrival of a Russian naval force in the Pacific by a southern route. The moment had arrived to play that hand, before a European power made a serious new move in those localities which Catherine herself viewed as a Russian zone of economic influence, that is, the waters east of Kodiak or north of the Pribylovs. Byron, Wallis, and Cook had all been sent to the Pacific to augment the wealth and power of the British Crown and government through trade.[130] The North-west and the North-east Passages to the Pacific and its wealth remained unsighted. The international search for the former was most likely to bring other foreign subjects to the region of Kamchatka.[131]

BRITISH AND FRENCH AWARENESS OF RUSSIAN ENTERPRISE ON THE PACIFIC

There had been British naval officers and shipwrights in the Baltic, and in Russian pay, since the middle of the sixteenth century.[132] For British naval officers, historical, financial, and political factors favoured the Anglo-Russian nexus, of which commerce formed one strand, exchange of personnel another.[133] Among those who played minor roles—as Spanish officers did not—in the process of acquainting Russian government officials with the opportunities yet to be taken by the Russians in the East, two will be mentioned: John James Blankett and Charles Knowles.

John Blankett had a lively interest in the existence of a North-west or, as second-best, a North-east Passage to the Orient and Indies. It had been aroused in him when, as a midshipman, he had been present at the taking of Quebec in 1759.[134] Long before his working visit to St. Petersburg, where he collected information about Arctic exploration off Kamchatka and the latest cossack voyages to the Aleutians, he had been disturbed by thoughts of Russian maritime and economic hegemony in the far North-East of Asia. He proposed that news and rumours of expanding Russian strength in the North-East and of discoveries by Russians off America be verified as a preparatory step to exploitation of that strength by British interests, in ways to be discussed in Cabinet. The Admiralty gave him leave to proceed on a brief fact-finding mission, to St. Petersburg, where British stock stood high on his arrival.[135] Returning to London, Blankett wrote an elegant report in which he emphasized that, in the future national interest, the British should attempt to make an ally of the Russian sovereign. On Russia's Baltic shores alone, there was sufficient standing timber to supply the Royal

Navy for many years to come; but in the easternmost possessions of the Empire grew even greater forests. Were the empress's Pacific and American resources and her harbours in the East not of potential value to her friends? And why should an alliance not be formed between the empress and the British for the purpose of excluding French and Spanish influence from North Pacific ports and markets?[136]

Admiral Charles Knowles, unlike John Blankett, entered Catherine's employ (March 1771). Although acquainted with the king and a full admiral, he had only modest prospects in his own country. He was, besides, in urgent need of money. As a specialist in ship and dock construction, he was welcomed by the empress and became responsible for the administration of construction programmes in all regions of the Empire. His salary and personal allowances were princely.[137] Between 1771 and 1774, he held ultimate responsibility for progress or the lack of it in the areas of building and repair on the Pacific shore. Okhotsk was the least of his concerns. Nevertheless, his term of office had significance for Russia's naval future in the East, as in the South. In two long memoranda to the empress of the early weeks of 1774, he drew attention to the need both to reorganize harbour and dock administration and to standardize ship-parts specifications, cables, guns, and even stores in every region of the Empire from Reval to Okhotsk.[138] Such programmes were impractical, no doubt; but for the first time at so high a level, the remoteness and attendant inefficiency of naval operations at Okhotsk had been discussed, and ways had been proposed of shrinking outlay by administrative means.

Neither Spain nor France drew comfort from the influence exerted at St. Petersburg, and in the Fleet especially, by men like Knowles and Samuel Greig of Inverkeithing, an efficient Scot who, disappointed in his hopes of a lieutenancy in Britain's peacetime navy of the mid-1760's, had been well rewarded for his services to Catherine, at Chesme in particular, and who was now of some political significance.[139] French apprehension at the thought of a concerted Anglo-Russian naval policy in the Pacific did not manifest itself, however, until 1776. In April of that year, a rumour spread that with assistance from the Royal Navy, Russians planned the conquest of Japan. The rumour is of interest as the precursor of the great Pacific scares of the next century.[140] It also serves to introduce the propagandist work of Count Benyowski.

Maurice Augustus, Count Benyowski (1746-86), an Austrian by birth, had fought for Poland, fallen prisoner to Russia, and been exiled to Kamchatka. There, in June 1770, he had led a local rising. With a rough and motley crew, he had escaped in a small vessel. After numerous adventures, he had made his way to France. In 1776, Benyowski recollected having seen "in Kamchatka," certain papers that related to the founding of a Russian colony on an Aleutian Island, whence Russians might proceed, he insisted, with the conquest of whole or part of Spanish California. Benyowski did not claim that any document that he had seen at Bol'sheretsk concerned *specific* projects or invasion plans. Nevertheless, he now believed that at some future date the Russians might attempt the annexation of a part of Alta California.[141] His views came to the notice of officials in the Ministry of Foreign Affairs in Paris and resulted in at least one memorandum on the prospects for an Anglo-Russian maritime entente in the Pacific Ocean, to be secretly or openly directed against France as well as Spain. Here are extracts from *Memoir no. 9* (*Angleterre,* Vol. VI: 1776) in the French ministerial archive and appended "Observations":

The Secretary of the Russian Embassy in London, when questioned regarding connections of his Court with that of England, let it be known that they were considering a project that would astonish Europe . . . 1st: For some time, England has been proposing to Russia to take possession of the Japanese Empire. 2nd: The Court at London promised that Captain Cook, after repatriating his Tahitian [Omai], would voyage along the coast of California pretending to seek a northern passage, and that he would call at Kamchatka under this pretext. 3rd: That he would explain to the Russians the route that he had followed. 4th: That he would investigate the Russians' dispositions . . . 7th: That he would leave at Kamchatka all the workmen and carpenters, of whom he had an abundance in his crew . . . Russia has promised that if the expedition should succeed, she would aid England with as many ships as possible and would keep the ports of Japan open to commerce . . .

If this was the only information, and entirely unsupported by any other source, it might be regarded as chimerical; but we have authentic proof that in 1768 Russia ordered great preparations in Kamchatka under pretext that she feared an invasion; that she thereafter planned with England to send ships to Kamchatka; and that extensive preparations were being made. It is Baron Benyowski who has procured this proof for us . . . . Altogether, indications seem to warrant the belief that there exists not only a plan on Russia's part, but also an agreement between that Power and England. As for the object of the combined expedition, M. de Benyowski had thought it might be California, but the latest data establish the likelihood that it concerns the Japanese Empire, or at least the conquest of some of the numerous islands of which it consists. Spain has been warned of the storm which is brewing.[142]

The memoir rests on two unnamed and two named sources. The latter are Benyowski and Jean Benoit Scherer, a Strasbourg savant who was long in Russian service. On returning to his own country in 1774, Scherer had brought with him a library of works and manuscripts relating to the far North-East of Asia and Siberia as well as Tartary. He made good use of them,[143] and he could well have given useful information to the French. His contribution to the memoir was, however, plainly smaller than Benyowski's; and the memoir is in any case a patchwork of improbabilities. And if the nameless Russian Secretary was not, in fact, Benyowski's alter ego, could he not have built on the foundations of a modicum of knowledge about cossacks in Kamchatka and the newspaper accounts of Cook's instructions? Possibly as a result of certain doubts about that secretary, or Benyowski, or the pair of them, the memoir bore no fruits. The French, however, did not lose their dark suspicion that the British and the Russians *were* conspiring to exclude all other powers from the North Pacific region and its trade, by realizing latent naval strength. How should the government of France parry that blow, except by sending a French squadron to Japan? Iron and weapons could be offered to the Japanese in exchange for trading privileges. Thus, in times of relative tranquility in Europe, could a hint of joint imperial activity by Russia and Britain in the North Pacific send a diplomatic ripple round the courts of France and Spain.

4

Cook's Final Voyage and the Billings and Mulovskii Expeditions

Cook's final expedition with the *Resolution* and *Discovery* in 1776-80 had its particular significance for the development and shaping of the Russian naval presence in the North Pacific region. The appearance of the British first on Unalaska Island in October 1778 and then in Petropavlovsk harbour, April-May and August-October 1779, served as a forceful reminder of the relative defencelessness and economic value of Kamchatka and the North Pacific islands.[1] Later former members of the expedition entered Russian naval service and played their parts in drawing Catherine's attention to the far North-East and East and to the wonderful potential of the oceanic otter trade, which Cook's men had begun, almost by accident, while at Canton in 1779-80.[2]

News of the enormous sums that Chinese merchants were prepared to pay even for torn sea-otter skins from the Pacific rim launched many speculative voyages from Britain, New England, and Bengal to the localities that Cook had charted and described. Even official scientific and exploratory ventures in the North Pacific Ocean were affected by the lure of accessible "soft gold," as the *promyshlenniki* fondly termed sea-otter peltry. Of the purely speculative voyages, reports of which served to sustain and even heighten Russian consciousness of the importance of asserting Russia's rights in the Pacific, none annoyed the Russian government more deeply than the first, that of the *Sea Otter* in 1785 (Captain James Hanna). Of the broadly scientific expeditions of the last years of the century that likewise drew attention in St. Petersburg to the need for action by the Russians, thereby stressing basic lessons taught by Cook, suffice to mention that of J. F. de G. de La Pérouse (1785-88), which, in September 1787, also put briefly into Petropavlovsk.

CLERKE AT PETROPAVLOVSK: THE REACTION

Shortly after Cook's violent death the *Resolution* and *Discovery*, commanded now by Clerke and Gore, entered Avacha Bay to water and provision.[3] It was time, once more, to seek the North-west Passage home to England. All was silent in the settlement; below it, ice extended from the shore. Alarmed by the arrival of two unfamiliar and unexpected ships, the little garrison of Petropavlovsk— thirty soldiers and a sergeant at the time—looked on as King and Webber, the *Discovery*'s artist, landed on the ice-sheet and proceeded up the shore. All guns were loaded. But the crisis quickly passed. As soon as the visitors made contact with the governor of the peninsula, Magnus von Behm (1727-1806), who had travelled up in haste from Bol'sheretsk, they perceived that they were fortunate to have encountered him. Behm was a generous and widely read official, a Livonian by birth. On his instructions, Clerke was given all he needed to repair and victual his ships. Clerke handed a packet containing his own latest reports and other documents by Cook, King, and Bayly to the governor for forwarding to London overland. The governor proved worthy of the trust;[4] and he was equally obliging when the foreigners returned to Petropavlovsk and on 26 August buried their captain.[5] For the second time, the British were assisted and supplied on Behm's instructions.[6]

Behm reported on the first of Clerke's two visits in mid-May in a despatch for Colonel F. N. Klichka in Irkutsk. The despatch was promptly forwarded to A. A. Viazemskii, then procurator-general, who showed it to the empress. Viazemskii received further despatches from Siberia relating to the double British visit to Kamchatka of 1779,[7] placing it in the most sinister light. As a result, orders were issued for more guns to be transported overland to Petropavlovsk. Catherine's own attitude towards the recent British visits and the possibility of others was reported diplomatically by Sir James Harris in a long despatch to Sandwich dated 7 January 1780. "The Empress," wrote the British minister, "feels the great utility which must result from such a voyage, & is anxious to promote its success—she expressed a very *earnest* desire of having Copys of such Charts as may tend to ascertain more precisely the extent & position of those remote and unexplored Parts of her Empire,"[8]

Catherine might well have wished for copies of such charts. The Russian government itself had all too few that covered waters to the north of St. Lawrence Island; and since Russia had no warships in the far North-East and East, how was even the Aleutian Island chain to be regarded as a safe, still less integral, portion of her empire? There were disadvantages, as well as great advantages, to any policy involving private traders as the instruments of Russian penetration down the Kurile and Aleutian Island chains and to the North.

JOSEPH BILLINGS'S ARRIVAL IN THE BALTIC

With the aid of English merchants in Canton, John Gore disposed of peltry gathered casually on the North-west Coast of North America for about £2,000.[9] Two seamen fled their ship, taking a boat, in hopes of entering the Coast-to-Canton fur trade on their own account.[10] Even the better-educated entertained such notions. The Connecticut marine John Ledyard and Lt. James Trevenen, among others, later formulated projects for the exploitation of the North Pacific fur trade.[11] Joseph Billings, too, was very probably impressed by the facility with which the £2,000 had been earned. Typically, however, he refrained from writing projects on that basis: he was not a writing man.

Much is obscure about the relatively humble early life and work of Joseph Billings. His biography has yet to be attempted. Even so, of all the subsequent successes won by young or minor members of Cook's final expedition, none may properly be said to have been larger or more brilliant than his.

On his return from the Pacific with *Discovery,* Billings immediately vanished from the Admiralty records, re-emerging two years later as the mate of a British merchantman (1782-83). On reaching Russia, at the age of twenty-five, he was accepted in the Baltic Fleet as a midshipman. Shortly thereafter he was given his lieutenancy. Even the social disadvantage of modest origins, which would inevitably have impeded his professional advancement in his native land, was thus removed in Russian sight.

Billings successfully impressed upon the Admiralty College that he had in early life been Cook's "companion" (and "astronomer's assistant" in *Discovery*).[12] There had, moreover, been developments in the remote North-East and East since he had joined the Russian Navy which had made the Russian government more conscious of the possible utility of such experience as he and James Trevenen had to offer. Along with significant developments in shipbuilding and trade—the three-year, capital-intensive hunting voyage to the waters east of Kodiak was growing commonplace—had recently come news of La Pérouse's sailing with the frigates *Astrolabe* and *Boussole* from Brest in August 1785.[13] What more logical than to employ a man like Billings on the North Pacific littoral? He was the able former servant of a rival state, Great Britain, and a seaman of experience though he was not yet twenty-eight years old. Thus, because he had "already been there," Billings was given the command of a sub-Arctic North Pacific venture.

THE BILLINGS EXPEDITION: PREPARATIONS

The Billings expedition was, in essence, an Imperial response to news of Spanish, British, and now French activity in areas where members of the Commerce and Admiralty Colleges agreed they should be halted. A. R. Vorontsov and other members of the Commerce College, in particular, were growing conscious of the threats posed to the Russian island fur trade by the Spanish and the British.[14] In the strictly naval context, Billings' Arctic and Pacific expedition marked a step in the long process by which members of the Admiralty College were now staking out a claim in the Pacific for the Navy.[15]

As a response to danger signals and developments in the remote North-East and East, the expedition lacked originality. Like the Krenitsyn-Levashev expedition, it was secret theoretically, but not in practice. When at length its existence was acknowledged, it was formally described as a new survey of the coastline of Siberia and of a scattering of islands between Asia and America.[16] Again like the Krenitsyn-Levashev expedition, it was planned in St. Petersburg by men who only grudgingly conceded that immediate conditions might determine the unfolding of events in the sub-Arctic. And like Bering's, Billing's orders, which at first came under twenty-seven heads, gave evidence of their composers' inexperience of exploration such as he was to attempt.[17] Thirdly, his expedition too was to seek information needed if the state was to continue to participate in and control whatever fur and other trade could be developed in the far North-East of Asia and, if possible, beyond in North America. Little had changed since 1771 in the official Russian view of what the state should be attempting to achieve on its remote north-eastern fringes. Unofficially, much had been changing in the 1780's, and such men as P. P. Soimonov, secretary to the empress, A. R. Vorontsov, and A. A. Bezborodko were conscious of strategic, as well as economic factors in the new Pacific fur trade, thanks to La Pérouse and Hanna.[18] Lastly, the Billings expedition, like the others, was to start before relations between leader and Siberian officialdom or, for that matter, between servants of the Navy and *promyshlenniki* had been specified by proper regulation. As a consequence, it too was troubled by dissensions arising from overlapping areas of competence and from the absence of precise delimitations of authority.

The orders for the Billings expedition were prepared within ten weeks of La Pérouse's sailing.[19] Was a "geographical and astronomical," that is a charting and descriptive, expedition, the appropriate response to more encroachments by three European powers on a Russian sphere of influence? The empress and the Senate thought so. Vorontsov and Bezborodko had some reservations; both were coming to believe that a more visible response might be more suitable.

Lieutenant Gavriil Sarychev left the capital with a small vanguard, which included several shipwrights, in the middle of September and pressed east throughout the winter. When he reached Okhotsk in March 1786, he and his party set to building solid vessels to a plan that had been furnished by another Englishman, Lamb Yeames. Billings came four months later, and still later, with provisions, came Lt. Robert Hall, also an Englishman.[20] Among others in Billings's detachment travelled Martin Sauer, German secretary to the expedition and its annalist.

As it proceeded, the detachment grew from 40 to 140 men, of whom two dozen were acknowledged specialists in their respective fields of wilderness survival, science, medicine, linguistics, and sub-Arctic navigation.[21] Now the Admiralty College had a choice of applicants for most positions on a major expedition to the North Pacific region.

Billings's instructions were numerous and complex. The Academy of Sciences, the Admiralty, and the Commerce Colleges had somewhat different hopes of the whole venture. As a consequence, there were both Arctic and Pacific projects, naval and commercial plans and studies. "Special attention should be paid to little-frequented and to quite unknown islands lying to the leeward of the North American coast and east of Unimak, e.g., Sannak, Kodiak, Lesnoy."[22] If new peoples were discovered, every effort should be made to "bring them all under the Russian sceptre's sway," by kind persuasion; "for most certainly, no Europeans will yet have embittered or annoyed those natives, so the first task must be to spread among them a fair impression of the Russians."[23] But while they were distributing trinkets to persuade the natives to become Russian subjects, Billings and his people were also "to acquire information on the tribes' different customs, mores, languages, traditions and antiquities." And he was also instructed to discover a navigable passage eastward from the Lena and around the furthest tip of Asia to Kamchatka. Clerke's assertion that the quest for such a passage would be vain was once and for all to be refuted by the Russians. "Explorations and sea-voyages should be extended by all means, as far as circumstances, safety and the requirements of the service itself shall allow . . . . Accurate charts will be prepared, and all locations seen will thereon be indicated . . . . Sketches should everywhere be made." When the expedition reached those areas, all extant Russian maps should be examined, in particular, all Russian maps showing the Kurile Islands and "the Chinese coast down to Korea" should be checked against the expedition's own solar and lunar observations. On the voyage to the Kuriles or returning thence, the expedition should in passing make a study of the islands seen by Clerke between 40° and 50°N. Watch should be kept, day in day out, for unknown islands. Geological and astronomical, botanical, linguistic, and commercial data would be gathered, most especially about the Chukchi country, of which not enough was known.[24] The very presence of a naval expedition should be veiled in secrecy. "Never, under any pretext whatsoever, are you to reveal to anyone the ends or operations of this venture."[25]

The main party reached Iakutsk on 29 May 1786. Arrangements had been made there to supply and to convey the two divisions into which the expedition was to split to their respective starting points: the valley of the River Kolyma and Okhotsk. Lt. Hall was to command the latter group, Lt. Christian Bering, the former. Billings went to Okhotsk from Iakutsk in mid-July. Having seen that work progressed on vessels which would subsequently take him to the shores of North America, he then made quickly for the Kolyma.[26]

THE VOYAGES OF *PALLAS* AND *IASASHNA*

Billings's arrival on the frozen upper reaches of the River Kolyma coincided with the onset of the early winter storms. It was an augury of coming tribulation, partly caused by the extreme cold, partly by a shortage of provisions. However, preparations for the Arctic voyage went ahead, and on 25 May 1787, the expedition boarded the two small but sturdy craft that had been built during the winter, the *Pallas* and *Iasashna*. Billings took command of *Pallas* and Sarychev of *Iasashna*. The expedition reached Nizhnekolymsk on 17 June. After a pause for procuring and stowing fresh-killed meat, it pressed on north into the ocean.

As so often in the study of the Russian enterprise in the Pacific, Arctic matters here obtrude. They inevitably do so, for the Russians, and the Admiralty College more especially, still hoped in Billings's day to force a way *down* to the North Pacific Ocean from the North. The College as a body and the government at large had yet to recognize the wider possibilities inherent in the opposite approach from Kronstadt to the South Pacific Ocean and thence up. Viewed in a certain light, indeed, the very history of Russia's naval effort in the North Pacific area is a reflection of the struggle between "northern" (eighteenth-century) and "southern" (nineteenth-century) approaches to the problem of controlling its resources, shores, and islands.

Billings and Sarychev steered due east along the Arctic Ocean's shore. Not for a day could they relax their vigilance. Their companies were soon exhausted. Billings ordered halts repeatedly at night and when the ice conditions threatened more than usual. They pressed on east until 25 July; but from 2 July onward, neither captain managed to stand even twenty miles offshore. The narrow strip of open water before them now expanded, now contracted, before finally betraying them completely. "Enormous, high icebergs now covered the entire sea ahead, and we could see no end to them. Waves crashing against these made an awful roar."[27] An observation showed a latitude of 69° 35′N, long. 168° 54′E. Billings called a council of all officers. At its end, he issued orders for both vessels to return to the known estuary of the River Kolyma.[28]

Despite a basic tendency to view Sarychev as the true and proper hero of the Billings expedition, recent Soviet historians of Arctic exploration have taken issue with such earlier historians as V. N. Berkh and I. F. Kruzenshtern, who wrote of Billings's Arctic effort as the enterprise of an irresolute incompetent.[29] These writers, comments M. I. Belov, would assuredly have tempered their attacks if they had had a just idea of the conditions in which Billings and his people found themselves by mid-July 1787 off Cape Bol'shoi Baranov.[30] It is certain, nonetheless, that the decision to abandon all attempts to force a passage to Kamchatka in the *Pallas* and *Iasashna* or in stout open *baidars* with only half a dozen men in each, as was suggested by Sarychev, greatly lowered the morale of Billings's men.

And spirits did in fact sink lower when the expedition reached Iakutsk after this failure. Many stores and some equipment that should long since have arrived there were still awaiting transport in Irkutsk and other places. Like another Vitus Bering, Billings saw no choice but to spend time over arrangements for moving his equipment and supplies. Obliged to linger in Iakutsk, he made a virtue of necessity, living in comfort. Using expedition monies then in trust with him, moreover, he bartered for provisions and some luxuries with local Iakuts and with merchants of the place, showing considerable acumen or sharpness in his dealings. It was less the acts themselves, which are obscure, than the way in which he acted that eventually discredited him. Billings continued to co-ordinate the expedition's scientific work during these months. But in the end, a new governor-general of Eastern Siberia, I. A. Pil', judged it proper to instruct him to travel to Okhotsk without delay. "Mr. Billings," wrote the governor to A. A. Bezborodko in St. Petersburg, "had been in Iakutsk quite needlessly almost till the day of my arrival. But the preparation of the vessels at Okhotsk, and everything connected with their readying, was under his command. Inasmuch as subordinates do not attend to work given them in the absence of their leader with the zeal and diligence that such a venture as this may well demand, I leave to your own judgement what is to be expected of this expedition."[31]

In fact, the Billings expedition had been swaying in the balance for some time in St. Petersburg. Billings himself now almost finished it by handing weapons to its critics. On 20 June, the Admiralty College had dispatched to Pil' by courier "Instructions Concerning the Return of Captain Billings and the Whole Command Now with Him." Catherine was always a pragmatist where expeditions were concerned. Gladly anticipating conflict with the Porte, she recognized that Billings and his officers and men might well be useful on the Black Sea front. The Pacific still had the lowest priority when war imposed a strain on the resources of the state. Before either Bezborodko or the Admiralty College could react to Pil''s report, Billings had actually reached, and was about to leave, Okhotsk. To his credit, I. A. Pil' voiced reservations about cancelling the venture altogether. In his view, it was too late to cut its costs, and its political significance within the North Pacific context was increasing in proportion to the presence of non-Russians in the North Pacific fur trade.[32]

OKHOTSK: THE SAILING OF THE *SLAVA ROSSII*

Okhotsk had changed a little since the time of Krenitsyn. Saltworks had been established near the settlement and were producing several tons each year.[33] The magazine and dockyard, which the Admiralty Office had continued to control, had been expanded; several vessels had been built in recent years, and more repaired. There was tolerably frequent, though irregular, communication with Kamchatka, and Okhotsk-built galiots sailed out to the Aleutians every season. Martin Sauer left a detailed and vivid picture of Okhotsk, and of the galiots, well laden with their trading knives and hatchets, rough tobacco, victuals and liquor, beads and drunkards.

> The city of Ochotsk . . . is built on a neck of land five versts long and from 15 to 150 fathom wide, its direction due east. It is chiefly composed of sand, shingles, and driftwood, the whole thrown up by the surf. The town occupies the space of about one verst in length, contained 132 miserable wooden houses, a church and belfry, several rotten storehouses, and a double row of shops. . . . The main channel of the Ochot is only navigable for small empty vessels one mile upwards, for in many places the depth is only ½ to 2½′, 6′ to 8′ at high water. The sudden check that the stream receives from the sea is the cause of a bank in the form of a crescent, SSW. and W., the distance of a mile and a half out: a bar continues westward leaving a channel 5′ deep at low water, 30 fathom wide but frequently shifting. A very violent surf constantly breaks over the bar and all along the shore. At the time of the equinoctial gales, the spray wets the houses of the town.[34]

Though no seaman, Sauer recognized immediately Petropavlovsk's great superiority. With its deep and sheltered water, it could easily accommodate "six or eight" warships, anchored "head to stern."[35] But there was nothing to be done about the natural conditions at Okhotsk. Returning there, Billings was able to report at least that Hall had been most diligent, keeping his people hard at work, "some equipping the vessels lately built, some on their armament. . . . All are in good spirits."[36] The two vessels in question had been named *Slava Rossii* and *Dobroe Namerenie (Glory of Russia* and *Good Intent).*

But again, omens were black: *Slava Rossii* made the open sea in safety, but disaster struck the second craft. *Dobroe Namerenie* had hardly left Okhotsk roads under tow at high tide on 8 September, before a storm followed a period of calm. A giant wave picked up the vessel and cast her on a sand-bank. She was broken and half-flooded. *Slava Rossii* was reladen in the course of the next week with the supplies that had been saved. While the shipwrights who had only lately built her watched, the *Dobroe Namerenie* was burned for her iron. On 19 September, the expedition put to sea again.

Slava Rossii reached Avacha Bay after a two-week voyage, in the course of which a little rocky island was discovered in the Sea of Okhotsk, which Billings named Sv. Iona. In Kamchatka, winter was at hand. Billings gave orders for his ship to be unrigged and for the local serving men to help their guests prepare to winter.

Early in March 1790, an unpleasant piece of news reached the peninsula by courier. The Russo-Swedish War had spread from Europe to the North Pacific Ocean in the shape of a small privateer, the *Mercury,* commanded by an English rogue and smuggler called Coxe.[37] It had been known for eighteen months that Captain Coxe was flying Swedish colours; now, it seemed quite likely that *Mercury* would show herself on the Aleutian chain. If Coxe met Billings, he was likely to be hostile. Here is part of Pil''s despatch to V. I. Shmalev, now governor of Kamchatka, dated 29 February 29 1790:

You will take steps to see that no foreign vessel can near the harbour [of Petropavlovsk] until we, for our part, have discovered what the strangers have in mind for us. . . . You will note, with great care, what flags are flown on such foreign ships, also the nationality of their people; for persons hostile towards Russia have at times insinuated themselves as her well-wishers. I pass over the English in silence—*they* have long been attempting to steal treasure belonging to Russia, not to them.[38]

Billings was to give chase to Coxe if he sighted him and to impress upon his countryman the dangers inherent in his "plundering. . . . within the limits of lands subject to Russia." Billings decided that the risk of meeting *Mercury* was too remote to justify changing his plans for the next season. Unwilling to meet trouble in advance, he sailed from Avacha Bay on 9 May 1790 as intended. The expedition stood due east. After twenty days, they sighted Amchitka Island, and on 1 June, *Slava Rossii* anchored in the lee of Unalaska, from which Aleuts finally came off on 3 June. So, slightly later, did a cossack in a long, eight-oared *baidar.*[39]

The cossack, Stepan Cherepanov, had no recent news of Coxe. He led the expedition to an anchorage and safe supply of water in Bobrovoi Bay, which Sarychev and a little party charted for the next ten days.[40] Billings once more turned to geological, botanical, and ethnographic work aided by Sauer and all others who were scientifically inclined, including Merck, Main, Krebs, Robeck, Leyman, and Allegretti. Ethnography was given much attention. As a naval precedent, the stress was important, for it was followed not only to the last week of the Billings expedition, but on many later Russian expeditions to the North Pacific area. Unfortunately Billings's journal, with its numerous word-pictures of the life of groups of Aleuts, Koriaks, and Chukchi of the later eighteenth century, remains unpublished.[41]

Slava Rossii put to sea again on 17 June, sailing north-east.[42] Three Aleuts went along. One of the men spoke halting Russian, and from him, Billings and

Sauer learned the names of six or seven of the reef- and rock-surrounded, inhospitable Shumagin Islands. ''Not the smallest bush was to be seen, not a single large tree. The lower areas seemed verdant, but the higher land and hills had a dark hue.''[43] Between and round the islands, sunken rocks promised immediate destruction for the careless mariner. Billings went on, making no landings, to the Semidi Group. More bare and rocky shores, without apparent habitation, sunk all spirits. Here, however, the Russians were approached by a flotilla of *baidarki*.[44] In one sat a *promyshlennik* sent out, he said, from Kodiak. A calm set in. Billings decided to explore one of the islands rapidly. He landed, noted osiers and granite, gathered flora, spotted geese, and hastened back. Within the hour, he was standing out for Kodiak, which he reached on 29 June.

Here, for the first time, Billings met an educated man. Evstratii (Eustrate) Ivanovich Delarov was a Greek by birth, a man of sense and, so it seemed to Sauer, who was disgusted with the overbearing manner of the Unalaska hunters towards Aleuts, of compassion. The expedition's portable tent-church was raised at Three Saints' Harbour to inspire thoughts of piety in all.[45] Delarov proved a mine of information. That year, he said, he had sent out six hundred *baidarki* in six parties of about two hundred Aleuts each. They were expected to do well; the sea-otter were plentiful again. Delarov gave the visitors a lesson in the local hunting schedule: seal and fur-seal from mid-February to late April; sea-otter until June or slightly later; then seal and fish again. The hunting parties would return about October. Fifty cossacks, more or less, wintered on Kodiak. At Three Saints' Harbour, five large cabins had been built. On the beach there were two hunting vessels, of approximately eighty tons, both guarded constantly as a precaution against arson by the natives. Billings, Sauer, and Sarychev all took notes, little suspecting to what use their observations would be put by future officers, notably V. M. Golovnin, anxious that Navy men, not ''traders,'' should direct in the Aleutians.[46]

Billings sailed from Kodiak with ''manager'' Delarov aboard after eight days. Probably he learned something about the plans and operations of Delarov's employer, G. Shelikhov. According to the Aleuts, a frigate had been seen entering Kenai (Cook) Inlet. It was thought that she was Spanish. Billings decided to investigate; but wind and currents thwarted his intentions. After three vain days of tacking off Afognak, the notion of a meeting with the Spaniard was abandoned.[47] Delarov left the ship in the Barren Islands. *Slava Rossii* pressed on north, in due course entering a bay on Montague Island where Cook had halted twelve years earlier. Here, a boat-party was landed. The Russians came on natives who, when certain of their peaceable intentions, made grave accusations against recent hunting bands. However, their timidity and deep respect for muskets did not stop them from attempting theft when opportunities arose.[48] Billings now assumed the rank of captain of the 1st rank as his orders gave him leave to do.

So began August. Billings called a council of his officers. To the astonishment of Gavriil Sarychev, he now insisted that the expedition's safety was dependent on a speedy return to Petropavlovsk. Too experienced to argue, Sarychev and the others held their peace.[49] But this time, subsequent events showed that Billings had been right to be so cautious; five weeks passed, and still *Slava Rossii* was at sea. Conditions worsened. Storms brought down the foremast and destroyed the mainmast spars. Water and victuals grew short. A young native interpreter attempted suicide. But Billings held his course and brought his company into Avacha Bay on 14 October. All but a few men were already weak from scurvy.

THE CONTINUATION OF THE BILLINGS EXPEDITION (1791-92)

For the seamen who were sick, the coming winter brought no comfort; for the fit, it brought no rest. Another ship had to be built. Nizhnekamchatsk was fixed on as the place for a new, temporary shipyard. As before, work went ahead on a new vessel under Hall's able direction in conditions of unmitigated hardship. To the credit of his men, and while others were more fortunately placed at Bol'sheretsk, Hall had the vessel named *Chornyi Orel (Black Eagle)* launched within six months. By May, she was ready to set sail.

Misfortune stalked the Billings expedition. *Slava Rossii,* too, was readied for an early start when spring, with human help, broke up the ice-crust that immobilized all craft at Petropavlovsk. Navigator Bronnikov having collapsed, another pilot had been found, the same Pribylov who had found the fur-seal's breeding-grounds (Pribylov Islands). Spring came relatively early, as was hoped. But day after day vexatious high winds made it impossible to stand away from Petropavlovsk. Not until 29 May 1791 did Billings and his men reach Bering Island, the appointed rendezvous with Captain Hall. Hall was not there. They decided to go on to Unalaska, where Hall was to proceed if he had not seen *Slava Rossii* between 25 and 30 May at Bering Island. On the way, the Billings party made a landing, on an island of which little had been written: Tanaga (Sitanaka). They could not find a single man. At length, an aged woman was discovered, cowering. A cossack party led by one Lukanin, she informed them, had carried off all able-bodied hunters and enslaved the younger women. Rape and slaughter had been widespread. "The youngest and the comeliest of Aleut women," noted Billings in his journal, "are selected for their services, but are not asked for their consent to this. Everything for the subsistence of the hunters, the natives are forced to provide, though they themselves often know hunger. . . . They have roots and berries as their staple foods."[49] Billings and Sarychev, among others, took down details of alleged atrocities committed there and elsewhere. Having watered and revictualled as far as possible, the expedition sailed for Unalaska on 25 June. Hall was not in sight when it arrived.

Could a single vessel, *Slava Rossii,* make the thorough search up Kenai Inlet which Billings had been planning to attempt with two? He decided not, and was unwilling even to listen to other opinions. Whereas Bering had inclined to ask his officers for their opinions more persistently as pressure on him grew, Billings was tending to shut out possibly contrary advice. In consequence his isolation grew more obvious as time progressed. It may be useful to recall here that Billings had not passed his early years in expectation of eventual command. Uncertain men are rarely flexible.

For Sarychev, the abandoning of plans to work up Kenai Inlet was a blow; but there was nothing to be gained by argument with a now stubborn Billings. Orders were at once dropped off for Hall, fresh meat was stowed, the *Slava Rossii* made all sail towards St. Lawrence Bay: Billings had decided that en route for winter-quarters he would call at an Alaskan bay for water and provisions, then cross over to Chukotka and explore it.[50]

After a brief pause at Cape Rodney and a meeting with a friendly group of natives, Billings headed north. The expedition reached its highest latitude, 65° 23′, on 2 August. They sighted islands in the Bering Strait, and the next day *Slava Rossii* stood at anchor in St. Lawrence Bay. From there, Billings planned to lead a party overland in the direction of the River Kolyma, while Sarychev took the ship to Unalaska. Preparations quickly went ahead for the land journey. More than once, Billings had angered his lieutenants by his cautious, even dilatory conduct. Now, almost perversely, he seemed anxious to embark upon a new and major venture, out of sight of any water. With its sleds of stores and instruments, his party struck inland on 13 August. Shortly afterwards, Sarychev sailed for Unalaska Island. He had limited supplies of food aboard; but anxiety for Hall made it unthinkable that he should pause at Petropavlovsk. He was troubled about Hall and about Billings.

Hall had in fact reached Unalaska very shortly after Billings's departure. He had thence sailed for St. Lawrence Bay, as ordered, and then back, not having seen *Slava Rossii* in the North. The anchorage selected for the *Chornyi Orel* and *Slava Rossii* for the winter was a cove on the west side of Illyukyuk Bay. Shore huts were built for the convenience of officers, though some preferred to sleep on board.[51]

Expecting that at least one of his vessels would be wintering at Unalaska, Billings had left orders to prepare at least dried fish. Even so, the two ships' companies were ill provided for the winter, and within a month the first victims of scurvy, like the spectres of Levashev's men of twenty-three years earlier, collapsed. In the new year (1792), effects of scurvy grew more terrible. Towards the end of February, Hall was burying at least one man a day and sometimes three. Given the circumstances, it was greatly to Sarychev's credit that he pressed

ahead with scientific work and, in mid-February, started on a survey of the island's jagged littoral. For forty days, he and his Aleuts edged their way around
the coast in skin *baidarki,* taking bearings as they went. The results were excellent; Sarychev was a competent hydrographer, and to his own exhaustive work at
Unalaska he was able to append that lately finished by the cossack Khudiakov
who had surveyed Sannak and Unimak on his instructions.[52]

But for all Sarychev's energy, the *Chornyi Orel* and *Slava Rossii* were readied
for the homeward voyage to Kamchatka with the greatest difficulty. Not until
mid-May did they set sail, with the sick and feeble seamen in the holds. They
reached Petropavlovsk safely on 21 June. *Chornyi Orel* sailed for Okhotsk some
ten weeks later, undermanned. After a winter in Siberia, Sarychev left for European Russia in July 1793.

BILLINGS'S MARCH THROUGH CHUKOTKA: WORSENING AFFAIRS

Seventeen seamen died on Unalaska. None of Billings's men were actually
murdered by the Chukchi; but their march was grim indeed once they had left the
coast. Harrassed by Chukchi, whom so many cossack parties had tormented,
stripped of clothing, wracked by hunger, they stumbled west for almost twenty
weeks. As for their instruments, the natives either confiscated them or prevented
their exhausted quasi-prisoners from using them effectively. Luka Voronin, the
artist, Dr. Merck, the scientist, and others were reduced to subterfuge to keep a
record or make sketches of their sorry situation. They hid their notes from their
lordly Chukchi "guides." It was a bleak end to a major, state-sponsored, expedition. No less wretched was the further evidence it gave of maladministration and
disease at Petropavlovsk, where as many as one hundred men lay prostrate from
the slow effects of scurvy and exposure to the cold.

A recent incident typified the mismanagement of economic life and men's affairs at Petropavlovsk as in other small north-eastern outposts. When the *Slava
Rossii* had arrived there, she found an English trading vessel, the *Halcyon,* at anchor. Her captain, Barclay, had been trying to persuade the local cossacks to buy
or even barter for at least a portion of his cargo of chandlery and ironware. The
cossacks had informed him that they had no right to buy it on their own authority,
and though his wares were badly needed, they had forbidden him to sell even a
fraction of them, telling him to leave for other parts. Sarychev vainly argued for
acquiring the ironware; Barclay's price was not exorbitant. The *Halcyon* departed with her cargo. Shortly afterwards another foreign merchantman arrived,
La Flavia, flying the tricolor of revolutionary France. She brought a quantity of
liquor to Kamchatka.[53] She, her crew, and supercargo, Herr von Torckler, of
whom more was to be heard by Russian officers in Asia,[54] were enthusiastically

received. *La Flavia* remained at Petropavlovsk for nine months, wreaking much havoc with the local cossack liver.[55]

Billings's decision to march across the Chukchi country was bold but ill-advised. However, it yielded precious ethnographic data about both the deer-herding and the coastal Chukchi groups and, as a bonus, about dealings between Chukchi and "Americans."[56] The ethnographic precedent had thus been re-inforced.

THE BILLINGS EXPEDITION: AN ASSESSMENT

Such, in outline, was the Billings expedition. There has been considerable controversy among scholars about whether, in the context of its objects and its officers' instructions, it was truly a success, or a failure. Certainly, there were officials in St. Petersburg at its conclusion who were lacking in the Vorontsovs' and Soimonovs' sympathy with far-flung trade and maritime adventure and who viewed it as a costly disappointment. Their criticism has been echoed ever since.

Assuredly, the expedition had its less successful sides. Chances were missed. Billings's leadership qualities were doubtful, and they were questioned at the time. And yet in three respects at least the Billings expedition did prove advantageous to the Crown and to the Navy in particular, although the Admiralty College did not recognize these gains for several years. First, practical experience was gained by whole ships' companies and by such officers as Bering, Hall, and Gavriil Sarychev. Secondly, there was the timely acquisition of Sarychev's, Hall's, Daurkin's and Khudiakov's various charts, surveys, and maps of the Pacific rim. This benefit was much augmented by Sarychev who later brought his own and others' cartographic work together in the *Atlas* that accompanied his narrative account (1803) of his experiences under Billings. Of especial value was his large "Mercator Map Showing the Northeast Portion of Siberia, the Arctic Ocean, Eastern Ocean, and Northwest Coasts of North America," on which the coastline of America was traced as far as Bristol Bay. Not only did it rectify most of the blunders made by I. B. Sindt, removing many non-existent islands; it also introduced a higher level of precision to the survey of the far North-East itself. "To have true charts of all those seas," observed Sarychev, "one must, as it were, chart gropingly; and to that end, one must do survey work in skin *baidars* or rowing boats which, by their shallow draught, are suited to work right by the shore and can take shelter from high winds in little streams and shallow bays."[57] Sarychev was a worthy successor to Nagaev. Thanks to him, the work of other men, such as the cossack Gilev, the interpreter and educated Chukchi N. Daurkin, and the naval officer Ivan Izvekov was collated in the Admiralty College's own drawing-room (*chertezhnaia*) and made available to central and Siberian officialdom.[58]

Also presented to the government was information on the cossacks' real treatment of a people whom, in theory, they viewed as fellow subjects. This was a third and major benefit obtained from Billings's and his people's work, published and otherwise. Abuses that continued to be practised in the islands were ventilated publicly by educated officers of rank.

But would the government respond to revelations of abuse in the Aleutian Islands by increasing naval influence in the remote North-East and East, placing the oceanic fur trade under naval jurisdiction or surveillance? There were many in St. Petersburg, as there had always been in Moscow, by the mid-1790's to oppose such a response. Already, mercantile and naval interests in the Pacific were becoming, if not as yet incompatible, at least distinct; nor did the area of overlap seem likely to increase, since as agents of the Crown, naval officers showed themselves ready to expose cossack abuses of the Aleuts and other native peoples. The question thus remained: how was the violence of hunters to be curbed in a *de jure* eastern province of the Empire? The most logical and the most economical approach, argued a merchant group led by Grigorii Ivanovich Shelikhov and his partner, Golikov, would be to cede complete control of the fur trade in the islands and in parts of North America to one strong company, whose board would be responsible to Catherine for its subordinates' and local agents' conduct. Thus Billings inadvertently hastened the process by which there was finally created in July 1799 a monopolistic company for exploiting the fur and other natural resources of the North Pacific area and, theoretically, for sheltering its threatened native peoples.

Billings's own relations with Shelikhov and his rivals in the new Pacific fur trade of the period 1786-92 are obscure. Some have argued, inconclusively for want of first-hand evidence, that certain understandings were arrived at between Billings and at least one group of merchants who had interests in areas that he initially intended to investigate, for example, Prince William Sound. It is significant, perhaps, that many of Billings's papers were "mislaid" during the 1790's. Not a fragment of his journal, moreover, went to press; and though he lived till 1806, he voiced no public criticism of activities by merchants and their agents in the oceanic fur trade.[59] Large investments were at stake. It would have been surprising had they not been well defended. Who defended them and how are questions that deserve separate study in the light of correspondence between G. I. Shelikhov and his manager on Kodiak, A. A. Baranov ("Billings has apparently told them many things"), and between Shelikhov and Lt.-General I. A. Pil'.[60] The answers are uncertain. What is sure is that the Billings expedition coincided with and hastened those entanglements of mercantile and naval operations in the North Pacific Ocean which had started in the 1760's. For another fifty years, it would be pointless to consider the advancements or reverses of the fur trade in the far North-East and East without some reference to naval influence and naval aspirations in the area.

OTHER NORTH PACIFIC PROJECTS (1782-87)

In the period immediately following Cook's final voyage, which sent echoes from Kamchatka to St. Petersburg, several Russians and at least three foreigners offered their projects or their services to Catherine II, with the North Pacific Ocean and its latent wealth in mind. One was John Ledyard (1751-89), the Connecticut marine.[61] Another was the Anglo-Dutch adventurer and propagandist, Willem (William) Bolts (1740?-1808.) On 17 December 1782, Bolts sent a memorial from Austria to I. A. Ostermann with a proposal fully worthy of John Ledyard in its scope. Russia, he argued, should annex certain Pacific islands "with a view to the establishing of sugar plantations." The sugar could be taken to Kamchatka and exported at a profit on the European market. "I would trust to make more profit from a single voyage round Cape Horn, than Russians might from twenty expeditions from Kamchatka."[62] Not surprisingly, given his tactless presentation, Bolts's services were speedily declined.

Within two years of Billings's departure from St. Petersburg a third Pacific planner arrived there from abroad: Lt. James Trevenen (1760-90.) Trevenen's "Russian plans"[63] derived from personal experiences on the North-west Coast and, shortly afterwards, in China. For a single broken buckle, as he later told Charles Vinicombe Penrose, his brother-in-law and first biographer, he had obtained an otter-skin which fetched $300 at Canton.[64] In 1784 Trevenen was on half-pay and depressed about his prospects in the Navy. He proved luckless in his dealings with the merchants of the City, men of "charters and monopolies," whom he was hoping to involve in Coast-to-China trading ventures or in schemes for New South Wales. The time was ripe for an approach to S. R. Vorontsov (1744-1832), the Russian minister in London.

From Trevenen's point of view, there could have been no better Russian representative; nor could the timing of his letter to the minister have been more fortunate. Not only was Vorontsov an influential anglophile, he was also well aware of Anglo-Russian naval links, present and past, and had connections of his own in British Admiralty circles. He was following developments both in the international search for the elusive northern passage to the Orient and in the North Pacific fur trade with considerable interest. Recently, he knew, Fedor Ivanovich Shemelin, an agent of Siberian fur interests, had drafted plans to send a European vessel to Kamchatka, the North-west Coast, and China. The vessel was to carry bulk provisions for Okhotsk and Petropavlovsk. She should certainly be Russian-built and manned, if possible; but otherwise, an Anglo-Russian venture might be contemplated.[65] Vorontsov had also learned of Captain Hanna's trading coup; within six weeks of his arrival on the Coast from India, the English captain had collected five hundred otter-skins in prime condition. He had sold them to the Chinese for some 20,000 piastres.[66] Now, the hunt for the sea-otter was proceeding in a region to which Russia had a claim. An edict had been issued on the subject on 22 December 1786 which he had read only days before Trevenen's letter reached him. Peltry, poaching, and the North Pacific fur trade were in consequence still on his mind. In recent weeks, more British vessels were reported to have traded with the Aleuts and the Tlingit Indians, whom Russians called Kolosh, exchanging guns, powder, and ironware for skins. The expedition led by La Pérouse was one more factor in a troublesome equation. Who could better guard the Russian North Pacific interest than the ex-servant of the British Board of Admiralty? At least one of Cook's former subordinates was in the Russian naval service. Given the empress's new stance towards the British and Bostonian fur poachers, Trevenen's plan to send three vessels from St. Petersburg to deal with them seemed promising. Less than eighteen months before, the empress had been wary when confronted with the distant possibility of conflict between Russians and the subjects of a European power in the North Pacific area. Her latest edict was assertive.

Trevenen's plan, or "North Pacific Project," was designed to catch the eye of Vorontsov and, later, Catherine II. It was basically commercial in its objects, yet it lent itself to other, more warlike ends. Being adaptable, it answered to the needs of the new policy. The minister approved the plan. Trevenen urged that Russia should equip three ships, one of 500 tons, the others of 300, and send them from the Baltic round Cape Horn to Petropavlovsk. The ships should carry trade goods for the natives, shipwrights, and smiths. They should leave during September, revictual and water at a South Pacific island, and proceed for "that part of the Coast which is north of California, and employ the summer in collecting furs the whole length of the Coast." Two of the three vessels should leave the Coast in time to reach Kamchatka, "disembark the artisans and all provisions for that colony, and be ready to depart by the beginning of September." The third should spend the whole summer collecting otter-skins, since the Chinese were prepared to buy great quantities of them at handsome prices. The passage south from Petropavlovsk to Canton might take six weeks. To keep the trade "in train," one or two ships should be sent to the Pacific from the Baltic every season. Commerce with Japan would very probably result from steady trade and intercourse between the North-west Coast and China and from dealings between Japanese and Russians on the Kurile Island chain, "for it cannot be imagined that . . . they shall any longer maintain their separation from the nations, or lock up their treasures in the bosom of their country." Other benefits would follow:

Russia will be supplied with all the produce of the East Indies in her own ships, it will afford a considerable exportation of her own manufactures, and create an equally considerable nursery of seamen. . . . It will become as necessary as advantageous to Russia to keep always a respectable force at Kamchatka. . . . The Empress will have the glory of . . . rendering the geography of the globe perfect.[67]

Trevenen's project was prophetic of the future and in many ways prefigured that adopted by the Russian government in 1802-3, when the *Nadezhda* and *Neva* were readied for their voyages to the Pacific. As he had urged, those vessels watered and provisioned at a European port in South America and proceeded round the Horn to fertile ''islands in the South Sea'' (the Marquesan and Hawaiian Islands). They carried trading goods of the variety envisaged by Trevenen, and their officers strove to initiate trade with Japanese as well as Chinese merchants. Finally, their voyages did lead to various discoveries ''in the immense extent of the South Seas'' and did indeed serve as ''a nursery for seamen.'' The British Board of Admiralty, meanwhile, had granted Trevenen leave of absence for twelve months, starting at once (mid-February). Catherine's approving response to S. R. Vorontsov's despatch came shortly afterwards. ''Being very willing to employ this officer in my service, I leave you to forward this affair; and as there is nothing to intercept such an expedition as he proposes . . . he may rest assured that by quitting the English service he shall not only lose nothing, but shall find it *much* to his advantage.''[68]

Trevenen broke a leg on his hurried way across Livonia. He lay immobile in a little roadside inn for fifty days, wracked both by fever and by panic lest a golden chance of earning fame be lost. Not till September did he reach St. Petersburg, in shaken health; and on the road he had heard things to sink his spirits. On 9 September the empress had at last issued a counter-proclamation to the Porte's declaration of hostilities five weeks earlier. It had thus become unlikely that a squadron that could serve against the Turks would be released to sail to the Pacific. Even more depressing was the news that for some weeks four vessels had been fitting out at Kronstadt for a voyage to the North Pacific Ocean, if they had not sailed already, thus conceivably avoiding an Imperial embargo that could now well be expected. One Mulovskii was to lead, or would have led, that four-ship squadron.

THE PROPOSED MULOVSKII EXPEDITION: THE BACKGROUND.

Captain G. I. Mulovskii's squadron, which consisted of two larger vessels, *Kolmogor* (600 tons) and *Solovki* (530), and two smaller ones, the *Sokol* and the

Turukhtan (both of about 450 tons),[69] had been commissioned ten months previously on the White Sea for a voyage of discovery. In fact, as could at once have been deduced from their acknowledged destination and the scope of the vessels' reconfiguring, Mulovskii and his men were to comprise an armed deterrent in an area to which the Russian Crown laid claim, and which it now perceived as threatened by encroachments of three European powers.

From the time that she had first been told of it, the empress had regarded La Pérouse's expedition as an openly imperialist probe for distant riches.[70] The Spaniards' brief appearance off the shore of Kodiak in the *Favorita* in 1779 had left a lasting memory. By not detecting Three Saints' Harbour, Bodega y Quadra had averted a fresh Russo-Spanish crisis. Recent Spanish and French advances on the Coast and the Aleutians might, in short, have been presented as a reason for a Russian expedition to the North Pacific Ocean. But the naval arm of England, too, had now become a factor. British officers had even made good use of Russian subjects to have documents conveniently forwarded to London. News of Captain Clerke's two visits to Kamchatka had impressed even those members of the Admiralty College who were not (like the intensely anglophobic Count Chernyshev) unfriendly towards England. In effect, Cook and his companies had slipped into a wealthy Russian province undetected. Even worse, he had renamed a dozen places on the Empire's fringe. True, that process was inevitable because Cook had seldom known the native names. Nevertheless, the Russian government deplored it. Yet more recently the full effect of Cook's last voyage on the fur trade had become apparent in St. Petersburg itself.

Catherine's secretary, P. P. Soimonov, reacted somewhat faster than the Admiralty College or the Senate to the escalating problem in the east. He sent a memoir headed ''Notes on Trade and Hunting in the Eastern Ocean'' to Count A. R. Vorontsov, head of the Commerce College, and at the same time he sent a copy to Chernyshev at the Admiralty College.[71] Both officials liked its message: that the influence of foreigners was growing in Canton and would quite probably result in the decline of Kiakhta-Mai-mai-ch'eng as an important fur-mart; that the British had designs both on Japan and on ''the Russian forts and islands'' to the north where seal and otter were abundant; and that commonsense dictated the dispatching of armed vessels from the Baltic to the North Pacific Ocean. It was fortunate that Captain Billings's shipwrights at Okhotsk were building ships to Mr. Yeames's plan; but those ships, even if small, would not be ready for some time. What was wanted was a squadron, to proceed as soon as possible and to remain in the Pacific for some time.[72]

The reasoning seemed sound to Vorontsov. The matter was presented to the empress. A committee was formed, orders were drafted and the ukase of 22 December 1786 was promulgated. In its text were these instructions for the Admiralty College: ''The College . . . will send from the Baltic Sea, and forthwith, two vessels armed like those employed by Captain Cook and by other mariners on discovery, together with two small armed sloops. The latter shall be Navy craft or not, as the College may think best."[73]

Under pressure, the Admiralty College acted promptly. The *Kolmogor, Solovki, Sokol,* and *Turukhtan* were speedily commissioned at Arkhangel'sk, refitted and reinforced to some extent. It was proposed that they should next be sheathed with copper, but at this point, parsimony intervened: wooden strips coated with pitch were instead fixed to their hulls below the waterline.[74] That this was to be different from all preceding naval undertakings in the North Pacific area was plain enough upon comparing the minor role that the Academy of Sciences was playing in its generally well-ordered preparation, with its role in the preparing of the Bering, Chichagov, and even Krenitsyn-Levashev expeditions. The sciences were not neglected, to be sure: P. S. Pallas wrote a scientific programme for Mulovskii and his officers to follow in the North Pacific Ocean and at "distant Russian factories". An invitation to accompany the expedition went to Georg Forster, who had sailed with Cook in 1776-79. But Peter Pallas's instructions and opinions did not dominate proceedings as Delisle's had in the 1730's or as Lomonosov's had during the 1760's. If Mulovskii's expedition had departed, as it nearly did, its members would no doubt have undertaken useful scientific work. Yet the fact that Georg Forster did not join the expedition was significant. It was an accurate reflection of the venture's proper purposes, which hardly called for quills and academic expertise.

Assisted by officials of their choosing, Vorontsov and Bezborodko started work on detailed planning of the venture that Mulovskii was to lead early in March 1787. A committee drawn from members of the Admiralty College and the Senate next decided how the squadron should advance. From the Baltic, it should sail to South America, then east and under Africa towards New Holland. Skirting New Holland, it should make for the Hawaiian (Sandwich) Islands. Having watered, revictualled, and rested, it should split into two forces. Two vessels would proceed with an investigation of the Kurile Island chain and of the Amur estuary and the island or peninsula, whichever it might be, of Sakhalin (Sagalin-anga-gata). Meanwhile, commanded by Mulovskii, the other two would make for Nootka Sound. Sailing from there to the latitude where, almost fifty years before, Captain Chirikov had first sighted land, Mulovskii would possess himself of "the whole littoral" in Russia's name, here and there leaving behind small iron crests marked with the year 1789, 1790, or 1791. Should he discover "crests or signs of other Powers," he should have his men "both level and destroy them."[75] The whole coastline of America above 55°N. should be annexed with proper ceremonies.[76]

Mulovskii's orders are replete with points of interest: three in particular reflect the growth of Russia's interest and strength in the Far East. For many years, the likely value of a port at the mouth of the Uda, south of Okhotsk, had been discussed in naval circles. By the late 1770's support for the idea was in danger of collapse west of Irkutsk. Mulovskii's orders however were to speed up building at Udinsk by every means. Plainly, the government foresaw a future for the place, which was doubtless safer for shipping than Okhotsk.[71] Second, for several generations, landsmen in St. Petersburg and Moscow had been arguing whether or not the Navy's servants in Siberia should be officially expected to perform tasks for which sailors were not trained. The matter had been aired during the planning of Mulovskii's expedition, and settled on the lines of common-sense: "From the sailors and cannoneers offering themselves for this service, only those shall be selected who possess a trade beside their own, e.g., carpentry, joinery, boilermaking, caulking, foundrywork. No man is to be taken who cannot wield an axe."[78] The Navy should assist the local cossacks to develop Russian military strength. By extension, naval officers and seamen were to exercise some functions and to execute some policies beyond Kamchatka that had long been recognized by the Siberian colonial administration as its own. Like Siberian officials on the "mainland," Navy men were to annex new lands to Russia; to survey, sketch, and describe them and their natives; to obtain oaths of allegiance to the sovereign, without resort to violence;[79] to make good use of serving men and private hunters in the national interest;[80] and to examine, if not supervise, activities by merchants. Obviously, the Navy's growing role in the Pacific Ocean *differed* from the role of the Siberian administration on the "mainland" of Siberia given the temporary nature of its presence in a given area, its lack of involvement with the building of *ostrogs*, with local enterprise, and with the gathering of *iasak*, and the larger international implications of its growth.[81] Significantly, even so, Mulovskii's orders nowhere specified whether, or in what circumstances, servants of the Navy would take orders from a cossack or civilian authority. Where ordinary seamen were concerned, no doubt, the problem would be academic; they would recognize authority, cossack or otherwise. But what of the commissioned naval officer ashore? These questions of authority were begged only to rise again, in far more urgent form, in 1802-4.

Thirdly, that section of Mulovskii's orders which relates to the adopting of foreign naval practices at sea, merits attention. What could be borrowed from the English should be borrowed, an improved "nautical stove," for instance, for distilling sea-water into pure[82] and the maps recently published with Cook's *Voyages*. V. P. Fondezin of the Admiralty College had instructions "to collate maps showing voyages and new discoveries by English, Russian, and all other navigators in the Eastern Ocean and in portions of the Arctic Ocean and Okhotsk and Penzhinsk Seas."[83]

Also of interest are several points arising from the Vorontsov and Bezborodko memoir to the empress on the question of her sovereignty in the North Pacific area. That memoir rested on the view that

> to Russia must belong the following: 1. The American coast from 55° 21'N. and extending thence northward, which was skirted by Captains Bering, Chirikov, and by other Russian mariners; 2. All islands lying off the mainland of America and by the Alaska peninsula, discovered by Bering or by Cook, i.e. Montague, St. Stephen, St. Dalmatius, the Shumagin group, and others which lie between Bering's and Cook's courses and the mainland; 3. All islands that stretch westward in a chain, known as the Fox and Aleutian Islands, and all others further north which are annually visited by Russian fur-hunters; 4. The Kurile Islands of Japan, discovered by Captains Spanberg and Walton.[84]

Vorontsov and Bezborodko claimed that it was necessary to declare that most or all of Cook's discoveries between America and Asia had no "validity" as true discoveries. It should be spelled out in an edict that *all* islands on the North Pacific Ocean's northern fringes, like the North-west Coast itself north of the stated latitude, belonged to Russia and, moreover, that no foreign hunting vessels were to visit them. Because so bold a declaration would have to be supported by a show of Russian strength, "lest it in some way even jeopardize the dignity of Russia's Crown and Court", it was essential to maintain a naval squadron in the East.

It was proposed, then, that the government strengthen its hold on many islands, including those referred to by the authors of the memoir, without any apparent sense of incongruity, as "Kurile Islands of Japan." Here, Vorontsov and Bezborodko merely followed an approach that had been taken in Siberia for half a century. In St. Petersburg as in the East, all Japanese pretensions to the Kurile chain as far as and including Uruppu were to be ignored.[85] This being so, Mulovskii's role in the development of contacts with the Japanese could only have been highly delicate.

There is also plain expression of a feeling that had long influenced Catherine's Pacific policy—that blunt assertions of authority or sovereignty in the North Pacific Ocean might "in some way even jeopardize the dignity" of Russia. But now two high officials of state were quite prepared to meet objections to expression of Imperial intention realistically; and for a few weeks, the empress apparently believed the risk worth taking. Her recent forward policies had served her well. Her progress with the Emperor Joseph II through the newly conquered "southern territories", and her chaffing of her guest about the shortness of the voyage by the Black Sea, where the keels of Russian ships were being laid, to Istanbul-Constantinople, conspired to put her in an enterprising mood where military or maritime expansion was concerned. That she kept her sense of balance was soon shown by the decision to cancel the Mulovskii expedition when the Porte had been goaded into war.

Lastly, the memoir serves as evidence that an essential difficulty in the effort to maintain a naval squadron in Pacific waters had been grasped: lacking serviceable dockyards in the far North-East, the Navy was obliged to send ships around the world and keep on sending them at heavy cost. The moral was straightforward. Either adequate facilities for the construction and repair of naval vessels of some size must be acquired, or the Crown must bear the burden and accept the inconvenience of sending warships to maintain its own authority and "dignity" so far away. As P. P. Soimonov justly emphasized, "the equipment of three or four frigates in those waters is just as costly as that of a whole fleet in European waters, and furthermore no little time would be needed for such an undertaking [as their building and equipping]."[86]

RUSSIA AND SPAIN IN THE PACIFIC (1787-90)

The sudden cancellation of Mulovskii's expedition could not have been foreseen by foreign diplomats then in St. Petersburg until, perhaps, July 1787. Pedro Normande, Spanish minister at Catherine II's increasingly expansion-minded court, was one of several diplomats who had grown more anxious in proportion as they thought they knew the full extent of Russia's North American ambitions.[87] The information that Normande sent to Spain was less than sound. He could not read Russian and depended on informants who could. As is evident from his distortions of a dozen Russian surnames, for example, "Captain Moloski," the results were poor. But, as more than once before, a Spanish minister's exaggerations and mistakes were in themselves to prove politically significant and to result in fresh activity by Spain in the Americas. "Captain Moloski," wrote Normande to the Conde de Floridablanca on 16 February 1787, was assuredly a bastard son of Count Chernyshev, vice-president of the Admiralty College, but he was also highly capable as a sea-officer. As to the plan which he was soon to carry out as commander of a four-ship squadron, it was frightening in scope. Catherine was said to favour a ukase declaring Russian sovereignty over North America from Mount St. Elias on the Pacific to the shores of Hudson's Bay. The ukase had been prepared; the announcement or assertion would be made in the near future, together with a statement that Moloski's well-armed squadron was to strengthen Russia's hand in North America. Two frigates and two sloops-of-war were to rendezvous with Captain Billings's vessels at Okhotsk.[88] Floridablanca sent a copy of Normande's despatch to Mexico in April 1787, requesting Galvez to investigate the matter of the Russian threat. His own concern about the march of cossack influence along the coast of North America had been increased by news of Billings's expedition; nonetheless, it had remained a very minor and peripheral anxiety. Now, it grew larger. He approached the king. Carlos III did not dismiss Floridablanca's apprehensions. On the contrary, he too sighted the distant thundercloud. Instructions followed on 25 January 1788 for the launching of a fourth maritime expedition to the threatened northern littoral of Alta California, to what the English vainly called New Albion and even further to the north. The instructions reached New Spain in time to darken Galvez's last days; he died on 17 June 1788.[89]

Originally to have been commanded by a local officer, José Camacho, since both Heceta and Bodega y Quadra were in Spain, the expedition that in due course put to sea to look for Russians in the *San Carlos* in June 1788 was led by Esteban José Martiñez, a younger and more energetic man. Martiñez, who was Kendrick's, Gray's, and Colnett's future adversary in the Nootka Sound affair, had clear instructions.[90] He should reconnoitre north of 61°N. and thoroughly investigate all cossack settlements or factories observed. He should on no account incite hostilities, but he should reaffirm Spanish possession of the mainland, including Alaska, which was merely an extension of the Spanish Californias. And he should do so by performing "proper ceremonies" and by leaving iron marks.[91] Master of *San Carlos* on the voyage was to be Gonzalo Lopez de Haro, who had recently arrived on the Pacific station from Havana.

Over the ensuing weeks, Lopez de Haro had great trouble with the arrogant Martiñez, who both meddled with the running of the ship and spurned advice from all subordinates. Indeed, Lopez de Haro grew disgusted with his captain and was glad to call at Kodiak without him, when Martiñez had gone off to Unalaska with a party of his own. That there were Russians on the island was apparent: the Spaniards saw their buildings and the signs of their activity. Anchors were dropped, and soon Lopez de Haro and his men were being entertained by Billings's former host, Evstratii Delarov. After lengthy courtesies, the Spaniard came to business. Had the subjects of the empress built a fort at Nootka Sound? Delarov said that they had not, but he declared that he expected the arrival of a major expedition from Kamchatka—two frigates if not more—which was to occupy and hold that very sound.[92]

Martiñez meanwhile had been entertained by Potap Zaikov, then in charge at Unalaska. He, too, had fished for details of the Russians' strength and movements in the area. Zaikov rose to the occasion. An intelligent native Siberian who had commanded vessels in the East since 1772 and even wintered in Prince William Sound,[93] he understood completely that Martiñez was an agent and, as such, hungry for "solid" information. He assured him that "after Bering and Chirikov, none of his nation had passed beyond Cape St. Elias; but that the next year he awaited two frigates from Kamchatka which, together with a schooner, would go to settle the port of Nootka."[94] His superiors, he added, had resolved to take the step because a British trading vessel [Hanna's] had sailed to Canton from Nootka Sound three years before laden with valuable skins. Not only, in short, did both Zaikov and Dèlarov know of Billings's expedition, they were also delighted to embroider what they knew and to exaggerate the Russians' local strength. In seven settlements about Alaska, said Zaikov, there were something like five hundred Russian subjects. A sloop was on its coast.

Martiñez's report produced alarm in Monterey, a stir in Mexico, concern in Spain. Orders were sent to garrison the sound of which he wrote and to collect both more and better information on the true extent of cossack influence. To gain that information Salvador Fidalgo took the *San Carlos* out from Nootka Sound on 4 May 1790, heading north. In Kenai Inlet, he observed a rough-hewn Russian strongpoint, and he did not pass unnoticed. *Slava Rossii* was not far away. Billings was told of the arrival of a foreign frigate, as was earlier related, and attempted to make contact. He did not succeed, but he sent a native to Fidalgo with a letter in English inviting him to join *Slava Rossii* in Prince William Sound. This letter reached Fidalgo, but he judged it best not to reply to it. The non-encounter was symbolic. For Russians and for Spaniards equally, the time was gone when either could reasonably view the other as the main potential rival on the Northwest Coast.[95] For both, a far more serious and growing threat was offered by the English-speaking world.

TREVENEN, MULOVSKII, KRUZENSHTERN: 1788-90

Trevenen's and Mulovskii's North Pacific hopes collapsed with the eruption of hostilities against the Turks and against Sweden. As usual in Russo-Turkish wars, it was supposed that full control of the Black Sea would bring immediate strategic gains to the controlling side. To reinforce the squadron at Sevastopol, the soundest elements of Russia's Baltic Fleet were ordered south; plans had been laid to do again what had been done by Greig and Elphinston a generation earlier. This time, fifteen warships were to enter the Mediterranean Sea.[96] One was Trevenen's ship, the *Rodislav*. But yet again Trevenen's situation was abruptly changed by a political development. The Swedish declaration of war led to an action between Swedish and Russian ships within two weeks of the departure of the latter from their base. Trevenen and Mulovskii both did well in the ensuing thirty months or so. In mid-July 1790, Trevenen received a thigh wound that proved fatal.[97] Before he died, however, he met Mulovskii several times. He also met on at least one occasion, a midshipman serving in the *Mstislav* with Mulovskii called von Krusenstern or Kruzenshtern. He was to realize large portions of Trevenen's thwarted North Pacific plan. As for Mulovskii, he was also soon to perish in the war against the Swedes.

MOUNTING PRESSURE ON THE NORTH PACIFIC OTTER: IMPLICATIONS

Cossack pressure on the varied fur resources of Aleutian Island groups, on the Pribylovs, and on Kodiak, Afognak, and the Kenai Inlet area did not grow uniformly in the last years of the century. But everywhere, it grew appreciably. As a result, the regional resources of the islands and Alaska were depleted. Neither cossack hunting parties, least of all *promyshlenniki,* nor the English-speaking traders gave a thought to conservation. Sea-otter killing, in particular, became so intense that the total otter catch for several seasons in the area of Sannak, for example, and in Kenai Inlet barely reached five hundred skins. Even in 1792, Martin Sauer could predict that the sea-otter would become extinct in fifteen years or less around the coast if hunting patterns did not change—and he was ignorant of recent devastation south of Iakutat.[98]

Faced with diminishing supplies, the hunters saw no option but to move on south and east or to witness the decline of their whole trade. The hunting operations became larger, and the voyages grew longer. Need for capital alone forced private traders and small partnerships into more permanent, larger associations. More than this, the time and cash that were required for a hunting expedition far away from any base led to a greater need for speed which, in its turn, led to forced labour by whole villages of natives. Aleuts, in particular, were mercilessly beaten and exploited by the agents of Shelikhov's and Golikov's new "Northern Company" and by their rivals.[99]

Such trends were self-perpetuating. Violence engendered hatred. The Shelikhov company's success in holding profit levels steady was won at the expense of rivals, natives, and resources.[100] But at least Sarychev, Billings, Hall, and others had recorded, even documented these excesses, in the empress's own name. By doing so, they reinforced a precedent that their successors would assiduously follow. It was hardly possible, however, to observe the movements of the cossack hunting vessels from a solitary ship; nor had Siberian officialdom the means to end all cruelty and licence in the waters between Asia and America. In short, the day was fast approaching when the Golikov-Shelikhov "Northern Company," its struggles with its rivals at an end, would be reborn as a monopolistic enterprise, Rossiisko-Amerikanskaia Kompaniia.

5

The North Pacific Fur Trade and the Navy: Growing Strains

G. I. SHELIKHOV'S "MEMORANDUM ON THE PRIVILEGES OF HIS COMPANY"

The Russian-American Company, with which so much of the activity of Russian naval officers and vessels in the North Pacific area was to be linked for half a century, was granted its monopolistic charter by Tsar Paul I in July 1799. Its origins, however, lay in plans developed twelve years earlier by the most wealthy and successful of the traders in Kamchatka, Grigorii Ivanovich Shelikhov (1747?-95), and submitted by Shelikhov and his partner, I. L. Golikov, first to Governor-General I. V. Iakobi (Jacobi), then, eight months later in January 1788 to the Commerce College in St. Petersburg.[1]

For seven years Shelikhov, who had once worked at the customs house in Kiakhta and whose shrewd investments in the new maritime fur trade brought him wealth,[2] considered how to rid himself of competition from his rivals in that trade most quickly and conveniently. He pondered the equation between profit and consolidation of specific hunting areas for given companies in the Aleutians and along the Northwest Coast of North America. He spent some months on Kodiak and was impressed by its potential as a base.[3] A man of vision, he appreciated that his problems could be solved only by carefully relating private interests to those of Russia as a whole. So he impressed on I. V. Iakobi:

Without the approbation of our Sovereign, my labours would assuredly be most unsatisfactory to me and of but little moment to the world, since the main end of my enterprise has been to bring newly-discovered waters, lands, and islands into our Empire before other Powers occupy and claim them, and to undertake new ventures to augment the glory of our Empress and bring profit both to her and to our fellow-countrymen. I trust that there are grounds for hope that wise measures will be taken to bring government and security to those distant regions.[4]

Encouraged by Iakobi, Shelikhov and Golikov the elder then submitted their petition to the empress in February 1788.[5] Their first request for state assistance, to the sum of 200,000 roubles, was denied. The sum was large, and Catherine perceived the international implications of her openly supporting such a company. Clearly Shelikhov had in mind a Russian company to exploit and to annex islands and parts even of North America that would in some respects resemble the Honourable East India Company. He felt, for instance, that his company should have full jurisdiction "in its own domains" and be untrammelled in its hunting operations by the dictates of Siberian officials; yet at the same time it should be regarded as subordinate, in principle if not in practice, to a government department to be named by Catherine. Again, it should have troops "to hold the forts that have been built, and to defend and shield the peoples who, in the name of the Company, have been brought by me under the rule of Her Imperial Majesty."[6] Shelikhov argued that the empress had good reasons for preferring to make use of a commercial company rather than a government department in an area where foreign ships and traders were becoming numerous. A single company could be made accountable for all that passed so far from European Russia far more easily than a group of smaller rival partnerships. Second, a trading company would be unlikely to be hindered in its hunting operations by the diplomats or vessels of supposedly affected powers. If, indeed, "a Crown administration were established in the colonies," assuming that the empress had accepted fealty from all the native Aleut chiefs or *toyons*, then "a trifling conflict" might abruptly escalate into an international crisis.[7] Spain had three times ordered warships to the waters claimed by Russia; might the king not now be ordering a fourth and much more formidable naval expedition to the North with the intention of expelling foreigners? Iakobi thought it very possible, and forwarded a long despatch in which he heartily approved of the proposal to send warships from the Baltic Sea [Mulovskii's four-ship squadron] to protect the national interest in the Pacific.[8]

However, there was one great difficulty in establishing a Russian variant of Western European companies for trading overseas: Russia lacked a merchant fleet and had no maritime-cum-mercantile traditions of the sort so long exploited by the British and the Dutch. She had no corps of merchant seamen to develop trade (or empire) in the Pacific or the East excepting that made up of men who, like himself, had learned from personal experience. The future state-assisted company might use the services of men trained in the Baltic, White, or Black Sea Fleets, perhaps; but there was little to be gained from closer contact with the Admiralty Office at Okhotsk.

The place then came to life only when special expeditions were victualling at Okhotsk—those of Krenitsyn, Billings, Laxman. The poor quality of rigging and building materials, a shortage of experienced shipwrights and seamen, and finally an insufficient knowledge of the sea itself, all made the navigation of the Sea of Okhotsk extremely risky. From the time that shipbuilding had started at Okhotsk up to the '90s, no more than 50 vessels had been built there.[9]

Here Admiral Veselago does not exaggerate either the baseness of a number of the local commandants of the last quarter of the eighteenth century or the impediments to the development of an efficient port and depot at Okhotsk: the shallow water, shifting bar, dangerous current, fickle wind, and soggy spit. True, the more recently constructed galiots had iron parts—and so were known as *gvozdeniki*, "nailers"; but often they were casually built, leaky, and dangerous even when not on the Okhota, where the ebb-rate touched four knots.[10]

Viewing the maritime position at Okhotsk, in the Aleutians, and along the North-west Coast, it was apparent that assistance was required from an outside source of expertise, for want of any other Russian agencies, the Navy. Even certain merchants recognized the need and spoke of possible secondments from the Baltic Fleet for officers prepared to command a trading vessel on the run between Okhotsk and the Pacific factories.[11] For generations, there had been naval officers who were prepared to serve the state in the Pacific. Even those merchants who most clearly understood that the arrival of trained servants of the Navy in the East might serve the North Pacific enterprise at large, however, did not *welcome* the idea. Already, the inherent lack of sympathy between mercantile and naval attitudes towards the spread of Russian influence in the Pacific was evident.[12] It was a lack the more suggestive for the sketchiness of naval influence in the remote North-East and East and for the unaggressive motives that had led to the arrival in Siberia of Billings, Sarychev, and their people.

In reality, Shelikhov deprecated the idea of any influence exerted by the well-born naval officers within his company. Nor was it evident that naval officers would be seconded to a trading company in a professional capacity. In his "Memorandum," Shelikhov therefore wrote in terms of hired specialists and of a modest, independent flotilla with its harbour at Udinsk. "Among the men needed are . . . two master anchorers and various experts in shipbuilding: two shipwrights or apprentices, two seamen versed in rigging, and a patcher."[13] Using Aleuts and Ainu when expedient, the company would send its vessels to "Japan, China, Korea, India, the Philippines," and even California. His plans were grandiose. But were they practical without assistance from the Navy? Given local pilots' records, it was improbable that they could systematically deliver cargo to Manila as proposed.[14] Renewed hostilities in Europe meant that no one was obliged to put his personal opinion on the matter to the test, for Catherine now consciously delayed over the matter of according an exclusive trading privilege to any company.

PIL' AND THE PILFERING OF RUSSIA'S TREASURES (1790-91)

Delay, however, only placed increasing pressure on the Russian hunter-traders; and the pressure took the form foreseen by Iakobi—increasing numbers of both English and Yankee trading craft, often in sight of Kodiak or Unalaska, growing boldness by their masters in response to a diminishing supply of the most valuable furs, and to the Russians' own invisibility, and then the coming of the *Mercury*.[15] In the interim, General Iakobi had been replaced by I. A. Pil'. Therefore, on 11 February 1790, by way of opening a fresh attack on high officialdom, Shelikhov sent to Pil' a new report on the achievements of his company and the growing foreign menace.[16] "In the past two summers," he asserted, "thirty foreign vessels" had been sighted "from our factories"; there was no need to seek them out, they came quite brazenly to Russia's doorstep.[17]

Such considerations weighed with Pil', and in despatches to St. Petersburg on 13 and 14 February 1790, he "defended with great fervour the necessity of lending aid to the Shelikhov company."[18] Over the next two years, Pil' was to ponder rather frequently how best to foster Russian interests, to guard Russian investment, in particular on Kodiak, of which Shelikhov had been painting rosy pictures,[19] and to spike the guns and plans of foreign traders in the seas between Kamchatka and the North-west Coast. It was a sign of changing times.

February 13 1790 Irkutsk.

It is known to Your Majesty's Ministry that the French flotilla which visited the Kamchatka coast in 1787 reported that, during the course of its cruise in the Eastern [Pacific] Ocean, it had spotted neither Russian settlements nor even Russian hunting vessels . . . . As for the East India Company traders, their greediness for trade and for the hunt among the natives, which would bring them substantial profits, gives me reason to believe that . . . they will lay their hands on a considerable part of the wealth [of the North-west Coast]. I believe that if the vessels that the Shelikhov Company now has on hand were all combined with the other Russian trading vessels . . . and if all were to agree that their essential object should be . . . full participation in the task of curbing the activity of foreign hunter-traders, only then might the audacity of the Europeans in the pilfering of Russia's treasure decrease.[20]

But, added Pil', even supposing that a merchant fleet were able to discourage the activity of foreign traders and their agents in an ill-defined and unprotected region claimed by Russia, such a fleet could not oppose armed force. Thus, "the profitable progress of the company along the coastline of America may be expected to continue only when, a port having been founded at the mouth of the River Uda, our military strength there has increased."[21] As a result, Pil' now believed that the construction of Udinsk should be the first priority. Shelikhov hastened to concur. No disagreement with the governor would serve his ends. A Captain Fomin and a party of surveyors hastened out to the Uda.

A. A. BARANOV, N. P. REZANOV, AND THE NAVY: THE TACTICS OF DELAY

Shelikhov, meanwhile, laid his own plans for Aleutian and American expansion and control before the man whom he had chosen to replace E. I. Delarov as manager on Kodiak, A. A. Baranov.[22] The appointment proved a happy one for both. Like the emergence of Shelikhov's son-in-law, N. P. Rezanov, as a powerful official in the capital, however, it increased the probability of struggle between mercantile and naval interests in the Pacific settlements. Neither Manager Baranov nor Rezanov was disposed to see control of the Shelikhov trading interest, which went by changing names after his death (American Company, 1795-97; United American Company, 1797-99; Russian-American Company, 1799), pass to the Navy. On the other hand, neither was able to pretend that some assistance from the Navy was not needed, if the Company was to achieve its own objectives in the North Pacific region.[23] Both, in short, regarded naval enterprise and aspirations to an independent presence in that region very coolly.

Baranov was a man of energy. He did fail to build a *city*, "Slavarossiia," on the mainland of America;[24] and he did not have the means to curb the pilfering of peltry by New Englanders, who were becoming very bold about the Coast. He did, however, make extensive preparations for the founding of a main company outpost there, and in due course even supervised the building of a settlement and fort on Sitka Island. And he showed himself resourceful and adaptable to both political and economic change.

Shelikhov's death had been a signal for a bitter public feud between his heirs and beneficiaries and those who joined with N. I. Mylnikov, a former rival. The Imperial Commerce Commission then approved amalgamation of the Mylnikov Irkutsk Company and Shelikhov's American Company. Shelikhov's widow, I. L. Golikov, and Mylnikov intrigued against each other and against their rivals'—and their own—principal shareholders. But the commission's will prevailed, thanks in large measure to influence then wielded by Rezanov in St. Petersburg, as in Siberia.

Rezanov, who was now to play his own, important part in the postponement of the spread of naval influence in the Pacific, had originally chosen a career in the small judiciary division of the Senate, the supreme court of the state. In early life, he had served briefly with a regiment of guards, but the military life did not appeal to him. For a time, his new career showed promise; but he clashed with Platon Zubov, the empress's last favourite, over a peculation case and judged it best to leave the capital. He travelled to Irkutsk where he encountered the Shelikhov family. He then accompanied Shelikhov on a journey to Okhotsk, and his mind was seized by the enormous possibilities confronting Russia in America. Shelikhov's eloquence and younger daughter, Anna, both induced him to consider the development of Russian North America, and not the Senate, as his true cause. He was confirmed in that opinion, on his marrying Shelikhov's daughter, by the present of a handsome block of shares in the Shelikhov Company.[25]

For Paul I, it was almost a point of principle that men, as well as policies, protected by his late mother were suspect. Thus while turning against Russian North America, Paul looked benevolently on Rezanov, Zubov's victim. Connected with a project that the emperor condemned, to the extent that he devoted any thought to it whatever in the first part of his reign, Rezanov's situation was again most delicate. The blooming of his fortunes and the founding of the ultimate, monopolistic Russian trading company for the Pacific, have been well described elsewhere.[26] Suffice it here to note that he became the force behind its founding; that he argued that the Company should exercise authority south to 55°N. for twenty years, after which time the Crown would either renew its charter or itself assume control of all its colonies; and that the story has extremely sordid chapters, some with bedroom overtones. At its conclusion, he was the ruler of a new company's board.[27]

Indeed, from April 1801 Rezanov was—as procurator general, company "correspondent," and a personal acquaintance of the emperor—the sole official intermediary between Senate, court, and company directors. Unavoidably, his views on matters such as founding and provisioning new settlements and seeking the secondment to the Company of naval personnel were influential. As it happened, Rezanov shrank away from the idea of immediate assistance by the Navy in developing the new trading flotilla which, he publicly acknowledged on 5 August 1797,[28] was essential if the Company was to succeed. He did not have a high opinion of the Admiralty College or the Navy. For the first time in perhaps three generations, the proponents of Russian economic and political control over the North Pacific region had a formidable advocate at court; but as a consequence both of his temperament and personal experience of aging naval officers and of his wide-ranging political and private interests, Rezanov was assuredly no ally of the Admiralty College. In itself, the fact went far towards delaying, for approximately twenty years, the day when naval officers became the governors of Russian North America.

For thirty months (1800-1802) while he continued to acknowledge the need to build a hunting-trading fleet in the remote North-East and East, the only step Rezanov took to solve the Company's Pacific problems was to send three midshipmen, with local servants, to Okhotsk. Nevertheless, the youthful Company seemed flourishing: in 1800, the value of a 1,000-rouble share trebled to speculators' joy. But such prosperity was only superficial; the rise in paper value was a consequence not of new enterprise but of financial "expertise."[29] Nor was it possible to hide the basic cause of inefficiency in the collecting and delivering of furs indefinitely. By the spring of 1802, it was apparent that the cause was lack of officers and competent deep-water seamen for the passage to the colonies and back to Petropavlovsk or Okhotsk. Both the vessels on the run and the majority of charts were quite unsatisfactory. If the Company had a corps of trained, efficient officers and men at its disposal, the problems would have been far less acute.[30] Rezanov raised the matter in the Senate, and a report was sent to the new tsar, Alexander I. "A rescript enjoined the release from the Navy, for service with the Company, of an unlimited number of sailors, naval officers, and pilots, half their salary being paid by Government."[31] For administrative purposes, all on secondment would be viewed as though on active naval service.[32]

Even by 1800, undercurrents carried the affairs of the new Company towards an end that was already growing clear. One way in which the "plot" might be considered has been shown; for five full years, Rezanov was in virtually personal control of policy for the whole Company and was its contact with the higher echelons of government. One consequence was that the Navy's part in new events in the remote North-East and East was both diminished and delayed.

The same developments, however, may be viewed from quite a different perspective. In the late 1790's, the merchants party led by Mylnikov lost influence over the fortunes of the company of which their own had formed a part. Shelikhov's heirs then lost *their* overwhelming vote in its administrative councils as Rezanov's star ascended; but his period of power was not long, viewed in the context of the growth of the Pacific fur trade and of Russian influence therein. Even by 1802, his personal authority over the Company was growing shaky, notwithstanding his acquaintance with the tsar. At length, he lost his exclusive rights and powers. A triumvirate replaced him, two of the three being selected by the shareholders, and one by Alexander; and among those now appointed to the board was the ex-minister of the marine, Admiral N. S. Mordvinov. To be sure, such an appointment might be looked on as a gesture to the new liberalism rather than towards realities obtaining at Okhotsk and in the settlements. More plausibly, it may be viewed as an expression of a fact that had, by 1804, been obvious for years in Siberia—that *lacking* aid from the professional, trained servants of the Navy, the new Company could never reach its aims.[33]

Alexander neither wished, meant, nor expected to annoy another power by his policies for the Pacific. He had many more immediate concerns and interests closer to home and was, besides, poorly informed about the North Pacific ocean and its trade.[34] That there were major Russian interests to guard in the Pacific, on the other hand, was obvious from the existence of the Company.

How was the state to lend the Company more aid and at the same time strengthen Russia's position in the East, while other powers were preoccupied with Europe and Napoleon? By 1802, the question preoccupied a number of the Russian naval officers who had served with the British in the 1790's in India or China, and so understood the meaning of control of the supply of furs to China. Certain facts, asserted one such officer, Ivan Fedorovich Kruzenshtern (1770-1846), were indisputable. To build a solid ocean-going vessel at Okhotsk or in Kamchatka was prohibitively costly, in money and in labour. The appearance of more Russian trading vessels in the waters between Asia and America would cause no stir in foreign chanceries, as might the coming of a well-armed naval squadron. He approved of seconding pilots, mates, and officers from Kronstadt to Okhotsk there to take charge of trading vessels;[35] but to build up the efficiency and profits of the Company and to control the foreign share of the immensely lucrative new China trade, more than a scattering of Navy men were wanted. Several merchantmen should sail for the Pacific from the Baltic Sea with chosen naval officers and crews.

I. F. KRUZENSHTERN: EARLY PACIFIC INDICATORS

In Kruzenshtern, commander of the earliest of Russian seaborne ventures round the globe, that of *Nadezhda* and *Neva* in 1803-6, the North Pacific outlooks and ambitions of Trevenen and Baranov were united with the happiest of consequences for the Russian Crown, which had itself done precious little to encourage naval officers to think in North Pacific terms. In him, moreover, was embodied the connection between Anglo-Russian maritime entente and Russian mercantile-imperial ambition.

Born at Haggud (Gongund) in Estonia (Estliandiia), Johann-Anton von Kruzenshtern (in Russian: Ivan Fedorovich) came of a noble Baltic family of distant German origin.[36] It was the custom for the younger sons of Baltic German families long settled in Estonia, to join the Navy or, more commonly, the Guards.[37]

Haggud lay relatively close to Reval. Kruzenshtern enrolled in the *Morskoi Kadetskii Korpus* in his fifteenth year and shone in every class.[38] When the Russo-Swedish war broke out, he was released "before his time" and placed in *Mstislav* (74 guns) as a midshipman. The captain of the *Mstislav* was Mulovskii. Thus, in May 1788, was forged the first link in a chain of circumstances and events that was to bind him to the North Pacific enterprise for thirty years; that Mulovskii spoke to Kruzenshtern and others in his ship of the aborted expedition that he was to have commanded is virtually certain.[39] Kruzenshtern was with Mulovskii when he died. Also in *Mstislav*, at this time, were Iakov Bering, Vitus Bering's lineal descendant, and Lieutenant A. S. Greig, son of the admiral. A godchild of the empress and created midshipman in infancy, Aleksei Greig was in 1789 to return to England, and from there to reach Calcutta and Canton. While in the Orient, he was promoted. Returning to the Baltic, he was yet again promoted, before setting out for England for a third, but not the last, time.[40] There were lessons to be drawn from such examples of success: that there was nothing to be lost by an awareness of Eastern trade and promise, for example, and that Portsmouth was as good a gate as any to professional advancement for a young, ambitious Russian. It remains to mention V. Ia. Chichagov in this connection of the early growth of Kruzenshtern's awareness of the East and the Pacific. Formerly commander of a naval expedition to the ice north-west of Spitzbergen but not, as he had hoped, to the Pacific, Chichagov now led the squadron to which the *Mstislav* was attached. Mulovskii and Trevenen, Bering, Greig, and Chichagov: there was a pattern of suggestion and example round the youthful Kruzenshtern. But such awareness of the East and the Pacific as had grown in him whilst in the Baltic, was increased almost immediately on his reaching London in 1794.

KRUZENSHTERN'S DEVELOPING PACIFIC PLANS: THE VISIT TO THE ORIENT

Kruzenshtern was sent to England as a Russian Volunteer at the age of twenty-three. Such secondment to an active foreign navy was a mark of high professional ability or a reward for naval services already rendered in the North. Most Volunteers spent their periods abroad, generally for about three years, in British service. Kruzenshtern was placed in *Thetis* (38 guns); his friend Iu. F. Lisianskii was appointed to *L'Oiseau*.[41] Both sailed for North America with Rear-Admiral George Murray, whose brother was commanding *Thetis*, on 17 May 1794.[42] George Murray, as the Russians quickly learned, had won distinction and advancement in the actions fought off India by Edward Hughes and de Suffren (1782).

For the "group of '94," the squadron's sailing marked the start of several friendships—with Charles Vinicombe Penrose, brother-in-law to James Trevenen, J. P. Beresford, and other officers with either knowledge of the East or Russian interests.[43] Kruzenshtern, Lisianskii, and their travelling companion and compatriot, Baskakov, saw a number of the British Caribbean and Atlantic colonies (Barbados, Antigua, Guiana), and they took a lively interest in their administrations and economies. They were reminded that the Russians, too, had island-colonies. They sought extension of their leave, which was granted, though without pay. From the West, they turned their thoughts to the East Indies. Kruzenshtern returned to England with Lisianskii and Penrose after an absence of some thirty months.[44] Wasting no time, he sought assistance from S. R. Vorontsov, now full ambassador in London, in developing a plan that he had nurtured: to proceed to the East Indies and, if possible, to China; to examine how the English, with the backing of their navy, were effectively controlling certain sections of the China trade; and to see what measures could be taken to strengthen Russian economic influence in the Far East.

For several years past, [wrote Kruzenshtern a few years later], the confined state of the active trade of Russia had occupied my thoughts. During the time that I was serving with the English Navy in the revolutionary war of 1793-99,[45] my attention was particularly excited by the importance of the English trade with the East Indies and with China. It appeared to me by no means impossible for Russia to participate in the trade by sea with China and the Indies. The chief obstruction . . . was the want of people capable of commanding merchant ships . . . . I determined upon going myself to India. Count Worontsow soon procured me an opportunity of doing so.[46]

Captain Charles Boyles of *Raisonnable,* then at Spithead, was informed that three young Russians would take passage in his vessel to Cape Colony. Kruzenshtern, Lisianskii, and Baskakov sailed for Africa on 21 March 1797.[47]

At first, on Baltic duty, the Russians' links with officers who had experience or knowledge of the East and the Pacific had been, in the main, coincidental. As they served with British ships against the French, the factor of coincidence decreased, for there were numerous such officers around them, and they came to seek their company. Now, at the Cape, they were alert to sights and incidents that underlined the value of "the English trade with the East Indies." Admiral Sir Thomas Pringle, officer commanding at the Cape, had, as it happened, served with Duncan and Makarov in the North Sea in the recent past.[48] Few men knew more about the movements and the commerce of the Dutch in the East Indies. He received the Russians civilly. Lisianskii, in particular, became his debtor. A fever that he contracted (so he thought) in Antigua in the cane-fields ("*never* would I have believed that Englishmen could deal so cruelly with men, had I not witnessed it in person")[49] struck him down again. Kruzenshtern sailed on alone aboard *L'Oiseau* to Calcutta. In due course Lisianskii reached Bombay aboard the *Sceptre* (Captain Edwards). There, much to his sorrow, he received an aged order to return at once to Kronstadt. But in all events, he had arrived too late to travel on with Kruzenshtern to China.

Kruzenshtern had made some useful contacts in Calcutta, before sailing to Pulo-Penang, aboard *L'Oiseau*. He had fallen in with that same Torckler whom the Billings expedition had encountered in Kamchatka eight years earlier.[50] And he had also met the representatives of leading trading houses: the associates of J. H. Cox, of David Reid, and, above all, of Thomas and Daniel Beale.[51] Torckler was informative about Kamchatka and the North Pacific fur trade, the others, about the Bengal Fur Society. Such contacts, and such knowledge of the "country trade" as Kruzenshtern now gained, at some expense both to his health and to his pocket, since he was not receiving Russian pay, proved very useful six years later in Canton, when he arrived there with *Nadezhda* and *Neva*.[52] It was on China, indeed, that all his thoughts were focused now; nor, when he reached it after many weeks of illness and frustration in Malacca did it disappoint him.

Even before he reached Canton Kruzenshtern knew that little vessels based on Indian as well as North American and European ports were making fortunes for their owners taking sea-otter and other skins to China from the North-west Coast. From the accounts of Cook, Marchand, and others, he knew something of the market conditions in Canton. Whereas the servants of the newly formed United American Company were limited in vision by their failure to have visited Macao and Canton, *he* had been lacking, until recently, in knowledge of conditions in Kamchatka and the North Pacific colonies. Torckler had emphasized the lack of ships and seamen to take valuable peltry from the factories and outposts on the Coast direct to China and the cossack traders' maritime incompetence. All seven vessels used by the Shelikhov company during the 1790's had been lost. On average, they made only two voyages between Kamchatka and the Coast. There were so many rotting vessels at Okhotsk that soon a commandant, Captain Min-itskii, would be speaking of a regular museum of the local shipwrights' art.[53] Often, two years would elapse between the sending of supplies and foodstuffs from Irkutsk to the Pacific and the day that they arrived in Kodiak, commonly spoiled by a drenching.[54] For a quarter of a century, there had been talk of build-ing a new port on the Uda, or in Aian Bay, but nothing had been done.[55] And that incompetence at sea which made the sending of supplies to the Pacific settle-ments so perilous, made it effectively impossible for Russia to compete with other powers in the Canton mart. Indeed, the British and Americans were bound to dominate it by conveying furs direct from Nootka Sound or from the countries claimed by Russia on the Coast, while Russian merchants were obliged to carry furs inland to Kiakhta—where trade had been suspended for seven years between 1785 and 1792, and where it could again be halted by the Chinese government at any time.[56] They would continue to control the seaborne fur trade until Russia did at last "open her own route to Canton."[57] All that Kruzenshtern had gathered in Bengal, he quickly verified while in Canton. During his stay, more than one vessel came with furs straight from the Coast. Among them was the *Caroline,* ex-*Dragon* (Captain Lay),[58] a little sloop-rigged craft of barely 50 tons.

> She had been fitted out in Macao. The whole voyage did not occupy above five months, and the cargo, which consisted entirely of furs, was sold for 60,000 piastres. . . . It appeared to me that the advantages would be infinitely greater if the Russians were to bring their goods to Canton direct from the Islands or the American coast. During my voyage from China [in the Indiaman *Bombay Castle*] I drew up a memoir with the intention of handing it over to M. von Soimonoff, at that time minister of commerce. . . . I proposed that two ships should be sent from Cronstadt to the Aleutic islands and to America, with every kind of material necessary for the construction and outfit of vessels; and that they should likewise be provided with skilful shipwrights, workmen of all kinds, a teacher in navigation, as well as charts, books, nautical and astronomical instruments. The money obtained from the sale of furs in Canton should be appropriated to the purchase of Chinese wares, which could be sent to Russia in ships fitted out in the Eastern Sea. . . .
>
> I had scarcely arrived in Russia but I wished to present the memoir in person[59] to M. von Soimonoff; but I could not obtain permission to go to St. Petersburg. In the meantime, Soimonoff was dismissed. Count Kuscheleff [Koshelev] being at this time minister of the marine, I determined to present my memoir to him; but the answer he returned deprived me of all hopes of my plan being adopted. My endeavours to interest private persons in such a speculation were alike unsuccessful.[60]

Kruzenshtern was thus rebuffed on his return to Baltic duty. The very situation was symbolic of the reign of Paul I. Frustrated, even angry, Kruzenshtern thought of retiring, of buying an estate, even of teaching at the *Domschule* in Reval. But he hesitated, loath to see his hopes and plans all spurned. He had only to wait eleven months. The tsar was murdered. Captain Kruzenshtern's return had coincided with the climax of a set of power struggles in St. Petersburg. One had been fought between Lopukhina and rivals for the emperor's irregular affections, another between Nikolai Petrovich Rezanov and Lopukhin and their allies in the Senate and at court, a third between the ageing Soimonov and his foes. With the accession to the throne of Alexander, another age began. A liberal, N. S. Mordvinov, succeeded Koshelev as minister of the marine, and Kruzenshtern immediately "rearranged" his memoir. He sent it to Mordvinov. "In May, I received an answer that my paper met with his entire approbation."[61]

THE BACKGROUND TO THE KRUZENSHTERN-LISIANSKII EXPEDITION

For Kruzenshtern, Mordvinov's rise to power was most timely. The North Pacific project pleased the admiral, who showed it to Rezanov of the Company and to Rumiantsev, of the Ministry of Commerce, future chancellor of Russia. Both men signalled their support. Rumiantsev's interest was crucial and, together with Mordvinov's, sufficed to bring the memoir to the notice of the emperor himself. Mikhail Buldakov, as chairman of the Company's board, later vainly asserted that the company directors had themselves "thought of a new and better method of conveying foodstuffs and equipment to Kamchatka and the colonies."[62] It was an old idea, given shape and impetus by Kruzenshtern, propelled into effect not by the Company but by the chancellor, Rumiantsev, to whom Kruzenshtern was, very rightly, grateful.

Yet Rumiantsev's interest in the America-to-China enterprise was in itself perfectly calculated to redouble the confusion of its naval and commercial elements.[63] There were good reasons, commercial and otherwise, for sending Russian vessels to the colonies from Kronstadt. For Rumiantsev, however, as in due course for the Company itself, an expedition to those colonies must be essentially commercial though ships be armed and officers all servants of the Navy. Nevertheless the servants of the Navy who were shortly to be sent to the Pacific could hardly be expected to regard the Navy's function in an altogether mercantile perspective, or to overlook its service and strategic implications. In the nineteenth century as in the eighteenth, in short, strife between mercantile and naval (service) interests in the Pacific was inherent in the very personalities of the defenders of those interests. In place of Billings and Shelikhov now stood Kruzenshtern and the *chevalier* Rezanov.

Open conflict still lay some way off in 1802, however; and for Kruzenshtern, as for Rezanov, everything was promising that summer. On 7 August he was named commander of a full-scale expedition to the North Pacific Ocean, in which Company and Crown would both invest. An age of caution and neglect, it seemed, had ended. Within weeks of the decision to send servants of the Navy on secondment to the Company's possessions in the North Pacific Ocean and America, another had been taken that would lead to the arrival of more Russian ships and crews in the Pacific—from the south. Decades of planning and of hope were to be crowned.[64]

6

The Kruzenshtern-Lisianskii Voyages

Kruzenshtern received a jolt within a week of his appointment. While awaiting confirmation from the Naval Ministry of his extraordinary status as an officer responsible in some ways to the company directors, in others to the ministry itself, he was informed that he would leave for the Pacific that same year. Not all had changed with the new century and reign, it seemed: Bering and Wilster, Krenitsyn and Chichagov had all, in other times, been given orders to proceed almost at once to the remote North-East or the East Indies. Kruzenshtern drafted a sober memorandum to Mordvinov on the inadvisability of haste. He judged the admiral correctly, and a civil correspondence on the subject of the coming expedition bore results acceptable to him and to the Company. Two ships, it was agreed, would sail the following summer. The Company and state would share the total cost incurred, in a proportion to be fixed by a committee, while the Navy readied ships and chose their officers and men. The Crown would grant the Company a 250,000-rouble loan at modest interest; the Company would purchase and equip one of the ships. Both would be laden with its goods.[1]

Kruzenshtern offered the position of second-in-command of the whole venture and command of the smaller of the vessels to Lisianskii, who accepted both the offer and the Company's conditions, which, however, he succeeded in emending in his favour.[2] The two then chose subordinates from those who had already volunteered or were highly recommended; and the search began for vessels.

But there were no vessels suitable for such an expedition in any Russian port. Lisianskii and a shipwright named Razumov were accordingly dispatched to Hamburg where the Company supposed they might be purchased. But the Russians saw no vessel while at Hamburg, or at Copenhagen, that would answer to their needs. They crossed the Channel. On the Thames, they found the craft that they were seeking. Drawing an order on the Russian government for more than £ 20,000, Lisianskii hastened into business. The 450-ton *Leander,* built in London two years previously, and the 370-ton *Thames,* fresh off the slipway, became Russian property.[3] A further sum was offered, and Lisianskii had the vessels somewhat modified for lengthy ocean voyaging. The work proceeded rapidly. Sailing through the North Sea ten weeks later, *Nadezhda* and *Neva,* as the *Leander* and the *Thames* were known already to the Russian Naval Ministry, maintained the creditable rate of eleven knots. Both entered Kronstadt roads on 28 May 1803.[4]

Kruzenshtern, meanwhile, had been adjusting to a second piece of news, this time delivered by Rumiantsev, whose preoccupation with the furtherance of Russian interests in the Far East had very properly increased since his appointment to the Ministry of Commerce. *Nadezhda,* Kruzenshtern had been informed, was to face wider challenges than had been planned: she would not only undertake both scientific and commercial missions, but would also take a personal acquaintance of the emperor, Rezanov, as envoy to Japan. The routes, too, had been changed. Instead of keeping company to Sitka Sound and thence west to Uruppu in the Kuriles, where Kruzenshtern was originally to build a small fur depot, try to form a trade link with the Japanese, and look at local whaling prospects, *Nadezhda* was to sail alone to Nagasaki and Kamchatka, while *Neva* made for the North-west Coast direct. They would part company in mid-Pacific, and Lisianskii would enjoy his own command for many months.

Everything had always been complex for the naval officers in the Pacific. Bering, Chirikov, Krenitsyn, and Billings, had all struggled to complete a range of very different, and sometimes unconnected, tasks. But at least all four had acted independently both of the Senate and of wealthy merchants' agents. For Kruzenshtern and Lisianskii, that measure of autonomy was not to be available. Company clerks, F. I. Shemelin and N. I. Korobitsyn, were to sail aboard *Nadezhda* and *Neva* as passengers. It was an augury of coming complications: for the clerks were shrewd and educated men and not admirers of the Navy. Ten years earlier, Shemelin had negotiated with the London merchants, Macintosh and Bonner, with a view to their delivering supplies to Petropavlovsk or the colonies by sea.[5] No contract had resulted; but the fact was illustrative of the clerks' knowledge of men and of affairs.

Kruzenshtern discovered what he could about Rezanov and his diplomatic mission while the ships were fitting out. A year before, he learned, the latest tsar had asked Rezanov to reorganize the Senate's First Department on less oligarchic lines. Even while he had been doing so, Rezanov had been fostering the plans of other men for the Pacific. Among the several designs with which his name had been connected in 1801-2 were one for opening the Amur River to commercial navigation, one for sending new trade missions to both China and Japan, and one for sending Russian vessels round the world; that is, the Kruzenshtern proposal.

There had been no thought, however, of his travelling himself. As procurator-general, as correspondent of the Company, and as a man in frequent contact with the emperor, he had enough to keep him busy in the capital. Then, in November 1802, his wife had died as a delayed result of childbirth. Rezanov entered a decline, and Alexander with the kindliest of motives decided to dispatch him to Japan with the *Nadezhda* and *Neva*. He had, after all, repeatedly insisted that the North Pacific colonies might be provisioned from Japan with great economy and ease, if only the authorities at Edo (modern Tokyo) would countenance a modicum of international trade. Rezanov was appointed Russian Envoy to Japan, and made a chamberlain at court to add more lustre to his name.[6]

In life, Shelikhov's daughter Anna had sustained and reinforced Rezanov's interest in the Aleutian and American possessions. Now, her death brought him in person to the settlements that he had read about in company reports for three full years. His presence in the Kruzenshtern-Lisianskii expedition, in the joint capacity of envoy to Japan and influential company official, was symbolic of a coming confrontation between Company and Navy in the North Pacific Ocean. On *arrival* in Japan or in the colonies, he would command. Meanwhile, the officers and men of *Nadezhda* and *Neva* regarded Kruzenshtern alone as their commander, and Rezanov as an arrogant and interfering passenger.[7] Again, tension and crisis were inherent in a blurring of the edges of authority.

FINAL PREPARATIONS AND DEPARTURE (1803-4)

Kruzenshtern selected Lisianskii as his second-in-command because he knew him to be a loyal, unemotional, and accomplished officer.[8] Similarly in "inferior commissioned officers," he looked for steadiness of temper and a first-class service record. Makar' Ivanovich Ratmanov, whom he took as first lieutenant in *Nadezhda*, had commanded ships of war for fourteen years. Second lieutenant Romberg had achieved success while with the frigate *Narva*, Golovachev, third lieutenant, while at Kronstadt. Fourth lieutenant Löwenstern had served with Ushakov in the Mediterranean.[9] All four were specialists, devoted to the service. It was solely on the basis of their records that such officers as F. F. Bellingshausen, V. N. Berkh, and Golovachev gained their berths. So too with surgeons, pilots, ordinary seamen; Kruzenshtern attempted to exclude the malcontent and to compose, to the extent that he was able, a harmonious society. It was with thoughts of Captain Bligh in mind, as well as of the need to run a calm and ordered ship which could for months or even years serve as laboratory and office for the expedition's scientists, Wilhelm Gottfried Tilesius von Tilenau, naturalist, Johann Caspar Hörner the astronomer, and Espenberg, *Nadezhda's* surgeon, that he emphasized the virtues of "attachment and obedience."[10]

In the same humane, pragmatic spirit, he next saw to it that all received the very best available supplies. On his instructions, even mattresses were issued to each member of both crews. He intended to establish an *esprit de corps* by hand-some pay, good food, consideration, and lofty expectations, not by isolated acts of generosity. From the beginning, he proposed to place his crews apart from or-dinary seamen in less favoured ships. As for the officers, their pay, to which the Company contributed, set them apart from all but a few of their fellows in the Baltic. Both the Navy and the Company, in short, meant that the new Pacific ser-vice should be special, with an enviable promise of advancement for a few.

To what extent this was the case became apparent in the course of 1803. The expedition was a novelty not only on the maritime, but also on the economic and administrative planes. The Naval Ministry did not have full control over its plan-ning. Complication seemed, indeed, to be its essence and was manifest in the confusion as to who was the commander of the venture as a whole. The naval of-ficers with Kruzenshtern spoke of the imminent "Kruzenshtern Expedition"; yet Rezanov, it was known, had been invested with authority over all aspects of the enterprise save those of discipline, the handling of vessels, and arrangements for the scientific work.[11] Could the ambassador give orders to the captain on his deck? Certainly not, since his authority did not extend to the handling of vessels. But the captain might be occupied with discipline or nautical affairs whilst ashore, or could in all events make that assertion. Such division of authority made tension probable, especially aboard *Nadezhda,* in which the envoy and his suite were to take passage. To increase the probability, the captain and the envoy had their own sets of instructions; and while Kruzenshtern's instructions had been written by Mordvinov's naval staff in consultation with Rumiantsev's, Re-zanov's, which were not revealed in full to Kruzenshtern, had been drafted at the Ministry of Commerce by Count A. R. Vorontsov on behalf of Alexander, who had signed a formal document addressed to the Mikado of Japan.[12]

At first, these blurrings and peculiarities seemed actually to assist the prepara-tion of the expedition; for they made it almost certain that whatever was regarded by the Company or Navy as conducive to the expedition's ultimate success would be provided by one government department or another. Where the officers and seamen were concerned, this strange phenomenon was further reinforced by the participation in the venture of a trading company and the Academies of Sciences and of Arts. Shemelin and Korobitsyn were well treated by the board: the latter sailed from Kronstadt with the sum of 16,000 piastres "for expenses" on the voyage. The Academy of Sciences provided splendid maps and many books for the two wardrooms. Admiral F. Miasoedov of the Admiralty yard at Galley-Port sent brand new rigging to *Nadezhda* and *Neva* without delay. Thus assisted by so many institutions, Kruzenshtern directed preparations that pro-ceeded practically without a hitch in July and August 1803. Recently ordered goods arrived from Hamburg, Helsingförs, and Zürich. Instruments were checked at the Academy of Sciences. The tsar himself evinced a certain interest and travelled out to Kronstadt to inspect the preparations for departure. Kru-zenshtern had reason to "conceive himself particularly fortunate," for on this visit, Alexander gave instructions that the revenues of an estate, ''amounting to the yearly sum of 1,500 roubles,'' should be paid to his wife for twelve years.[13] Lisianskii, meanwhile, supervised the stowing of a quantity of foodstuffs, instruments, ''antiscorbutic remedies.''

But what of personal relations between Kruzenshtern himself and the ambassador, who now delayed his embarcation? A little of the truth may be discerned even from Kruzenshtern's cool prose:

In the fitting out of my ships, it was necessary to provide for the different objects of the voyage, the combination of which was attended with many inconveniences. The ship belonged indeed to the Emperor and was destined for the embassy; but it was allowed to the American Company to lade it with their goods. Of this lading and of the many presents destined for Japan, I could obtain no previous information. With regard to the latter, I continued in ignorance until the last moment. I was in the roadstead and effects were still arriving, which I was not a little puzzled how to stow.[14]

Kruzenshtern was deeply irritated by Rezanov's late appointment both as envoy to Japan and, more injuriously to himself and to his officers, as the leader of the mission in a vague and cloudy sense. Rezanov's coming on the voyage had deprived him and Lisianskii of a certain sum of money, which the Company had promised them beyond their already high pay, and of prestige. Then the ''effects'' came to the roadstead, far too late to be conveniently stowed: paintings, mirrors, model boats, a thousand books, numerous bulky trunks of clothes, musical instruments. The gifts for the Mikado were valued at 300,000 roubles. Most were delicate. When the *Nadezhda* and *Neva* finally did weigh anchors on 4 August, the wind moved to the west, further delaying their departure.

Nadezhda and *Neva* made poor time west to Copenhagen, which they reached on 17 August. But a halt was necessary; many casks of salted beef, though newly purchased, were already spoiling. Kruzenshtern called at the local arsenal, observatory, and admiralty chartroom till at last, on 8 September, having been joined by Langsdorf, Hörner, and Tilesius, the squadron could again make sail. After a slow and painful voyage, they made Falmouth, where again casks were inspected and rejected while her carpenters examined the *Nadezhda*'s hull. Fresh meat was bought, the hull recaulked; the crews were either exercised aloft or given leave to stroll through Falmouth, which did not impress the Russians. *Nadezhda* and *Neva* kept company throughout the crossing to Brazil, making one stop, at Teneriffe.

During the winter of 1803-4, the Russians made their way from Santa Cruz to the Marquesas Islands via Santa Catharina Island and Cape Horn. Almost immediately after their departure from the port of Santa Cruz, where fresh supplies were purchased, Kruzenshtern imposed a strict routine on both ships' companies. Henceforward nothing but disaster was to halt the clockwork rounds of testing, sampling, and measurement, which now filled the time of J. C. Hörner and the German naturalists. Repeated reckonings of latitude and longitude; checkings of compasses and other instruments; testing of air and water temperatures, humidity, ship's headway, water content (why, for instance, did the surface water sparkle in one region of the South Atlantic? "It is not occasioned merely by the motion of the water, but is in fact produced by organized beings . . . fiery bodies, in the form of crabs"):[15] all proceeded under watchful eyes, though not Rezanov's, since the envoy had elected to remain aloof after a first and clumsy effort to exert his own authority over the naval officers had been rebuffed by Kruzenshtern at Teneriffe. Week after week, the work went on under conditions of increasing sultriness. Moisture appeared on the wardroom walls.[16] Then, in December, clouds of butterflies were sighted off Brazil. From Cabo Frio, *Nadezhda* and *Neva* slipped easily along the coast, finding their way into the strait dividing Santa Catharina from the mainland. They halted by the settlement of Nossa Senhora do Desterro, a place replete with parrots, pigs, bananas, cinnamon, and even alligators for Tilesius von Tilenau. The Portuguese commander, Dom José de Carrado, made the Russians more than welcome.[17]

Kruzenshtern had reckoned on staying in Brazil just long enough to water and revictual. He was depressed to learn that, though *Neva* needed new masts, the local timber was too hard and heavy for the purpose. Trunks of 120-foot trees were therefore dragged more than a mile to the picturesque cascade by which *Neva* was watering.[18] The carpenters worked constantly: the passing days made it more likely that the expedition would encounter stormy weather at Cape Horn. The Russians took their leave at last in February, with relief and some regrets (for Langsdorf, Brazil had seemed a botanist's and naturalist's paradise). Days were alternately extremely cool and very hot. But on the crucial day, 3 March, the winds proved calm and friendly, and *Nadezhda* and *Neva* rounded the Horn. Some six weeks later, after the two had been parted in a storm, Lisianskii caught a sight of Easter Island where he planned to get provisions. He approached on 19 April and could soon see that a landing would be perilous: the coastal surf was high and boiling white. He put a boat off, and Lt. Povalishin managed to barter Russian knives, mirrors, and trinkets for a fair amount of produce. Povalishin gave descriptions of banana groves, reed houses, giant figures made of stone, and Lisianskii noted the absence of a serviceable harbour.[19] Meanwhile, Kruzenshtern had moved into the balmy latitudes of the Marquesas Island group. At 5 P.M. on 7 May 1804, *Nadezhda* came to rest in Taio-hae Bay ("Anna-Maria") by the shore of Nuku Hiva.

KRUZENSHTERN, LISIANSKII, AND THE SOUTH SEA ISLANDERS (1804)

Kruzenshtern passed eleven days (7-18 May) at the Marquesas Islands.[20] His arrival was significant politically and scientifically. It forged a much-delayed and geographically improbable connection between Slav and Polynesian. For the first time, a whole Russian company had dealings with a group of South Sea Islanders, and vice versa. The event had, understandably, been exercising Kruzenshtern, to whom it was apparent that such visits needed careful management, if all the errors that had clouded the relations between other Europeans and such peoples were to be avoided. For a guide, he turned to Cook, honoured exemplar of the navigator's and commander's highest qualities for many younger Russian naval officers, including leaders of Pacific expeditions of the future, for example, the *Nadezhda*'s fifth lieutenant, Bellingshausen, and cadet, Otto von Kotzebue. Kruzenshtern bore witness to his deep respect for Cook both in his published narrative of 1809 and by his orders to the people of *Nadezhda* as they closed on Nuku Hiva, which were modelled on Cook's own of almost fifty years before. In themselves, as reminders of the dangers facing European captains in the South Pacific Islands—petty theft, overfamiliarity, and lethal retribution by the gun—and as the touchstone for all subsequent official dealings between Russians and the natives of the Washington-Marquesas and Tuamotu Island clusters, the "Marquesan Orders" merit quotation here:

The principal object of our calling at the Marquesas Islands is to water and take on fresh provisions. Though we might well achieve all this without the consent and goodwill of the natives, risks for them and for ourselves prevent our having recourse to such approaches. And I am certain that we Russians shall depart from the shores of a tranquil people not having left a bad name for ourselves. Our predecessors, describing the islanders' temper, represent them to us as a peace-loving group—they parted from them with all the signs of friendship. We too shall endeavour, by our humane conduct, to inspire a lively sense of thankfulness toward ourselves and so to prepare, for our countrymen who follow us, a people aflame with friendship for the Russians.

In order to avert all unpleasantness that could possibly be caused by our sojourn in these islands, and to achieve the main end of our stay, I have thought it necessary to lay down the following code. It will be very natural if, on our arrival, unfamiliar objects provoke in many a desire to have them; and you, for your parts, would gladly barter European goods, consisting for the most part of trinkets, for the various curios of these people.

But lack of caution here might have highly undesirable results—for the islanders, anxious to possess objects of ours and obtaining them in plenty in exchange for things of little value to them, would end no doubt by wanting things that we would not be able to surrender to them—before they would satisfy our genuine needs. It is therefore prohibited for anyone to barter with the natives on the ship. Once we have furnished ourselves with all the provisions necessary for the continuation of our voyage and for the preservation of the health of our whole company, I will give sufficient notice for every man to be able to exchange his things for others, in accordance with his means and inclination. For the orderly purchasing of foodstuffs for crew and officers alike, Lieutenant Romberg and Dr. Espenberg are hereby appointed. Only through them are exchanges to be made. For this reason, one of them is always to be on board the ship.

It is emphatically reaffirmed that no member of the lower deck is to use a firearm, either on board or ashore, without special orders to that effect from the officers.

Kruzenshtern[21]

Nadezhda had not anchored before islanders encircled her and Kruzenshtern was dealing with the problems he had foreseen. The islanders were friendly and accommodating. Some proposed to barter fruit for iron. Here, the Russians could oblige, having a stock of cracked or broken iron hoops which had been carried from the Baltic for the purpose. Others, driven on by curiosity, as Kruzenshtern supposed, swam round *Nadezhda*'s stern, while several clambered up her sides onto the bowsprit and the deck. Among the visitors were women, some of whom had more than fruit to sell the Russians: they were naked or had practically no covering over their private parts. That they were happy to expose their charms was evident from gestures which the Russians thought lascivious and lewd.[22]

And yet, to a remarkable extent judging by subsequent accounts of the Marquesan visit, Kruzenshtern succeeded in preserving Russian seamen from temptation as embodied in these nymphs and in averting all the troubles he had properly anticipated. There were thefts; but these were calmly, if not tolerantly, viewed.[23] A rumour spread to the effect that Russian seamen planned to seize a local chieftain, to "go man-fishing," in fact, as the islanders did themselves; but when the author of the rumour was found, accused, and named before the chieftain, all was amicably settled. There were other awkward moments and alarms—when Kruzenshtern, for instance, was not present to accept a hog that had been brought him by the chief and when two European castaways, a Frenchman and an Englishman, denounced each other bitterly as liars, whom the Russians should not trust. (In fact, they trusted neither altogether, but inclined towards the Englishman.[24] The Frenchman, le Cabry, who took an unexpected passage in *Nadezhda,* was eventually landed in Kamchatka, whence he travelled on to Paris, Rennes, and sideshow poverty.) As to liaisons between Russians and the girls whose very fathers were prepared to sell their favours to the highest bidder,[25] it would seem that not one Russian fell from grace.

Russian descriptions of the physical conditions and political and social situations that obtained in Taio-Hae and adjoining bays and valleys, are commendably objective. As such, they have significance today for the historian of Oceania of the immediate post-contact period. Like Cook, the officers and scientists with Kruzenshtern prized accuracy. So did their successors in the South Pacific Ocean; not a few of whom were also Baltic German. Russia's total contribution to the scientific study of the South Pacific islands and their peoples was a valuable one. It was extensive thanks in part to the example set during the course of the first Russian expedition round the world.

In general, the Russians with *Nadezhda* and *Neva,* which had arrived at Nuku Hiva on 10 May, found the Marquesan Islanders, many of whom were rather larger than themselves despite their custom of not nourishing an infant with its mother's milk but with raw fish, fresh fruit, and water, a sympathetic people. They were cannibals, indeed, and indulged in gross sexual licence. But they were intelligent as well as generous toward their guests.[26] One of their several fishing techniques, by which the fish were dazed by scattered crumbs of belladonna root, was as original and subtle as their style of body ornament. Various Russian goods were bartered for a range of local artifacts, many of which can now be seen at the Academy of Sciences' Museum of Ethnography and Anthropology in Leningrad.[27] Again the influence of Cook had proved significant. Nor in the strictest naval terms was the arrival of the Kruzenshtern-Lisianskii expedition at the island devoid of meaning. Sent to sketch its southern shore, Lieutenant Löwenstern came on a sheltered bay, which Kruzenshtern named after Chichagov, the former naval minister.

But did *Nadezhda* and *Neva* in fact leave the Marquesans all "aflame with friendship for the Russians" as opposed to other visitors? Though the Russians had been treated, as Lisianskii put it, "like old friends,"[28] so had many other foreigners before them. So would many more before, in 1813, Captain David Porter and the men of the United States Ship *Essex* reached the place. After that sorry episode, in which a number of the Islanders (who had been welcomed to the "great American family" by their imperialist-minded visitors) were killed or maimed by them, the Russians, like the British, French, and Dutch, were to find themselves regarded with a coolness that no European had yet sensed at Nuku Hiva when *Nadezhda* called for water and supplies.[29] All Europeans had been tarred by the same brush.

FURTHER DEVELOPMENTS ABOARD *NADEZHDA*

Developments aboard *Nadezhda,* meanwhile, had been black. The simmering dislike between Rezanov and the naval officers came to the boil when after Kruzenshtern had ordered Dr. Espenberg to barter with the natives for provisions to be stowed for later use, Rezanov gave instructions to his aides also to barter—for more implements of ethnographic interest. At first, Kruzenshtern countenanced this gesture, which would not exactly thwart his own intentions. Then perceiving that Rezanov had expected acquiescence and was testing his authority, he chose not to co-operate. Both men grew very heated. There was shouting. Then, the morning following, the two had a dramatic argument. So much is clear from the extant evidence, which on the whole places Rezanov in as poor a light as possible and must be treated gingerly.[30] Kruzenshtern, it seems, entered Rezanov's cabin, where the latter made the error of proclaiming that the captain of *Nadezhda* was, by rank and by appointment, his inferior. News of the clash soon reached *Neva*. Taking a boat, Lisianskii crossed to the *Nadezhda* and, exasperated, wondered aloud whether Rezanov might not be a charlatan. It was now obvious that the ambassador had no supporters in the crews of either vessel, and he went below, supported by the members of his suite. Kruzenshtern, however, would not grant him quarter and demanded that he read his secret orders. Tempers mounted. Rezanov saw no option but to go onto the quarterdeck and do as he was bid to put his taunters in their places. The performance did not end, as he imagined that it must, in his triumphant vindication. The lieutenants were not cowed. When he had read his secret orders, there was laughter, even doubt as to their authenticity. Rezanov took the setback very badly, and fell ill. He withdrew to his cabin for the best part of a week and remained there while the *Nadezhda* pressed on north.[31] Thereafter, Kruzenshtern was treated unambiguously as commander of the venture as a whole, for it was clear that authority rested with him.

Time was now pressing. Kruzenshtern decided not, as he had previously planned, to make directly for Japan from the point of separation with *Neva* but to proceed to Petropavlovsk and from there, in the same season, to hasten south to Nagasaki. Steady north-westerlies made it unlikely that the expedition could reach Nagasaki or Kamchatka till it met the southeast trade-winds. Kruzenshtern provided reasons for his move: it was important to deliver iron bars and naval stores to Petropavlovsk with the minimal delay; much of the cargo would be spoiled in the course of a long sojourn in Japan; "it was a matter of doubt whether the embassy would meet with the success that was expected from it"; and his people's health would certainly be shaken by September monsoons, if he proceeded as was planned. Better by far "merely to bring to for a couple of days off the coats of Owaihi whence . . . natives will come out 15 or 18 miles to sea, to barter their provisions"[32] and to hasten to the North.

Kruzenshtern's views on how most suitably to deal with Rezanov may be sensed through protestations that the crew's health, or the Company's own interests, were paramount in his considerations. But the passages in question were composed for public scrutiny some time after the events that they described or, rather, prudently did not describe, had flared up and died away in the Pacific.

Nadezhda and *Neva* covered the last stage of their cruise in company quite swiftly. By 25 May, they had already left the Southern Hemisphere. A leak caused by a line of rotted hemp in the *Nadezhda*'s hull grew worse, with the result that many men were forced to pump until fatigued. Hawaii proved a disappointment: the first native canoes to reach *Nadezhda* set the pattern. The Hawaiians offered nothing in exchange for iron, cloth, mirrors, and baubles, but some fruit and one small pig. Not even axes were of interest to these sophisticated islanders, who had had twenty years of dealings with commercial travelers from Europe and New England, and were loath to part with meat. On the south shore of Hawaii too, the natives looked for money or for "articles of luxury."

Kruzenshtern's comments on the islands' wealth, luxuriance, abundant fruit and serviceable harbours were precise although, indeed, not unaffected by his disappointment there. True, the Hawaiians were themselves but "one degree below the brute creation,"[33] grasping, sullen natives. But their manners were of no concern to hungry mariners, and the Hawaiian group was geographically well situated to meet the victualling needs of vessels sailing north to China or the North-west Coast. It formed the hub of the Pacific, being almost equidistant from Japan, Alaska, and New Spain. For Russian vessels running north to Petropavlovsk or the North Pacific colonies from Chile, it could be extremely useful. Barely ten years later, Russian guns were actually to be mounted on the shores of Kauai.[34]

LISIANSKII ON THE NORTH-WEST COAST (1804)

Nadezhda and *Neva* parted company on 10 June. For Kruzenshtern especially, time was short. Lisianskii was instructed to proceed to Kodiak without undue delay. He decided first to satisfy his curiosity by looking at the beach where Cook had died. He did so, finding several flattened bullets in the trees behind the spot where Cook had fallen. Small-scale bartering continued for five days aboard *Neva,* which stood at anchor in Kealakekua Bay: eleven hogs for 90 pounds of iron, fruit for axes, yams for clothes.[35] Hearing that "sickness" was reported on Oahu, Lisianskii decided to avoid it, and set course for Kauai Island on 16 June. He reached it three days later and was met almost at once by "King Tomari" (Kaumualii), who spoke broken English. Kaumualii sought the Russians' armed assistance in his fight for independence from Kamehameha, who, he knew, was planning an attack with a flotilla from Hawaii. "In return," noted Lisianskii," he would gladly have agreed to come, with his island, under Russian domination. . . . We were not in a position to agree to the king's plan."[36]

Lisianskii would in any case doubtless have left without involving Alexander I in a distant native war. (Rezanov's absence was the pretext that he offered to Kaumualii as he hastened on his way.) In the event, he now acquired extra reasons for proceeding to the Coast: he had received wholly unlooked for confirmation and indeed amplification of the news that had reached Russia twelve months earlier, first, that the settlement on Sitka had been taken by the Indians and, second, that the Company's position on the Coast had been enfeebled by the fact.[37] The *Neva* sailed on for Kodiak, where company supplies still in her hold were to be signed for and unloaded and where far more recent news was to be had. For twenty days, Lisianskii kept on north through rain and fog. At last, Chirikov Island showed on the horizon. Four days later, Neva was towed by numerous *baidarki* into the "harbour" or main inlet of St. Paul.[38] "At two after midnight, the manager of the Kodiak office, Mr. Banner, came aboard. As we entered, the Russian flag was raised."[39]

Neva's arrival was the cause for celebration on the part of Ivan Banner and his men. She came with food, as well as tools not to be had from Petropavlovsk or Okhotsk, and was a source of entertainment for the hunters, some of whom had, like the manager himself, been in the settlements three years or even more; and while she stayed, she represented strength. Too often in the settlements' short history there had been panic when a foreign ship was sighted. Peter Puget of the *Chatham* in Vancouver's expedition had in fact rendered a service to the servants of the embryonic Company at Iakutat, who had been hungry and beleaguered when he came. Nevertheless, the very presence of the British on the Coast had caused alarm at Petropavlovsk and on Kodiak. It was supposed that British forces were about to take possession both of Kenai Inlet and of several other regions rich in furs.[40] Trading vessels from New England or from Britain had repeatedly sent tremors of alarm through Kodiak. Then, in the spring of 1800 and again in 1801, there had been repetitions of the *Mercury* alarm, only now it was a nameless Spanish frigate, not an Anglo-Swedish raider, that was feared—for Baranov had been given details by *Enterprise,* out from New York—of fresh hostilities in Europe in the wake of the creation of a Second Coalition. France and Spain were allies; Spanish forces were expected to attack the Russian outposts on the Coast. When Baranov heard this news, the storehouses at Three Saints' Harbour, Kodiak, were full. They were immediately emptied, and the furs were all concealed. While *Neva* remained at Kodiak, even a well-armed Spanish frigate was unlikely to attempt a raid.

It was, however, not from French or Spanish guns that Ivan Banner was anticipating violence in 1804; nor was it Kodiak, to which *Neva* brought welcome guns and ammunition, that demanded Lisianskii's attention. Company Chief Manager Baranov, though himself not present to receive his fellow-countrymen, had left a paper for the captain of *Neva,* of whose approach he had been formally advised by the head office. It described the Sitka situation:

Mr. Banner [wrote Lisianskii] begged my assistance in opposing the savages and restoring things to their former state [at Sitka]. He gave me further to understand that the commander-in-chief, Mr. Baranoff, had gone there himself with an equipment consisting of four small ships, manned by

120 Russians, and of 300 bidarkas containing about 800 Aleutians, and that he was still there. . . . I complied with his request and resolved to prepare for sea immediately.[41]

The disaster that had struck at Sitka two years earlier had, as Lisianskii recognized, shaken morale throughout the company possessions. Since its founding in May 1799, the Sitka Island outpost of Mikhailovsk (Novo-Arkhangel'sk from 1804) had cost the Company too many lives. Thirty *baidarki* were lost with all their crews in stormy seas on the initial approach; nor had the local Tlingit Indians been taken by surprise. Twenty-six men had been abducted on the night of their arrival in Sitka, then tortured, if not slaughtered. Afterwards the Tlingit had not tried to stop the building of a strongpoint in their midst, chiefly, it seems, because of nervousness about the movements of other Europeans in the region. Henry Barber, of the *Unicorn,* was only one of several traders in this period who would entice a group of Indians onto his deck and then hold them to ransom for a quantity of furs.[42] Baranov and his men entrenched themselves, but they were faced by an unpleasant summer season. The Tlingit congregated in the woods around the Russians and their Aleuts and prepared for open war. No sooner had the latter built their fifty- by seventy-foot strongpoint with its simple palisade than two New Englanders arrived in the vicinity hoping to barter skins for guns and ammunition: Crocker in the *Hancock* and Breck in the *Despatch.* Other New Englanders arrived within the season. All had the advantages of great mobility and speed; they had no forts to try to hold.

By 1801, out of sixteen ships on the Coast all but two were Bostonian . . . On making his landfall, a Boston Nor'westman came to anchor off the nearest Indian village, bartered so long as he could do business, then moved on to another of the myriad bays and coves until his hold was full of valuable furs. It was a difficult and hazardous trade . . . In 1803, the natives near Nootka Sound attacked the Amorys' ship *Boston,* Captain John Salter, and slaughtered all the ship's company but two. Besides swivel-guns on the bulwarks, the vessels were armed with six to twenty cannon, kept well shotted.[43]

By Sitka Sound especially, the Indians proved dangerous. Within twelve months of the construction of the palisaded strongpoint at Mikhailovsk and in Baranov's absence, they attacked in force. The place was burned. Of 450 souls, not 50 lived. Half the *baidarka* fleet from Kodiak was also fired, and the Tlingit took the muskets of the dead. Already short of men and craft, Baranov lacked the means to take revenge. Then came O'Cain.

New Englanders had caused Baranov great anxiety over the previous ten years. Now a Bostonian, Joseph O'Cain, provided him with what he needed most: the means of recapturing Mikhailovsk. The two had met when, as the mate of *Phoenix* (Captain Moore), O'Cain had come to Nuchek in 1792. The traders had been favourably treated and invited to return. O'Cain, at least, in due course did so. 1801 found him at Sitka as the mate of Captain Hubbel's *Enterprise,* the quintessential Boston trader of the period, well-built, heavily manned, just under 80 feet in length, and copper-bottomed. Once again, O'Cain was welcomed by Baranov, and the visitors took on two thousand skins. In 1803, and once again in 1804, O'Cain returned to Sitka as the master of his own vessel, the newly built and fast *O'Cain.* He carried muskets, hand-guns, tools, and ammunition as well as dried foodstuffs and liquor. But Baranov now lacked skins with which to trade, and O'Cain could not give credit. They quickly came to terms: O'Cain would take a group of Aleut hunters to the coast of California, where the sea-otter were plentiful. The Aleuts would take orders from a Russian foreman. The Company would halve the total profit with O'Cain, purchasing guns and ammunition from its share. When the American returned after four months, he had peltry to the value of $160,000. Now Baranov had the vessels and the weapons to attack the Sitka Indians, and he left with his flotilla. Such in outline was the situation when *Neva* came on the scene. Lisianskii anchored by the ruins of Mikhailovsk and waited. Silence reigned.

> I never saw a country so wild and gloomy: it appeared more adapted for the residence of wild beasts than of men . . . I learned that the inhabitants of Sitka had fortified themselves and were resolved not to suffer the Russians to make a second settlement amongst them without a trial of strength. . . . From the day of our pursuit of a canoe, no natives made their appearance till the 31st at noon, when a large boat was observed under the shore rowed by twelve naked men, whose faces and bodies were painted. . . . In the meantime, Captain Okeen [O'Cain], returning from the woods, was attacked. I instantly sent the armed launch against the barbarians; but they escaped. . . . Their skill as marksmen was apparent from the shattered state of Captain Okeen's launch, as well as from the collar of his coat, through which a bullet had passed. . . . In the morning of September 8, Captain Okeen set sail on his voyage homewards. In the afternoon of the 19th, Mr. Baranoff arrived from his hunting expedition in the ship *Yermak.* We had been more than a month in this unfavourable climate, anxiously expecting his return.[44]

So matters continued for another week, in constant watchfulness. Day after day, Russians and Tlingit fenced and parried, each uncertain of the other's strength.

Canoes slipped by the shores, where "native warriors" were audible, and some-times visible, "writhing and twisting, singing, beating on a broken bottle." Still the Russians made no move; nor was it evident who was to order an attack—neither Lisianskii nor Baranov was prepared to act in a subordinate capacity when finally the moment came.

Lisianskii's attitude toward Baranov is understandable. As a naval officer, ex-perienced in war, he was accustomed to command. *Neva* was an essential part of the combined Aleutian-Russian force. He recognized Baranov's standing and would not affront his dignity, but he regarded the command of an assault as his prerogative. To understand Baranov's prickly attitude toward Lisianskii fully it is necessary to know to what extent he had been vexed since 1802 by other servants of the Navy. Baranov was of merchant antecedents, not a nobleman. Neverthe-less, he was invested with authority extending, theoretically at least, over all pilots, crews, and naval officers in the employment of the Company in the Pa-cific area. In 1801 Rezanov had suggested that a few young naval midshipmen be sent to the Pacific, on secondment with the Company.[45] Two were immediately sent, and quickly saw that they alone of company employees in the far North-East and East were nobly born. They proved unwilling to obey Baranov's orders, for they scorned him as an officer. Despite this and a public scene involving Mid-shipman Gavriil Talin, who threatened Baranov with death if he should step onto "his" vessel, Baranov held his peace. Within the year, Talin perished in the packet-boat *Orël*. The disaster cost the Company a ship, five lives, and 20,000 roubles' worth of furs. The other midshipman was connected in Baranov's mind with *Feniks,* built at Kodiak under conditions of considerable difficulty, which was also lost at sea.[46]

Meanwhile, the skirmishing at Sitka, feint and counterfeint, grew more in-tense. In mid-September, more Aleuts joined Baranov who, in council with Li-sianskii, agreed that an attack should now be launched without delay, unless the Tlingit gave their word (backed up by hostages) not to oppose the building of a second, larger fortress in their midst. The *Neva* was towed a little closer to the shore. Shamans were heard. On the next day, 29 September, the Russians took possession of an empty Tlingit village situated on a hill beside the sound. This was the future site of Novo-Arkhangel'sk. Still unopposed, the naval party dragged a pair of long six-pounders up the hill. A Tlingit war-canoe was sighted, fired on, and blown out of the water. Evening came, and the Russians waited on their hill. But there was no attack. Instead, a native envoy came with peaceful overtures. The Russians' terms were carefully explained. Several times over the next two days, the envoy came and went, until Lisianskii's optimism and impa-tience were in balance and Baranov's moods, erratic. Finally, after white flags had been shown both on *Neva* and by the Indians, but still not one native had shown himself to start negotiations, Lisianskii gave the order for a volley to be fired at the fort. At the same moment, Lt. P. Arbuzov took a party to destroy na-tive canoes that had been beached. Afterwards, he advanced upon the fort. Still there was silence. Baranov now resolved to land himself, together with a pair of heavy guns. He joined Arbuzov and his seamen with 150 of his own men near Mikhailovsk. That night, Baranov ordered an assault. The Tlingit had been waiting, holding their fire, and many died. The Aleuts on the guns took to their heels.

> Their commanders, left with a mere handful of men belonging to my ship, judged it prudent to retire and endeavour to save the guns. The natives, seeing this, rushed out in pursuit of them; but our sailors behaved so gallantly that, though almost all were wounded, they brought off the field-pieces in safety. In this affair, out of my ship alone a lieutenant, a master's mate, a surgeon's mate, a quartermaster, and ten sailors were wounded, and two killed. And if I had not covered this unfortunate retreat with my cannon, not a man could probably have been saved.[47]

Frontal attack had failed. The failure brought about an alteration in Lisianskii's public attitude toward Baranov. Issues that had earlier been cloudy, became clear. First, it was patent that the Tlingit were a formidable enemy and that their marksmanship was good. As a result, Lisianskii grew more serious about an operation which, at first, he had imagined would be brief. Second, the value of *Neva* to the attack was now unquestionable: it was Navy guns and men, and not Baranov's people, that have staved off total tragedy at Sitka. Finally, Baranov himself now grudgingly conceded that, being no longer young and, more especially, being without experience of warfare on the necessary scale, he should yield to the authority of naval rank and gunnery. Though wounded in the arm, he sent a note to the *Neva* to that effect. On 2 October at dawn, Lisianskii took his chance, and fired on the fort. The Tlingit sued for peace during the afternoon, bringing their hostages and promising the prompt release of Aleut prisoners. The fort, however, they retained. Lisianskii took the hostages, repeated his demands, and moved his ship closer inshore. More envoys came and went, and plans were made to storm the fort:

> But when morning came on the 7th, I observed a great number of crows hovering about the settlement. I sent on shore to ascertain the cause; and the messenger returned with the news that the natives had quitted the fort during the night, leaving in it alive only two old women and a little boy . . .
> Had the plan of molesting the enemy from the ships, cutting off their supply of fresh water, and hindering them from having communication

with the sea, been followed, I am persuaded that our wishes would have been obtained without the sacrifice of a single man. But Mr. Baranoff was . . . led into the error of placing too much reliance on the bravery of his people, who had never been engaged in a warfare of this kind before.[48]

It is not certain that Lisianskii had, as he asserts, clearly presented such proposals to Baranov when he first reached Sitka on 19 September. But however that may be, it is as undeniable today as then that guns, not bravery, had proved the vital element in victory over the Tlingit. The moral, that the Company itself must bring more guns to North America, was evident to all. No less apparent was a major implication: that the question of authority in places where Baranov and commissioned naval officers were to co-operate must be resolved. Lisianskii, for his part, had to the last treated Baranov with forbearance; but authority such as Baranov claimed called for respect and open deference, even from naval officers.

EVENTS AT PETROPAVLOVSK (1804)

Events at Petropavlovsk, meanwhile, had been hardly less dramatic, though less bloody, than developments at Novo-Arkhangel'sk. On the *Nadezhda*'s passage from Hawaii, there were continued signs of strife between Rezanov and the naval officers. Lieutenants Romberg and Ratmanov, in particular, insisted that the envoy—who was keeping to his cabin—was indeed a charlatan: and Kruzenshtern himself had ceased even to exchange civilities with him. Rezanov's various attempts to override naval authority at Copenhagen, Teneriffe, and Nuku Hiva had resulted in a heavy shipboard atmosphere.[49] Trouble erupted when *Nadezhda* reached Kamchatka. In accordance with tradition in the place, the arrival of a friendly ship led to a festival.[50] Most of the visitors and hosts, but not Rezanov, were caught up in a mood of celebration. Kamchadals put on a bear-dance for the seamen, and Tilesius wrote down the tune. Rezanov sent a courier to Major Koshelev, governor of Kamchatka, to request that extra infantry be sent from Bol'sheretsk to Petropavlovsk. In the meantime, he set about removing Kruzenshtern from his command.

The situation grew extremely difficult for Captain I. Krupskoi, the commandant at Petropavlovsk. He steered a careful course between Rezanov, who had moved into his quarters, and the senior lieutenants of *Nadezhda*. Koshelev at length arrived, exhausted, with his brother and sixty soldiers. All at once explained the situation from their various perspectives. To his credit, Koshelev informed Rezanov that, as governor, he would permit no sudden trial and removal from command of the sort that was envisaged. Once again, Rezanov read his orders of 10 July 1803, by which the emperor gave him authority over the officers and seamen in the Company's employ—within the controversial limits noted earlier.[51] The governor refused to be faced down and read through Kruzenshtern's instructions from the company directors dated 21 May 1803 and his orders from the Naval Ministry.[52] He saw that Kruzenshtern had been in an ambivalent position from the outset but had been correct to claim that he and not Rezanov should command where naval matters were concerned. The Naval Ministry, he also saw, had differed from the company directors in its broad interpretation of the captain's powers. While he reflected, Rezanov took measures of his own, making it known that he would name another officer to the command of *Nadezhda,* on his personal authority as correspondent; and he actually offered the command to the lieutenants. Now offended for their captain and the service, one by one they refused the questionable honour which, indeed, was not Rezanov's to bestow, since Kruzenshtern was under contract with the board. The strife between the disappointed envoy and the captain thus assumed a broader character.

Rezanov's suite stood by him. In particular, Lieutenant of the Guards Fedor Tolstoi was coolly insulting when confronted with the practical reality of Kruzenshtern's authority. The symbolic clash was ended far less easily than Kruzenshtern gave his compatriots to understand some five years later. "Trifling changes," he suggested, had occurred "in the ambassador's own suite." In fact, the troublesome Tolstoi, Surgeon Brykin, and the artist Kurliandtsev left *Nadezhda* and set out across Siberia for home, to be replaced by Captain Koshelev of "the Kamchatka Battalion" (the governor's brother), and a group of infantry.[53] Tolstoi, who had been difficult for weeks, had actually been dismissed by an exasperated Kruzenshtern.[54] Brykin's health had been shaken by the voyage and the recent crises; and shortly after his arrival in St. Petersburg, he died. The *Nadezhda's* stay at Petropavlovsk was, in sum, a sorry one.

Yet, for the lower deck especially, the sojourn (15 July to 7 September) did have brighter aspects. There was relative physical comfort: it was summer, and their beds were dry. There was no shortage of provisions at the time, and the environs of the settlement were green and welcoming. Nor from the maritime, and even strictly naval, viewpoint was the stay wholly fruitless: it much improved morale at Petropavlovsk and it strengthened its defences in the longer term. As a result of Kruzenshtern's extremely critical remarks about the place, never again would the authorities on the peninsula be left at liberty to let a ship like Billings's *Slava Rossii* rot and founder in a dozen feet of water. And, of course, soundings were made across and round Avacha Bay, all the advantages of which had, as in Billings's time, impressed themselves on officers, certain of whom were later to exert great influence, thereby ensuring that the government would not forget the harbour altogether.

NADEZHDA IN THE KURILE ISLANDS AND JAPAN (1804-5)

Nadezhda left Kamchatka on her diplomatic mission to Japan (Dezima, Nagasaki) on 7 September 1804. She was provisioned generously,[55] but the mood aboard was sober. It grew more so as the rain and fog persisted on the passage to a port where none expected to be welcomed. One month after sailing from Kamchatka, the ship stood at anchor by the shore of Nagasaki.

Large enough though they had previously seemed, Rezanov's troubles now expanded. To Japanese officials his presence, and the presence of all Russians, was unwelcome. If the tsar wanted the friendship of Japan, why had he sent a well-armed vessel full of soldiers? If *Nadezhda* was a merchantman despite appearances, she should depart immediately, as had other uninvited foreign traders. Rezanov argued that *Nadezhda* should be treated merely as the vessel that had brought him, the ambassador from Russia, to Japan. If an exchange of goods could also be arranged, he would be pleased, but he had come not as a trader, but as representative of Russian friendliness. He had credentials and small gifts for the Mikado. The Mikado, came the answer, did not need the little gifts of other rulers; and by what authority, since they did not possess a letter from Japan and were not Dutchmen, had the Russians dared to visit Nagasaki? If a Nagasaki permit had been granted their compatriot named Laxman more than ten years earlier, as they had claimed, why had it not been used? *Nadezhda* should be gone.[56]

It was a terrible beginning; but Rezanov persevered. He claimed to feel unwell, and he demanded leave to land both for his health's sake and as envoy. Reluctantly, permission was accorded, and the Russians were allowed to stretch their legs within a fenced and guarded compound by the shore. At this point an official approached Rezanov and asked if he would bow extremely low to an exalted Japanese plenipotentiary, as Japanese custom required. He refused at once, indignantly. As Russian envoy, he could not abase himself as he had seen the local Dutch do.[57] Not surprisingly in view of this, ''our intercourse became more limited,'' ''less intimate,'' as days and weeks dragged by.[58]

After three months of fruitless waiting and civilities, Rezanov had the Shogunate's response to his initial invitation and request: ''It is our Government's will not to open this place. Do not come again in vain. Sail home quickly.''[59] Rezanov lost his temper with the Japanese officials present, speaking of insult to the Russian Crown and fearful retribution. The officials were embarrassed; he seemed to wish them to oppose, even to criticize the Shogunate. After a day or two, Rezanov saw the pointlessness of anger. He attempted to save face by not accepting certain foodstuffs which, he gathered, the authorities were sending out to hasten his departure: fifteen thousand pounds of rice, more than two thousand bags of salt, and other victuals. Even this pleasure was denied him. If he failed to take the gifts, it was explained, the local governor and numerous subordinate officials would be forced to meet that insult by an act of disembowel-ment *en masse*. They were prepared to accept such a contingency, but could the Russians not make use of the supplies? The rice and salt were duly stowed and, on the morning of 18 April 1805, the *Nadezhda* sailed.

No understanding had been reached, no trade begun or even cautiously dis-cussed, and no Russian had so much as seen the capital. Such, noted Kruzen-shtern, were the results of an expensive embassy of which so much had been ex-pected. "We gained no new advantages, but even lost those we possessed."[60] The naval officers made much of the ambassador's apparently unmitigated fail-ure.

Certainly, Rezanov's failure had been merited, though it was also very likely unavoidable, given the Shogunate's official xenophobia. Rezanov had prepared himself efficiently enough for his appointment, reading widely and consulting high officials at the Ministry of Commerce (June to August 1803). He was no tourist in the Orient, as his detractors later claimed. Nevertheless, his tempera-ment, regardless of all other, local factors, guaranteed disaster. In Japan, he made no effort to conceal his deep antipathy towards the Shogunate itself.

But the rebuff at Nagasaki wore a very different appearance from the stand-point of the Shogunate, for Kruzenshtern and modern naval weapons were con-nected with Rezanov and intrusion from the north in the official mind. Linked with the Shogunate's immediate—and future—apprehensions where the Rus-sians were concerned was the reality of Russia's naval presence in the East.[61] In 1806-7, Russian officers, Davydov and Khvostov, were to lend substance to these early apprehensions.

Nadezhda was thus freed from a debilitating, fruitless spell of idleness by the ambassador's failure. His discomforture, however, quickly ceased to gladden Kruzenshtern's, Ratmanov's, and his other critics' hearts once Nagasaki had dis-appeared from view. The naval officers addressed themselves with genuine relief to plans that Kruzenshtern had polished in Japan. The voyage once again as-sumed a scientific and exploratory nature.

As it seemed unnecessary for *Nadezhda* to reach Kamchatka before the end of July, I was desirous of employing these three months in filling up the gaps which . . . La Pérouse was compelled to leave for want of time. . . . To explore the north-west and south-west coast of Japan; to ascertain the situation of the Straits of Sangar; to examine the west coast of Jesso . . . to take an accurate plan of the island of Sakhalin from Cape Crillon to the north-west coast from whence, if a good harbour were to be found there, I could send out my longboat to examine the supposed passage which divides Tartary from Sakhalin: all this came into my plan, and I had the good fortune of executing part of it.[62]

Nadezhda edged her way north-west. The "isle of Tsus and Jesso" came in sight. Arrowsmith's chart, then La Pérouse's, ceased to be of any help. Bearings and soundings, measurements of currents, rapid sketchings of a dozen capes and promontories—steadily the work went on. Kruzenshtern's and Langsdorf's narratives both give descriptions, *inter alia,* of meetings with the Japanese and Ainu on the Kurile Islands, of Aniwa, and of eastern Sakhalin. A fragment from the Kruzenshtern account dealing with "avaricious Banjos" and control over Aniwa Bay speaks eloquently for itself:

> With regard to taking possession of Aniwa, this could be done without the smallest danger, as the Japanese, owing to their total want of weapons of every description, would scarcely think of resistance. . . . Two cutters of 16 guns and 60 men would be quite sufficient, with a moderate air of wind, to sink the whole Japanese fleet, had it even 10,000 men on board. The capture of Aniwa is therefore no perilous undertaking.[63]

Charting as they went, the Russians closed on Sakhalin (20-21 May), then, the thermometer at freezing point, sheered off towards the Kurile chain. They passed between the twelfth and thirteenth islands on 29 May, bore north, and spent a week charting the chain.

Rezanov, who had spent most of the past five weeks below-deck in his quarters, was in one essential way unlike his Russian-born or sponsored predecessors in Japan, Lovtsov and Laxman.[64] As the former correspondent of the Company, a friend of Alexander, and a government official with authority extending over many ships and crews in the Pacific, he was *able* to avenge himself on those who, in his view, had offered insult to the Russian Crown. His expectations of Japan had been too great; but there is evidence that as an envoy he impressed the Japanese far more than he or his compatriots supposed in 1805. The Marquis Shigenobu, among other Japanese historians, has argued that Rezanov went some way towards convincing an unwilling Shogunate of the need to open up Japan to foreign trade.[65] However, all such evidence was hidden in the future and could hardly mollify the thwarted envoy who now, to his disgust, found himself virtually trapped aboard *Nadezhda.* Long frustrated in Japan, the naval officers headed by Kruzenshtern thought it their duty and their privilege to undertake hydrography along the west coast of that empire and through Tsushima Strait. One may usefully imagine the position from Rezanov's point of view.

Day by day he frets on board, impatient to arrive at "his" possessions in the North. *Nadezhda* is a hostile country: in Kamchatka, he will come into his own. Two weeks elapse, and there is still no sight of land.[66] *Nadezhda* is accompanied by fog. Rezanov's patience wears away. At last, a course is laid due east. At

39° N., the Russians slip into the Sangar Strait (Tsugaru), and eventually move in close to land. Rezanov comes on deck and sees a city: Matsumae (modern Fukuyama). It is spread around "a very open, insecure bay"[67] and has no visible defences. He remembers Nagasaki. Thus, perhaps, did the *Nadezhda* bring his hitherto vaguely belligerent and vengeful feelings into focus. In the next few days, he also saw Aniwa Bay, where Russians briefly landed, and a group of undefended Kurile Islands.[68]

Rezanov and his suite reached Petropavlovsk on 17 June. They left *Nadezhda* with impatience and relief. Kruzenshtern, having unloaded both the rice and salt obtained at Nagasaki and a quantity of Russian stores, set his ship to rights as speedily as possible and left to chart the eastern shores of Sakhalin, telling the commandant of Petropavlovsk to expect him back in August.

THE FURTHER MOVEMENTS AND RETURN TO KRONSTADT OF *NADEZHDA* AND *NEVA*

Within a month of his departure from Kamchatka, Kruzenshtern had proved that Sakhalin and Karafuto were a single island. That important hydrographic service to his government, however, was in due course counterbalanced by a failure to correct the misconception, spread by La Pérouse, that no large ship could safely pass between it and the Asian mainland. To the general astonishment of the inhabitants of Petropavlovsk, who were unaccustomed to such punctuality, he had returned there on 30 August 1805. Such was the nature of the work performed off Sakhalin and down the Kurile Island chain, and such the dampness of the climate, that *Nadezhda*'s rigging needed much attention. She was duly unrigged and, in view of the considerable voyage back to Europe that was now to be performed, also unladen, cleaned from stem to stern, retouched, recaulked, and carefully reladen. On 4 October she was ready to depart. Anchors were raised after the briefest of adieus, for the *Nadezhda*'s officers and seamen were alike growing impatient to be home.

After a slow but uneventful passage south, *Nadezhda* reached Macao on 19 November, dropping anchor in the Typa, a roadstead two miles or so out of the sorrily, yet beautifully, decayed Portuguese town. The governor received the Russians kindly. As the Japanese had been confused by the *Nadezhda*'s function as a trading Russian warship and uncertain how to deal with her, however, so the Chinese now reacted with uncertainty. Kruzenshtern explained the situation, more than once, with some assistance from the local Dutch and British merchants. Nonetheless, he was refused permission to proceed, as he had planned, up the Whampoa to Canton. Making the best of things, he had repairs carried out aboard *Nadezhda* in the Typa, while attempting to bring influence to bear on appropriate officials in Canton. Then, on 3 December, the *Neva* arrived. Lisianskii's statement of the reason for his visit and description of his vessel, and perhaps even the cargo that he carried, changed *Nadezhda*'s awkward status in the sight of Cantonese officialdom, though not immediately. Only on 25 December, after wearisome, repetitive discussions and exchanges of civilities, did Kruzenshtern at last take the *Nadezhda* up the bustling Whampoa and proceed to business with the two company clerks in close attendance. As was natural enough, he had by then not only listened to Lisianskii's and his officers' accounts of their activities about the Coast since mid-September 1804, but had also read (and thoroughly approved) Lisianskii's full written report. It was an interesting document.

Lisianskii and his men had wintered safely and productively on Kodiak in 1804-5. They had meticulously mapped the island and, moreover, been intelligent and catholic observers of Pacific custom, spectacle, and natural phenomena. (A glance over the motley section-headings of Lisianskii's published narrative—identical with Kruzenshtern's in title, but unlike it in both tenor and pace—reveals the lead he gave: "Plants: beasts: birds: number of inhabitants: customs: dress: food; burials: manner of catching fish; wild animals and birds: instruments used: shamans: games: building of bidarkas," and a dozen more.[69])

Nine months had passed since the destruction of the Tlingit stronghold there, when *Neva* re-entered Sitka Sound. Lisianskii and his officers were favourably struck by the results of the chief manager's resolve that a new settlement should rise beside the ashes of the old. Eight solid buildings had been finished in a winter; and work had started on a drying-shed, a bath-house, and a smithy. Groups of men were clearing land for kitchen-gardens.[70] N. I. Korobitsyn described the scene:

> The fort at Novo-Arkhangel'sk is situated on the high south-east promontory of the island. The fortifications consist of gabions placed around and interspersed with twenty cannon of various calibres, including four 24-pounders. . . . Inside the fort there is, first, the Manager's residence, together with his office and kitchen. Then there is a house for the naval officers in the service of the Company and for the ship's masters, consisting of four suites of rooms. . . . At a distance of 700' from the settlement, a site has been designated for a dock. Riding at anchor in Novo-Arkhangel'sk harbour were the Company ships *St. Paul, Ekaterina, Yermak,* and *Rostislav.* . . . On August 5, the Company vessel *Elizaveta* arrived from Okhotsk with a cargo of 50,000 fur-seal skins. That same day, two United States vessels, the *Juno* and the *Maria,* sailed into the harbour.[71]

But the Navy party doubted if the place on which such toil and so much blood had been expended would be left to raise its hens and pigs in peace. "It was understood that other tribes had been busily employed fortifying their settlements . . . so that, it is to be feared, our countrymen here will in a short time be surrounded by very formidable neighbours."[72] But this was not Lisianskii's problem, and after Baranov handed him a packet for the company directors in St. Petersburg, he saw no reason for remaining on the Coast. On 20 August, therefore, *Neva* set sail for China on a course which her captain thought was likely to result in the discovery of unknown specks of land.

Lisianskii's hopes were realized in a dramatic fashion. He learned of his success as it was threatening to turn into his doom. At 10 P.M., 16 October (lat. 26° 2′ 48″, long. 173° 42′ 30″), the *Neva* received a shock:

All hands were summoned upon deck and set to work; and upon sounding, we found that we had touched on a coral bank. I now ordered the guns and the heaviest articles that we had stowed in the booms, to be thrown overboard, but with such precaution that they might be recovered should circumstances admit. The ship being thus lightened, we succeeded in getting her into deep water. Then we perceived, at a distance of about a mile, a small low island to the WNW, and to the SW some high rocks. . . . Desirous of examining the place which, by its situation, appeared to be of the greatest importance to navigation, I went on shore in the morning with several of my officers. . . . The surf was so great that we could only with difficulty land at a small bay, where we found numerous birds of different kinds and seals of an enormous size. . . . Towards evening, having examined everything worthy of notice, we fixed a high pole in the ground and buried near it a bottle containing a description of our discovery.[73]

Lisianskii or Lisiansky Island still appears on the map of the Pacific at the westermost extremity of the Hawaiian archipelago; and it remains much as it was in 1805: a low and reef-encircled spot, its sand practically "overgrown with creeping plants and grass." The U.S. Navy visits it at intervals.

Two more adventures followed as *Neva* approached the Marianas. In the third week of November near Tinian, the Russians met a hurricane. Then they found that more than thirty thousand pelts bound for the Canton mart had grown so putrid on the voyage out, it was essential to jettison them. Grief was tempered by relief as the appalling stench grew weaker. When the *Neva* dropped anchor at Macao on 3 December, junks stood around her by the dozen. Lisianskii went ashore to seek out Kruzenshtern.

For Kruzenshtern especially, the meeting was a happy one: inadequate reports had reached Kamchatka of the "battle" with the Tlingit and the victory at Novo-Arkhangel'sk. Kruzenshtern explained why the *Nadezhda* rode at anchor with the other foreign vessels at Macao and had not sailed in to Canton by the Whampoa. Theoretically, it was because she had displayed a naval pennant on arrival and was thus regarded as a warship. In reality, commercial factors were at work.

In the event, the reunited Russian visitors discharged their business with considerable difficulty in a city where, it seemed, the merchants' agents had their agents, and where only a few members of the *hong* enjoyed the privilege of even purchasing the cargoes of barbarians, for whose behaviour they then became responsible. Appreciating that he needed more assistance, Kruzenshtern again contacted Thomas Beale, whom he had met six years before and who was now in partnership with Messrs. Shank and Magniac.[74] Would Beale and his associates exert their influence on his behalf to find a member of the *hong,* who would accept responsibility for two whole Russian companies? The English merchants offered acceptable terms.

At length, a young merchant named Lucqua, the junior of the *hong,* supported by Messrs. Beale's credit, ventured to become security for both ships. The cargo of *Neva* was sold to him for 178,000, and that of *Nadezhda* for 12,000 piastres. But the most valuable sea-otter skins, each of them being worth two and three hundred roubles apiece at Moscow, were reshipped.[75]

With the profit from the furs, the two company clerks bought teas, nankeen, and chinaware. In fact, Lucqua had stipulated that the Russians take a quantity of tea instead of cash. Lading began. Beale took a 5 per cent commission.[76] Kruzenshtern, Lisianskii, and their crews gazed at local Chinese scenes the more attentively as the reality of imminent departure for the Baltic dawned.

Enormous crowds living afloat, somehow subsisting on the offal of the river, squalid temples, heavy lacquered idols, and, in gardens of the wealthy, stagnant ponds: in Kruzenshtern's as in Lisianskii's narratives, condescension, curiosity, and deep distaste are obvious. *Nadezhda* and *Neva* weighed anchor in the second week of February 1806, making for home via the Straits of Gaspar and of Sunda, St. Helena (in *Nadezhda*'s case), Portsmouth (in *Neva*'s), and so at length the Gulf of Finland. Kruzenshtern reached Kronstadt on the morning of 19 August 1806, after an absence of three years and twelve days. To his vexation, his subordinate Lisianskii had preceded him by thirteen days after a rapid (and later controversial) non-stop voyage from the East.

RECKONING RESULTS

The conclusion of the first Russian circumnavigation of the globe was inevitably followed by a reckoning of benefits accrued to its supporters and its sponsors: the Company, the Navy, and the Crown. They might well have seemed exiguous to the dispassionate observer. The expedition's diplomatic objects in Japan had undeniably misfired—the government explained Rezanov's failure, to itself and to the world, in terms not of its own deep ignorance of the conditions and conventions of the empire of "His Tenjin-Kubo Majesty,"[77] but rather of intrigues by Hendrik Doeff and the Dutch at Nagasaki. As a trading venture, certainly, the Kruzenshtern-Lisianskii enterprise was disappointing; for the skins that had been sold, not tossed away, low prices had been paid in a depressed and glutted market.[78] Chinaware and a few hundred pounds of tea had been conveyed by sea to European Russia rather faster than they might have been imported via Kiakhta. To have brought them overland would not, however, have increased the cost of transport, and the goods would not have suffered on the journey. Indeed, Canton officials asked why Kruzenshtern had not dispatched his pelts to Kiakhta as his countrymen had done for many years. The risk, they said, would not have been increased thereby, nor would the profits have been smaller.

It was not judged a failure by the emperor or by the Company's board. Why? Partly, no doubt, because Pacific voyages had fine associations with the early Spanish voyages and Cook and La Pérouse, but more especially because, for all the venture's poor commercial success and diplomatic failure, it had succeeded as a naval exercise. Achievements of a naval and a scientific kind had cast an aura of success over the venture as a whole.

The expedition, it was emphasized, had ended with the ships in good condition and with officers and crews in splendid health. Much useful hydrographic work had been completed in the areas of Sakhalin, the Kurile chain, and Kodiak especially. *Neva* had played her part in a variety of battle and had won a kind of victory. That such a voyage round the world would offer admirable training opportunities for companies of seamen and their officers had always been contended. The reality had matched the expectation. On returning to St. Petersburg, the officers and seamen of *Nadezhda* and *Neva* were almost certainly the best-trained in the Navy. They had demonstrated clearly to the Naval Ministry and to the Company that sea communications between Kronstadt and the North Pacific colonies were practical and, possibly, commercially viable.[79] As a result, the board no longer wondered whether it should send another vessel to the colonies with stores by the oceanic route: the question was not if, but when. The Naval Ministry was also now alert to the Pacific challenge. And as Kruzenshtern's awareness of Russia's prospects there had grown apace between 1804 and 1806, so had his standing in the Navy.

There was food for thought in Company and Admiralty circles in the fact that one small ship had fired guns to such effect along the Coast. Lisianskii's "victory" at Novo-Arkhangel'sk, indeed, raised certain questions. The *Neva* had carried modest armament as was befitting in a modest merchantman, but her commander had behaved as the captain of a Russian ship of war. He had supposed that his professional superiors would wish him to, for company and naval interests were consolidated in the person of Mordvinov. Was a naval officer always to act in the Pacific as a servant of civilians at hand? The *Neva*'s actions had tipped the balance of control along the Coast towards Baranov and the Company. But might the Navy not itself aspire to represent Imperial authority in North Pacific waters, more especially if in the last analysis, exerting that authority depended on it? By extending the Navy's role, all panics might be ended in Kamchatka and the islands.[80]

Neither Kruzenshtern nor any of his officers had had instructions to reflect on future policy and action in the North Pacific Ocean or on Russia's naval prospects there. Yet it was almost unavoidable that they should do so and report on Petropavlovsk and Okhotsk. Lisianskii strongly advocated an extension of the Navy's presence in Kamchatka. Naval shipwrights, Kruzenshtern asserted, should be sent without delay to build decked vessels to be based at Petropavlovsk and at Novo-Arkhangel'sk. Moreover, little craft of stout construction should be carried to Kamchatka, not Okhotsk, from Russian Baltic yards. They were needed to assist in unlading vessels that would call at Petropavlovsk in the future and for carrying freight along the coast.

Besides, there should be constantly a naval officer having five and twenty or thirty men under his command, as well as carpenters, smiths, locksmiths, sailmakers, caulkers, and other necessary workmen: in short, there should be a small naval arsenal at Kamchatka . . . Nor do I think it superfluous, but indeed even necessary as the place bears the title of an Imperial port, to keep there constantly a small ship-of-war of 18 or 20 guns.[81]

Lastly, brief comments may be added on the scientific value of the Kruzenshtern-Lisianskii expedition. That value was not questioned at the time and has remained beyond all doubt. Kruzenshtern's own learned work based on his 1803-6 journals and notes ranged over areas of maritime astronomy, geodesy, linguistics, physics, and hydrography. Hörner and Tilesius both published their results at state expense, and both were honoured. Gratified by Langsdorf's published work, the Russian government in due course sent him to Brazil, as he desired, as the Russian consul general. It was, in sum, a most respectable result, particularly considering that the venture was not planned as an encyclopaedic scientific one. Indeed, its scientific objects and potential had been treated by the government as altogether secondary to diplomatic, training, and commercial ends. It was to Kruzenshtern's credit that, in 1803 as later, he had emphasized the academic aspect of the enterprise to the extent that he was able. Moreover, he had taken the position that his officers themselves could do a good deal of the scientific work and not neglect their other duties. He was mindful of unhappy French examples of the dangers attached to an excessive use of outside specialists.[82] Again, he followed Cook.

SCIENCE AND PRESTIGE: THE BALTIC GERMAN ELEMENT

Kruzenshtern was able to select his own subordinates. It was, perhaps, predictable that he should favour Baltic Germans like himself; and a degree of local pride was proper in a scion of the German nobility based in Estonia—it wielded a political and social influence in Russia as a whole quite disproportionate both to its size and to its wealth, and was a source of able servants of the state.[83] Ratmanov and Golovachev, first and third lieutenants of *Nadezhda,* were of ancient Russian stock, like Povalishin and Arbuzov of *Neva.* Nevertheless in both ships, as in the upper ranks and postings of the Guards and in the Baltic Fleet, the Baltic German element loomed large. Fourth and fifth lieutenants of *Nadezhda* were Hermann Ludwig von Löwenstern and Fabian Gottlieb von Bellingshausen, later to command an expedition of his own.[84] Löwenstern's counterpart aboard *Neva* was V. N. Berkh, or Berg, future recorder of the Russian enterprise in the Aleutians and America.[85] Also with Kruzenshtern went sons of August von Kotzebue, German playwright and a Russian counsellor: the family was now living in Reval. The two, Otto and Moritz, were supported by the emperor himself.[86] Simply by taking Bellingshausen and the Kotzebues with him, Kruzenshtern went far towards ensuring that the academic emphases that he himself so valued would persist in the Pacific naval service.

For contemporaries, however, such names had social and political as well as academic overtones. In 1843, the German traveller and writer J. G. Kohl thus commented on Baltic German dominance of Russia's court and military services, and on their consonant prestige:

The ranking of the classes of nobility, even the rules of Court etiquette have been transferred from Germany or partially imitated from German models. Princes of the Russian Imperial family have married German princesses . . . . And by the St. Petersburg Court Calendar for 1837, it appears that of 600 of the highest posts in the Empire, no fewer than 130 were filled by German names . . . . But the whole nobility of the Baltic Provinces, so exceedingly important and influential, constitute only a small population of about 8,000 souls.[87]

Kohl's remarks would have been equally correct in 1803. Its German element, in short, gave to the Kruzenshtern-Lisianskii expedition a yet more prestigious aura than it would in all events have had because of Alexander's interest.That aura grew more unmistakable at its conclusion. Alexander and his mother went to Kronstadt separately to congratulate Lisianskii and to stroll around *Neva*, the first of the two vessels home. Both were impressed and entertained by what they saw. The Empress Dowager left golden snuff-boxes and watches for the officers, "ten ducats" for the sailors, and "a costly diamond ring" for the commander.[88] Later came a shower of promotions, pensions, prizes for the two ships' companies.

Thus the link between Imperial benevolence and naval enterprise in the Pacific which Peter I himself had forged was reinforced. Promotions, pensions, snuff-boxes and watches were acceptable, of course. But it was contact with the emperor that was especially significant for the returning men. Personal contact with the Crown betokened future advancement, if all went well. Lisianskii's star, like Kruzenshtern's, ascended. Shortly after his return, he was commanding the Imperial yacht squadron in the Baltic.[89] As director of the Naval Cadet Corps and a member of the Admiralty Board, Admiral Kruzenshtern exerted influence in Russian naval councils for another forty years.

KAMCHATKAN PROSPECTS

Within a month of her return, *Neva* was readying at Kronstadt for another voyage out to the Pacific. There were several applicants for the command, which went to L. A. Gagemeister, yet another Baltic German,[90] for officers had learned that the promotion prospects for those connected with such voyages were quite as good as in the Baltic Fleet or better. They were certainly far better than for officers like A. V. Mashin, who had lately been seconded to the Company and stationed in the far North-East or East. It was a paradox. For those who took the oceanic route, the North Pacific promised both prestige and prompt advancement since the voyages themselves were now regarded as a likely source of "honours" for the Crown. By contrast, naval officers *based* in the North Pacific region, whose runs between Kamchatka and the colonies were risky, whose responsibilities were growing, and whose lots were extremely hard, were far less likely to win favour. Yet better naval officers and companies were needed in the far North-East and East. Lt. Mashin's crew, reported Langsdorf, had arrived in Petropavlovsk from Okhotsk in sorry state; they did not even know the names of ropes and sails.[91] Petropavlovsk's state, from the naval point of view, was described by Kruzenshtern:

The first prospect might raise in the mind of a person newly arrived, and ignorant of the history of this Russian settlement, the idea of its being a colony founded a few years before but recently abandoned . . . . Not only Awatcha Bay, but the three adjoining ones also, are entirely forlorn and uninhabited; nor is the beautiful harbour of St. Peter and St. Paul [Petropavlovsk] enlivened by a single boat. Instead of this, the shores are strewn with stinking fish . . . . You perceive the wreck of a three-masted ship bearing evident marks of having been in its present condition for some years.[92] It is upwards of a hundred years since Russia first obtained possession of this province, which might become of infinite importance—if all the advantages of which it is capable of affording were derived from it.[93]

It was a desolate and scurvy settlement, its very name pronounced by Europeans and by Russians from St. Petersburg "with horror and disgust." And yet, "it might become of infinite importance." True, Kamchatka's climate was severe and its soil none too rich. But even so, there were some parts that were "invariably very fruitful," bearing "many kinds of vegetable" and "grains of every species."[94] "Might become" and should become: it was an attitude in which Rezanov, last seen at Petropavlovsk, and such energetic Navy men as Kruzenshtern, Lisianskii, and Ratmanov could concur.

7

Rezanov and Baranov: Response and Legacy

N. P. REZANOV IN KAMCHATKA AND THE COLONIES (1805-6)

N. P. Rezanov's situation was immediately changed on his arrival at Kamchatka in June 1805. Notwithstanding the imbroglio with Kruzenshtern and Koshelev, his rank was recognized by the authorities.[1] The settlement itself, by contrast, seriously disappointed him. Chest pains compounded his depression. It was fortunate that Langsdorf was accompanying him as a private surgeon, having seized the opportunity, so unexpectedly presented, of examining Kamchatka and the North-west Coast.[2] Two little vessels stood at anchor in the harbour, which would quite comfortably have held the Russian Navy. One was *Fedoseia,* galiot, which had arrived with foodstuffs from Okhotsk; the other was *Mariia,* or *Mariia Magdalena,* brig. She had barely limped to safety in Avacha Bay, Rezanov was informed, before subsiding on the mud. A local carpenter had patched her leaking hull.

Rezanov spoke at length with the *Mariia*'s captain, Lt. A. V. Mashin, who told him that both he and the other Navy men lately seconded to the Company, Lieutenants Sukin and Karpinskii, all regretted their decision to come out to the Pacific. Another officer, Borisov, had in 1804 taken *Elizaveta* with a cargo of supplies to Kodiak and had been forced to spend six months on Unalaska, where eight seamen died of scurvy. Men died annually from disease or even hunger in the settlements. Rezanov weighed what he was told against the spectacle around him. *Mariia,* bound for Kodiak by way of Unalaska, did not inspire confidence. Her crew Langsdorf described as "drunkards, bankrupt traders, criminals in search of a fortune."[3] He reflected, then gave orders for his books, paintings, and instruments to be deposited on board the evil-smelling brig:

There was not an inch left between decks for upwards of 50 persons. These were therefore obliged to sleep on deck . . . . Hammocks they had none: everyone lay down where he could, in his clothes, and of these there was the greatest want. Filthiness and laziness were the general characteristics. Some few wore shirts, but most, in spite of the heat of June, were wrapped up in greasy furs . . . . Seamen in the service of the American Company lead a most wretched life. It cannot be a matter for surprise if under such circumstances, and in a cold, foggy climate, the strongest man should fall a victim. Even of water there is frequently the greatest scarcity.[4]

The *Mariia,* a two-masted vessel of about 200 tons, was not the worst of Company-owned brigs then on the Petropavlovsk-St.Paul-Unalaska-Kodiak-Slavorossiia-Novo-Arkhangel'sk mixed cargo route. Nor was her crew the worst provided for. To the good fortune of Rezanov, two young naval officers, Lieutenant Nikolai Khvostov and Ensign Gavriil Davydov, both on temporary service with the Company, were also bound for Kodiak. Their presence in *Mariia* made the voyage tolerable, and relieved to have the chance, Rezanov spoke at length of his experiences in Japan and of the sights seen to the north. Within the week, he was regarding the two officers as likely instruments of his revenge. Davydov and Khvostov were both adventurous by nature and acknowledged the extent of his authority. Rezanov spoke, at first in abstract terms, of sudden raids along the Kurile Island chain, then more specifically of Matsumae and Aniwa Bay. Even suggestions from a man of such importance could be treated as instructions, and the pair were willing to regard them in that light.

Only Rezanov could have had Russian naval officers commit aggressive acts against the Japanese, with whom the Russians were at peace. There were no admirals or captains in Kamchatka or Okhotsk who would oppose the stated wishes of a friend of Alexander. Only Rezanov could embroil willing agents of the Navy in a raid along the Kuriles; and he chose to do so.[5]

DAVYDOV, KHVOSTOV, AND THE KURILE ISLANDS RAIDS

The *Mariia* entered Sitka Sound in August 1805. By then, Rezanov had developed further plans, and in Baranov's private rooms, he wrote a wonderful despatch to Alexander, touched with paranoia, patriotic fervour, and Imperial ambition.[6] After all the settlements in Russian North America were strengthened and more ships built, he wrote, it would be feasible to force the Japanese to trade with Russians as the ordinary Japanese desired. Meanwhile, he had devised chastisement for the Japanese authorities at large: they, not the people of Japan, had offered insult to the Crown. With the assistance of Davydov and Khvostov, Russia would demonstrate quite clearly to the Shogunate that she should not be trifled with. The Japanese would be expelled from Sakhalin. Japanese buildings would be burned at Matsumae. And, deprived of needed fisheries and food supplies, the Japanese authorities would have no choice but to behave as common sense dictated and to trade. It was the first and last time that the Company would so abuse the Navy in the East.[7]

The situation was unique because Rezanov's position was unique. It was not that the ideas of extending Russia's presence on the Kurile Island chain or of annexing Sakhalin were not acceptable in Admiralty circles. One small warship, Captain Kruzenshtern had noted, would suffice to hold that island and Aniwa and to cow the Japanese into a politic passivity.[8] What was troubling, when the authorities eventually learned of his activities, was that on his own initiative a civilian had vessels built and armed with warlike acts in mind. "We require," Rezanov informed Davydov and Khvostov from Novo-Arkhangel'sk on 10 September 1805, "two new armed vessels, a brig and tender. . . . I ask you to proceed at once to examine drawings by master shipwrights and, when you have approved some, to supervise construction so that both vessels are ready by late April."[9] Rezanov had himself then purchased *Juno*, a New England trading vessel (though indeed less for the hull than for the food she was carrying as cargo), so that only one more craft "had" to be built. *Avos'*, tender, was duly launched at Novo-Arkhangel'sk on 7 July 1806. Her name (*Maybe*, in English) was perhaps an indication that Rezanov's plans had yet to take a firm and final shape; but by mid-August, all was ready for a raid if he decided to proceed.

Rezanov had been thinking of a June or July raid on conveniently sited, that is, coastal, Japanese establishments. It was already growing late for an attack even on fisheries. He hesitated, wrote fresh orders for Khvostov, changed them again, then cancelled them. Should he perhaps postpone the venture and not risk the *Juno*, now *Iunona*, or himself go to Okhotsk? Again he vacillated. There was no one to consult. At last, the die was cast, and in mid-October, Khvostov arrived off Sakhalin ready for action. In Aniwa Bay, he found a small Japanese vessel. She was anchored off the settlement of Kushunkotan. Khvostov and a boat-party made a landing and, confronting a bewildered group of Japanese, read out a proclamation. The Japanese perceived at length, from gestures, that the strangers were demanding trade or barter. Khvostov then had his men seize four guards and carry them on board *Iunona*. The Russians pillaged one or two small warehouses, removing rice and salt as well as liquor. What they did not want, they burned, destroying fishing boats and nets which they observed along the beach. Well satisfied, Khvostov then sailed for Petropavlovsk, where Davydov welcomed him. They wintered there together. On 16 May 1807, they cut their way through ice and sailed again to "free" the Ainu from the "tyranny" of Japanese oppression and to pick up further booty in the process. On 30 May, they came to Etorofu. Two days later, from Naibo Bay, they landed and attacked, discharging cannon as they rushed across the sand. Again, they sought to rob the

Japanese and to appease the Kurile Islanders. Again, they did so hurriedly and crudely, burning, looting, and departing. They carried on in this fashion for forty days. At Shana, where they were met peaceably, they committed murder. On Uruppu, they found nothing to destroy. At Hakodate, they fired on a "war junk," which did not retaliate. On coming to Rishiri Island, they encountered four well-laden merchantmen which they plundered and destroyed. And so, weighed down with booty, *Iunona* and *Avos'* set sail for home and reached Okhotsk safely on 28 July. The sorry episode brought no credit to the Navy, to Rezanov, or indeed to the defenders of Naibo Bay and Shana. Its impact, nonetheless, was very great. Attacks by Russian craft were feared in many coastal areas. The popular imagination firmly linked the Russians with the terrible Red Devils of Buddhist imagery, and the Japanese prepared to meet fresh onslaughts.[10]

Unlike their reception in the Kuriles, in Okhotsk Davydov and Khvostov met trouble. The commandant in 1806-7, was Bukharin, an extremely hard and avaricious officer. Davydov, Khvostov and all their men were arrested and imprisoned on the pretext that the raids had been performed without authority. They languished under guard for several days. At length, a pair of local men helped Davydov and Khvostov to flee their damp and noisome little prison. Only their youthful strength and vigour (they were twenty-three and thirty-one respectively in 1807) saw them safe across the hinterland in autumn. They reached Iakutsk on 25 October emaciated and in tatters. Fear of arrest went at their heels till at last they reached the capital. But even in St. Petersburg their fate hung in the balance: Rezanov, on whose orders they had burnt and pillaged settlements had lately died. N. P. Rumiantsev, now minister of foreign affairs, ordered an enquiry into the raids, and in the end their actions were condoned by a committee which he personally chaired. Both officers, he noted, had been following instructions from Rezanov. If they wished to lay complaints against Bukharin, they should do so formally at the Naval Ministry. They did so; and the ministry convened a special court to hear the case. It went against them, but the judgment had yet to be pronounced when the pair left St. Petersburg again, this time for Finland.[11] Having served against the Swedes with great distinction in a mobile gunboat unit, both were drowned at 3 A.M. on 16 October 1809, right in the middle of St. Petersburg. Recklessness killed them in the end, after a happy drinking bout in Langsdorf's quarters on Vasil'evskii Island. The carousal was to honour the arrival in the capital of Captain John D'Wolf, from whom Rezanov had acquired *Juno* on the Coast.[12]

N. P. REZANOV AT NOVO-ARKHANGEL'SK: WIDER AMBITIONS

By the time he entered Sitka Sound in the *Mariia*, in August 1805, Rezanov understood to what extent he and the board had been misled, or had perhaps misled themselves, about conditions in the colonies. There were no doctors to care for the disabled and the ailing who were everywhere in evidence. On every island visited, company servants went in rags. At St. Paul in the Pribylovs, seals were slaughtered in the middle of the breeding season. Rotting animals gave proof of hunters' habitual improvidence. Even at Kodiak, supposedly a major Russian colony, there was no bread. As for the missionaries, not only had they not established missions on the lesser islands; with the solitary exception of Father German, they had failed even to learn the Aleut tongue.[13]

At Sitka, meanwhile, Baranov and his people had been toiling on a strongpoint so positioned and defended that no Tlingit Indian or hostile ship could ever take it.[14] Baranov was exhausted, and he proposed to gain permission from Rezanov to retire. He was fifty-eight, troubled by arthritis,[15] and tired of the effort of asserting his authority over the officers in company employ. Ivan Kuskov, his second-in-command, had been assaulted by a drunken midshipman whom he would not allow more liquor.

When Rezanov arrived, Baranov welcomed him but lost no time in listing problems that confronted him and the insults that he and his deputy had borne too long at Navy hands. It seemed indeed that though Davydov and Khvostov had broken records by delivering a cargo from Okhotsk to Kodiak in 1802 in just eleven weeks (in the *Elizaveta,* galiot) and had returned with equal speed the summer following, the services of other naval officers had not improved the local record of disasters. *Feniks* had been lost with more than ninety Russian lives, as well as that of the efficient shipbuilder, James Shields, and more than 500,000 roubles' worth of stores. Also in 1802, the *Severnyi Orel* had been abandoned on a run from Iakutat to Three Saints' Harbour, Kodiak, with more than 20,000 roubles' worth of cargo.[16] Not one vessel brought a cargo from Okhotsk to Russian outposts on the mainland of America between 1801 and 1804.[17] As a result of frequent shipwrecks, the men often went hungry.[18]

Rezanov heard Baranov out. He looked for confirmation of the facts from other Russians then at Novo-Arkhangel'sk.[19] It was provided, readily, with details of stores and peltry lost through naval arrogance. He wrote a letter to the company's main board.

With regard to my conclusions where the naval side is concerned, I must add, with some distress, that it would be infinitely better for the Company to recruit foreign seamen, or retired sailors not previously in Crown service, than to continue as we do. His Imperial Majesty's goodness is limitless, but perhaps as a result of the training given our naval officers, or perhaps because of the remoteness of the parts in which they are serving, where anything may seem permissible, the Company stands to lose a great deal by them—and the Fatherland to lose its American possessions. Scorn of trade, which has struck such deep roots in our Russian nobility, has made them all masters here. But, as you know, too many cooks spoil the broth. There is here a Governor of some rank, and he attained that rank through the most commendable service. Yet the fact that this Governor is of merchant antecedents means, in the eyes of our brethren here and unhappily for the Fatherland itself, that he is a good-for-nothing. To them, to take orders from such a man seems sheer mendacity.[20]

Some individuals seconded from the Navy, he observed elsewhere in this same letter (presumably with special reference to Gavriil Terent'evich Talin), were declared to have provoked "no little violence" and to have taken for themselves practically everything imported for the use of all the servants of the Company at Kodiak. As a result, company servants had at times been forced to purchase goods from traders like the Winships and O'Cain.

There is evidence besides this striking letter that Rezanov and Baranov understood each other well and trusted each other, in itself a striking thing given the context of the meeting and their pasts. Each drew some comfort from the other's long involvement with, and expectations of, Russian America. Both knew the full importance to the Company, moreover, of immediate expansion southwards—southwards, because there lay the potential for both farming and continuing profitability from furs; immediate, because the energies of Britain and France would not forever be absorbed in wars such as had made it possible in recent years for New Englanders to take the lead in the Pacific seaborne fur trade.[21]

Baranov had long been conscious of the need to gain some influence and even territory further south than Sitka.[22] More than once, his people had depended for essential food supplies on the goodwill and business instinct of Americans. If these had carried only foodstuffs up the Coast, there would have been no reason for complaint; but most traded in guns, powder, and spirits for their furs. Washington was far away, and Congress was untroubled by Americans' activities along remote Pacific shores. (Nevertheless, it must be noted, such New Englanders as Kimball, Ayres, and O'Cain were viewed as friends as well as long-term trading partners by Baranov.)[23] As to likely hunting benefits of any southward move, they were beyond all doubt. By 1800, the Novo-Arkhangel'sk "counter" or area accounted for three-quarters of the whole sea-otter catch in what was then Russian America.[24] The animals were scarce even in Kenai Inlet and in Bristol Bay.[25] Rezanov too had, for at least five years, been conscious of the probable advantages—a regular supply of grain, smaller expenditure on foreign staples, an increased sense of security at Sitka—of expansion to the south and of the mounting danger of delay. On 18 April 1802, for instance, he had baldly written to Baranov from St. Petersburg that "all work is to be halted in the northern area, nor are fresh efforts to be made there until we have strengthened our hold on our possessions adjacent to the English territory."[26] Neither man had then supposed that the establishing of a new fortress at Mikhailovsk, on Sitka, would delay southward expansion for eight years.

Where should new hunting-farming settlements be placed? As his detractors emphasized after his death, Rezanov's plans of 1805-6 were vague as well as grandiose.[27] Four areas seemed to him suitable for the establishment of farms which might provision the Pacific settlements more easily, and also more abundantly, than areas in Transbaikalia: the shores of Gray's River Columbia, which were reported to be temperate as well as rich in furs; "New Albion," "the English territory"; Upper California, if the weakness of the Spaniards was sufficient to reduce them to passivity; and the Hawaiian archipelago. In conversation with Baranov in the first weeks of his stay, Rezanov's schemes developed. All they lacked was concrete detail: places, timing, means of execution. Winter on the Coast had soon convinced him that the details, too, must quickly be arranged: by mid-October, food supplies were very low at Novo-Arkhangel'sk, and by November, everything was rationed. One pound of bread per day per man. Because the well-armed Tlingit waited in the sound, it was impossible to fish. Eagles, crows and other birds were shot and eaten hungrily. So, too, were cuttlefish and vermin.[28] Constant rain, interminable threats of an attack by Tlingit raiders: all combined with the result that, as Rezanov candidly remarked in a despatch dated 6 November 1805, he and Langsdorf lived at Novo-Arkhangel'sk chiefly in hopes of leaving it.[29]

Then came the *Juno* (Captain D'Wolf). As seen, Rezanov did not hesitate to purchase her complete with cargo, which included beef, pork, flour, bread, rice, sugar, and molasses.[30] The price, $8,000, was a trifle in the circumstances, and the crisis eased, albeit briefly. By mid-February 1806, the settlement was once more growing desperate for food and Rezanov now resolved to send to Spanish California for provisions. He knew that international trade was banned there by Madrid, but hoped that even so a little trade might be transacted with connivance by the Spanish Californian missionaries, who were "in fact principal agents in exchange of contraband."[31] The plan was rather desperate; but hunger was a potent advocate. *Juno* was laden, and on 8 March, Rezanov, still accompanied by Langsdorf, Davydov, and Khvostov, put out to sea. Weakened by hunger and disease, barely half the crew were fit for duty; but to hesitate was probably to die.[32]

So began that series of encounters with the Spaniards on the shores of California, in which, thanks to the grandiose but hunger-driven projects of Rezanov, naval officers would often play a part over the coming twenty years.

RUSSIANS IN UPPER CALIFORNIA: REZANOV'S DEATH (1806-7)

Following Vancouver's charts, copies of which had reached the colonies with Kruzenshtern, Khvostov took *Juno* south. Langsdorf describes the voyage well[33] and makes it evident that *Juno*'s failure to investigate the mouth of the Columbia, as tentatively planned, was not the fault of the lieutenant.[34] A debilitated crew and fickle wind gave him no help. Moreover, his good sense cooled Rezanov's mounting ardour to make land and found a colony at once, after a period of danger off Cape Adams. Though adventurous, he and Davydov both disliked the sight of surf. "They therefore represented . . . that it was better not to lose more time, but . . . to sail away directly for San Francisco," where they would be "among civilized people."[35] By mid-March, having reached Cape Disappointment, Khvostov had in reality no further choice of action. He had too few healthy seamen to turn back or to head out towards Hawaii and the certainty of food. A change of the moon at last brought favourable winds, however, and by 4 April *Juno* was standing off the heads of San Francisco Bay. Next morning, the exhausted mariners ran straight into the harbour on the tide with all sails set.[36] No guns were fired. When challenged, they simply shouted "Russkie." They were at length allowed to anchor. At a nervous shipboard conference, it was arranged that Dr. Langsdorf and Davydov, both of whom spoke fluent French although not Spanish, should be landed first, to parlay with their hosts, or enemies. An armed group would escort them in a boat. Rezanov, who did speak halting Spanish, would remain on board lest it emerge that Spain and Russia were at war.

Fortune smiled on the Russians. Arrillaga, the provincial governor, and Argüello, the regional commander, were away at Monterey. The latter's son, deputizing for his father, was an amiable youth who had received instructions that a Russian squadron led by Kruzenshtern might be expected and was friendly. He welcomed Langsdorf and Davydov civilly. Rezanov was accepted as a guest at the presidio at which, over the next few days, he made a politic but honourable conquest of the daughter of the house. Maria de la Concepcion. When Argüllo returned, sick Russians were recovering, friars were attempting to arrange illegal barter, and a Russian officer was courting his daughter.[37]

Argüello was polite. Because Rezanov was not a Roman Catholic, a marriage was impossible, no matter how high his rank might be, unless he waited for a special dispensation from the Pope and for the king of Spain's approval. Rezanov agreed to wait; and Arrillaga gave consent to the betrothal and to the purchase of a quantity of grain, for specie. There is another, drier version of events at the presidio, in which the sequence of the governor's approval of the trade and the betrothal are reversed. "It must," says Bancroft justly, "be confessed that this celebrated courtship had a solid substratum or superstructure of ambition and diplomacy. . . . And it was not until all other expedients had failed that Rezanov pressed his suit so far as to propose."[38] For his part, Langsdorf was also sceptical. Rezanov's marriage to Maria would, perhaps, be a "vast step gained towards promoting the political objects he had so much at heart";[39] yet it was hardly probable, in Langsdorf's view, that it would lead to steady, profitable Russo-Spanish commerce in the area, unless a nearby Russian settlement were countenanced by Spain, and that was most unlikely.

But however that might be, the Russians' first and keenest wants had now been satisfied. The *Juno*'s cargo was unloaded and her hold was filled with various provisions to the value of about $5,000.[40] Rezanov's name nowhere appeared in local records of the trade. After six weeks, *Juno* set sail for Sitka Sound. Rezanov told Maria de la Concepcion that he would take her to St. Petersburg, to fame and luxury, within two years. First he must arrange a formal Russo-Spanish understanding on the vexed matter of international trade in California, after the necessary meetings with the tsar and with the king of Spain. Whilst in Madrid, he would of course seek royal sanction for his marriage to Maria.

She waited many years before at last joining the convent of St. Catherine, Benicia.[41] Rezanov reached the North-west Coast, but then delayed at Novo-Arkhangel'sk to supervise the building of *Avos'*. Not till the last days of September did he finally proceed towards Okhotsk, as a result of which, torrential autumn rains found him en route for Krasnoiarsk. Ignoring swamps and freezing spells, he hurried on. Worn out and no longer in Langsdorf's company, he took five months to reach Irkutsk whence, late in February 1807, he went on towards his death on 1 March. Maria heard the details of his death only in 1842, from Sir George Simpson, who was then on his world tour.[42]

Rezanov was the single Russian government official who, in the first decade of the century, not only could but did delay the process by which power in the settlements passed to the agents of the Navy. For Baranov, he remained a presence several years after his death, having bequeathed shadowy projects in Hawaii, by the shores of the Columbia, in Upper California, all destined to preoccupy company servants. In his overall design for the new Russia overseas, a central role had been assigned to the chief manager and smaller parts to naval officers. At least his death had put Baranov and the Company at liberty to husband the resources that they had and to adapt half-finished blueprints for expansion to material and maritime realities of which Rezanov had, from first to last, had only the most tentative of grasps. And this Baranov did, with the result that after early and expensive disappointments, the Company did not persist on the Columbia, but concentrated mainly on the North and, since supplies of grain were vital, on the coasts of California and on Hawaii.

As a courtier and as a landsman with a fine unwillingness to trouble with minutiae for one trained in the law, Rezanov stood apart from his successors as the leading Russian actors on the North Pacific stage. He had admirers in the Company who stressed the wideness of his vision, not his tendency to act high-handedly; and he has found some advocates in recent times.[43] But by the members of a generation that was young in 1800, he was treated harshly. ''An impetuous, quick-tempered individual,'' in the opinion of V. M. Golovnin, ''he was a fruitful scribbler; a great talker; a fellow better able to build castles in the air than to realize a well-laid plan—in sum, a man completely lacking in the patience and ability to realize large, distant goals.''[44] The comments are unjust.

What is significant, however, is that Captain Golovnin spoke for an unofficial party, had a brief, and so expressed himself *à thèse*. In his own circle, he had won his case already; for within it, both Rezanov and Baranov were regarded as anachronistic agents of civilian supremacy and enemies of naval influence. Rezanov had postponed the day when naval officers, not managers, would run the North Pacific colonies, but he had done no more. That he had done even so much was thanks in large measure to attitudes and policies adopted, and adhered to until his own death, by the company chief manager at Novo-Arkhangel'sk.

Baranov did his best to give reality and substance to the grandiose designs that were Rezanov's legacies. Because those projects lacked a solid underpinning of materiel and manpower, however, they could only be adventures in the true sense of the word. Indeed, as K. T. Khlebnikov observed in his biography and study of Baranov, whom he personally knew and highly honoured, it was never possible that he could realize a half of what Rezanov had in mind. "He had to struggle with both cold and hunger, needs of every kind, and with internal and external foes."[45] It was these problems that impelled him to support or to initiate adventures in strategically untenable positions such as Kauai and Bodega Bay. He had no choice but to attempt to take advantage of a temporary absence of effective European opposition and to press on south and build. By 1812, Russians were settled on the coast of California (Mad-shui-nui, known as Ross or Fort Rossiia). Three years earlier, a tentative beginning had been made in the Hawaiian Islands. True, the Russian presence there was ephemeral; and even Ross was only held for thirty years. But the Russians had at least made the attempt, without encouragement from any central ministry, moreover, to establish new Pacific colonies. From one source or another, Russian outposts in the North had to be fed. In these respects, Baranov's personal achievements were considerable.[46]

THE VOYAGES OF *NIKOLAI* AND *KAD'IAK* (1808-12)

In September 1808, Baranov sent two company-owned vessels south to trade in California: *Nikolai*, schooner (Navigator Nikolai Bulygin), and *Kad'iak*, ex-*Myrtle*, brig (Navigator A. Petrov). With the *Nikolai* went, besides Bulygin's wife and several Aleut women, a hunting-trading party led by V. A. Tarakanov. The arrangement was that *Nikolai* would investigate the mouth and lower reach of the Columbia to barter with the Indians and with a view to colonizing (as Rezanov had proposed in 1806),[47] then join the *Kad'iak* at Gray's Harbour and proceed to California.

Kad'iak, with Baranov's second-in-command, Ivan Kuskov, aboard, had a relatively easy passage south to Bodega, where Aleut hunters caught some nineteen hundred otter.[48] But the *Nikolai,* caught by winds and currents, was destroyed close to Olympic Peninsula, off Destruction Island. Most of her company were killed by Quillayute or Makah Indians, poisoned by fungi in the woods, or simply lost. Anna Bulygina was taken by a Makah chief as a temporary wife, and a handful of survivors were eventually rescued by the *Lydia* of Boston (Captain Brown). Bulygin and his comrades were restored to Novo-Arkhangel'sk on 9 June 1809, after some fifteen months of slavery and beatings. Bulygina was said to have committed suicide. Nothing was saved from *Nikolai*'s hold.[49]

Kuskov produced a very full and positive report on Bodega Bay, where he had managed to establish good relations with the Indians and to erect a group of temporary buildings. On the strength of it, Baranov asked the company directors to petition Alexander to induce Spain to remove the ban on international trade in California and to countenance a modest "southern outpost."[50] The mention of an outpost was received with equanimity. The board did seek Imperial permission to establish a new settlement, but in "New Albion," not in California. Probably the company directors were conveniently vague as to the limits of New Albion in arguing the case.[51] In all events, Imperial assurance of support in case of trouble with the Spaniards was considerably less than watertight. The board, nevertheless, regarded it as a clear signal to proceed, and once again Baranov sent Kuskov to California.

This time, however, the reliable Kuskov met with ill-fortune and was forced back north by winds and hostile Indians. The setback had political results, for he was carrying a lengthy proclamation from the company directors to inhabitants of Upper California.[52] Couched in friendly and conciliatory terms, it stressed the mutual advantages of trade. It had been signed on 15 March 1810, but was not destined to provoke concern in Mexico or Spain for several years. In its tardiness lay much of its significance.

Kuskov returned to California in 1812 with "all deemed necessary" for founding the new establishment.

There were in the company 95 men of Russian blood, and probably 80 Aleuts. . . . In the course of a few months, a fortified village had arisen on the shore. The site, selected probably during the previous visit, was some eighteen miles above Bodega Bay, called by the natives Mad-shui-nui, in latitude 38° 33', long. 123° 15'. . . . The fort, with its ten cannon, was erected on a bluff some 100' or more above the sea.[53]

Thanks to Baranov's bold decision to co-operate with North Americans in mutually profitable poaching of sea-otter on the coasts of California and to Kuskov's pragmatic industry, matters looked promising in California at least. From the voyage of *O'Cain* alone, under the terms of an agreement reached in 1809 with Winship, the Company acquired 2,728 prime skins—a good return on an investment of the services and time of ninety hunters.[54] Baranov came to terms with four or five New Englanders. By 1812, those foreign partners had provided him with 7,000 skins.[55]

In short, Baranov had successes in realizing Rezanov's dreams. Always, however, he was struggling with the historic problem of provisioning; always, resources were extended to the limit in the colonies. And in themselves these harsh realities, which were compounded in their gravity by an incessant lack of seamen and of ocean-going vessels, merely served as ammunition for those servants of the Navy who contended that the Navy should control the North Pacific settlements.

Before considering the growth of that opinion in St. Petersburg, however, it is useful to survey one final venture that was also, and par excellence, Rezanov's legacy. Not only was that venture undertaken for the Company in 1808 by a commissioned naval officer, Lt. Leontii Adrianovich Gagemeister (German: Ludwig Karl August von Hagemeister); it also marked the start of a new phase in the development of Russian naval influence in the Pacific.

GAGEMEISTER AND *NEVA* IN THE HAWAIIAN ISLANDS (1808-10)

On being offered the command of the *Neva* at the age of twenty-six, Lieutenant Gagemeister had already given evidence of great ability. His early years of service had in fact followed a pattern reminiscent of Lisianskii's and, especially, of Kruzenshtern's. An ancient Baltic family;[56] the Naval Corps; a spell of Baltic duty; early contact with the British: it was all familiar. In 1802 he was in action in the Caribbean Sea (St. Lucia, with *Argo*);[57] in 1804, with Collingwood and Nelson.[58] Commended to the Russian Naval Ministry and wreathed in glory of the shade that the dying Nelson had bestowed on every officer around him, he returned to Baltic duty and was thereupon promoted in June 1805. Soon afterwards, he was successful in obtaining command of the *Neva,* just back from China. His orders were to sail to the North Pacific settlements with iron, naval stores, and an assortment of supplies. He was a circumspect commander, and the voyage was conspicuously slow. A late departure from San Salvadore (9 March 1807) led him to choose the eastern route to the Pacific, and he paused to water, revictual, and rest his men in New South Wales before proceeding on 1 July for Sitka.[59] Baranov welcomed him in mid-September.

Since Gagemeister seemed at the outset to reciprocate Baranov's sympathy, all went more easily than might have been expected. Baranov, who was more than twice his age, appears to have looked on Gagemeister as an erudite and earnest officer. Baranov then gave orders for *Neva* to take supplies to Kodiak, and also mentioned the Hawaiian Islands project. Gagemeister gathered that Rezanov had proposed that, both to guarantee a food supply for northern settlements and to improve the Russian Company's position *vis-à-vis* the North Americans, a settlement, a depot-cum-plantation, should be founded in the Islands. Ostensibly, the Russians would arrive only to purchase salt and other needed foodstuffs. By coincidence, salt was already badly needed. Gagemeister took his sailing orders from Baranov and proceeded on 10 November 1808 first to Kodiak, then to Oahu.

> He stayed there (comments K. T. Khlebnikov) three months, after which he visited the islands of Maui and Kauai, loaded a considerable quantity of salt, and arrived at Petropavlovsk on June 8. . . . He returned to Sitka on September 2 1809.[60]

Viewed as a record of Hawaiian-Russian dealings in the early part of 1809, this passage is a masterpiece of politic omissions. As for Gagemeister's letters to the company directors, dated 1 May and 20 June, describing what had passed during his visit to the Islands, they were certainly misleading. In the former, which he wrote aboard *Neva* just after he had left Oahu, he had this to say:

> One of these islands can produce foods in quantities sufficient to supply a large part of Asiatic Russia. . . . The Bostonians spread rumors on these islands that the Russians wanted to come and settle there. At first, King Kamehameha was afraid of us, but now he says: "Let the Russians come; we have lived without them, we can also live with them."
>
> If we were to undertake a settlement, we should start it on the island of Molokai, which is more fertile than the others. In the southern part, there is a port for small boats, and near this island are the best fisheries. The king would be willing to sell us either this or some other island. . . . If we cannot occupy the whole island now, it is possible to buy part of the land from the king. . . .
>
> For defence in this locality, it would be sufficient to maintain one or two towers with one or more cannon each. To occupy this territory would require only about 20 Russians for defence and about the same number for agriculture. The writer is sure that these islands can be occupied by friendly methods; but if force is necessary, then two ships would be sufficient.[61]

False notes are audible throughout. What king, the chairman of the board, M. M. Buldakov, might have asked, would sell "us" Molokai? Did Kamehameha say that he would let the Russians come and build a tower or a fort and bring their cannon and their ships? Why does an island now decrease in size to part of one, now swell to several islands? But above all, it is Gagemeister's use of the conditional that interests the modern reader: had he, or had he not, arrived with orders to attempt to purchase land for a plantation and a fort?

Numerous students of the period have reinterpreted such evidence as is available for and against Russian designs in 1809.[62] Claims that Baranov did indeed intend that Gagemeister's visit should result both in a settlement and in a Russian *point d'appui* were soon put forward—by Archibald Campbell, who had been on the spot, among others.[63] Campbell was a Scot who had been given working passage on *Neva* from Kodiak. In an account of his Pacific wanderings, published in Edinburgh in June 1816, he stated:

It would appear that the Russians had determined to form a settlement upon these islands; at least, preparations were made for the purpose. The ship had a house in frame on board, and intimation was given that volunteers would be received.[64]

There is no reason for mistrusting Campbell's evidence. Though he was not a great admirer of the Russians, he had no anti-Russian animus or private axe to grind. And at least one of Lisianskii's officers of 1803-6, Vasilii Berkh, is known to have considered that a colonizing effort should be made without delay. ("These islands do not belong to any European Power, and must belong to Russia.")[65] He and others in *Neva* in 1804-5 had doubtless emphasized the value of the Islands as a food base to Baranov. Berkh, at least, claimed that "one Russian naval vessel should be sent down to those Islands *every autumn,* from Kamchatka. She should winter in the Islands and return to the peninsula in May."[66] All things considered, it seems probable that Gagemeister's orders were to act only if circumstances favoured an attempt at semi-permanent colonization.[67] Obviously the political realities obliged him to abandon such ideas and, moreover, to reject an alliance with "Tomari" (Kaumualii), who again sought Russian aid against Kamehameha.[68] With the blessing of Kaumualii, the Company might well have gained a toehold in the Islands. But the cost would have been high: Kamehameha's enmity.

It was an error on Baranov's part not to have gone himself to meet Kamehameha. Yet, his reasons for dispatching Gagemeister on so delicate a mission were adequate. He was no longer young or even fit. He had enough logistical and other problems to exhaust him in the northern settlements without venturing further afield. Lt. Gagemeister spoke good English, which Kamehameha and his rival understood, and was an officer of wide experience. Finally, Gagemeister seemed to recognize the complex nature of his mission in the Islands and the value of a well-defended mid-Pacific farm.[69]

In reality, the young lieutenant's knowledge and experience of foreigners, in peace or war, had no bearing on the Islands. What was needed was a good and recent knowledge of the social, economic, and political conditions there—a knowledge of the kind and depth that even the *promyshlennik* Sysoi Slobodchikov, who had visited the Islands in 1807 in the *Nikolai*, had not had time to gather. Gagemeister was acquainted with the *Voyages* of Cook, Vancouver, and Broughton;[70] even Broughton's information was outdated for his purposes. All of this moreover was completely incidental to Lt. Gagemeister's underlying and profound unsuitability as an executor of the Rezanov scheme. He was, at best, a lukewarm advocate of the extension of the Company's authority. Indeed he was only concerned about it to the extent that Russian influence in the Pacific was essentially dependent on the welfare of the Company. What was more, his attitude towards the Company as agent of the state had somewhat changed since his arrival in the colonies as a result of all he saw. It was the pattern of the future.

The actual results of Gagemeister's four-month sojourn in the Islands, apart from the acquisition of some salt and the surveying of a half a dozen bays, are summarized by Bradley:

In February 1810, thirteen months after the arrival of *Neva*, an English whaler touched at Honolulu. When it departed early in March, it carried Archibald Campbell, to whom Kamehameha entrusted a letter to George III. In this letter, the British monarch was reminded of the promises made on his behalf by Vancouver, and he was requested to send a man-of-war to the Hawaiian Islands. In August, Kamehameha addressed a second communication to King George, acknowledging himself to be "a subject of His Most Gracious Majesty," and again requesting some tangible evidence of British protection.[71]

Possibly incidents occurred after *Neva* sailed for Kamchatka and before the whaler came that gave Kamehameha reason to believe that he was threatened by an outside force. The island of Hawaii itself had twenty-three white residents even by 1800,[72] and the number of Americans was growing. All in all, however, it is likely that Kamehameha's interest in British suzerainty was a consequence of pleasant memories of other times coupled with happenings during *Neva*'s stay at Oahu. That the king never again regarded Russians with an open friendliness has been well shown by recent students of the rise and fall of Georg Anton Schaeffer as the petty-king of Kauai (1816-17).[73] Even by 1810, friendly relations between King Kamehameha and Baranov had collapsed. Baranov sent no word of explanation or apology for Gagemeister's attitudes or actions, and Kamehameha was disposed to credit rumours that the Russians had, indeed, future designs upon Hawaiian independence.

Baranov's failure to respond to the Hawaiian situation, which was certainly significant in the development of Russian naval influence over the colonies, largely resulted from his personal position at the time, that is to say, in 1810 when Gagemeister was replaced as naval visitor at Novo-Arkhangel'sk by Captain V. M. Golovnin, of the *Diana,* sloop of war.

V. M. GOLOVNIN'S FIRST CONTACT WITH BARANOV (1810)

Baranov had been planning retirement for years by 1810. In 1805, he had discussed it with Rezanov. Three years later, Buldakov had requested him to stay until a suitable replacement should arrive. Baranov had reasons other than his health for considering retirement. He had learned of the death of his first wife and so could consider a return either to Kargopol' or to Siberia escorted by his native wife and their children.[74] The fort at Novo-Arkhangel'sk had been completed in essentials. Kuskov was competent. Lastly, he knew that there were those who wished him dead: in 1809, nine of the hunters then at Novo-Arkhangel'sk, being miserably fed like all the servants of the Company including the chief manager himself, had plotted a revolt *à la* Benyowski. The men had hoped to seize a vessel and escape, with thirty women and the best part of the edible supplies, to Easter Island. Baranov made a terrible appearance in the room where Naplavkov, the leading spirit of the malcontents, and his associates were actually signing a pathetic note of general defiance.[75] But the situation shook him, and he wrote to the main office yet again about retiring and, in the early part of 1810, drank heavily. ''For safety,'' he dispatched his wife to Kodiak. Suspicious, irritable, and in constant expectation of his replacement, Johann Koch, who died en route to the Pacific, Baranov cut an unimpressive figure when V. M. Golovnin first met him on 30 June 1810. It was not, indeed, as a result of his appearance that Golovnin assumed a public attitude so hostile both to the Company itself and to its trading operations on the Coast. As is clear from his subsequent reports,[76] Golovnin's opinion of the Company had taken shape while he was still in Europe and had crystallized during the winter in Kamchatka. On the other hand, Baranov's state and swiftly changing moods certainly strengthened Golovnin's hostility towards the Company and did so at a crucial time.

8

V. M. Golovnin and *Diana*

Like Kruzenshtern, Lisianskii, and Gagemeister, Vasilii Mikhailovich Golovnin (1776-1831) had served in British warships as a Russian Volunteer.[1] In the process he had grown more conscious than before of Russia's Asian and Pacific opportunities. His service contacts with the British were particularly close. As an orphaned adolescent, he had fallen under James Trevenen's influence when both were serving in the ship *Ne Tron' Menia*. It was almost as if Reval were the centre of a North Pacific club and Kronstadt a creche for the Pacific plans and projects of young officers. Trevenen's influence led Golovnin to master English thoroughly. He read Cook's *Voyages* in the original. Twice in the 1790's, his facility in English and his competence in signalling resulted in his serving as liaison officer between the Russians and the English in the Channel, where both were on blockade.[2] Admiral Makarov's favour followed him. He served with Collingwood and Nelson (1802-5), seeing action in *Plantagenet, Ville de Paris,* and *Prince of Wales* against the French. When not in action, he performed repeated guard and convoy duties and visited Jamaica.[3] Like his predecessors, he examined the colonial administration of the Caribbean islands that he saw; did well in battle;[4] and requesting an extension of his foreign secondment, agreed to go unpaid. Within a month of his eventual return to Baltic duty in August 1806, he was appointed to *Diana,* sloop, with sailing orders for Okhotsk and Petropavlovsk.

Diana's voyage was, officially, one of provisionment, surveying, and discovery in North Pacific waters. In reality, as was made clear to Golovnin, the Naval Ministry had one more end in mind in sending her around the globe. The further object was to demonstrate effective Russian hegemony over certain tracts of water between Asia and the Coast. In build, *Diana* was a storeship displacing 300 tons, and in keeping with her function as supply ship (*inter alia*) for the Pacific settlements, she was especially capacious for her length (84 feet). Both in

Russia and abroad, despite all this, she was regarded as a warship; and indeed she mounted fourteen six-pounders, four carronades of eight-pounders, and half a dozen falconets.[5] Moreover, Golovnin took orders from the Naval Ministry, as represented by the nationalistic P. V. Chichagov, not from the Company. But some things seemed unchanging, and, as usual, too little time was given for the preparations vital to a lengthy voyage. Thirty days of almost frenzied yard activity were ended by an order that postponed the sailing date by nine whole months.[6]

As his second-in-command, Golovnin chose P. I. Rikord (1776-1855.)[7] Their relationship confirmed and fixed the pattern formed in 1802-3 by Kruzenshtern and Lisianskii. They, too, had met at Reval (in 1793); their paths had likewise crossed during a "North Sea Period." Both men had served under Khanykov for two years; and both had had a series of encounters between 1796 and 1799 with Aleksei Greig, back from the Indies and Canton by way of London.[8]

As Golovnin's instructions made apparent, Russia's naval and strategic objects on the Coast and in the Kurile Islands were quite different by 1807 from what they had been in 1802. Yet it was not the total outline of the Navy's interests in the Pacific that had altered since Trevenen's and Mulovskii's day. It was merely that some aspects of the overall design had gained more emphasis in altered national circumstances. Exploitation of Pacific fur resources; providing material support and moral aid to Russia's agents in the far North-East and East; discovery; hydrography and the pursuit of other sciences; convincing the world of Russia's influence and strength in certain North Pacific waters; and the furtherance of diplomatic aims: such were the pieces of the pattern both in Golovnin's own time and in Lisianskii's. What had gained in emphasis since 1802 was the assertive element.

THE VOYAGE OF *DIANA* (1807-9)

Golovnin and Rikord sailed from Kronstadt on 25 July 1807. *Diana* had a crew of fifty-five, excluding officers and, as the latter numbered only six, was sparely manned and handsomely provisioned on leaving the Baltic. Like Kruzenshtern, Golovnin was deeply conscious of the value of such missions as "a nursery for seamen," and while the *Diana* carried only one lieutenant, Rikord, there were two midshipmen and three naval cadets.[9] It was a young and energetic company. The cargo was mainly naval stores: rigging and cables, canvas, iron, anchors, tools, and also foodstuffs. Heavy stores were even used as ballast to increase the cost-efficiency. At Petropavlovsk, they were always in demand and short supply.[10]

The political position on the Continent was tense when Golovnin set out from

Kronstadt. It was not supposed, however, that events would move so fast as to affect the voyagers. In fact, the Russians saw a British naval squadron shell the forts of Copenhagen, and they were sobered by the sight. Cannonballs from Kronberg fell not far from the *Diana,* and a drifting, blazing ship threatened to set her afire. Watched from Nelson's flagship, but unhindered, Golovnin went on his way to Helsingör and so to Portsmouth. Copenhagen set the tone for his whole voyage.

Britain and Russia were at peace in mid-September 1807. On the other hand, the meaning of the pact arranged at Tilsit had been obvious for weeks. But *Diana* needed scientific instruments ordered in London in advance. In the event, the Russian company was well enough received on reaching Portsmouth; nor were difficulties made when Golovnin, having delayed almost eight weeks while he provisioned for the passage to Brazil, decided suddenly to sail on 1 November. He had no doubt received intelligence that gave him reason to depart; and, shortly afterwards, news of a break between the Russian and the British courts was duly published and the government sent orders to the stations where *Diana* might put in for water and provisions to detain her. It also cancelled papers, lately issued to her captain in London at the Russian embassy's request, which guaranteed a safe, unhindered passage through all regions where the British writ then ran.

Golovnin crossed the Equator on 20 December and reached Santa Catharina Island on 10 January 1808. The Portuguese authorities were friendly, and *Diana* and her company, well rested, headed south across the mouth of the La Plata. They rounded Cape Horn on 12 February; but here, the weather turned ferocious. For thirteen days and nights, the Russians fought to make a mile of headway westward. Finally, the elements prevailed. Golovnin set course towards South Africa. Even the longer eastward passage proved a hard and stormy one; but on the morning of 21 April, *Diana* entered Simon's Bay in safety and dropped anchor. She was boarded that same hour, and her people were arrested and removed by jolly-boat. Armed British sailors stayed aboard her.

The Russians were detained for thirteen months at Cape Town. They would certainly have languished longer still, had Golovnin, insulted by demands that his subordinates reduce their rations, angry that his sloop had not been mentioned in despatches sent from London, and concerned about collapsing morale, not made a daring escape on 16 May 1809. The wind was high. Only the frigate *Proserpina*'s sails remained unfurled; all other vessels in the bay were unprepared to put to sea. "At half past six, in a rainy squall and in overcast weather, I ordered cables cut . . . . By 10 o'clock, we were in the open sea. Our detention had lasted a year and 25 days."[11]

For fifty days *Diana* pressed on east, avoiding land. By mid-July, they had rounded Van Diemen's Land and crossed the Tasman Sea, coming at last into the latitudes of the New Hebrides. Golovnin dropped anchor in the inlet shown on

European maps as Resolution Bay, in Tana. All around lay heavy jungle. Now and then, volcanic rumblings could be heard. The native craft which soon approached were just as Cook described them, and a stilted, friendly dialogue ensued. Barter began: fruit, hogs, and firewood for Russian mirrors, knives, and beads. One way in which the barter differed from the Russians' trade at Nuku Hiva five years earlier was that it gave no place to native artifacts or thought to ethnological collections. Though a regular compiler of all proper information, which included local customs and resources, Golovnin was no savant. In this respect, he differed basically from Kruzenshtern, Otto von Kotzebue, and the later Bellingshausen. His intelligence was of a political complexion.

Barter soon provided *Diana*'s company with an abundance of bananas, yams, and coconuts, and Golovnin relaxed a little. Armed watch was maintained nevertheless. Next morning, once the native group had laid their weapons down, about twenty casks were filled with water from a lake described by Cook. Barter expanded, as did local confidence in Golovnin's intentions: for a dozen coconuts, an iron nail; for a pig, a shirt or hatchet. By the fourth day of her stay, more than a thousand coconuts, more than a hundred pounds of sugar-cane, and quantities of breadfruit had been stowed aboard *Diana*. Peace continued to the last. Having arrived in a condition of emotional and physical exhaustion, Golovnin set sail from Tana reinvigorated on 24 July 1809. For Golovnin especially, but also for his men, the Tana sojourn was a respite after months of strain, a brief hiatus between tension in South Africa and strife in the Pacific. Following too long a voyage out from Kronstadt, all approached Avacha Bay with great impatience in the third week of September. For many, it was thoughts of life ashore that protracted the *Diana*'s final passage to Kamchatka; for Golovnin, it was the wish to test his views on both Kamchatka and the colonies and harbours to the east against the litmus of reality. Even on arrival in Avacha Bay, he was convinced that in the Russian national interest Imperial authority should now replace the jurisdiction of a merchant company in the Pacific.[12]

GOLOVNIN IN KAMCHATKA AND THE COLONIES

Golovnin spent two peripatetic and extremely active winters in Kamchatka (1809-11), taking notes as he proceeded from one area of maladministration to another. Shipping, commerce, buildings, everything was in a sorry state. At Petropavlovsk, there were still outbreaks of scurvy, though the cure was common knowledge. Peculation, sloth, and drunkenness were to be found, he insisted in reports of 1810, in the most flourishing condition in those areas where trade and agriculture had been put aside. At length, on 10 May 1810, he left Kamchatka for the Coast and an encounter with Chief Manager Baranov. His subsequent account of the meeting and of Novo-Arkhangel'sk made his opinions very plain:

At one in the afternoon, Mr. Baranov left us and returned to the shore, having invited me and all my officers to dine with him. Those officers whose service duties permitted them to quit the sloop, had the honour of so doing. On our reaching the fort, at 2 P.M., Mr. Baranov did us the entirely unexpected honour of a seven-gun salute . . . . What most astonished us in Mr. Baranov's dwelling was an extensive library in almost every European language and a collection of masterly paintings. I concede that I am no judge of art. Even *I,* however, could appreciate that such paintings deserved to be hung in some better place than this . . . . Observing my amazement, Mr. Baranov explained that the company directors had judged it necessary to send the paintings out.[13]

But pomp and luxury where they were inappropriate, and made the more so by surrounding destitution, were the least of many aspects of the Sitka situation that distressed him. First, the place had not in fact been made impregnable against attack by Tlingits or by hostile foreigners. Second, it had no school, however humble. Third, it had no hospital, no store of basic medicines, no doctor. Fourth, there was no priest, despite the Company's repeated protestations of concern for the salvation of so many natives' souls. But, Golovnin asked rhetorically, had not Buldakov's and Baranov's Company conspicuously failed even on the level of mere *trade,* being dependent for supplies on foreign traders? But for North American self-interest, Baranov and his people might have starved:

On coming to America, we feared to find the Company outpost in a pitiable state for want of food. And so it would have been, were it not for citizens of the American republic. . . . And this was the extent of the directors' foresight: not having so much as assured supplies for their own settlements from their resources, they insisted that no foreigners bring food to those same settlements! Had the American government been empowered by its own constitution to place the requested interdict on its citizens' activities . . . then hunger must have led to the most dreadful consequences in the settlements. For even last year [1809], a total want of bread was the cause of various illnesses, which led to quite a few deaths of Company servants. And on one of the Company's vessels, almost half the crew—of seamen from the Imperial naval service—died of hunger.[14]

The presence of American free traders had at times been very fortunate for the beleaguered, ailing servants of the Company. But, argued Golovnin, the Russian government should not suppose that "Boston captains" would support a starving outpost if their own financial interests were not served.[15] For many years the

Company's incompetence to guard its own (and Russia's) interests against the depredations of New Englanders like Ayres, Winship, Peacock and O'Cain, had led to incidents such as the *Mentor*'s walrus massacres. In Russian waters, out of season, that Nor'wester's crewmen had disposed of several thousand walruses, then traded guns for other peltry in the area of Novo-Arkhangel'sk. It was inevitable, Golovnin believed, that such events would recur till Russian strength was used in the defence of Russian interests.

Such, then, was his position at the close of 1810. The shift of regional authority from Manager Baranov's to the Navy's hands might have been rapid notwithstanding Golovnin's comparatively modest rank and lack of influence at court, had he returned at once to European Russia. But he stayed. He was not destined to express his strictures on the Company in contexts that would make them irresistably effective for another seven years. Together with four sailors and two other naval officers, he was held captive by the Japanese on Kunashiri Island and, later, Hakodate, for twenty-seven months. The experience convinced him of the need for Russian warships to be permanently stationed in the North Pacific area and heightened the respect with which his opinions on all North Pacific matters were heard out when he did return to European Russia. His fortunes thus delayed the final ousting of the Company from its position of executive authority over the settlements, yet, at the same time, made the outcome far more probable.

THE JAPANESE CAPTIVITY OF V. M. GOLOVNIN

In March 1811, orders reached Kamchatka for *Diana* to proceed from Petropavlovsk on a survey of the southern Kurile Islands, Shantar Islands, and "the shores of Tartary" north of 53° 28′N. Golovnin's enviable task was to finish work begun by La Pérouse, Sarychev, Broughton, and particularly Kruzenshtern, not one of whom had covered more than portions of the sea north of Japan. *Diana* sailed on 8 May, edging her way through broken ice, and made for Ushishiru, Ketoi, and Uruppu.[16]

The ship flew no flag, for Golovnin did not intend to provoke the Japanese unnecessarily. Despite that gesture, he was soon in an uncomfortable position. On 29 June, when they were off the shore of Etorofu, the Russians saw a group of men rushing about, gesticulating. They supposed them to be Ainu, and Golovnin sent Ensign Fedor Mur (Moore) and Assistant Navigator Vasilii Novitskii in a boat to question them. A little later, Golovnin himself went in a boat. He was surprised to find that Mur was making halting conversation with a group of Japanese: the Japanese could speak a little Ainu, and the Ainu understood a little Russian. Soon, more Japanese approached. All were in armour and had swords and heavy muskets. Ishizaka Kihei, who was in command, asked Golovnin why he had come. If the Russians wished to trade, he added sensibly, they should proceed along the coast until they reached a larger settlement, where there was something to be had.[17] The Japanese were courteous, but wary. "Such a people," Golovnin observed in retrospect, "cannot conceive what business it may be of foreign countries to send vessels to describe alien lands out of mere curiosity."[18] He therefore happily accepted the commercial explanation of *Diana's* presence. Next, the Japanese referred, somewhat obliquely, to the enmity created towards Russians by Davydov and Khvostov. Golovnin replied that "such attacks upon them by two craft of tiny size could hardly have been launched at the behest of the monarch of a great and mighty State."[19] The two young officers had acted independently of orders from St. Petersburg. Though tense, the meeting passed off fairly well, and at the end of it, the Japanese offered their visitors a drink.[20] Next morning, Golovnin crossed over to the east shore of Uruppu; with him went an Ainu, one "Aleksei Maksimovich," who spoke good Russian. From him, Golovnin learned of a settlement and harbour on the sheltered southern shore of Kunashiri where supplies might be obtained. He decided to proceed there without delay, especially because he wished to chart the harbour and the strait between the island and Hokkaido.[21]

Not till mid-July did currents, winds, and fog relent and let *Diana* make her way into this strait. Almost immediately, when she did so, fires blazed beyond her on the capes. A sound of guns came through the mist; two cannon-balls fell near her bow. The scene was set for a small international incident, which ended unheroically when Rikord found an empty fishing village, seized some fuel, fish, and rice and, anxious not to earn the name of thief, left a few articles behind him on the beach. Golovnin returned next morning to make sure that these were gone; and so they were.

What can be said of these non-meetings, which continued like a game of hide-and-seek among the mists, for five full days (18-22 July)? Only, perhaps, that Golovnin would have done better not to think that the Khvostov-Davydov raids would be so easily dismissed and that the message of abandoned fishing villages, cannon, and bonfires was plain: no Russian visitors were wanted. Golovnin was not disposed to read that message. On 23 July, his importunities led to the expedition's downfall. Again he made a landing accompanied by Mur, and again he met a group of Japanese. This time, they were expecting him. He was invited into Kunashiri fortress, which he entered with Mur, Navigator Andrei Khlebnikov, the Ainu "Aleksei," and four sailors. He was shocked to see standing in ranks around the inner fortress walls about three hundred armed Japanese and many hundreds of Ainu.

The Japanese commander, Nasa Masatoki, had been waiting for some time. He asked the Russians many questions, and the answers were recorded. Golovnin was asked how many men *Diana* carried and whether there were comparable vessels in the area. He patriotically inflated the crew to 102 and asserted that the Russian Navy had a number of large warships at Okhotsk, at Petropavlovsk, and along the North-west Coast. Mur noticed that while Golovnin was speaking, naked swords were being issued to the soldiers. Finally, the Russians panicked and rushed towards the fortress gate. Yelling, the Japanese closed in and took them prisoner. That night, they were taken in a small boat to Hokkaido and incarcerated in a set of zoo-like cages in a dark and massive jail at Hakodate. They were brought before the commandant of Hakodate on 22 August for the first of many long interrogations.[22]

Often, the commandant's questions were embarrassing. How, for example, could the Russians justify Khvostov's giving a heavy silver medal to the Ainu chieftain on the west shore of Aniwa Bay on 12 October 1806 and taking Sakhalin and all its people under the "protection" of the tsar?[23] It was impossible, declared the commandant, that a lieutenant should have dared to do such things unless he had orders; therefore, Alexander knew about the medal and Khvostov's infamous letter of October 1806. To Golovnin's good fortune the commandant could read no Russian and relied upon his prisoners' translation of the letter: they could try at least to modify the meaning of the operative phrases, and they did. *Iunona*, Golovnin proposed, although indeed described as "frigate" in the letter, had in fact been a mere merchantman. The Russian word was a generic one. As to the medal, the lieutenant (whose behaviour he himself deplored) had doubtless purchased it. The Russian flag and naval ensign that Khvostov had drawn in ink at the conclusion of his letter were, no doubt, mere decorations. For the prisoners, the situation was unpleasant. It became still more so when the Japanese brought to their cages wooden boards inscribed, "Diana: Golovnin: 1811." These, observed the commandant, had been discovered on the shores of Kunashiri and Etorofu, prominently posted. Were they signs of territorial assertion? Wretchedly, the Russians pleaded that the boards were not assertive but informative: if *Diana* had been wrecked, their compatriots could readily have traced her route.[24] No doubt her failure to return to Petropavlovsk had already caused concern. The air was thick with disbelief.

And yet the Russians underwent no harsher treatment than before the wooden boards had been produced. They were, indeed, visited daily by a stream of friendly Japanese, whose conversation gave no hint of what their fate might be. But they already knew that developments elsewhere had not been favourable to them. Matsumae was demanding that the commandant extract more information; and the Ainu were attempting to protect themselves by claiming that the Russians had compelled them some years earlier to reconnoitre settlements along the Kurile chain in preparation for a raid by seven Russian warships full of troops. Seven was the number hazarded by Golovnin three weeks before, when he was striving to impress the Japanese with the resources of the port of Petropavlovsk. The commandant continued to be civil while Russian nerves grew seriously strained.

Then, on 8 October, the prisoners were roped around the waist and escorted into Matsumae. After a four-day journey, they were cast into a shed in the shadow of the castle. In the shed were two small cages with heavy wooden doors, so low that Golovnin and his subordinates were forced to crawl through on their stomachs. Two days later on 14 October, they were led before the governor of Matsumae, Arao Shigeaki. He amicably asked them questions running the gamut from the Rezanov expedition to the burials of poor and wealthy Russians.[25] Golovnin perceived the governor's benevolence as a device to keep his prisoners' morale above that point at which all might have thought of suicide. His mood infected all the Russian prisoners; but though they now considered death a possibility, nothing occurred. At the suggestion of the governor, they laboured for a month on a document requesting their repatriation, but in February 1812 the plea was still in Matsumae. Next, they planned to break out, and on 6 May they actually made a mass escape. They were speedily recaptured and returned to their dark shed, where their conditions were made harsher. Then, in mid-September 1812, they were presented with two letters. Both had come from Kunashiri with a special guard. One was addressed to Golovnin, one to the officer in charge on Kunashiri; and both were signed by P. I. Rikord.[26]

THE RESCUE OF CAPTAIN GOLOVNIN (1813)

To Rikord, Golovnin's and his subordinates' imprisonment came as a shock. The *Diana* moved in closer to the fort at Kunashiri and even opened fire on the walls. Heavy fire was returned. Angry and fearful for their countrymen, the officers all signed a letter, which they placed in a cask and then threw overboard. (''My God! Will these lines reach you, and are you alive?'')[27] Explaining what they meant to do, they left the ''Bay of Treachery'' (Zaliv Izmeny) for Okhotsk.

In command there in 1810-12, was Mikhail Ivanovich Minitskii (1772-1829), an acquaintance of both Rikord and Golovnin: all three had served as Volunteers with the British. As his appointment indicated, the time of drunken rascals and of tyrants at Okhotsk was finally over there, though he himself was doing battle with the former, month by month.[28] He and Rikord were united in their anxious wrath and equally determined that the prisoners be freed, by strength of arms if need be. Both accepted, on the other hand, that to attempt a raid and rescue operation of the kind that they envisaged was beyond their own authority. It was essential that the government be made aware of the disaster and their plans at once. Minitskii wrote to the *de facto* governor-general then at Irkutsk, Nikolai Treskin. Rikord started out, without his servants, for St. Petersburg. Reaching Irkutsk, he learned that Treskin had already reported the disaster to St. Petersburg. Rikord should remain a little longer in Siberia to plan the needed rescue

operation. Treskin himself felt that a special expedition would be needed to re-
cover and avenge.

The central government did not agree that any raid on Hakodate was in order.
That Russians had been captured by the Japanese on Kunashiri Island was deplorable. But there were worse calamities to deal with; the Napoleonic armies
had already crossed the Niemen. Moscow burned. It was no time for distant,
risky expeditions that could well result in war on yet another, ill-defended front.
Rikord was told to curb his anger with the Japanese, whom he was not in a position to attack, and to proceed as best he could with survey work, stopping at
Kunashiri Island to enquire after Captain Golovnin.[29]

Rikord returned to the *Diana* at Okhotsk and put to sea early in August. Accompanied by the *Zotik,* transport (Lt. A. Filatov), and carrying a dozen extra
seamen and a half-a-dozen castaways whom he hoped to exchange in Japan for
his compatriots, he headed south. Among the castaways was Nakagawa Goroji, a
victim of Khvostov's earlier raid, who had twice tried to escape from
Bol'sheretsk. On the passage to the Kurile Islands, Rikord had the pardonably
bitter Nakagawa translate a warning paper, signed by Treskin and addressed to
the officer in charge at Kunashiri. Certain castaways, it said, had been returned
with the *Diana* as a friendly gesture; Russian captives would no doubt be set at
liberty in an exchange. If they were not, then Russian warships would arrive the
season following. The venture proved a failure from the start. Fourteen new guns
had been erected in the so-called Bay of Treachery, Nakagawa fled, and the commander of the fort would not appear.

Could Rikord take measures to "induce" the Japanese to set their prisoners at
liberty? The Russian government, preoccupied with European crisis, had already
shown its unwillingness to countenance adventures in the East. Firm steps could
very well be treated as a challenge by local Japanese authorities; but on the other
hand, *Diana's* very presence might be saving Golovnin's and his companions'
lives. Crisis approached in the shape of a small merchantman. Now desperate for
solid information about Golovnin, Rikord gave orders to the gunners to arrest
and take her. None of her passengers and crew had anything of interest to say
about the captives, and Rikord had committed an open act of war. The die was
cast, so when a larger trading vessel, *Kanze Maru* approached, she was similarly
seized. Her wealthy owner, Takadaya Kahei, was aboard. Unwittingly and reck-
lessly, Rikord had found a key to the eventual release of Golovnin. Takadaya
Kahei was taken up onto *Diana.* Perceiving his intelligence and rank, Rikord
treated him with courtesy. The Japanese responded with an unexpected zeal and
throughout the stormy three-week passage to Avacha Bay stayed close to him.
He even plunged into the study of the language, trade, geography, and history of
Russia, insofar as this was possible in the unlikely circumstances. Rikord, for his
part, bemoaned the deep misunderstandings that subsisted between Russia and
Japan. Takadaya then exclaimed: "I perceive in my misfortune Providence,

which has chosen me for its instrument. Without important reasons for going into Kunashiri Bay, I entered there by chance . . . and thereby caused you to desist from your intention of attacking the settlement; consequently, I became the saviour of tens of Russians and several hundreds of Japanese."[30] Takadaya offered to aid Rikord in his negotiations for Golovnin's release, for he was certain that more serious hostilities between the Russians and the Japanese must be averted in the interests of both. He kept his word. For several months, he served as intermediary at his own expense. Finally, in August 1813, the preliminaries to a mutually satisfactory conclusion to the drama were complete. In October, *Diana* entered Hakodate harbour with papers from Minitskii. Points of protocol having been settled and the letter from Minitskii which explicitly condemned Khvostov having been translated into Japanese and read, Rikord left the *Diana* with a retinue of twelve, making his way up to a decorated hall. The silence was profound. Officials stood in heavy silks with swords. Rikord declared that he considered himself to be at home with friends. He was correct, answered the governor, to think so. Russian vessels had alarmed the Japanese for far too long; now, peace would reign. Golovnin and his subordinates were freed. Four days later on 23 October 1813, *Diana* was at sea. From Petropavlovsk, Golovnin traveled by dogsled, reindeer, horse, carriage, and water to St. Petersburg. He reached it on 3 August 1814, exactly seven years after his departure. He and Rikord were promoted, and both were granted pensions.[31]

RUSSO-JAPANESE RELATIONS: GOLOVNIN'S REPORT

How was the pattern of Imperial activity and growth on the Pacific changed or modified by Golovnin's imprisonment? What were the consequences of his trials for the Navy's own Pacific aspirations? Neither question can be answered without reference to Golovnin's own *Notes (Zapiski),* with their passages on Russo-Japanese relations and his own, recent experiences as a prisoner.

Unlike Rezanov, Golovnin had no desire to avenge himself on Japanese officialdom, though he had suffered far worse at its hands. As to the Japanese in general, he openly conceded that his treatment had been good.[32] His observations, on Japan present and future, were impressively objective and acute.[33] What Kotzebue, Kruzenshtern, and Bellingshausen did for South Sea islands, he and Rikord did as eloquently for Japan. "In later years," adds G. A. Lensen, Golovnin's opinions and remarks were neglected and "accounts which doted on the quaintness of the Japanese" would gain attention in St. Petersburg. "But with the onslaught of the Russo-Japanese War, authorities were to remember Golovnin's most penetrating observations, and regret that his remarks had not been taken more seriously."[34]

Golovnin disputed the contemporary European view that the Japanese were a cowardly and cunning race. He stated that they were both courteous and brave and no less civilized than the inhabitants of European states. Disputes among them, for example, seldom led to violence, since arguments were by tradition settled calmly and with deference to social status. By and large, again, the Japanese were an hospitable, well-educated, honourable people. They possessed no gunboats that a European squadron would have treated with respect, but that did not reflect a lack of national valour. "If the Japanese are timorous, it is a consequence of the peace-loving nature of their very government, and of the calm in which, having no wars, the nation has rejoiced for many years."[35] That such a situation still obtained should not lead Russians to suppose that it would always and inevitably do so. If the Japanese should choose, for any reason, to transform themselves into a naval power, there was not the slightest doubt that they could do so.

For if the Japanese Government *should* desire to build a navy, it would be quite simple to establish one on the European model and to bring it to a high pitch of efficiency. The Japanese have only to invite to their country two or three good shipwrights and several naval officers—they have excellent harbours for naval establishments, all the materials necessary for building and arming vessels, a multitude of able carpenters, and alert, brave seamen. Japanese seamen put on a European footing, could in a short time match their fleet with the best of Europe.[36]

In Golovnin's considered view, the Russians should be circumspect in dealing with the Shogunate. From its base at Petropavlovsk, the Navy might perhaps exert some pressure on the Japanese in future; and Japan should be encouraged, in a manner that did not affront its pride, to open trade with foreign states. But any pressure should be carefully applied. Russia gained nothing by provoking such a nation into armament.

More efforts were in fact made between 1812 and 1817 to persuade the Japanese to trade with Russians, and the Navy played a certain role in these. That it was not a smaller one was a result more of insistence by Siberian officials that the Navy be in evidence, than of a policy adopted by the Naval Ministry. But, in the main, naval involvement in the Kuriles and in Japanese affairs was discreet. Gone were the days when any peaceful Japanese could be attacked by Russian vessels. The authorities also opted for caution in regard to Japanese claims to control some Kurile Islands: Etorofu and all islands further south, Treskin proposed, should be regarded for the present as belonging to Japan. Nor should a Russian fort be raised on Sakhalin, lest that precipitate a crisis between Russia and Japan or even possibly endanger Russo-Chinese trade in ways not well fore-seen. Lastly, the Company should be directed not to trade, hunt, or push its influ-ence by any other means beyond Uruppu. Treskin's sensible proposals were en-dorsed by an edict from the Crown.[37]

In August 1814, Navigator V. Novitskii sailed to Etorofu Island in a trans-port, *Boris i Gleb,* in hopes of finding a reply to a brief letter sent by Treskin to the governor of Matsumae and delivered the preceding summer by *Diana.* The letter reasserted that the pillages committed by Khvostov had been unauthorized and opened the topic of an international boundary, perhaps at Etorofu or Uruppu. Though he sailed along the shore of Etorufu for a day and was quite visible, No-vitskii made no contact with the Japanese. Some two years later, it was Assistant Navigator Srednii's turn to sail, unbidden and in vain, to Etorofu. In the transport *Pavel,* Srednii took a message from Lt. Rudakov, late of the *Diana* and now commanding at Petropavlovsk, to the Shogunate. Again an answer was requested to the letter sent in August 1813 to the governor of Matsumae. Once again, si-lence was the reply.[38]

Should servants of the Navy still be used to bolster trade between the Ainu and the Russians? The apparently inevitable dwindling of that trade offered an answer. At the time of the *Nadezhda*'s visit, Etorofu, Kunashiri, and the whole of Sakhalin had been effectively controlled not by the government at Edo, but by Lords of Matsumae, who had tolerated trade as being useful to themselves. By 1812, the Shogunate was fully in control of all those areas, and new officials stamped out trade in which the Ainu were the middlemen—a trade that linked Kamchatka and Nemuro Bay, Okhotsk and Kunashiri. Much was to be lost and nothing gained from yet another Russo-Japanese maritime incident. The fact was recognized by Treskin in the course of 1817, and by the company main board a little later. In the future, it was ordered, shipwrecked Japanese were to be sent only as far as the middle Kurile Islands; from there, they would make their own way home. No Russian warships called again for many years where all too often their appearance had provoked dismay.

To this extent, then, Golovnin's captivity and subsequent position on the question of Japan, Russia, and power in the East had altered matters in the East; for several years, starting in 1804, the Japanese had viewed the Russian Navy as a dangerous, aggressive force, and with some reason. In the period from 1813 to 1825, there were no incidents, nor did a single Russian vessel cause alarm at Hakodate or in any other district of Japan. Golovnin's position on the question of the proper Russian attitude towards the Shogunate (and the Mikado) comple-mented his position on the matter of the North Pacific colonies. The Navy, he in-sisted, should not press the Japanese too closely, for fear of harming future Rus-sian interests. But at the same time, it should recognize the parlous situation that obtained on the Aleutian Island chain and on the Coast. And *there,* certainly, the Navy had a duty, to the state and to itself, to grow in strength. Here is an extract from that part of the *Zapiski* in which Golovnin's "American" and "Japanese" opinions were set forth:

No matter how firmly the aversion to everything foreign is rooted in the Japanese Government, a complete alteration of its system should not be regarded as simply impossible. They are people; and in human affairs, nothing is permanent. What the Japanese might not wish to do, they might be forced to do. For example, repeated attacks by neighbouring States would, of course, oblige them to weigh all means by which they could prevent a handful of foreigners from troubling a populous nation. And this would in itself be an inducement for the introduction of warships on the European pattern; and from those, whole fleets would soon come into being. . . . It seems to me, therefore, that one must not provoke this populous, intelligent, patient and imitative people. Moreover, if ever there should rule over that people a monarch like our own Peter the Great, he would not need many years to permit Japan to lord it over the whole Pacific Ocean. And what would happen then to coastal regions in the east of Asia and the west of North America, so distant from the countries that must needs defend them?[39]

As it was, the Russian colonies were set about and undermined by "citizens of the American republic" and, in lesser numbers, by "King-George men." They might *hope* that, from the Japanese at least, they were secure; but they should act in such a way as to increase the probability. The Russian Navy should be ready to defend all Russian outposts, in America as elsewhere in the world, against attack from any quarter. Golovnin's main problem was to rally the support of men of influence for such a view. He spent five years from 1814 to 1818 doing so.

9

The Company under Attack

For several years after *Diana* sailed from Kronstadt, war made further Russian voyages to the Pacific settlements imprudent, if not impractical. In St. Petersburg, alarm and jingoism alternated; in the company main building (72 Moika Canal), inertia reigned after the *Grande Armée* crossed the Niemen. As a consequence of these developments in Europe, Baranov found himself once more in personal control of all the Company's affairs on and about the North-west Coast. By now, however, there were officers, including Lisianskii, Gagemeister, and Ratmanov, who were ready to assert, with Golovnin, that the Navy, not the Company, should represent the state in the Pacific settlements. The question was: could they find allies in St. Petersburg to plead the cause of naval aggrandizement in the far North-East and East and on the Coast on those same economic and strategic grounds which for the past half-century had led the Crown *not* to regard the Navy as its agent in the North Pacific area? Meanwhile, the Company itself wielded an influence that could assist a naval officer in his career (Gagemeister) or, conversely, gravely damage it (Lisianskii).[1] Allies must perforce cope with the power the board could still, in 1812-14, exercise at will through its supporters in the Senate and at court. Members of the emperor's family held shares. For all these reasons and because communications between Sitka and the capital were infamously slow, Baranov had not yet become aware of the virtual campaign that Golovnin was to conduct against him.

In the event, matters went better for Baranov in these years of war in Europe and America than the directors had a right to expect—better on the economic plane, at least. He handled problems of supply posed by the war between the

British and Americans pragmatically. He did not look upon American free-traders as his foes simply because their government was at war with Britain, Russia's ally in the European struggle. For years, certain Bostonians had dealt with him correctly. News of happenings in Europe took some months to reach the Coast—a war could meanwhile have erupted between Russia and another power. American merchantmen were idling at Canton and other ports on the Pacific Ocean's rim in 1812, fearful of capture by British men-of-war if they departed. Baranov passed the word that if Americans could reach the colonies, they and their crews would all be hired and might sail under the Company's own flag. Within five months, five Yankee masters had arrived in Sitka Sound. Baranov bought two vessels outright, the *Lady (Il'men)*, brig, and the *Atahualpa (Bering)*, a three-master. So little did the War of 1812 impinge on company activity that in that year he hired both an English shipmaster, George Young, and two Bostonians.[2] Thanks largely to the war, he had by March 1814 some seven ocean-going craft at his disposal—an unusual state of affairs. One was sent to Monterey, one to Hawaii, one to Kodiak, one to Manila. Suddenly, the Company's affairs were going well again. Aleuts caught otter off the shores where, once again, Ivan Kuskov had purchased foodstuffs from the Spaniards. In the north, walrus and otter were plentiful by recent standards. Hired American seamen proved efficient. Russian peltry could no longer be disposed of at Canton under the flag of the United States, so furs were sent to Kiakhta overland via Okhotsk in the old manner. But the loss of that convenience, a tolerable setback, was the only loss sustained in the Pacific by the Company as a result of the war. Company profits for 1814 touched on a million silver roubles: extra dividends were paid. How was the Navy to respond to such improbable success?

LT. M. P. LAZAREV AT NOVO-ARKHANGEL'SK (1814-15)

In Mikhail Petrovich Lazarev, the next young naval officer to reach the North Pacific colonies, those pressures first exerted on the Company's authority by Golovnin and by Lisianskii, but which war had greatly eased, found the most thoroughgoing agent whom Baranov had yet met. His ship *Suvorov*, a handsome, French-built merchantman of 337 tons or slightly less had sailed from Kronstadt on 9 October 1813. From Rio de Janeiro, Lazarev had headed east on 23 May, reaching Port Jackson in Australia on 13 August. *Suvorov* was the second Russian vessel in Australia, and since he brought the news of Blücher's entry into Paris, Lazarev was even more hospitably received by the new governor, Lachlan Macquarie, than Gagemeister and his men had been by Bligh in 1807.[3] *Suvorov* entered Sitka Sound in mid-November, anchoring under the fortress on the seventeenth. Lt. Lazarev reported to Baranov, and at first matters went well as they had at the beginning of Lisianskii's and Gagemeister's visits. The supplies he

Isaac West Commander

Plate 8. Sitka in the 1820's, showing "Baranov's Castle." The settlement had also been known as Novo-Arkhangel'sk sir 1804. Attacks by local Tlingit Indians led to the construction of the palisades and watchtowers.

Plate 9. A. A. Baranov (1746-1819), the resourceful chief manager of the Russian-American Company possessions in the North Pacific, supervised the building of Novo-Arkhangel'sk and struggled for twenty years to supply his men with foodstuffs and the Company with furs.

Plate 10. N. P. Rezanov, a favourite of Tsar Paul and son-in-law of the fur-trader G. I. Shelikhov. He travelle with the Kruzenshtern-Lisianskii Expedition to the Nort Pacific as envoy to Japan and developed grandiose desig to provision company possessions from Hawaii, New Albion, or Alta California.

Plate 11

Plate 12

Plate 11. Iu. F. Lisianskii (1773-1837), Kruzenshtern's second-in-command in 1803-6, took the *Neva* straight to the North-west Coast from the Marquesas and Hawaii.

Plate 12. I. F. Kruzenshtern (1770-1846), commander of *Nadezhda* in 1803-6, was one of many Baltic Germans who attained flag-rank in Russian naval service.

Plate 13. L. A. Gagemeister (German: Hagemeister) commanded the *Neva* on her second voyage out to the Pacific in 1807, and in 1817, he replaced Baranov as the chief Russian official in the North Pacific settlements.

Plate 14. V. M. Golovnin (1776-1831) served as a Russian Volunteer in assorted British warships. On his voyage to the Pacific he was detained at Cape Town for thirteen months, and in July 1812 he was captured by the Japanese.

Plate 15. M. P. Lazarev sailed in the *Suvorov* in 1813. At Sitka he clashed with Baranov.

Plate 13

Plate 14

Plate 15

Plate 16. A view of Sydney and Port Jackson from the north in 1820. Russians were well received there, at least till 1829; their presence in the North Pacific basin made the British government increasingly unhappy.

Plate 17. "Two tropical fish," caught in Port Jackson, by *Vostok*'s artist, Pavel Nikolaevich Mikhailov.

ates 18-19. Also by P. N. Mikhailov, two drawings of Maoris, who were met in Little Waikawa Bay, Queen Charlotte Sound, New
aland (June 1820). Russians also collected native artifacts in other parts of the Pacific.

ate 20. A *haka,* or Maori dance, being performed in Queen Charlotte Sound for Bellingshausen and his men. Captain Cook had
ded near this spot. Russians had read and been influenced by his *Voyages.*

Plate 21. An idealized drawing by Louis Choris of the reception of *Riurik*'s officers by King Kamehameha I, on Oahu, in November 1816. Inset: *Riurik*'s youthful ~~~~~ ~!~~ Otto von Katzebue (1797-1846), son of the German playwright, who had sailed with Kruzenshtern in adolescence.

Plate 22. *Vostok* and *Mirnyi* sailed for the Antarctic under Bellingshausen and Lazarev in 1819. Bellingshausen (inset) actually sighted Antarctica. The Bellingshausen Sea commemorates his voyage.

Plate 23. A late view of Novo-Arkhangel'sk, with the fort on the right. By this time, Russian government interest in the place had waned; but the sale of Russian North America to the

brought and the account of the collapse of the Napoleonic Empire were both welcome. Baranov was hospitable by nature;[4] and the mood was very festive for three days (18-20 November).

But Lazarev reflected an increasingly familiar Pacific-naval pattern. Like Lisianskii, Gagemeister, Kruzenshtern, and Golovnin, he had seen action (Riga, Danzig: 1812-13) and had served in British vessels. Like them, he nurtured patriotic hopes and aspirations which his travels and experience abroad had greatly widened. He refused from the beginning of his time at Novo-Arkhangel'sk to recognize civilian authority, that is, Baranov's, over the *Suvorov* or the elderly chief manager's prerogative to make such use of the *Suvorov* as he chose while she remained about the colonies and Coast. "Navy" and "Company" adherents quickly demonstrated their respective loyalties. Temperamental incompatability between the principals only exacerbated what both parties rightly understood to be a basic clash of forces. Lazarev did not conceal his feelings on the matter of the Company's relations with the Navy. Passions mounted when Baranov ordered Lazarev to the Pribylov Islands to collect a store of skins. Lazarev declined to sail at once, and indeed did not proceed to St. Paul till April 1815. No sooner were the skins brought back to Sitka than another argument broke out. Judging by extant evidence, which is both biased and fragmentary, Baranov again wished the *Suvorov* to make sail and was openly defied; and once again, tempers grew frayed. At length, a Yankee merchantman arrived and paid respects to the commander of the frigate that he saw. Her master was informed, while on *Suvorov,* that the ultimate authority at Novo-Arkhangel'sk lay with his host Lt. Lazarev. Then came the *Pedler* (Captain Wilson Hunt). Hunt had at one time been employed by J. J. Astor at Astoria on the Columbia. During the War of 1812 he had even found a refuge with the Russians, who, however, had good reason to regard him with disfavour by the time of this untimely reappearance in their midst on 17 July 1815. He had been trading guns and powder for the Tlingits' otter-skins and had enraged Governor Sola by poaching close inshore at Monterey.[5] Baranov ordered *Pedler* seized, and she was boarded by a group of loyal hunters. Her sails and ammunition were removed. Meanwhile, the fortress guns were trained, not on the unexpected visitor, but on *Suvorov*!

That night, Baranov wrote a full, angry report on the whole set of incidents involving Lazarev, accusing him of many heinous things. He woke next morning to discover that *Suvorov* was already under way. Russian gunners are asserted to have opened fire,[6] but the ship was out of range. Lazarev was gone, leaving behind him as a pledge of future troubles for Baranov an imperialist-minded and intelligent but quarrelsome physician, Dr. Georg Anton Schaeffer, moving force behind the imminent Russian adventure in Hawaii. Just as Kruzenshtern had rid himself of the officious Count Tolstoi, so Lazarev ejected Schaeffer. In his wrath, Baranov levelled yet more damning accusations, charging Lazarev with damaging the Company's Pacific interest, and sent them to St. Petersburg at once. He hoped they would arrive before his new antagonist.[7]

PREPARATIONS FOR THE VOYAGE OF *RIURIK* (1814-15)

Otto von Kotzebue's voyage in the *Riurik,* brig, showed yet more clearly than Lazarev's, that the final restoration of political stability to Europe had announced another era for the Russian and for other Western navies in the North Pacific region. More than this, it demonstrated that the principal non-diplomatic objects of the Kruzenshtern-Lisianskii expedition of a dozen years before—resupplying and supporting the North Pacific settlements both physically and morally and furthering trade, hydrography, discovery—were to be energetically, but also more selectively, pursued in a new era.[8]

Kotzebue (1787-1846), who had sailed with Kruzenshtern while still an adolescent, was the living measure of the change of emphasis which had grown evident in Russian naval thinking at the end of the Napoleonic Wars. His voyage was designed to bring new glory to the state, as well as useful commercial and strategic knowledge, and as such it expressed in a new way the international rivalry that had for decades been pursued by other means. New emphases, on commerce and the sciences connected with discovery, were not to break the underlying continuity of outlook among forward-looking servants of the Navy. Like Kruzenshtern's, Otto von Kotzebue's orders showed that, once again, parts of the pattern of an overall intention had been rearranged by war and its conclusion. As a result, he became the representative of change and continuity alike in the Pacific naval context. Like his mentor Kruzenshtern, he was a native of Estonia, a pupil at the *Domschule* in Reval. Like Lisianskii, Gagemeister, and Golovnin, he did well at the Cadet Corps, read voraciously, and felt strong foreign influences. Though he never served abroad, he was based for several years at Arkhangel'sk, the Russian port with the most ancient connections with the West and with the North. Finally, at only twenty-seven, he was offered the command of *Riurik.*

His reputation, as became a Baltic German protégé of Kruzenshtern, was that he was an extremely able scientific seaman, and the mission he was chosen to conduct was basically a scientific one.[9] Indeed, the voyage of the *Riurik* to the Arctic and Pacific set new patterns where the Russian scientific expedition was concerned. Yet at the same time, it revived past naval practices and old preoccupations. In the first place, it was organized to solve the ancient problem of a navigable passage to the Orient. The Russian government still claimed that land did not seal off the Arctic Ocean to the north of Bering Strait and that the failures of past mariners to penetrate the barrier of ice were hardly proof that there was not a summer passage, possibly concealed by an icy fringe and often choked by it. In the second place, it had been very largely planned by Kruzenshtern, Rumiantsev, Hörner—men of 1803, linked with *Nadezhda.* Thirdly, by extension, it was *sui generis* an offshoot of the western expeditionary experience since Anson's day. And Count Rumiantsev's lively interests in maritime and scientific questions were not new: they had been nurtured and sustained to some extent by Kruzenshtern himself. With the return of peace to Europe, they had put out new shoots. As chancellor, Rumiantsev thought it fitting to encourage any project that was likely to redound to Russia's honour.[10] By comparison, the Naval Ministry had no such attitude towards discovery. Since 1812, under the elegant mismanagement of Jean-François de Sausac, marquis de Traversay (1754-1830), who had replaced Admiral Chichagov the younger as the Russian naval minister in June 1811, it had lacked the will even to plan a distant venture. Here are extracts from the lengthy introduction to the Kotzebue *Voyage of Discovery into the South Sea and Beering's Straits,* of 1821, written by Kruzenshtern in 1818.

Even previous to the dreadful war of 1812, 1813, 1814, the political situation of Russia had rendered it quite impossible even for the Government to undertake such an enterprise [as a new search for the northern passage]. The count, however, did not give up the idea of it and . . . I undertook, according to his wish, to draw up a view of all Polar voyages since the first attempt of the celebrated Sebastian Cabot in the year 1497. . . . As soon as the war was concluded, the count resolved to proceed to the execution of the plan, at his own expense.

Even supposing that the wished for discovery of a connection between the two seas [Pacific and Atlantic] should not be made in the intended voyage, many important advantages would accrue from it to the sciences and especially to navigation, viz.: 1) The conviction that it *is* impossible to penetrate farther north from Beering's Straits than Cook and Clerke have done, and consequently that no passage to the Atlantic Ocean can exist there. 2) The examination of the coast of America, which was not seen by the celebrated English navigator on account of the shallowness of the water. 3) In case the examination of the coast of America northward of Beering's Straits could not be continued . . . the prosecution of the examination by land. . . . 4) The crossing of the South Sea twice, in quite different directions, which would certainly not a little contribute to enlarge our knowledge of this great ocean, as well as of the inhabitants of the very numerous islands scattered over it; and a rich harvest of objects of natural history was to be expected, as the count had appointed an able naturalist to accompany the expedition.[11]

As adviser to the chancellor on naval matters, Kruzenshtern was privileged to decide, within wide margins, the questions to which Kotzebue should address himself in the Pacific and the North. A second point also arises from this extract. So long as the Napoleonic Wars lasted, writes Kruzenshtern, the government had been unable to send ships on "such an enterprise" as Kotzebue's. But Russia had already been at peace with France for months when work was started on the *Riurik* in a Finnish yard. Even in March 1814 the tsar had been in France as conqueror, yet it was not till June 1815 that Kotzebue had his orders. Then again, N.P. Rumiantsev was a wealthy man; yet it is striking that it fell not to the Crown, but to an individual to guard the honour of the state in the area of seaborne exploration. In these contexts, the comment that, for several years by 1815, the political conditions in the state had rendered it "impossible" for Arctic or Pacific undertakings to be launched requires more examination.

In 1818, Kruzenshtern in fact no more than hinted at the pitiful reality of Russia's naval weakness and failed altogether to mention that the government had long been allowing it to develop. There had been some small successes in the south since 1809: at Ruschuk, in Silistria, at Varna under Hall.[12] But what of Kronstadt, and the ships judged to be capable of "open-water voyaging"? "In mid-October 1812, a squadron of 15 ships left under Tate. . . . On reaching England, Tate and his squadron placed themselves under the orders of Admiral Young. The Russian warships stood at Blackstairs, on the River Medway, for some time."[13] Not till July 1814, in fact, did they return to the Neva. Within three years, "all ships at Kronstadt were literally rotting, painted and prettified on one side only—and along that side, during reviews, the monarch was invariably led."[14] Here is F. F. Veselago on Jean-François de Sausac, marquis de Traversay:

> Traversay, a French emigré, had been received into our galley fleet in 1791 as captain, and had reached admiral's rank within ten years. . . . Unsuccessful management of the Black Sea Fleet did not prevent his being appointed Naval Minister . . . for he succeeded in winning the good opinion of necessary persons, including the all-powerful Arakcheev and other grandees close to the tsar. Amiability and an ingratiating manner won him sympathy. . . . In the first part of his ministry, Traversay's activity was chiefly directed towards changing or annulling everything achieved by his predecessor. With the exhausting of material on which to produce this negative effect, there began a time of inactivity, reflected in the stagnation of all branches of the naval administration, and in the Fleet itself.[15]

In the postwar period, more than ever, Pacific service was distinct from other branches of the Russian naval service. It was connected yet more firmly with prestige and with expenditure unthinkable to the majority of Admiralty bureaucrats and also with the sciences. What Traversay would not disburse on *Riurik* and on other vessels like her, Count Rumiantsev would. Meanwhile, he and his helpers, led by Kruzenshtern, looked to the Company as much as to the Navy for assistance:

It was resolved to have a vessel of 70 or 80 tons, with movable keels on the plan of Captain Shank, built of oak in the Imperial dockyard by the able shipbuilder Razumov. This plan, however, could not be executed as there is no private dockyard in St. Petersburg and oak timber is the exclusive possession of the Admiralty. The only alternative was to purchase abroad a ship built of oak timber, which would have been too expensive, or to have one built of fir. . . . Lt. Kotzebue accompanied me to Abo, and at the latter end of May 1814, I contracted with a shipbuilder named Erik Malm to build us, for the sum of 30,000 roubles, a vessel of 180 tons burthen, which should be launched at the beginning of May in the following year. I bespoke the astronomical and physical instruments in England, of the justly celebrated Troughton.[16]

The admiral also ordered in London two telescopes by Tully, a log and sounding-machine by Massey, maps by Horsburgh, Purdy and Arrowsmith, and maritime provisions. Appointed to the *Riurik,* at Rumiantsev's personal expense, were Lt. Gleb Shishmarev of the Navy, who had long known Kotzebue and was recommended by him to the count; the young French artist Louis Choris; the Franco-German soldier-savant Adalbert von Chamisso (1781-1838); and, as surgeon, the Dorpat entomologist and doctor Johann-Friedrich Eschscholtz (1793-1831). Kotzebue's company was cosmopolitan and young. As if to emphasize the point, *Riurik* gave passage to Avacha Bay to the young Danish naturalist, Wormskiöld. In short, old chords were struck repeatedly during the course of preparations for the voyage of the brig and on the passage: the use of English instruments and expertise and charts; the major Baltic German contribution; invitations sent abroad; the appointment of a wholly Russian crew; hopes of discovering a northern passage. Kruzenshtern explained what was *un*traditional and novel in the first of Kotzebue's two Pacific expeditions:

No objection can well be made against the utility of a voyage of discovery to the South Sea as far as the sciences are concerned. . . . But at a time when, thanks to the generous sentiments of Alexander, Russia will enjoy the blessings of a durable peace, how *could* our sailors be better employed? Only two of my companions on board *Nadezhda,* besides the commander of *Riurik,* are now [1818] employed, though they possess all requisite qualifications.[17]

One thinks of the contemporary outlets for the British naval officer seeking adventure of the patriotic sort, fearful of unemployment in a shrinking navy: Arctic work, African work. Parry north-west of Davis Strait, Kotzebue and Vasil'ev (1820) north and east of Bering Strait: all three answered the unaccustomed challenge of a period of international peace by sailing north.

RIURIK IN THE NORTH (1816)

Kotzebue sailed from Kronstadt on 30 July 1815.[18] Rounding the Horn towards the end of January, he recuperated briefly in the port of Talcaguano on the coast of Chile before making for Kamchatka which, together with Alaska, he surveyed from close inshore. *Riurik* did well in shallow waters; nor did the frequent fogs and rain dampen the spirits of her company as Kotzebue headed north. By August, he was crossing the Alaskan bay still known as Kotzebue Sound. There was disappointment when it proved to be no passage to the east.

Riurik called at Petropavlovsk briefly. Thanks to the co-operation of Captain-Lt. Rudakov, her copper sheathing was efficiently and promptly patched with copper taken from *Diana*'s hull. High on the rocks above Avacha Bay now stood a telegraph to signal the approach of distant craft. The crew ate well. Wormskiöld disembarked to head off north into the Chukchi country.

Rather more needs to be said of Kotzebue's stay at Unalaska in September 1816; and his own remarks are eloquent. He and his people had been cheerfully received by Kriukov, who was managing the Company's affairs. There was a Russian bath, an ox was slaughtered, and the *Riurik*'s needs were all attended to, mainly by Aleuts at Illyukyuk and by Kriukov's kitchen-gardener, who dug up radishes, large turnips, and potatoes for the visitors. Then, as a final gesture of goodwill and hospitality, Manager Kriukov and Captain Benzemann of the *Chirikov* gave a dinner at Illyukyuk:

> We went to a large subterranean dwelling, where a number of Aleutians had assembled to dance. I readily believe that their dances and sports in former times . . . were very different from what they are now, when slavery has nearly degraded them to the level of brutes, and when this spectacle is neither pleasing nor diverting. . . . The sight of these people who, with mournful countenances, were obliged to dance before us, gave me pain.[19]

Unlike Golovnin, Kotzebue had not come to the Pacific settlements expecting to condemn; he was unprejudiced against the Company. Yet he was pained by what he found. At Illyukyuk, as in many other places in the Company's domains, the bloody past lived on to damn contemporary hunters, if the visitor would only watch and listen. These were only impressions, but they augured ill for Kriukov's company.

Riurik sailed from Unalaska on 14 September 1816, making not for Honolulu, as had earlier been planned, but for San Francisco Bay.[20]

RIURIK IN CALIFORNIA

Kuskov had been four years at Ross when *Riurik* arrived. He had been working in the face of sometimes theoretical, at other times practical Spanish opposition, to consolidate the Company's position. His men lived well by northern standards, and from year to year he managed to sustain a certain volume of illicit Russo-Spanish trade and barter. On the other hand, his chances of obtaining an admission from the regional authorities that he was anything but an intruder, which had always been extremely feeble, had diminished. Only recently, Northrop and Ayres of the *Pedler* and *Mercury* had been arrested and detained for coastal smuggling, by Spanish Californian authorities, although in fact Northrop had merely been provisioning Fort Ross from Honolulu.[21] Within the past few weeks, the further poaching of the sea-otter by Aleuts based aboard *Il'men* had much annoyed Governor Sola and the regional commander, Argüello. They had hunted them in clear view of a presidio. The vessel had been taken by the Spaniards at El Cojo, and Eliot de Castro, a polyglot company agent, had been sent to Santa Barbara. The Aleuts' foreman, Tarakanov, was imprisoned in Los Angeles. The time had come, said Argüello bluntly when his latest Russian visitor, Lt. Kotzebue, reached San Francisco Bay, for Russia to acknowledge Spanish sovereignty over Alta California and for all Russians to obey the laws of Spain when in that country. Ross was a sore that Spain had borne; she would apply the proper medicine. Almost as soon as he set foot in California, Kotzebue was required to be party to political discussions which, he recognized, could well have major implications for the future. In attendance at the "San Francisco conference" of late October 1816, were Kuskov and Kotzebue, Argüello, Sola, and von Chamisso, who spoke a fluent Spanish and so served as general interpreter

Argüello received the naval officers and scientific corps with every possible attention. . . . A bull and bear fight took place at the presidio. Sola came up from the capital to greet the foreign guests . . . and profited by the occasion to complain of his nation's grievance at the hands of Kuskov and the Company he represented. Kotzebue, of course, said he had no authority in the matter, but promised to bring the subject to the attention of his government; and finally he consented to summon Kuskov to the conference.

Kuskov came down on October 25. During the three following days, the conference was held at the presidio, the result being preserved in a documentary record signed by Kotzebue, Kuskov, Chamisso as interpreter, and Luis Argüello and José Maria Estudillo as witnesses. In this paper are narrated the circumstances under which the conference was held; Sola's complaint that Kuskov had settled in Spanish territory and neglected to obey the Viceroy's orders to depart or even to give any definite answer to the Governor's letters; Kuskov's declining to make any argument on the merits of the case, or to abandon the settlement without orders from Baranov; and Kotzebue's declaration that he had no authority to act but would submit the case to his Sovereign. It is evident enough, and in fact Chamisso so states, that Kotzebue recognized the entire justice of the Spanish claim; and it is equally certain that Kuskov was by no means pleased with the turn things were taking.[22]

Baranov too was much displeased when news arrived with the *Chirikov* of Kotzebue's interference in the Company's southern affairs. And yet, as Bancroft notes, "whatever Kotzebue may have *thought,* the document in question can hardly be deemed an admission of Spanish rights." What Kotzebue did in fact think was that Kuskov's and the Company's position, and the latter's claim to Ross, were shaky, but that Spain herself had shamefully neglected California as a whole. Potentially a rich and fruitful colony, it was a burden on the royal treasury and full of ragged soldiers, stupid Indians, and missionaries whose efforts to convert whole tribes to Christianity had brought more harm than benefit to the Pacific.[23] The kernel of Baranov's irritation, however, was the impropriety of a lieutenant's having put his name to *any* Spanish document; for by signing such a paper, Kotzebue had made it virtually certain that the Company's activities in Alta California would—as Sola wished—be subject to official scrutiny both in Madrid and in St. Petersburg. He had thus damaged Russia's interest at Ross, which was best served by total silence.

Baranov took some days to overcome his irritation. He then dispatched Iakov Podushkin, another naval officer in company employ, to undo some of the harm that had most probably been done. Podushkin sailed from Novo-Arkhangel'sk in the *Chirikov*. His credentials, in the form of a letter from Baranov to Sola, mentioned only the release of Aleut and Russian prisoners then held in California; but doubtless he was also told to raise the all important question of trade and to conciliate the governor. Podushkin was received politely by de Sola and allowed to load a cargo of provisions. On reaching Monterey, he was given fifteen prisoners, including Tarakanov, whom the Spaniards were finding too expensive to maintain. A number of the Aleuts captured with him at San Pedro on 9 September 1815 had obligingly embraced the Roman Church and even married local women. They remained behind.[24] Predictably, however, Podushkin failed to break the deadlock on the more important issues of the Russians' right to live and hunt at Ross and to conduct an open, regular, and mutually advantageous trade in Spanish California.

Kotzebue, whom Don Luis Argüello and de Sola had continued to treat civilly, left San Francisco on 1 November 1816. With *Riurik*, now in excellent repair and abundantly provisioned, went three Russians and a Portuguese in company employ, J. Eliot de Castro, whom the Spaniards had also captured on their beaches and imprisoned for illicit trading. Kotzebue set a course for the Hawaiian Islands. His departure was accompanied, bizarrely, by the howlings of innumerable sea-lions ashore.

RIURIK AT OAHU

After he reached Oahu in November 1816, Kotzebue wasted little time in disassociating Russia, and himself, from the imperial adventure then proceeding under Georg Anton Schaeffer on the shores of Kauai.[25] He was generously entertained by the "head chieftain" of Oahu, Kareimoku, and by John Young (1742-1835), still the powerful adviser of Kamehameha, whom, indeed, he had been warning against Schaeffer. Since the scientist had reached the Islands in November 1815, ostensibly to repossess the cargo of the company ship *Bering*, which had foundered in a bay of Kauai two years earlier or to obtain due recompense from King Kamehameha, the industrious but lordly Dr. Schaeffer had acquired territory both from him (on Lanai and Oahu) and from his foe Kaumualii (on Kauai). With Kaumualii, who had in May 1816 signed a pledge of loyalty to Alexander I seeking Imperial protection for his islands, he made four secret treaties. A fort had been erected, and Kaumualii had agreed to extortionate conditions—exporting to the Company two shiploads of sandalwood, at least one hundred hogs, fifteen or sixteen thousand taro roots per annum—in return for Schaeffer's promise to obtain a man-of-war with which the king might conquer all the Islands. In short, the Russian doctor had sided with Kaumualii against Kamehameha.[26]

It was well that Kotzebue had so soon declared his own position with regard to Schaeffer, for when Khramchenko, first mate of *Riurik*, set up poles with flags round "Hanarura harbour" with a view to charting it, he was surrounded by infuriated natives who remembered Schaeffer's poles and flags and desecration of an old morai (sacred area).[27] Khramchenko's poles were rapidly replaced by brooms.

Hawaiian skills proved very useful to the Russians. For example, local divers examined and repaired the *Riurik*'s hull, remaining underwater for some minutes at a stretch. Likewise, a number of the European residents, including Beckley,

Holmes, Francisco de Marini, and particularly, Alexander Adams of the *Albatross,*[28] proved helpful—once the Schaeffer situation had been clarified to King Kamehameha and to them.

Kotzebue's attitude towards the Islanders was as sensible as Schaeffer's was provocative;[29] nor did he stint his admiration of their skills as, for example, when he came on coastal reservoirs for sea fish made of coral-stone, and artificial taro fields. Relations with Kamehameha's "governor" over Oahu, Kareimoku, were cordial; and as a group, the Russians (some of whom were French or German) proved intelligent observers of the Islands scene. In Choris and von Chamisso, Kotzebue had assistants worthy of their predecessors, Langsdorf and Tilesius. The expedition was well managed on the level of technique, and it was fruitful in discoveries and on the scientific plane. Kotzebue had instructions to investigate a number of the islands seen by Jacob Roggeveen and other early Dutch explorers. He did so efficiently and in the process found a number of new islands: the Rumiantsev and Kutuzov groups, the Riurik chain, and New Year's Island.[30] Later, at Guam, he surveyed La Calderona Bay. Among the faulty longitudinal bearings that he rectified to the advantage of future mariners was that given by Arrowsmith for Christmas Island.

In good health and better spirits, Kotzebue left Manila, where the *Riurik* had been cleaned after her long tropical wanderings on 4 January 1818, and proceeded through the Sunda Strait towards South Africa, entering Table Bay on 29 March. After an amicable meeting with de Freycinet of *Uranie,* he pressed on home by way of Portsmouth, Copenhagen, and Reval. On 3 August, *Riurik* stood at anchor facing Count Rumiantsev's mansion on the bank of the Neva.[31]

Kotzebue's homecoming was gratifying both to him and to his patron. Traversay and the Academy of Sciences publicly recognized the expedition's worth, and Kotzebue was promoted shortly afterwards. And yet, the air of the reception was not altogether gay. There were no patriotic scenes as there had been aboard *Nadezhda* and *Neva* in 1806. There was no positive—or negative—reaction at the Naval Ministry or in the company main office to Shishmarev's and Kotzebue's detailed information on the Ross-Kuskov and Schaeffer-Kaumualii affairs. Officially, at least, nothing was done about the San Francisco document. If possible, reaction to their statements that Kamehameha had been told that Alexander had not ordered Schaeffer's actions and was very likely ignorant of them was even more equivocal.[32]

Though he could not have known it, Kotzebue had in fact returned to find the company directors in confusion and the Golovnin campaign against the board in crucial phase. Even while *Riurik* had been docking, Traversay had been arranging new political alignments *vis-à-vis* the directors and Captain Golovnin and his supporters, led by Admiral G. A. Sarychev. In the Pacific 1817-18 for the Navy and the Company alike was a turning point. *Kamchatka,* sloop, with Golovnin commanding, had already left for Sitka to deliver fresh supplies and naval stores.

There her commander was to gather yet more damning evidence for later use against the Company at home.

THE NAVY AND THE COMPANY: POLITICAL ARRANGEMENTS (1816-17)

Baranov, meanwhile, struggled for a modus vivendi with the several young naval officers in company employ. Lazarev's insults had not made it impossible for other more complaisant and more needy Navy men, like Lieutenants Z. I. Ponafidin and I. Podushkin, to serve the Company. In April 1817, Podushkin took *Chirikov* down to Monterey again on orders from Baranov. Navigator E. Klochkov brought her back with a cargo of more than forty thousand skins and victuals besides.[33] From the perspective of the shareholder, relations between Company and Navy looked quite satisfactory. By sending no supply ship to the colonies in 1814-15 and by bargaining with North American free-traders for supplies, the board and the chief manager respectively had much improved the balance sheet. The situation echoed that of 1800.[34] In June 1815, the Company paid out a 100-rouble dividend on each 500-rouble share. In June 1816, it was 150 roubles on the share; in 1818 slightly more. On the surface, the Company was flourishing, but in reality, it was in shaky health. The board itself acknowledged that in view of recent pressure brought to bear by Golovnin and his adherents, it must make amends for long neglect of its own interests. It was some time since yearly profits after dividends and taxes had been soundly reinvested.

Who would represent the Navy in the Company's Pacific settlements and harbours? Gagemeister, Golovnin, and Lazarev were all on active service in or near St. Petersburg from May to July 1816. All three had meetings with the aging Admiral Sarychev, who had lately been co-opted to the company main board in recognition of his almost forty years of active interest in the Pacific. Since returning from the Billings expedition in 1794, he had worked at frequent intervals on charts showing the waters, coasts, and islands claimed by Russia in the North Pacific area.[35] He had contributed a good deal to the planning of the Kruzenshtern and Kotzebue ventures. Finally, he had himself seen the results of earlier *promyshlennik* barbarity, and understood the opportunities that offered in the East and the Pacific. In Sarychev's judgment Golovnin's position that the Company had shown itself unable to fulfil its charter's terms was correct.

Thus accused in memoranda,[36] the board had to defend itself; silence might justly be regarded as acknowledgment of culpability, on many charges—failing to control its cossack agents, to encourage missionary work, to foster agriculture, to insist on independence from American suppliers, to defend the native interest, and so forth. The directors therefore took an angry stance; but from the first, they were defensive, even wary. It was soon being suggested that the blame for absent doctors, for non-existent churches, for dependence on republican suppliers, and indeed for all "discrepancies" between instructions and realities should rest with the chief manager. Buldakov hesitated, but political self-interest won out. It was agreed *in camera* that Baranov would be replaced by an appointee of the Navy who, together with his aides, would receive a block of shares by way of supplementary salary. The naval officers were to *direct* affairs at Novo-Arkhangel'sk. A civilian administrator and his clerks would *manage* business matters. The directors would remain. With naval help, and in conjunction with a nominee of O.P. Kozodavlev, minister of internal affairs, under whose overall control the board had theoretically been functioning since 1812, the present board would seek renewal of its charter, which was shortly to expire.[37]

The inherent flaws of this peculiar arrangement were as obvious by 1820 as they are today.[38] The socio-political prerogatives of officers were built into their terms of service with the Company. Business affairs would be treated as a matter for mere clerks, while their superiors concerned themselves, whether or not they or the Navy spelled it out, with Russia's naval-cum-political rapports with foreign powers in the North Pacific area. It might conceivably have worked, had the divisions of authority and station, which reflected class rather than functional distinctions, although also the latter, been accepted by the "clerks" as by the naval "gentlefolk." Much depended on the attitude of L. A. Gagemeister, who was now selected as Baranov's replacement as chief officer at Novo-Arkhangel'sk.

THE RETURN OF GAGEMEISTER TO THE COLONIES (1817-18)

Gagemeister travelled overland to Kronstadt from Kamchatka in 1810. In 1811 he was *kapitan-leitenant*, in 1812, director of the Admiralty Office in Irkutsk. There, forming a link between the Admiralty Office and the capital, between Minitskii at Okhotsk and General Ivan Borisovich Pestel', governor-general of Eastern Siberia, who then resided in St. Petersburg, he deftly organized developments far off on the Pacific littoral: the moving of the Admiralty Office at Okhotsk to Petropavlovsk; the rebuilding of Okhotsk itself as Golovnin proposed 400 metres from its present (second) site and on the far side of the mouth of the Okhota; and the building of an arsenal and yard at Petropavlovsk. If Gagemeister's efforts caused no stir within the Naval Ministry, then under Traversay's dead hand, at least they strengthened the impression in Siberia and at the company main office that his knowledge of conditions in the far North-East and East was sound.[39] Pestel's official representative *in loco*, and the day-to-day director of Irkutsk affairs, Nikolai Treskin,[40] worked harmoniously with Gagemeister for many months. Thus was yet another link inserted in the chain that stretched from 1810 to 1820; from *Diana* to *Kutuzov;* and from Rikord and Minitskii to Pestel'.

For Treskin wrote approvingly to his superior about both Gagemeister and, particularly, Rikord, who had visited Irkutsk a little after the Kurilian disaster had encompassed Golovnin.[41] Treskin and Rikord found each other sympathetic. Later Golovnin, too, made a good impression on the energetic Treskin, who appreciated energy in others. Pestel' himself then met both Golovnin and Gagemeister in St. Petersburg. Not long before, he had been named to the Imperial State Council. As a councillor, his views carried some weight both with the directors of the Company and with the courtly Traversay. General Pestel' and Treskin believed Gagemeister had a place in the ongoing discussions at the company main office, and Sarychev and Kruzenshtern agreed. Gagemeister was instructed to report to Moika Quay, where he was offered command of the *Kutuzov,* bound for Novo-Arkhangel'sk. He did not hesitate before accepting the command.[42]

Before *Kutuzov* sailed, the capacity in which her captain would be present in the colonies had to be finalized. M. M. Buldakov, chairman of the board, would not be party to a brusque and sharp removal of Baranov from his post, though he agreed that he must go. A compromise was needed. Whether Captain Gagemeister was invited to participate in the discussions of mid-August to attempt to find it or was merely an observer is unclear. The former seems more probable. At all events, he was presented with the following emotive document, dated St. Petersburg, 25 August 1816:

From the Board of the Russian-American Company, Established by Sovereign Edict, Now under the Protection of His Imperial Majesty: An Order to the Novo-Arkhangel'sk Office:

Coupled with the advanced age of Collegiate Councillor and *chevalier* Baranov, Chief Manager of our American possessions, his attacks of illness and 25-year service in those parts amidst constant cares and difficulties, have justified his making several requests to be relieved of his duties. Twice already, successors were in fact sent out to him: Koch and Bornovolokov. But death prevented their reaching the countries here in question, and the Board could not find a third suitable person for the post. Now, however, it has found a person worthy of the task, in the bearer of this document, Captain-Lieutenant of the Navy and *chevalier* Leontii Andreianovich Gagemeister, commander of the vessels *Kutuzov* and *Suvorov.* In view of this, the Board determines to write to Mr. Baranov and to direct him to surrender to the Captain, in proper order, his post, capital, and affairs. The Novo-Arkhangel'sk Office, all naval officers, and all other Company servants are to know of these developments, and are to obey the newly appointed head, Gagemeister, in everything relating to their duties, under pain (in the contrary event) of severe penalties according to law.

Given in St. Petersburg this 25th day of August 1816, and signed by
Gavrilo Sarychev, Ivan Weydemeyer, Iakov Druzhinin, Mikhail Buldakov, Benedict Cramer, Andrei Severin, Ivan Zelenskii (Secretary to the Board.)[43]

The compromise lay in the fact that Gagemeister was empowered to delay at Novo-Arkhangel'sk before revealing his true colours to Baranov and his men. *Kutuzov* (525 tons) and *Suvorov*, the latter under Zakhar Ponafidin, weighed from Kronstadt roads together on the morning of 8 September. First lieutenant of *Suvorov* was Semen Ivanovich Ianovskii (1789-1876), first lieutenant of *Kutuzov*, A. S. Selivanov.[44] Both vessels carried men whose future links with the Pacific and the colonies would last until their deaths: Dionisii Zarembo, Ivan Kislakovskii, Efim Klochkov, and Kiril Khlebnikov.[45]

Gagemeister's rate of progress was, as ever, comfortable. He paused at Santiago in the Cape Verde group, then in Brazil, and at Callao, and at Guayaquil. At last, after a final stop for watering at Tumbes, he proceeded north to "Port Rumiantsev,"[46] which served Ross. *Kutuzov* stood at anchor in Bodega Bay for two weeks from 17 September to 1 October, and then moved round to San Francisco. Here, the hopeful Gagemeister made an effort to resolve the hunting-trading difficulties of a now defensive Russian California. And, not withstanding Governor de Sola's absence, he did manage to secure the release of fourteen prisoners and to obtain provisions for Fort Ross;[47] but he could do no more. It seemed that Russo-Spanish trade was to remain a semi-secret, unofficial one, subject to Spanish whims and need, if not corruptability.[48] *Kutuzov* reached Novo-Arkhangel'sk on 21 November 1817. She had long been expected by Baranov: Ponafidin had arrived direct from Guayaquil on 20 July. Baranov's young assistant, K. T. Khlebnikov, later observed apologetically that the chief manager

was pleased with the supplies from California. But he was angered and openly protested that the Company ignored his persistent requests and refused to replace him, forcing him to continue under his heavy burden. His frequent complaints eventually persuaded Captain Hagemeister to assume the duties of Chief Manager of the colonies, for which he had provisionally been granted powers by the Main Office. But for personal reasons, he long hesitated, reluctant to accept these new and arduous duties, strewn with so many cares.[49]

One must be wary of such passages by Khlebnikov. Baranov's first biographer was also his admirer and, in general, he tended to omit what was unflattering to him and what suggested strife and discord. Though he wrote *à thèse,* however, one is grateful that he wrote at all, given the sparseness of contemporary records of events at Novo-Arkhangel'sk.

What, then, did happen in the final weeks of 1817? Most likely the supplies brought by *Kutuzov* were entrusted to Baranov, whom, however, Gagemeister thought incapable of making a professional inventory. Khlebnikov's services were offered and accepted, though at first he was effectively no more than the controller of the stores. Meanwhile Gagemeister tried to persuade Baranov to allow him to examine old account books, but Baranov took the line that the accounts should be inspected only by his own successor. Gagemeister then sought evidence of peculation but was thwarted once again. As twice before at Novo-Arkhangel'sk, a "Navy party" was surveyed with deep suspicion and hostility by a defensive group of company employees who had long worked with Baranov.

Then, in mid-December, the position was further complicated when *Suvorov*'s first lieutenant, S. Ianovskii, sought Baranov's daughter's hand in marriage. She was willing. He was anxious. Gagemeister was informed of the development and as senior official in the colony, was asked to give his blessing. Unexpectedly, but happily, he saw the answer to his problem with Baranov: bless the marriage, then appoint Ianovskii as the temporary governor or senior official. He himself had no intention of remaining on the Coast for years. The lieutenant was agreeable, and Baranov had no objection to an early wedding. Gagemeister had no more than to complete his part of the arrangement. He produced his secret orders from the company directors on 11 January 1818.[50]

So ended the initial phase of a deliberate campaign against the Company in the Pacific. Under the observant eye of Khlebnikov, accounts were checked for six or seven months. Baranov gave no trouble and explained his own procedures and deciphered aging notes. Gagemeister speedily "persuaded the *promyshlenniki* to relinquish the old method of payment by shares in kind, and to accept a monetary basis."[51] All workers in the settlements were to be paid 300 roubles annually in notes. Dissatisfaction with this change led Gagemeister to add one *pood* of flour monthly to each worker's pay. Other administrative changes quickly followed and Gagemeister departed.

At Monterey on 7 to 10 September 1818 he had a series of discussions with Golovnin, the commander of *Kamchatka,* who had been active in the second, even more successful phase of the campaign against the company ever since Gagemeister left St. Petersburg. Gagemeister then returned to Sitka Sound, while Golovnin returned to Russia via Hawaii.

Of the final weeks of Gagemeister's brief governorship, suffice to note that whilst at Monterey in California, in mid-September 1818, he had two or three days' talk with Golovnin, who had arrived in *Kamchatka.* He then hastened back to Sitka Sound, while Golovnin went on his way, via Hawaii, to St. Petersburg.[52] The second phase of the campaign was almost over.

10

Imperial Ambition in Peacetime:
Trade, Discovery, Science

THE VOYAGE OF *KAMCHATKA:* BACKGROUND (1817)

Since the middle of the eighteenth century, Siberian officialdom had known that hunting parties were committing crimes of violence in the Aleutians; nor had cossack persecution of the natives ended after Billings's and Sarychev's grim reports of March and June 1794,[1] or even ten years later. Although less so, to be sure, by 1812 than earlier, the Company still had good reason to avert too close a scrutiny of the activities of certain of its servants in the North Pacific region. Native memories were long, and oral traditions kept alive historic grievances.[2]

Theoretically, the Company was not responsible for cruel acts, "outrages and abuses . . . barbarities and plunderings,'"[3] committed in the later eighteenth century before its founding. In the Aleuts' eyes, however, its misrule stretched back for decades, and, indeed, a certain number of the company employees of the early nineteenth century were blood relations of Shelikhov's, Bechevin's, and Glotov's men.[4] That native attitude toward the outrages committed in the islands, some of which, for example on Sannak in 1771, had resulted in appalling retributions,[5] served the ends of Golovnin and his supporters.

Much had changed with the appointment of Minitskii to Okhotsk in 1809. From the beginning of his service, the new commandant had struggled to eradicate the violence still perpetrated far from all authority in the North-East, on the North-west Coast, and on the many barren islands in between. He sent well-documented, regular reports to his superior, the governor-general of Eastern Siberia, concerning witnessed and alleged irregularities in places under company control. Year after year from 1810 to 1816, copies of these went to St. Petersburg. Some allegations of misdoings in the islands were of small significance;

others reflected major crimes. A navigator called Dubinin had physically assaulted the *toyon* (chief) of Atka Island, a venerable man; and the chief had not recovered. In 1812, *promyshlenniki* from the company-owned vessel *Finliandiia* had raped a group of Aleut women in the Andreianov Islands and abducted them for forced labour. Some of the women later died as a result.[6]

Pestel' could not accept the thought of Russian subjects terrorizing native tribes who had been formally assured in June 1787 of "the continuing care and protection of the Crown."[7] Minitskii, Golovnin and Gagemeister struck him as intelligent and sober officers. Accordingly, Pestel' began in time to view the Company with some disfavour. Then, in 1816, he received a copy of a document sent by Minitskii to Irkutsk from Okhotsk on 24 September 1815. It gave details of irregularities in the Aleutians since Minitskii had arrived on the Pacific and cast a lurid light on certain company activities.[8] Next came the brief interrogation, in July 1816, by an admiralty court, of M. P. Lazarev, who had recently returned from Novo-Arkhangel'sk in the *Suvorov*. On arrival in St. Petersburg, Lazarev was faced with many charges, all preferred by the directors on the basis of despatches from Baranov, which had reached the capital by special courier. He was charged with immorality, with leaving Novo-Arkhangel'sk without permission, with abandoning a youthful supercargo and Schaeffer in the colonies, and with selling 60,000 roubles' worth of furs at Lima that were destined for St. Petersburg. He was acquitted.[9]

How should Pestel', under whose jurisdiction both Okhotsk and Petropavlovsk fell where all non-naval matters were concerned, react to the clash of interests between the company main board and naval officers? His sympathies lay with the naval party, and he decided to support it on the basis of official correspondence with Okhotsk. He wrote to Traversay, who had himself been watching progress in the company main office. Gagemeister's posting, the departures of *Suvorov* and *Kutuzov* for the colonies, the board's public admission that a third vessel would leave for Petropavlovsk very shortly under Admiralty orders all suggested the degree to which the future of the Company now lay in naval hands. If this had not been plain to Traversay by August 1816, it became so in December when, apparently without his intervention, the name of V. M. Golovnin, the arch detractor of the Company, began to be connected with another, and investigative, voyage to the settlements. And Golovnin was duly named commander of *Kamchatka*, the third vessel in question. The *Kamchatka* was a sloop-rigged frigate. She displaced 900 tons and mounted 32. For a warship, she was generously manned: 12 officers and a lower deck of 119 men. Since she was leaving on a mission of surveillance and inspection of the company possessions, she carried both an artist, Mikhail Tikhanov, and a captain's clerk.[10] When loading began, even the minister responsible for company affairs, O. P. Kozodavlev of Internal Affairs, saw fit to state that naval officers might very properly replace such men as Cramer and Buldakov, who were constantly complaining of the loss of their supposed prerogatives. At least the Navy was a section of the government with standard dealings with its many other branches, not a strange beast like the Company.[11] Thus, for a range of private or, more often, departmental reasons, Imperial bureaucracy perceived and reinforced the winds of change and drew advantage from them. Finally, Pestel' resolved to act. He wrote to Traversay again.

To the Minister of the Marine, Marquis de Traversay, from General Pestel', Governor-General of Eastern Siberia.

no. 1124   St. Petersburg, June 16 1817

It has long been known and recognized that servants of the Russian-American Company in many ways oppress and outrage natives of the Kurile and Aleutian Islands. In itself, this was the reason for the fact that, when the reform of the Kamchatkan administration was first envisaged [in response to Golovnin's representations of 1810-11], attention was paid to the state of the Company colonies not only on the westerly Aleutian and Kurile Islands, but also in America. To this end, it was established by an edict from the Crown (no. 86, para. 3) of April 9 1812, that "the Governor of Kamchatka shall dispatch a warship to the Kurile and Aleutian Islands and America, there to observe the native peoples subject to Russia, and a report on their condition and on that of the American possessions generally, shall be submitted to the Government." In that same edict, in connection with the situation in Kamchatka itself, it is further stated (no. 85) that "a transport shall be sent to Kamchatka from Kronstadt every other year, with essential supplies. At the same time, a warship shall be sent." In accordance with this stipulation, Captain of the Navy Golovnin is appointed to circumnavigate the globe and will shortly be departing in the vessel entrusted to him.

Taking the opportunity thus offered, and with a view to lightening the lot of the aforesaid unhappy natives, I most respectfully request that Your Excellency instruct Captain Golovnin to make a careful study, when in the Aleutian and Kurile chains and in other areas where the Company maintains colonies, of the oppressed condition of the natives, who have indeed suffered all manner of abuse and insult at the hands of commanders of Company vessels and from hunters.

I address you thus, dear sir, so that the Government's own objects may be served, by means of these requirements imposed on Captain Golovnin . . . and incidentally so that it may not be necessary to dispatch a warship to the Islands. I must add that, lest all this result in more abuse of the de-

fenceless islanders, I would judge it essential to give the Commandant at
Okhotsk full rights to subject to legal investigation, on their return to that
port from the Islands, those hunters against whom any complaint may have
been laid. Otherwise, and if the evil acts of Company servants continue un-
punished, (acts committed without fear in such remote parts), the Aleuts
may experience the final disaster, to save them from which is the Government's own business. Thus sending my thoughts to Your Excellency, I
would beg that you include them in your instructions to Captain Golovnin,
to assist him in his consideration of the means to be employed for the establishment of the true well-being of the natives of whom I write. I have
the honour to be, etc.,

Pestel'[12]

Traversay was cautious by temperament and training, but he did as he was bid.
Every week, it grew more evident that influence was sliding from the Company's
merchant interests towards the Navy's few, but very active, agents. Signs were
everywhere for the official who, like Traversay, had eyes for them. For instance,
A. A. Arakcheev, whose career was rising swiftly thanks to Alexander's public
recognition of his military "reforms," was willing to allow that inner slide to
continue—notwithstanding major efforts made in 1817 by I. V. Prokof'ev, the
manager in Moscow, to obtain his favour.[13] In addition, K. R. Nesselrode, the
rising figure in the Ministry of Foreign Affairs, was kindly disposed towards the
Navy.[14] Traversay took up his pen:

To General Pestel', Governor-General of Siberia, from Marquis de Traversay, Minister of the Marine.

no. 1348   July 14 1817

In accordance with Your Excellency's communication to me, no. 1124, I
shall not fail to instruct Captain of the Navy Golovnin that, when in the
Aleutian and Kurile Islands and in other colonies of the Russian-American
Company, he should undertake as detailed a study of the position of the natives in those places, as time and his circumstances may permit. . . . If he
should find cases of insult, oppression or abuse, he will make his findings
known to the Commandant at Okhotsk, with whom it will rest to take such
further measures as Your Excellency, through your head chancery directing all those countries [i.e., in Irkutsk], may then see fit to determine. I
have the honour to be, etc.,

Traversay.

From Golovnin's own point of view, matters could hardly have developed better. Traversay sent him a copy of the text of the request that he had had from General Pestel', and of his own response to it (12 August). Article IV of Golovnin's instructions read as follows:

> From the enclosed communication to me from the Governor-General of Siberia, and from my enclosed reply, you will see to what extent I am desirous of satisfying his request with regard to your examining the position of the natives in colonies belonging to the Company. It is for you to act in this matter, on the basis of my aforementioned response.[15]

Golovnin was to devote as much as two years to visiting those islands, bays, and inlets that had yet to be surveyed, using an extra-shallow vessel that the governor would make available to him, if needed, in Kamchatka. He was to learn what hydrographic work had been completed by Lt. Kotzebue in the *Riurik* and not duplicate it. On the voyage out, he would perhaps call at such places as Callao or Valparaiso, where, the government had reason to believe, royalist forces were increasingly pressed in by revolutionary insurgents. How the situation there would have evolved before *Kamchatka* came could only be surmised. But Golovnin would certainly be representing Russia at a time of mounting anti-Spanish crisis in the west of South America; and it would probably be known before he came to Valparaiso that Russia had supplied the Spanish government with five old sloops and three, half-rotten frigates, to be used against American insurgents. His welcome might be warm or very hostile.[16]

GOLOVNIN ON THE NORTH-WEST COAST (1818)

Kamchatka made a swift Atlantic passage, having watered and revictualled at Portsmouth. She reached Rio de Janeiro on 5 November and left after an active two-week stay. Her company was an exclusive one. Among *Kamchatka*'s midshipmen were Friedrich Lütke (1792-1882), later admiral and president of the Academy of Sciences, and future governors of Russian North America—Arvid Etolin, or Etholen (1799-1876), and Ferdinand von Wrangel (1796-1870), later captain of the round-the-world ship *Krotkii* and, like Lütke, a full admiral and eminent geographer.[17] Even more justly than of Kruzenshtern in 1803, it might be said of Golovnin, that he was carrying the future of the Russian naval venture in the North Pacific Ocean.

For twenty days, the voyagers were stalled by winds and waves about Cape

Horn. By New Year's Day, however, they had rounded it. Some six weeks later, the *Kamchatka* stood at anchor at Callao. The tranquillity that reigned there was a consequence of deep disturbances elsewhere in the collapsing Spanish empire. Shipments of grains and other foodstuffs from the port of Valparaiso had virtually ceased. Peru's celebrated mines were no longer being worked, nor was its mint in operation. Yet the regional authorities were calm, and the reception that the viceroy gave for Golovnin at Lima was a stately one. The Russians knew, nevertheless, that Spanish power was declining. They were forced to pay high prices for the victuals that prudence made them stow on board, despite the viceroy's order to the leading local merchants that the prices should be low. *Kamchatka* left Callao, with its earth tremors and hanging mist, on 18 February.[18]

Giving a wide berth to the beckoning Marquesan and Hawaiian Islands[19] and exploiting every hour of the tradewind, Golovnin made yet another rapid passage. By 3 May, *Kamchatka* was at anchor in Avacha Bay. Commanding at the port of Petropavlovsk was the captain's friend and former first lieutenant, P. I. Rikord. Much had changed on the peninsula since Rikord had assumed command with Petropavlovsk rather than Bol'sheretsk as his base. The very sight of the improvements (agriculture, schools, a simple hospital) introduced by Rikord only forcefully reminded Golovnin of all the tasks confronting him. He decided to combine Aleutian charting with a study of conditions under which the Aleuts lived and, he had earlier decided, suffered, in the company possessions. *Kamchatka* would proceed along the chain from west to east, and every officer would keep a full account of what he found. On 16 June, within eight weeks of her arrival, *Kamchatka* had sailed from Petropavlovsk for the now inhabited Komandor Islands.

Golovnin methodically followed his plan for thirteen weeks. Day after day a compound set of detailed records was compiled. Charts were amended, soundings made, *toyons* examined, Aleut villages described. The data multiplied. The exercise was simultaneously an objective and profoundly unobjective one, for Golovnin knew well enough what he proposed to "verify" and "determine" in the Islands. Steadily, the scent of maladministration, of injustice, of brutality and godlessness, alleged or real, drew him on along the chain to Kodiak and so at length to Novo-Arkhangel'sk (28 July 1818). He set to work on the initial draft of what in due course split, under its weight, into two connected onslaughts on the past and present workings of the Russian-American Company: "A Note on the Present Condition of the Russian-American Company," and "A Note on the Condition of the Aleuts in the Settlements of the Russian-American Company." In the following extracts from the former, having first summarized company history in the remote North-East and East, the author "asks himself" four questions: "What benefits has the Company brought to its shareholders? Of what use has the Company been to the State? Is the Company useful to society and to private citizens? What has religion gained?"[20]

A trading company that has received from the Government absolute rights of possession of extensive territories, with their natives and with everything discovered on the surface of the land or underneath it; a company that has the right to make new contracts and establish trade links with the peoples adjacent to its territories; a company, finally, with numerous privileges, many offices—all this is quite unheard of in Russia, but a phenomenon that we first beheld in the Russian-American Company. Grand title! "The Russian-American Company, Under Sovereign Protection" is familiar, now, to practically all our fellow-countrymen. But what exactly *is* this company, in essence? With what does it concern itself, how is its business managed, and what benefits does it bring to the State? . . .

Our naval officers have been witnesses to the activity of the Russian-American Company—many of them from as close a vantage point as myself. *They,* however, were in its service; and the Company imposes obligations on its servants to say nothing bad about its workings. The duty of the honest man, therefore, which is to keep his word, has not permitted them to write in detail and impartially about the Company. Captain Ratmanov, for example, who served with Captain Kruzenshtern, had occasion in Kamchatka to hear of numerous abuses committed by Company agents in America and the Aleutian Islands—abuses which should have been stopped at once. On his return to Russia, he presented observations on these matters to a number of Government officials. Some replied that it was not for *them* to look into such things. Others received Ratmanov's representations, which were just and philanthropic, very drily—which might no doubt have been anticipated, as this was the precise time when the Company's two vessels had returned to Kronstadt at the end of a successful circumnavigation of the earth. The honour for that achievement, of course, lay exclusively with the ships' officers; but the Company Directors were appropriating to themselves no little credit for the voyage . . . . Ratmanov proved unable to make headway.

Then there was Mr. Rezanov. This was an impetuous, quick-tempered individual, a fruitful scribbler and great talker, more able to build castles in the air than to realize a well-laid plan; in sum, a man who lacked the patience and ability to realize large, distant goals. In consequence, as we shall see, this person did the Company considerable harm; he himself destroyed the plans that he devised. . . .

Let us now consider how the Company Directors put their grandiose ideas into effect. First, they went diametrically against the rules which must be followed in such cases, and which builders of commercial institutions have invariably kept. Always, at the outset of a large commercial venture, foreigners observe the strictest secrecy, zealously concealing its true advantages and never revealing either their profits or their strength in distant parts. . . . But *our* Company acted entirely differently. The Directors had no use for guile against a rival. *They* needed to deceive a friend, in order to acquire shareholders. Suddenly, they unveiled tremendous plans, (which they had neither the resources nor the skill to realize). The trade that they proposed to engage in with China and Japan was announced to the whole world, and all the newspapers and journals started discussing preparations for tremendous embassies! A captain of the Navy and a shipwright were sent off to Hamburg and London to purchase vessels for a voyage round the globe. Foreigners knew all about it, in short, from its inception—and the English charged a minimum of 25% more for the ships than need have been paid, had the Company's mighty undertakings not been trumpeted abroad. Then the Company adjudged Russians other than shipwrights incapable of seeing *its* grand enterprises through. For high prices, it had clothing and footwear imported from London for the seamen, and quantities of various supplies. Even the salt-beef came from four States! Nor was this all: the Company showed that in Russia there were neither scientists nor surgeons, so Germans were produced from Germany—at a good salary. . . . As for the successes of the voyage itself, they included the fact that neither the Japanese nor Chinese government even received the ships sent out. But notwithstanding this, and huge expenditure, and losses incurred by errors or faulty reckonings, the Company still proposed to savour the glory inherent in the fact that its vessels could circumnavigate the earth. Rewards and praises that would not have been unworthy of Columbus, heralded "eternal glory" for such feats.

Having shown that the Company brings benefits neither to its own shareholders nor to the State, I will now turn to the third article: has the Company been of use to society, to the private individual? Dandies sporting beaver collars will say that, of course, it is useful. But I say to them that *even in this respect,* the Company is not only useless to them, but positively harmful. For if private citizens had the right to engage in trade in those parts where now the Company alone may do so, they could have bought their beaver collars for less. . . .

Lastly, what has religion gained from this Company? I mentioned that in 1794, the merchant Shelikhov took several monks to Kodiak Island and there left them, entirely unsupervised. Since then, alas, the Company has taken no care whatsoever of that mission, nor lent it even minimal resources. And the eccelesiastics, or most of them, have sunk into dissipation, taken native women, sired children, slipped into drunkenness—in short, made themselves despicable in the Aleuts' sight. The Chief Manager himself has not a little contributed towards their living that debauched life . . . . Many of the Aleut elders are indeed quite familiar with the Russian language. I myself asked them if they had any conception of what Christianity really is. They replied that they knew nothing of it, because nobody had instructed them. To my query as to why their people had allowed themselves to be baptized into a faith of which they had no understanding, they answered very frankly that many of them would gladly undergo baptism daily, since in that case the Company would reward them repeatedly with a shirt and a few leaves to tobacco. And here we see the advances made in religion in the Company settlements! In my view, this observance of the merest external ritual of Holy Baptism with the Aleuts is no less than an insult to the Divinity, which should strictly be prohibited. . . .

In conclusion, I think it my duty to observe that all described here occurred before Captain-Lieutenant Hagemeister assumed the direction of the settlements. It is not possible, in view of the brief time since he did so, that he should already have removed all irregularities. Even now, however, he is taking measures to improve not only the service conditions of the *promyshlenniki,* but also the lot of the natives—an endeavour in which, one may think, he will succeed.[21]

Golovnin made much throughout his "Notes" of objectivity and of his comrades' word of honour. In fact, he wrote a tract. The considerable portions of the "Notes" devoted to statistical analysis of the position in the colonies lent probability to comments interspersed among them. That the *figures* were correct has not been questioned since their publication, and they are accepted here— even though omission is the age-old ally of accountancy. Golovnin was already known in Admiralty circles as the author of well-balanced essays on Japan and the Kurile Islands. Nonetheless, he used his facts to suit his purposes. For instance, Golovnin well knew that it had been at Kruzenshtern's request and with the full collaboration of Lisianskii that *Nadezhda* and *Neva* had been provisioned largely from abroad, and not as a result of any policy laid down by the directors of the Company. Again, it is considerably more than faulty emphasis when he attributes the drunkenness and licence of the "monks" on Kodiak and elsewhere in the settlements not to the Church or to the board or to the missionaries themselves, but to Baranov. Certainly, the missionaries had not been too successful, with a handful of notable exceptions;[22] and certainly Baranov who viewed them as a nuisance, had neglected them for years.[23] But the reasons and effects of the beleaguered and often hungry missionaries' failures, were more complex than Golovnin cared to allow. Was he deliberately reinterpreting realities to fit his ends, as did the loyal Khlebnikov when he described the 1818 meeting between "worthy and respected Captain Golovnin" and the chief manager as though the pair were united by a mutual regard and amity?[24] It would appear so. That in the heat of indignation, he had lost his normal, calm and steady vision and in fact felt deeply hostile towards those whom he regarded as embodiments of maladministration, there can be no doubt.

BARANOV'S REMOVAL

While Golovnin worked eastward in *Kamchatka* in July 1818, Baranov was settling both personal and Company affairs in belated preparation for departure. His personal affairs concerned money, his son's uncertain future, and where to pass his last few years. At one time, he had thought of the Hawaiian Islands; now, he inclined to retire to Kamchatka, where his sole surviving close relation, a younger brother, lived.[25] Gagemeister was at hand when Golovnin at length reached Novo-Arkhangel'sk, and they conferred. Both saw the "need" to have Baranov leave the North Pacific area. By mid-September 1818, Golovnin had undertaken to sponsor Antipatr, Baranov's half-caste son, at the Naval Cadet Corps, and Baranov had agreed to settle in St. Petersburg, "where the Company . . . would undoubtedly undertake to provide him with all the perquisites of a peaceful and pleasant life."[26] Baranov sailed as a passenger aboard *Kutuzov*, under Gagemeister's care, on 27 November 1818.

They did not stop at the Hawaiian Islands, but they spent five weeks in the malarial and torrid climate of Batavia after a call at Port Umata in Guam, where *Kamchatka* had also lately been. Batavia was not a healthy place for the elderly Baranov, whose condition quickly worsened as the days stretched into weeks. While the choice of route and lengthy passage through the tropics almost certainly contributed towards Baranov's death, *Kutuzov* does appear to have left Batavia as soon as all her business was transacted with the local Dutch. In all events, a healthy Gagemeister had the privilege of lowering Baranov's corpse into the sea on 17 April 1819.[27]

Baranov's son was also dead within the year. His death was, like that of his sister within months of her arrival in St. Petersburg, symbolic of the father's unacceptability in certain Admiralty circles. Baranov's death and the appointment of his son-in-law, Ianovskii, as the temporary governor at Novo-Arkhangel'sk marked the beginning of the third phase of the Golovnin campaign against the Company. Like the second phase, which the arrival of *Suvorov* in the settlements in 1814 had initiated, it was doubly imperialist. Once again, the Navy was to further both its own and Russia's ends in the Pacific area as certain naval officers perceived them; and again the opposition was, on one level, embodied by the chairman of the board, M. M. Buldakov, on another by non-Russians on the North-west Coast itself.

Within six months of Golovnin's arrival in the capital on 8 September 1819, Ianovskii was reposted to the Baltic Fleet. His marital connection with the former merchant order was too strong to be ignored, and he left the colonies forever. With the naming of a naval officer of ancient family as "Governor of the Imperial possessions in and by America," it seemed that Russia was at last to be a power in the North Pacific basin.

SCIENTIFIC VENTURES IN THE NORTH AND SOUTH PACIFIC

Riurik was designed and built for scientific and investigative purposes. *Suvorov* had been modified for trading purposes. Neither had heavy armament, yet both had unmistakable political significance in North Pacific waters. In the post-Napoleonic age, as in the time of *Resolution* and *Discovery*, "the aims of science and of empire were essentially one and the same."[28] Knowledge was power.

Kruzenshtern having bespoken certain instruments and stores for him in London in July 1814, Lt. Kotzebue's voyage out in *Riurik* came as no surprise to Englishmen; nor was the slightest effort made to keep the expedition secret. Even so, it was disturbing, as was circumstantial news of the activity of Schaeffer and his men on the Hawaiian Islands, brought to England on 8 June 1817 by the *O'Cain* (Captain McNeil). It lent substance to the rumours of the previous twelve months and to Lt. A. M'Konochie's *Considerations on the Propriety of Establishing a Colony on One of the Sandwich Islands.* In Britain, no one knew what an impression had been made on Kotzebue and Shishmarev when they learned, while at Oahu in November 1816, that "a fine ship" was being built in New South Wales for King Kamehameha's use in peace or war.[29] Had it been known that Kotzebue viewed the building of that craft, *Prince Regent,* as a pledge of British readiness to intervene at once, should any power grow too bold in its pretentions in the Islands[30] and moreover that his view would in 1818 be accepted by the Russian Foreign Ministry, McNeil's news of 1817 would have been softened. As it was, rumour and apprehension flourished. There were Russians, it appeared, on the Kurile and Aleutian Island chains, by San Francisco, on Oahu, Kauai, Molokai, and along the North-west Coast to an uncertain point of latitude. The British were disturbed on three counts. First, Kamehameha, to whom warships had at no time been dispatched as he requested as "tangible evidence" of British protection,[31] was apparently experiencing pressure from the North. Second, with bases in America and Asia, Russian warships might become, almost at will, a larger factor than before in the Pacific.[32] Third, Russia enjoyed certain advantages over all other would-be finders and exploiters of whatever Northern Passage to the Orient and Indies might exist: control and knowledge of Alaska; ports and wintering facilities relatively close at hand, and yearly supplies from California, the Hawaiian Islands, and Siberia.

Profoundly though he scorned the Russian government, John Barrow, secretary to the Admiralty Board, was roused to action by the news of Kotzebue's Arctic enterprise. He had a long term personal involvement in the quest for the elusive Northern Passage, and a public duty to perform where exploration was concerned. It was vexing that the Russians had a grip on the Hawaiian Islands, or on some of them at least; but the Americans were also present. There were certainly no plans in 1817-18 to establish British rule at Honolulu.[33] Possible Russian domination of a navigable passage to the North Pacific Ocean, on the other hand, called for effective action. The mere *finding* of a passage by the Russians would be bad. "It would," wrote Barrow, "be mortifying if a naval power of but yesterday should complete a discovery in the nineteenth century which was so happily commenced by Englishmen in the sixteenth."[34] The Commons sympathized, mindful of Thomas Hurd's remarks in his capacity as chief hydrographer to the effect that all discovery and hydrographic work in the Pacific or the North might well bring naval, economic, or strategic benefits to Britain and moreover "keep alive the active services of many meritorious officers and would be the means of acquiring a mass of valuable information that could not fail of being highly advantageous in any future war."[35] Mindful also of the harm that Russian triumph in the North might do to Britain's China trade, the Commons offered a substantial prize for the discovery of any navigable northern passage to the Orient. The golden age of British Arctic exploration had begun. It bore directly on the launching in the spring of 1819 of the double Russian enterprise of Bellingshausen and Vasil'ev to the farthest South and farthest North respectively.

The time had come, it was agreed in May 1818 when news reached Kronstadt of the Buchanan-Franklin expedition with the *Trent* and *Dorothea* to the North and of the Ross and Parry venture in the *Alexander* and *Isabella* west through Baffin's Bay, for Russia also to win laurels and political advantage, if not profit, from another major scientific venture. What was needed was another, even grander undertaking on the lines of Kotzebue's but supported by the state. Where should the Russian thrust be made? Not to persist where Kotzebue had done well was hardly thinkable. Unlike the British, on the other hand, the Russians could not compensate for failure there by activity in South America, or Africa, or Asia, or Australia. The argument conduced to the adoption, by December 1818, of the notion of a double expeditionary effort.[36] While one Russian squadron sought a navigable passage in the North linking Pacific and Atlantic tidal waters, a second would be bound for farthest South where no European expedition had done any work whatever since James Cook's return in 1775. In Antarctica, a Russian naval officer might hope to emulate the hero of discovery and even complement his work.

For the Arctic venture, Captain-Lieutenant Mikhail Vasil'ev was appointed to the sloop *Otkrytie,* Lieutenant Gleb Shishmarev, late of *Riurik,* to the modified transport *Blagonamerennyi.*[37] Like their Russian, British, and French predecessors, they were to sail through Bering Strait and do their best to find a gap in the ice to the north-east. De Traversay offered command of the Antarctic expedition first to Kruzenshtern, who pleaded illness, then to Makar' Ivanovich Ratmanov, the former first lieutenant in *Nadezhda.* He too pleaded ill health and proposed the former fifth lieutenant of *Nadezhda,* Bellingshausen.[38] Though Bellingshausen thus received the command almost by default, his posting proved most fortunate. Again a sloop and reconfigured transport were allotted and refitted at considerable cost: Bellingshausen was appointed to *Vostok* and M. P. Lazarev to

Mirnyi. For both Bellingshausen and Lazarev, it was a second voyage to the South Pacific.

What Vasil'ev and Shishmarev hoped to do was an impossibility. But circumstantial factors made their Arctic failure the more certain. Neither was of Kotzebue's calibre as a scientific officer or the equal of Lazarev in terms of expertise and seamanship. Their vessels were less suited to their task than *Riurik*, and on coming to the North, they quickly parted. As Parry's and the Rosses' joint experiences showed, the Russians would most likely have gained more by keeping company north-west of Kotzebue Sound. In the event, Vasil'ev reached a point close to the modern Arctic settlement of Wainwright (by his far from certain reckoning, 70° 41'N., 161° 27'W.), before turning back from what he viewed as pack ice. On the Asian littoral, Shishmarev went no further than Cape Serdtse Kamen' before he met solid ice and turned away. The expedition had some small achievements. It discovered Nunivak, an island in the Bering Sea, while in the Carolines it sighted and surveyed a group of sixteen little islands—the "Blagonamerennyi cluster." In the main, however, the Northern expedition was a recognized failure. As a result, its people's journals were not printed by the government. To the frustration of ethnologists from Sydney to Alaska, ethnographic information has remained in naval archives to this day, gathering dust.[39] What the *Otkrytie* had failed to do was largely left for *Blossom* and Frederick William Beechey to achieve.[40]

The southern venture was, by contrast, a brilliant success; and Bellingshausen proved himself to be among the ablest of all maritime explorers of his age. "It would," as a recent writer comments, "be invidious to compare Cook and Bellingshausen. Cook has well been called incomparable; but no pioneer ever found a worthier disciple and successor."[41]

Fabian Gottlieb von Bellingshausen (Russian: Faddei Faddeievich: 1779-1852) came of a noble German family long settled on the Isle of Oesel (Saaremaa) in Estonia. Since his return with the *Nadezhda* in 1806, he had done well and won promotion twice. He was known as a meticulously thorough navigation officer. In that capacity, he had been serving on the Black Sea station and surveying poorly charted littorals: it was a version of Cook's service on the coasts of Newfoundland.[42]

Vostok and *Mirnyi* sailed from Kronstadt on 4 June 1819 and made for Portsmouth. Both were splendidly provisioned. In their holds were a substantial quantity of goods to barter with Pacific islanders for victuals and native artifacts, for once again ethnography was a prominent aim.[43] The departure date was earlier than usual, for it was not to a familiar Pacific that the pair were bound. Much was familiar, however, in the expedition's early stages: calls at Copenhagen and in southern England; purchases of charts, of new chronometers by Arnold, of tinned soup said to prevent effects of scurvy; an encounter with the aged Joseph Banks; and so to South America. But there, at last, the Russians put precedents aside. Leaving Sir Thomas Hardy's squadron outside Rio de Janeiro, Belling-shausen and Lazarev pressed south and sighted the South Georgia Islands on 27 December. Bellingshausen's tactics were profoundly scientific. Cook had approached South Georgia from the south and, passing between Willis Island and the mainland, had surveyed its northern coastline. Bellingshausen was approaching from the north. He therefore rounded Willis Island and explored the southern coast, charting minutely as he went. In such a spirit, and with all the diligence that Cook's lingering presence in those seas seemed to demand of them, Lazarev and Bellingshausen laboured for another fourteen weeks. From South Georgia, they proceeded to another sub-Antarctic cluster, the South Sandwich Islands, which they charted.

They then moved south-east, crossing the Antarctic Circle in longitude 1°W., and drew closer to the continent that they suspected to exist, perhaps concealed behind a fringe of ice. On 28 January 1820, the two vessels, which remained in company despite the *Mirnyi*'s sluggish sailing, thanks to Lazarev's efficiency and Bellingshausen's sense, came to within some twenty miles of modern Princess Martha Land. They turned aside, meeting a chain of mist-enveloped, icy hummocks. Three weeks later on 18 February the Russians were again in sight of frozen land or, more precisely, ice resting on land. They saw shining folds of ice-cap, stretching on to the horizon or, at least, as far as could be seen from either ship. It was Antarctica. But inexperience robbed Bellingshausen of his glory; he apparently supposed that what confronted him was only a series of enormous icebergs. Soviet historians of polar exploration have disputed this at length; but from the extant written evidence, it is apparent that the Russians failed to recognize—or to record the view, if they in fact thought it probable—that underneath the ice-caps lay a continent. The expedition pressed on east, remaining south of 60°S. for a full quarter of the circuit of that line of southern latitude. At last, when firewood and food were growing dangerously short, the expedition made its way towards Australia. At intervals, conditions were appalling. The sun did not appear for days on end. But work went on, regardless. Lazarev and Belling-shausen made their ways towards Australia by different routes to maximize their scientific usefulness. At last, on 11 April 1820, *Vostok* dropped anchor in Port Jackson at Sydney, to be followed four days later by the *Mirnyi*. The companies were cheerful but exhausted.[44]

Bellingshausen and his men were hospitably received in New South Wales; and with competent interpreters at hand, the visitors and host, Lachlan Mac-quarie, found it possible to go some way beyond the formal courtesies. While Bellingshausen and a group of officers rode up to Parramatta, where they stayed for several days visiting nearby townships, other members of the expedition sketched, made observations from a portable observatory on Kirribilli (''Russian'') Point, repaired and cleaned the ships, and sweated at leisure in a steam-bath on the shore.[45] Governor Macquarie had himself travelled through Russia, and after a number of collisions with provincial bureaucrats en route from Astrakhan to Moscow which had angered him (and even led to house arrest), he had been well received by courteous and friendly naval officers at Kronstadt in September 1807.[46] All were conscious of the twenty-year alliance between Russia and Great Britain, which had only been disrupted for a time by the events of 1807 which had led to Captain Golovnin's arrest at Cape Town, incidentally preventing him from visiting Australia himself.[47] It was a consciousness that had already shown itself in the hospitable receptions of *Neva* in 1807 and *Suvorov* in 1814. All passed off pleasantly once more. Well rested and provisioned, the expedition left Port Jackson on 23 May for an active winter voyage through the Tuamotu Archipelago. Again the precedent of Cook was borne in mind.

The archipelago was reached by way of Cook Strait and Queen Charlotte Sound, New Zealand, where the first of two collections of Pacific artifacts was made among the Maori, most probably a small group of the Rangitane tribe (30 May-13 June).[48] The arrival in the lee of Motuara and Long Islands by Ship Cove had not been plannned; high winds had driven Bellingshausen, who had meant to sail directly to Oparo from Port Jackson, to abandon the attempt to round North Island. Nonetheless, the Russians did fine ethnographic work while provisioning and watering. The ship's artist in *Vostok,* Pavel Mikhailov, and the astronomer, Ivan Mikhailovich Simonov, an academic voyager seconded to the expedition from Kazan' University, of which he was eventually *rektor,* both proved to be competent ethnologists. Nor were astronomy and botany neglected. Once again, after this friendly interlude among the Maoris, a people known to Peter the Great thanks to the Russo-Dutch connection (Witsen, Vinius) and admired by Golovnin.[49] Bellingshausen and his companies set out in hopes of making a discovery or two. Their hopes were quickly realized:

Bellingshausen's contributions to the discovery of the Pacific islands were as follows: on July 10 1820, he gave the first firm record of Angatau in the Tuamotu Archipelago. On July 13, he discovered Nihiru, on July 15 the Raevski Islands and Katiu, on July 16 Fakarava, on July 18 Niau, and on July 30 Matahiva, all in the Tuamotu Archipelago. On 1st August, Bellingshausen gave the first firm report of Vostok Island. On August 19 1820, he discovered Tuvana-i-Tholo and Tuvana-i-Ra, and either discovered or rediscovered after the *Bounty* mutineers, Ono-i-Lau in the Fiji Islands. Landings were made on Niau and Ono.[50]

All told, seventeen islands were meticulously charted. Guns were not used once, though natives were occasionally threatening. Well satisfied and healthy, the expedition made its way back to Port Jackson, where again *Vostok* and *Mirnyi* were refitted between 22 September and 12 November, and again all was goodwill.[51] Not until 1831, when news of Polish insurrection had arrived and been digested in Australia, was russophobia to raise its head at Sydney or in Hobart.[52]

But though able, Bellingshausen was a luckless leader. While in Sydney, he was told of the discovery of the South Shetland group by Captain William Smith, a year earlier: the news had just arrived in a despatch from South America. It was enough to make him hasten his departure. As a consequence, the Russians reached the Ross Sea mouth, as modern atlases describe it, in the first days of December and were faced by thick, uncompromising ice. Had they arrived a little later, most of the ice would have been loosened or dispersed.[53]

Now, as the year drew to its end, the Russians started on a final, major voyage of Antarctic exploration. For two whole months and through a distance of 145 degrees of longitude, *Vostok* and *Mirnyi* remained south of the 60th parallel, in sight of the Antarctic pack ice. At last, the expedition was rewarded for tenacity. Uncharted land was sighted on 22 January 1821, in lat. 68° 55'S., long. 90° 50'W. The island was in due course named in honour of the founder of the modern Russian Navy, Peter I Island. One week later, other shores were sighted on the starboard bow. The Russians were unable to approach nearer than forty miles or a fraction less, but perfect visibility permitted them to see that land extended from the shore to their horizon. Alexander I Land, as Bellingshausen called it, was in due course found to be an island, separated from the mainland of Antarctica by a long and narrow sound. Yet, as Frank Debenham observes, "it might be called the continent with more propriety than Bransfield's Trinity Land [discovered in 1820], which was a promontory 350 miles further north. It is therefore most fitting that the sea to the north and west of this discovery is now known as the Bellingshausen Sea."[54]

To the last day of the expedition, Bellingshausen noted what he saw with an exemplary precision. His description of the British and American sealing and whaling industries in the Antarctic is a vital one and was familiar to English readers many years before his other writings.[55] His chart of the South Shetlands, where the Russians had an unexpected meeting with the youthful sealing captain, Nathan Palmer of Connecticut,[56] was far more accurate than might have been expected from a rapid running survey in such waters. So too was a portfolio of sketches of Smolensk (Livingstone), Polotsk (Roberts), Beresina (Greenwich), and several other islands of the Shetland group. The Russians could not know that Edward Bransfield had so recently done portions of the work that they were doing, naming islands to his taste.

Unhappy timing and ill-luck, however, have not robbed the expedition of its fame. Soviet interest in the Antarctic, and specifically in regions of that continent around the scientific settlements or bases named after *Vostok* and *Mirnyi,* may be said to rest in large measure on Bellingshausen's work. And though his failure to have landed on Antarctica caused open disappointment in St. Petersburg, so that official, state-supported publication of his narrative was much delayed even by 1825-26 (when the arrest of K. P. Torson, late lieutenant in *Vostok* and a Decembrist, put it back for five more years),[57] Bellingshausen was not cheated of eventual professional success as great as Kruzenshtern's. Having commanded a division of the Baltic Fleet, he was named military governor of Kronstadt. In that post, he reached the rank of admiral and twice received high naval decorations. As for M. P. Lazarev, he was eventually named commander of the Black Sea Fleet. The rule was proved again: Pacific duty was a special naval service with its own, special rewards for the deserving. High standards of efficiency, and privilege, were self-renewing in the post-Napoleonic and Pacific naval context.

11

The Aftermath of Victory

Even while this grandest of the early Russian circumnavigations of the globe had been unfolding, Golovnin and his supporters had intensified their struggle with the Company-in-the-Pacific. Their success in undermining the authority of those whom they regarded as "civilians" and "merchants" in the colonies was the result of a political campaign. It both reflected and itself comprised a part of that political development which, only recently, had lent such weight to the opinions of Khvostov and Kozodavlev and caused the "merchants" to lose influence and status on the company main board. This process may be summarized as follows. In 1811-12, ostensibly at the request of the main board, which had already lost control of large political decisions to a "Special Provisional Committee,"[1] this last was made a permanent committee. In October 1813, this "new" permanent committee, which was called the "Special Council" of the Company, was charged not with complete responsibility for "all important questions, or those that require secrecy for political reasons . . . and which may sometimes prove perplexing to the Directors or be outside their power,"[2] but instead with obligations to confer with the directors and at all times to co-operate with them. The latter were mistaken in expecting to preserve their independence from the council even where strictly trading matters were concerned. In fact, the council was directing the directors cautiously in 1814-16, then with mounting confidence.

In other ways, too, the directors, now identified as backers of the merchants, saw their powers and prerogatives diminished. For example, the statute that established the council had provided that one of its three posts should be filled anew each year by a new government official. In reality, some members of the council, like Druzhinin, Sarychev, and Mordvinov, held their posts for many years. Thus, the "merchants" on the board became increasingly dependent on the power of the council, where the Navy was at all times and adroitly represented by Sarychev and Mordvinov and, in due course, Golovnin. Other political developments in the St. Petersburg of 1817-20 either aided Golovnin and his supporters on the council in their efforts to reduce the "merchants' " power in the North Pacific region or at least did not reverse them. For reasons unrelated to the Navy or indeed the North Pacific, for example, the Ministry of the Interior lost overall control of the activity of agents of the Company. The office that concerned itself with Company commercial enterprise (Manufacture and Domestic Commerce) was transferred in mid-July 1819 to State Finance. While the fact did not decrease the Navy's influence within the council or the Company at large, it put more pressure on the board, of which Buldakov was the longest-serving member, for its policies and actions were now scrutinized by government accountants and by other fiscal experts of the ministry concerned.[3] In all these ways, then, Golovnin was aided in his effort to replace merchants' authority on the Pacific by the Navy's. If the Company itself became a shell in which the Navy and the Ministry of State Finance itself could work conveniently, that is, if it became another "regular" Crown agency, the latter ministry would have regarded the development as sound.[4] In sum, the Golovnin campaign against the "merchants" and "civilians" unfolded, and could *only* have unfolded, as it did as part and parcel of a larger set of causes and political effects, by no means all of which related to the Navy.

It was true that the commercial vigour of the Company in the Pacific, to which naval crews and officers had long contributed, had been of value to the latter. Even this, however, was allowed for in the Golovnin campaign. It was with naval or some other departmental interests, not with the Company's commercial health in mind, that Golovnin's adherents had since 1812 or slightly earlier publicly criticized the Company, whose very name was found ridiculously "splendid" by its enemies.[5] Golovnin claimed that the service of his fellow Navy men had been of obvious advantage to the Company. Increased participation by the Navy in the Company's activities abroad was bound to bring advantages to both the Company and, more importantly, the state. So the naval case was put to Kozodavlev, Druzhinin, and officials of the Ministry of Foreign Affairs. Nesselrode, *de facto* foreign secretary, had only lately been involved in the conclusion of the Schaeffer-Kaumualii imbroglio.[6] It had disposed him to deplore the expansionist activity of the employees of the Company in the Pacific. Yet more recently, P.I. Poletika's despatches and reports from Philadelphia had lent more weight to Golovnin's assertion that the Navy must defend the dignity of Russia on the North-west Coast. American curiosity about the Coast, and more especially about the settlements, activities, and projects of the Russians, Poletika wrote on 21 January 1821, had "reached an intensity that truly amazes me."[7]

In fact, of course, the Navy and the Company alike had benefitted from their close association in the North Pacific region almost since the century began. Of late, the balance of advantages might have been judged by a dispassionate observer to have shifted, though still falling on the Company's side of the scales. By 1822 the scales were level. Year by year, thanks to the Company's continuing activity in the Pacific, Russian officers and seamen, most of whom were under thirty, made long voyages, visited foreign ports and cities, and did duty in the settlements themselves. In 1819, for example, the *Kutuzov* had no sooner docked at Kronstadt than she had been cleaned and readied for another voyage out to Novo-Arkhangel'sk under Lieutenant P. Dokhturov.[8] Three months earlier, the Company had bought another English vessel of 600 tons. Renamed *Borodino,* she too had been refitted and immediately readied for a voyage to the colonies under Lieutenant Ponafidin, late of the *Suvorov.* She sailed on 29 September 1819, *Kutuzov,* the following September. Both vessels were at Novo-Arkhangel'sk by mid-October 1821; *Borodino,* after a fever-ridden voyage through "the tropic zone," delivered documents that specified the nature of relations that the emperor desired to exist between the Company and King Kamehameha.[9]

In 1819-21, then, just as many naval officers and men were in the North Pacific area furthering both company and Navy interests as there had been during the period preceding the arrival of *Kamchatka* in the colonies. At the same time, Bellingshausen in the South Pacific Ocean and Vasil'ev in northern waters strove to purchase such advantages for government and tsar as were available to all in polar seas in peacetime: glory, knowledge, and the prospect of converting either one into another, harder currency—political advantage. Trade, embodied in the labourers taken to Ross aboard *Kutuzov* in 1821, together with the first phials of vaccine matter known to have been used in California;[10] science, embodied by the patient Bellingshausen in *Vostok*: both were important enterprises in themselves and did not need apologists. Science and trade had long been pieces in the European pattern of Imperial expansion overseas; now, Russia too had her Imperial design across the seas. Science and commerce were assuredly, however, not the main or central part of that design. That part, for Russia, was the North-west Coast and Novo-Arkhangel'sk, to which, perforce, affected powers turned their thoughts. Indicative of a new age, along the North-west Coast as elsewhere in the North Pacific region, was the fact that the United States was one of these, while Spain was not.

EMERGING INTERNATIONAL FACTORS

With the appointment of Captain Matvei Murav'ev as governor at Novo-Arkhangel'sk, it seemed that Golovnin's campaign had brought the Navy total "victory" in the Pacific and that Russia's naval presence might expand without delay over the North Pacific Ocean. It was not to be: the naval victory was hollow. As political rather than naval factors had resulted in that "victory" over the hypothetical or real merchant interest in company affairs, so in the 1820's factors in the wider sphere of international politics ensured that Golovnin's and Lazarev's designs would leak and founder. But the situation was familiar. Though contact with the British in particular, but also with the European naval states in general, had gone so far to reinforce Russian authority over the islands and waters between Asia and America during the later eighteenth century and to increase the Russians' consciousness of them, for fear of political reaction in Great Britain (or indeed elsewhere) that might damage Russian interests at home or on the European Continent, it had been difficult deliberately to *assert* that same authority through the deployment of armed vessels. It was not that Britain *had* reacted badly to intermittent news of Russian progress in the far North-East and East. It was the prospect that she might that had then counted in St. Petersburg—the shadow of political reality, which had its own reality. As S. B. Okun' notes, the Russian government "preferred not to push antipathy to the point where a decisive clash would have become unavoidable. The policy of tsarist Russia with regard to England in the Pacific was patterned substantially after her policy in the Near East."[11]

The problem of the hypothetical reaction of the British to an open demonstration and development of Russian jurisdiction over North Pacific coasts and islands, then, was old by 1820. It had exercised Baranov for a good part of his life. Not until now, however, and the full assumption of authority at Novo-Arkhangel'sk by naval officers did the historic problem seem intractable even to them.

There were three main reasons why political considerations which had after all attended every effort to expand the Russian presence in America for thirty years now loomed large. First, the Russian Navy's prominent new role in the Pacific, where it threatened to control the flow of shipping through the Bering Strait (such as it was), to put more pressure on "New Albion," and even to connect Fort Ross and Sitka with Siberia by regular communications, was a factor of political significance itself. Second, political developments in North America, specifically in areas with which the governor at Novo-Arkhangel'sk concerned himself in an official way, the North-west Coast and California, had been complex and dramatic since Baranov's death in 1819. Third, regardless of events in North America, Murav'ev had reached the colonies in 1820 with instructions to enforce an isolationist and even xenophobic policy well calculated to enflame whatever complications might already be developing in the Pacific basin as a consequence of Spain's decline as a world power.

M. I. MURAV'EV AT NOVO-ARKHANGEL'SK

Murav'ev began as he intended to continue in September 1820. On arrival, he gave orders for the building of additions to "Baranov's Castle"; made arrangements for the shipyard to expand and for *Chirikov* to be overhauled at once; and made it known that, in the interests of friendship with the Tlingit, he proposed to end the rule preventing them from living by the settlement. Within a month, numerous Tlingits were encamped beside the outer walls of Novo-Arkhangel'sk, causing anxiety. The nervousness was justified by earlier and later perfidy or, from the Tlingit point of view, by acts of rightful independence.[12] In the next five years, on Murav'ev's instructions, there were built another sentry station on the upper palisade, a structure to contain the offices of two company clerks, a doctor, and a priest, sick quarters and a drug-store, two large Russian bath-houses, a bakehouse, and new barracks in the lower settlement to house six dozen men. But it was building of another kind that caught the eye of those few foreigners welcomed at Novo-Arkhangel'sk in 1821-24: a new, two-storied arsenal, a new and longer quay, and, overhead, a battery of eight.[13]

Murav'ev's was a unique, motley command. Civilians, natives, and troops, as well as sailors and, to a degree, the missionaries fell under his orders. On the brig *Buldakov*, built at Ross for almost 60,000 roubles, were *promyshlenniki* guarding peas and barley.[14] Seamen mended rigging; Aleuts, the *baidarki*. Armourers cared for the cannon and the muskets of the colony, in which by 1821 there lived about eight hundred souls, more than a third of whom were Russians.[15] In no other company possession were so many Russians congregated or so many women. Infantry kept watch over *Otkrytie,* moored permanently by the quayside as a storeship since October 1820. She was full of grain brought by *Buldakov* or her sister-ship from Ross, the brig *Rumiantsev,* launched in 1818, but found unseaworthy by 1823.[16]

The new governor furthered policies adopted by his predecessors, for example, by distributing monthly chits as legal tender in the settlement for Aleuts and *promyshlenniki* and discontinuing of the old payment in kind save for a private flour ration,[17] and he instituted others of his own towards the schooling and care of the children of the settlement, for instance. He instructed that the children should have fresh and salted fish, as well as whale-meat and vegetables each day at company expense. Their teacher should have two assistants and a helper "to repair their clothes and wash them."[18] Essentially, however, Murav'ev's activities were bent towards a single end. Amidst confusion that was only superficial, he took measures to prepare for the contingency that his instructions made inevitable—semi-isolation from the outside world. His was the task of implementing a decision reached on Golovnin's and Gagemeister's earlier advice[19] and aimed at closing Russia's North Pacific shores and islands to intrusive foreign traders. In his orders lay the seeds of that disaster for the Russian Navy's hopes and aspirations in the North Pacific Ocean which Imperial ukases of September 1821 made the more certain. First, however, it is necessary to take note of certain naval implications, for the Russians, of contemporary revolutionary developments in Upper California.

CHANGING SCENARIA IN UPPER CALIFORNIA

When he called at San Francisco in October 1816, Kotzebue had been drawn into a dialogue with the provincial governor, Pablo de Sola, on the questions of Fort Ross and unofficial, "secret" trade in California at large.[20] No Russian officer who called there afterwards remained unconscious of the serious possible consequences of illicit Russo-Spanish trade and, worse, of Russia's seizing what some powers still regarded as a piece of Spanish territory. Gagemeister grew exceedingly aware of all these problems when he spent two weeks at Ross and four in San Francisco in 1817. Unlike Kotzebue, he believed it proper to become involved in them, at least to the extent of opening a correspondence with de Sola, whose despatches branding Russians as adventuring intruders had already led to the delivery of diplomatic notes to Nesselrode by the ambassador of Spain in Russia.[21] Golovnin's brief dealings with the Spanish Californian authorities at Monterey the following September are unclear. Evidently he involved himself in the discussion on the future and legality of Russian California. He is known to have contended in St. Petersburg at least that since an Englishman, Sir Francis Drake, and not the Spaniards, had found New Albion and since the latter had not built a single outpost to the north of San Francisco, Russia had a double right to found her settlement(s) at Ross. On his return with the *Kamchatka* in 1819, he argued on that basis in the capital, adding that by and large the Indians of Upper California were inimical to Spaniards but friendly to the Russians, whom they welcomed as a check and counterbalance to the lordly Californios. This argument was also pressed by Gagemeister.[22]

That Golovnin should have been drawn into discussion of these matters was perhaps inevitable. On 5 May of the preceding year Cea Bermudez, then the Spanish foreign minister, had made the strongest of his several demands that Russian subjects should abandon Fort Ross. Spain had already done her best to reach agreement on the issue with Kuskov and his superior at Novo-Arkhangel'sk, Baranov, but in vain; and Spanish patience was exhausted. The Russian Foreign Ministry, to which these Spanish notes were handed, had requested that the Company state its position, past and present, on the matter and assist it in explaining or, rather, justifying the existence of Fort Ross. The council, which was charged with the direction of precisely such political and international matters—in conjunction with the board, though this was almost a dead letter by 1817—handed the bomb to the directors. In a disingenuous report to Nesselrode dated 13 August 1817, the board claimed that the Company "had but availed itself of the same law as that adhered to by all European States, when settling their people in the West and the East Indies."[23] And indeed, Article II of the Company's own charter had specifically required that it "trade and hunt" both north *and south* of the 55th degree of northern latitude, "and occupy new lands discovered as Russian possessions, according to prescribed rules, if they have not been previously occupied by, or been dependent on, any other nation."[24] The argument was anything but watertight, for Spanish mariners had sighted the localities known as Fort Ross and Port Rumiantsev long before the Russians came. The board considered what more tenable position it might take. What was referred to by de Cea Bermudez as a "fortress," Nesselrode was told, was in reality an area surrounded by a fence. The guns there were mainly ornamental and provided an inadequate defence against an enemy; but Russian California was, happily, surrounded by its Indian and Spanish friends. As it happened, even while the board was casting round for better pretexts for company activities in Ross and the surrounding area, Captain Gagemeister was obtaining "legal sanction" for the "cession" of that settlement to Russia by the local native chiefs. Happy coincidence! Though months elapsed before the board appreciated it, its Spanish problem had been "solved" in the same month that it assumed its starkest form: September 1817.

Gagemeister had in fact drawn up a paper while at Ross and then persuaded several Indians to place their marks on it. The Indians thereby "confirmed" that they were pleased to have the Russians in their midst because they guaranteed tranquillity in the whole area. In gratitude, they were prepared to cede a plot of land belonging to their brother, Chu-gu-an, on which the Russians could erect their wooden buildings. Such was the sole document establishing the Russian right to Ross.[25]

And yet, the place had huge potential, not perhaps as the especially productive source of grain envisaged by Rezanov and Kuskov,[26] though even here, all was not black, because the Californios were often happy to exchange their grain for tallow, lard, small boats, or ironware,[27] but as the core of a considerably larger Russian colony or province and a mid-Pacific base for Russian shipping. Gagemeister had not gone to California with thoughts of helping the expansion of a province and strategically important port; he went to settle hunting-trading difficulties and, if possible, to guarantee a future grain supply for northern settlements. He soon *began* to entertain imperialist, that is, territorial, ambitions once in the country; so did other servants of the Navy who, in 1820-25, developed far more grandiose Pacific projects than Golovnin had.

Small wonder, in these changing circumstances, that officials in St. Petersburg and Russian subjects in the three countries most sensitive to an aggressively expansionist new Russian policy in the Pacific area, England, Spain, and the United States, treated the document of "cession" with a mixture of anxiety, silence, and scorn. Indeed, some Russians in politically significant positions, in St. Petersburg and elsewhere, scorned this claim. "So far from being evident," observed the minister plenipotentiary to the United States in a letter to Count Nesselrode, the Company's pretended "rights" in California were highly dubious. P. I. Poletika had considerable knowledge of American antipathies derived from postings under Pahlen (1810-12) and from recent and more aggravating brushes with the Philadelphians.[28] He explained that any atlas would reveal that "the colony in question," that is, Ross, "was wedged into the Spanish possessions in California and the territory next to them. In fact, one fairly long-established Spanish colony is situated scarcely thirty miles from Ross, towards the south, while the town of Monterey, chief town of Upper California, is at a distance of barely 1° away from it."[29] The British and Americans moreover might declare that the Russians, as some Russian naval officers were saying of the Spaniards, had forfeited all rights based on the fact of occupation: for the Company had not a single permanent establishment between Fort Ross and Sitka Sound. In the Russian Foreign Ministry, where Nesselrode himself perused Poletika's despatches, the prevailing attitude towards the end of 1820 differed greatly from that adopted by the forward Navy party where Fort Ross and its defenders were concerned. And whereas Nesselrode treated Poletika's remark that certain influential men in Philadelphia had noted that the Russians had no posts between Fort Ross and Sitka Sound as a good reason for a policy of caution in New Albion, Mordvinov saw it simply as a reason for establishing an outpost in New Albion at once.

But though Mordvinov, Kruzenshtern, and Gagemeister might not have thought of them as such in 1820, there were actually two good reasons for considering the danger of a forward naval policy from Sitka Sound to Ross. First, the United States had recently become an interested party in the far North-west and West of North America, having in February 1819 signed a convention with the court of Spain which recognized the 42nd parallel as the extremity of Spanish jurisdiction in New Albion or Upper California. North of that parallel, the British and Americans remained in harness. The convention was pregnant with significance for London and St. Petersburg alike. Secondly, even the need to *deal* directly with Madrid over the question of Fort Ross was growing smaller by the week, for Spain's authority was known to be diminishing in Upper California. Revolution in Madrid itself seemed possible, though not yet likely, to Tatishchev, then the Russian minister in Spain, who, like Count Stroganov in 1810-12, served Alexander well in 1820. What could Russia gain from a provocative new policy towards New Albion and Ross? She still supported Spain in Central and South America; and Spain had few enough supporters in her struggle with colonial insurgents. The most prudent policy in the opinion of Nesselrode and Kruzenshtern was to begin negotiations with Madrid over those areas at once. Ross might conceivably be closed if, as a compensation, Spain would guarantee specific trading rights in perpetuity in California to Russians who were authorized to trade there, that is, servants of the Company.[30] If both New Spain and California did throw off Spanish authority as Poletika thought probable by 1821,[31] then Russia would at least have gained those rights and could expect to see them swiftly reconfirmed by whatever new government emerged on the Pacific littoral. Again, if Spain sanctioned the existence of Fort Ross and its dependencies, would not that future hypothetical authority in Upper California concede the Russian right to hunt and farm and trade there?[32] It would hardly seek out trouble on its northern flank when it was young and insecure. Here Nesselrode and Kruzenshtern were wrong. When Hernandez de Vincent visited Ross in 1822 in the name of Iturbide, the new Emperor of Mexico, he demanded that the Russians leave the area within six months; was quite untroubled by the prospect that St. Petersburg would fail to recognize his master; and would certainly have failed to recognize whatever cessions had been wrested by the Russians from Madrid in 1820.

Now news of Spanish revolution reached St. Petersburg. Not only did it reawaken hopes throughout the Company that Spain would finally give formal recognition of Russian rights in California, it also nourished and enlarged all such ambitions.[33] In her present sorry state, Spain might repay Russia for comfort and support, present and past (monies were owing for the vessels bought in 1817-18),[34] by ceding all the coast between Fort Ross and San Francisco. True, the infant government in Mexico might well protest against the cession; but, wrote Kruzenshtern in a memorial to Nesselrode, that government, embattled as it must remain a little longer, would not venture on an international war in California. Indeed, it could be willing to "legitimize" Fort Ross in return for speedy Russian recognition of its own legitimacy.

Golovnin respected Kruzenshtern, but in this matter he could not agree with him. "It may be said with certainty," he argued in the council of the Company and then in writing to the Foreign Ministry, "that the cession made by the king of Spain will not be recognized by the republicans; and even though we should gain possession of the land, it would still be perilous to invest any capital in the improvement of Ross—for the republicans would no doubt desire to assert their rights, for reasons of their own. They will then . . . insist on the destruction of our establishments, and will perhaps even employ force."[35] In Golovnin's opinion, local agents of the Company should sound out independent Mexican and Californian views and, while St. Petersburg delayed its recognition of a new Mexican state, examine local attitudes towards Fort Ross and to the prospect of a larger Russian province, which might possibly extend to San Francisco in the south and far inland.

Alas, the Californian and indeed the whole Pacific situation had developed with a speed that made it late, by 1821, for any such "examining." In the case of California, revolution made it late; and over that, no foreign power had control. Conversely, Golovnin and a handful of his influential sympathizers were themselves responsible for no less sorry changes in the Russians' situation on the Coast.

THE UKASES OF SEPTEMBER 1821

Golovnin's object in his 1818 "Notes" had been to represent the agents and the actions of the Company in the Pacific in as negative a light as possible. With that in mind, he had insisted that though even Russians who were not in company employ were barred from hunting in the countries under company control, many Americans had done so for three decades (1788-1818) and that unimpressed as they indubitably were by the pretensions of a toothless company, they were unlikely to abandon such a profitable trade. "For the beaver trade has not escaped the notice of that bold and enterprising people—a people skilled in commerce and commercial seafaring."[36] In fact, the company main office had already taken measures to control the brazen pilfering of foreigners; in January 1818, and expressly to discourage them from coming to the area of Novo-Arkhangel'sk at all, company agents were forbidden to dispose of any peltry caught in company possessions to non-Russians.[37] (Board and council turned a blind eye to the selling of some furs to Californians.) But Golovnin, like Gagemeister, felt that merely depriving the Americans and other long-range traders of the Company's own furs, would not deter them from continuing to barter guns and liquor with the Tlingit. Content with modest profits on each single voyage (they suggested on returning to St. Petersburg),[38] American free-traders had succeeded in developing tastes among the Coastal Indians that almost guaranteed that they would never be rebuffed. The truth was that a number of New Englanders had recently been shot at from New England guns which they themselves had carried to the Coast. But it was not with such realities that Golovnin was dealing or indeed would now have cared to come to terms. He insisted that measures were needed to restrain the open insolence of foreigners. It damaged Russian trade, and it affronted Russian pride. The Company had undertaken more than it had power or resources to accomplish; but the Company's disgrace would disgrace the nation. Politically and economically, therefore, it was important to enlarge the Navy's role in regions that were theoretically under the Company's control.

So Golovnin was arguing when more despatches reached St. Petersburg from Novo-Arkhangel'sk. Still the Bostonians were bartering their weaponry for furs.[39] Almost immediately, in response to these pressures, the company main office reiterated its 1818 ban on sales of peltry to non-Russians. It was Golovnin's hour of influence. By August 1820, he had practically *carte blanche* in the main office, where events even as large as those in Spain and Mexico were over-shadowed by the fact that the first charter of the Company had lapsed on 8 July 1819. In his capacity as member of the council, Golovnin for months played an essential part in the involved negotiations with the Ministries of Foreign Affairs and Finance, the Senate, and the Naval Ministry that led to confirmation on 14 September 1821 of a markedly altered charter for the Company.

It was an interlude of influence that left its mark, for on the council's in-stances, the southern limit of the territory claimed for Russia by the Company was moved to 51°N. on the coast of North America, and 45° 50′ on the Asian lit-toral. Also, by the terms of the ninth article of the new charter, the employees of the Company were to be given all the rights and benefits enjoyed by persons in the armed and civil services. The Company, in short, could now attract both civil servants and, particularly, naval officers into its service with less trouble and, it hoped, in larger numbers than before. The stage was set for the ukases of 4 and 13 September 1821. By the first, Russia claimed sovereignty over territory in America down to 51°N., extending to 115 miles offshore on both the North American and Asian sides of the Pacific Ocean. By the second, which comple-mented it, the Company was granted a monopoly of fur-hunting, trading, and fishing in those seas, on islands of the Kurile and Aleutian chains, and on all other northern islands for a further twenty years:

Section 1. The pursuit of commerce, whaling, and fishery, and of all other industry in all islands, ports, and gulfs, including the whole of the Northwest Coast of America beginning at Bering Strait and down to 51°N., also from the Aleutian Islands to the east coast of Siberia, as well as along the Kurile Islands from Bering Strait to the southern cape of the island of Uruppu, viz., to 45° 50′N., are exclusively granted to Rus-sian subjects.

Section 2. It is therefore prohibited to all foreign vessels not only to land on coasts and islands belonging to Russia, as stated above, but also to approach them within less than 100 Italian miles. The transgressors' vessel is liable to confiscation, with the whole cargo.

Section 3. An exception to this rule is to be made in favour of vessels car-ried thither by heavy gales or by real want of provisions . . . . Ships of friendly Governments merely on discovery are like-wise exempt from the foregoing rule. In this case, however, they must previously be provided with passports from the Russian Minister of the Marine.

Section 14. It is interdicted to foreign ships to carry on any traffic or barter with the natives of the islands and the Northwest Coast of America in the whole extent hereabove mentioned. A ship convicted of this trade shall be confiscated.

Section 24. Foreign men-of-war shall likewise comply with the above regulations for merchant ships, to maintain the rights and benefit of the Company. In case of opposition, complaints will be made to their Governments.

Section 25. In case a ship of the Russian Imperial Navy or one belonging to the Company meet a foreign vessel on the above stated coasts, or in harbours or roads within the aforementioned limits, and if the commander find grounds by the present regulation for seizing that vessel, he shall act as follows:

Section 26. The commander of the Russian vessel, suspecting a foreign ship to be liable to confiscation, must inquire and search the same and, finding her guilty, take possession of her. Should the foreign vessel resist, he is to use, first, persuasion, then threats, and at last, force; endeavouring, however, at all times to do this with as much reserve as possible. But if the foreign vessel employs force against force, then he shall consider the same an enemy, and shall force her to surrender according to the naval laws.[40]

How had a naval captain come to wield such influence? No doubt, the fact that Nesselrode had been in Russian naval service as a youth (1796-97) before transferring to the Guards[41] and entertained residually friendly feelings towards Kronstadt and its staff worked to the Navy's benefit. Nesselrode could also see that Golovnin's position on the question of the Navy's proper role in the Pacific harmonized with Poletika's, despite some differences of opinion on specific issues such as the correct approach towards republicans in Upper California. And he had recently been vexed by company activity in the Hawaiian Archipelago. It was a matter first of reputation. Golovnin, like Kruzenshtern, was viewed as an authority on North Pacific questions. Second, Nesselrode approved of Golovnin's distinction between what should be attempted on the Coast, and what in California, in a time of mounting pressures in both areas.

A Eurocentric diplomat *par excellence,* Nesselrode was of German origin, though he was raised in half a dozen European cities. Nevertheless, he was ill at ease with North American and North Pacific issues. Republican ideals were decidedly not his, nor was he comfortable when dealing with remote anti-monarchical tendencies or factions, as in Chile and Peru. Still, in 1820-21, he made a conscientious effort to grasp the new and rapidly evolving situations on the far side of the globe of which the tsar himself was ignorant, a fact that would have tended to discourage such an effort in a diplomatic secretary or aide.[42] Given the time and very patchy information that had reached St. Petersburg by late December 1820, the decision to move cautiously in Upper California but decisively at Novo-Arkhangel'sk was sound enough. In theory, it was far easier for Company and Navy to defend their joint position on the northern *lisière* than in the South and no more difficult to hold it than for agents of a hostile state to overrun it. In reality, it was a deeply flawed decision.

First, it overlooked the simple fact that danger might approach the Russian outposts in Alaska from the landward side. Indeed, within six months of the announcement of the ukases of September 1821, the governor and committee of the Hudson's Bay Company resolved to push their own activities far north and westward of the Fraser River Valley and thus "to keep the Russians at a distance."[43] Secondly, it failed to take the government of the United States into account. The Russians had miscalculated on the basis of uncertain information and erroneous assumptions about attitudes that foreign groups and governments would likely take towards a new expansionism on the Coast. The tsar, who had himself shown little interest in these developments in the Americas, or even in Poletika's and Nesselrode's related correspondence of the previous twelve months, little suspected the offence and anger that his act would cause in London and in Washington when he initialled the ukases. Too late, their military and naval implications grew apparent to officials who had earlier regarded them as bearing less on Admiralty matters than on fishing, furs, and trade. If offending foreign ships were to be "confiscated" and if poachers were in fact to be detected and arrested in so vast an area, at least one squadron was immediately wanted for the duty.

All this was plain to Nesselrode by April 1822. Two British protests were then followed by a note from the United States. "That Government," wrote Nesselrode to D. A. Gur'ev of Finance on 3 June, "protests against what *it* calls the expansion of our territory."[44] The position was most difficult, for it was not in Russia's interest to clash with Britain over such an issue. Alexander's object at the time was to bring "order" to the Balkans as a whole: British neutrality was wanted. On the other hand, the Company for whose specific benefit the edicts had been promulgated was in deep financial straits.[45] And edicts were not to be ignored if the Imperial authority was to remain unquestioned in the company possessions as they stood. Measures were needed to lend weight to the Imperial authority where, as so often in the past, it lacked both ships and guns.

The measures taken would a few years earlier have been regarded as impolitic. *Apollon*, sloop (Captain Irinarkh Tulub'ev) had not long before left Kronstadt for the colonies. He was expected to arrive by August or September 1822.[46] Like the *Kamchatka* and *Otkrytie*, the *Apollon* was of about 900 tons and well equipped and manned. She mounted 32 new guns. She was the nucleus, at least, of a Pacific squadron. Tulub'ev's sailing orders had already specified that he should look for foreign poachers, on arriving at 51°N. and moving up to Novo-Arkhangel'sk. Orders now followed him, by courier across Siberia, expanding on those earlier instructions and requiring him "to cruise as close as possible to the dry land [the North-west Coast], though not beyond the latitudes in which the Russian-American Company at present enjoys all its prerogatives."[47] It was a start; but further action was required, if the rights so boldly claimed, but now disputed by the British and Americans, were to be guarded successfully. It was resolved to send two other Navy vessels to the Coast. The frigate *Kreiser,* mounting 36 guns, and the *Ladoga* (ex-*Mirnyi* of the Bellingshausen-Lazarev Antarctic expedition), a sloop-rigged reconfigured transport armed with 20 guns of varied calibre, were promptly fixed on. Mikhail Petrovich Lazarev was offered the command of the small squadron and accepted it at once, naming his younger brother, Andrei, to the *Ladoga.* Provisioning for eighteen months began. Both craft were readied at the Navy's expense, and they sailed from Kronstadt on 17 August. Lazarev's orders were to join the *Apollon* and to patrol the North-west Coast. The depredations of free traders were to end.[48]

KREISER AND *LADOGA:* THE VISIT TO VAN DIEMEN'S LAND (1823)

The voyage out to Sitka sealed Lazarev's professional success. Since 1812, he had been marked as a young officer of high potential; now, he made a move towards flag rank. His seamen, midshipmen, and officers formed a particularly able company. Among the officers were future admirals P.S. Nakhimov and E. V. Putiatin, four future captains, Pavel Murav'ev, future director of the School of Merchant Seamen, and a future chief staff surgeon of the Black Sea Fleet, P. Aleman. Two of the five lieutenants in the *Kreiser* had already served with Lazarev in *Mirnyi* in the South Pacific Ocean (Kupreianov, Annenkov).[49] Of all his company, however, only D. I. Zavalishin, the incipient Decembrist, was to equal or surpass him in celebrity in later years.[50]

Kreiser and *Ladoga* reached Rio de Janeiro in January 1823 after a slow and troubled crossing. Storms had twice damaged the transport, which was sluggish under sail even though canvas had been added on the instances of M. P. Lazarev, who well remembered her behaviour as the *Mirnyi.* The slow crossing to Brazil, where grain and sugar were acquired for the companies' own use and for delivery to Novo-Arkhangel'sk, had large results. Being unwilling to do battle with the elements about the Horn in March, when sudden storms could be expected, Lazarev chose the longer, eastward route to the Pacific. When at length *Kreiser* and *Ladoga* came to the colonies, the situation was quite different from what they would have faced some weeks before had they arrived by way of Chile. On 17 May 1823, after a storm-wracked, eighty-six-day passage from Brazil, they approached Van Diemen's Land. *Kreiser* and *Ladoga* dropped anchor in the Derwent, hard by Hobart Town, at 4 P.M., without great ceremony.[51] Both ships' companies were weary, and Lazarev was counting on the friendly welcome he received.[52]

Lieutenant-Governor of the young colony in 1823 was Colonel William Sorell. Because they posed no threat that he could see, Sorell received the 254 Russians, who described themselves as bound upon discovery,[53] with courtesy. They were a respite from his own preoccupations: bushrangers, new convict parties, building. *Ladoga* was beached a little higher up the Derwent, and the Russian officers were entertained by local worthies starved of European news: Bromley and Frazer, Scott and Loans.

A single incident, of which the details are uncertain, cast a cloud over this otherwise harmonious and tranquil interlude. A group of seamen sent inland to fell soft timber for the ships under the orders of two midshipmen grew restive, and apparently, four or five of them were insubordinate. The midshipmen were young. After so many weeks at sea, all had presumably been hoping for a respite in a town, only to find themselves sent off into the bush. A leading seaman, Stanislav Stankevich, then went missing.[54] Sorell was told the facts, or most of them, and a search was made. But the deserter, whom Lazarev describes—perhaps with relish—as "of Polish antecedents," was not found, nor was he ever heard of later. Most of what is known about this incident rests on the questionable evidence of an already paranoid Zavalishin, who dramatically describes it in his record of the visit, written later in Siberia, as a "rebellion" or "riot."[55]

Kreiser and *Lagoda* left Hobart on 9 June, without Stankevich. To the last, Colonel Sorell remained in ignorance of Lazarev's true mission on the Coast.

EVENTS AT NOVO-ARKHANGEL'SK

Lazarev proceeded to the colonies via Tahiti, where he victualled and watered. The five-day sojourn, from 15 to 20 July, passed pleasantly. In a despatch to A. V. Müller of the Naval Ministry, composed at San Francisco five months later on 10 December 1823, Lazarev described their subsequent activities:

On July 24, being in latitude 13° 34′S., longitude 210° 56′E., all dangers from the numerous low coral islands to the north of Tahiti being over, I decided that it would be advantageous to part company with *Ladoga*. I instructed her commander to proceed with her cargo to Kamchatka and, having unloaded there, to hasten to Novo-Arkhangel'sk on the Northwest

Coast. . . . We ourselves crossed the Equator on July 31. On September 2, we caught sight of the Coast, and next day dropped anchor by Novo-Arkhangel'sk, where we joined *Apollon* sloop; her commander was now Lt. Khrushchev, Captain Tulub'ev having perished on March 31 1822 on passage to New Holland from Rio de Janeiro.

I discussed with the Chief Manager of the Russian-American Company's colonies, Captain-Lieutenant Murav'ev, the waters in which my frigate should cruise. Having given Captain Murav'ev a copy of the latest two communications *I* had had from Government, one dated August 3 1822, the other August 13 (no. 1865), in which the Emperor's intentions on the matter of surveillance to be kept by Russian warships off the Northwest Coast were stated, I was informed by the Captain that, on pondering the Government's objectives as expressed in those instructions in the context of the present situation on the Coast, he regarded all patrolling by my frigate as superfluous. And, with a reference to the impossibility of getting any fresh provisions whatsoever in that season for my people, (let alone sugar or bread), he suggested that I apply to the ports of California, where both might very probably be had. . . .

However, in his next communication to me, Captain-Lieutenant Murav'ev informed me of a grave shortage of grains in California, news of which had lately reached him with the Company-owned brig *Buldakov,* just arrived from San Francisco. The *Ladoga* moreover, he observed, being provisioned from Russia for a voyage of two years, would shortly be obliged also to look for some assistance in the colonies. Because of the grain shortage in California, not only the colonies but I too might encounter difficulties in obtaining supplies in that province; and the *Ladoga,* being similarly in need of victuals, would only further embarrass our situation, while bringing no advantages to the colonies. For, as he said, he simply could not see the need for her presence on those shores.

I decided, in view of these representations by the Chief Manager, which were intended to ease the colonial supply situation over the coming year, to order the sloops *Ladoga* and *Apollon* back to Russia. *Ladoga* finally reached Sitka on November 9, having unloaded all her cargo for Kamchatka and Okhotsk at Petropavlovsk. Her commander reported that the sloop needed repairs to the rigging, and recaulking. As neither matter could be attended to at Sitka so late in the season, I resolved to waste no time but to set out, with her commander, for San Francisco.[56]

Lazarev is eloquent despite himself, and though he does not spell it out, he makes it plain that Murav'ev had grown dispirited after three years at Novo-Arkhangel'sk and that the Russians' situation on the Coast was an unhappy one.[57] *Apollon* had reached the colonies in mid-October 1822, bringing the text of the ukases of September 1821 in several copies. But already, the 1820 ban on trade with the Americans was showing its unfortunate effects. It was no longer possible to purchase what was needed, year by year; now, Murav'ev was forced to take what came from Kronstadt—it could hardly be returned as rotten, broken, or not needed. The system of supplying from the Baltic was an economic failure: goods from Kronstadt cost far more than the Americans had charged, arrived too late and often spoiled, and could only be dispatched if the political relationships of the great powers posed no threat to their delivery. Again, it cost the Company some 700,000 roubles to send a cargo with *Kutuzov* (1820-21) worth 200,000 roubles.[58] There was hunger in the colonies even in 1821, though its full rigour was not felt by those at Novo-Arkhangel'sk, but by the men at Iakutat, Attu, and the Pribylov Islands. But already, the directors had compounded all these problems on the Coast by agreeing, in response to a complaint from the Siberian administration that the Iakuts who delivered freight over the infamous Iakutsk-Okhotsk Tract were impoverished and wretched, to convey grains from the Baltic to the colonies in company-owned vessels. Of the rye sent in *Elizaveta* (1821), less than a half was bound for Iakutat, Attu, and other places much in need; nor did the Iakuts benefit. *Elizaveta* met a hurricane not far from the Cape of Good Hope. The vessel with her, *Riurik,* weathered it successfully, but the *Elizaveta* sprang three leaks and barely struggled back to Simon's Bay and safety. An examination showed her structure to be dangerously rotted; she was therefore sold with all the cargo that was saleable and fetched a miserable price.[59] In all, about 435,000 roubles were lost to no avail.[60] Then, early in 1823, news reached the colonies that since the Company was ordering the purchase of a vessel in New England to replace *Elizaveta,* no supplies would go from Kronstadt that season. A vessel of 400 tons, built at New Bedford and renamed *Elena,* was in due course bought and sent in 1824 with rye that spoiled on transit through the tropics, so that once again the servants of the Company gained nothing, and the board lost almost half a million roubles.[61]

The colonies were thus in evil case and the prospect of survival for a time on fish and seal-meat appeared inevitable. In these circumstances, "necessity altered the rules."[62] Governor Murav'ev appealed to the directors for additional supplies; in the interim, he sent Lieutenant A. Etolin to Oahu in the *Golovnin* to purchase fresh provisions. Calling at San Francisco on the voyage out, Etolin managed to exchange some furs for grain.

No grain to spare, almost no furs, no foreigners: such was the situation in the latter part of 1823, when *Ladoga* arrived at Novo-Arkhangel'sk. The elder Lazarev did not present it quite so starkly in despatches. He had spoken for the Navy and for prohibition of all commerce with Americans along the Coast during the earlier colonial debate, and any crisis would reflect unfavourably on the service, notwithstanding all extenuating circumstances. But the truth was not concealed in contemporary private letters, for example, those of Midshipman P. S. Nakhimov of the *Kreiser* to his friend, Lt. M. F. Reineke:

We finally reached Sitka on September 23 1823. It is a sorry place with a wretched climate—cruel winds, incessant rain. You can get practically nothing there, and even if you do, it's only for the highest price. No fresh food except fish, and precious little even of that, during the winter. But we had plenty of work. An amazing number of rats had bred on board, spoiling everything without discrimination. We had to unlade the whole frigate, fumigate her, then relade her. And *that* took three weeks.[63]

For the companies of *Ladoga* and *Kreiser,* as of *Apollon,* the voyage out to Sitka had been hard. But compared with the problems facing Murav'ev in 1822-23, those that the seamen had encountered in the form of storms and strain were small. Murav'ev did not rebel against his orders, but being at hand, he grew intolerably conscious of the suffering that they had caused and would continue to occasion. Finally he was constrained by his own conscience to infringe them. In 1824, the failures of the new supplying policy and of the ban having grown evident to all, the main office sent Murav'ev permission to resume trade with Americans and others, if such trade was necessary and would not, in his opinion, lead to loss.[64] By then, however, Murav'ev was, in the board's and council's sight, so closely linked with problems of supply and disappointing hunting expeditions that the notion of replacing him was attractive. For his own part, he had grown disillusioned with the Coast and his appointment and was ready to return to Europe. The decision to replace him had been reached some weeks before *Elena* sailed from Kronstadt for the colonies under Lieutenant P. E. Chistiakov on 31 July 1824.[65] By August 1825, when Chistiakov replaced him as the governor, thoughts of patrolling Russian waters off the shores of North America would have been utterly abandoned by a government whose understanding of the situation there was six months behind the current of events.

THE CALIFORNIAN SITUATION (1823-24): ZAVALISHIN'S PROJECT

The crews of the frigate *Apollon* and of the company-owned trader *Golovnin,* though very different in composition, were united in their high opinion of the port of San Francisco. All were quite at ease there and in splendid spirits, for relations between Argüello and their own captains were cordial,[66] and the amenities of San Francisco, which included ample sunshine and a fairly balanced diet, were most welcome. Since the collapse of Spanish power in the area local Californian authorities had given Russians, whom they knew and almost trusted, the considerable privilege of hunting sea-otter on shares, and since 1821, when Mexico had gained her independence, all the ports of California had been opened up to unrestricted trade.[67] Certain *padres,* like Duran, might do their best to fan suspicions of the Russians and their Californian intentions, but in 1824, the new authorities had other and more urgent matters to attend to than Fort Ross. Luis Argüello found himself at liberty to treat the Russians as he chose, and shortly after the arrival of the *Ladoga* and *Kreiser,* he chose to sign a twelve-month contract which produced some fifteen hundred otter skins to be divided.[68] Why should Russians in the country not be happy? Trade was adequate, and there was certainly no present danger from the regional authorities whom Argüello represented. For the first time, Russia even had the strength in California to dissuade local authorities from moving against Ross and its dependencies, if they should feel disposed to do so. Never had the Russian seaman been so much in evidence in California. Hardly had the *Volga* left for Sitka than *Buldakov* and *Golovnin* arrived. *Kreiser* and *Ladoga* then joined the *Apollon* at San Francisco, which was shortly afterwards revisited by *Riurik* and visited by *Predpriiatie* (Otto von Kotzebue) on her voyage round the world. *Baikal,* ex-*Arab,* a vessel lately purchased by Lieutenant Etolin on Oahu, was already on her way to Monterey. All these vessels were not present at one moment. Nonetheless, there was some reason for referring to a Russian fleet as Argüello did.[69]

At San Francisco, then, matters looked healthy in the early part of 1824. Perhaps a number of the Russian naval officers felt that the Californios, and certain *padres* in particular, were indolent and good-for-nothing, as did Kotzebue who arrived in mid-October to be entertained and influenced by J. M. Estudillo.[70] But at least they were prepared to trade on a considerable scale with the Russians, of whose strength in the Pacific they again had an exaggerated notion. Kotzebue, not surprisingly, did not discuss a change of orders that released him from the duty of patrolling Russian waters as a unit in a non-existent squadron and permitted him to concentrate once more, when certain stores had been delivered to Kamchatka (8-16 June 1824), upon scientific matters. As before, his was an academic company, and though the Spaniards might be struck by her two dozen new six-pounders, the true meaning of his enterprise lay in the presence of the naturalists Lenz and Eschscholtz, the astronomer von Preus, and the mineralogist Hoffmann. Like his first Pacific venture, this resulted in a quantity of scientific data and a number of discoveries.[71]

But Lazarev went on to Ross from San Francisco Bay. How matters had progressed there since 1822 was soon apparent: *Kreiser's* seven-gun salute was met by silence. There was not a single shell at Port Rumiantsev or at Ross, it was explained, to return such compliments. As for the settlement's other resources, the supposed main granary for all the northern settlements had long been disappointing expectations. Ross was a table, of approximately one square mile, cut off by ravines on all three landward sides. As Port Rumiantsev (Bodega Bay) had replaced the open and exposed Ross Cove as the colony's chief harbour,[72] so had land further afield replaced it in 1821-24 under the management of Carl Schmidt as the major source of grain. In 1823, twice as much wheat was planted as before, and the harvest proved sufficient for the colony's own needs. But there was nothing for the hungry men at Novo-Arkhangel'sk and further north; nor had the problems of the place—a salty soil and persistent dampness that encouraged blight, yearly depredations by squirrels and mice—yet been defeated. Furthermore, there was so little pasturage at Ross that stock could not be raised on any scale; and if cattle strayed away, they were invariably lost for weeks on end, or altogether. And the local redwood, pine, and laurel were ill-suited for shipbuilding. As the timber was not adequately seasoned before use in early days, the craft built there had never lasted well. In short, the colony presented a sad spectacle to those who understood its full importance to the northern settlements and to the Russian enterprise in the Pacific as a whole. Nevertheless, even a cursory inspection of the place, even a week or two with Schmidt or his successor, Pavel Shelikhov (1824), who had had his people sowing land two miles off, sufficed to fire the imagination of the officers of *Ladoga* and *Kreiser* and of Midshipman Dmitrii Zavalishin in particular. Despite the many failures, it was evident that Russian California could grow good grain as well as vegetables and fruit. Another era of intensive and extensive agriculture was beginning with the advent of Shelikhov: 1824 marked a beginning and an end—*Kiakhta* was the last ship to be built there at the Company's expense, and otter hunting was declining. Zavalishin thus arrived there at a watershed: past disappointments, recent changes that reflected new political realities, and future possibilities and hopes could all be seen by the perceptive visitor in a single panorama.

Lazarev and Kotzebue also saw the full significance of Ross for the whole Russian enterprise in the Pacific. Still, the problem was to feed the northern colonies. Both officers, moreover, were aware of the contrasting Kruzenshtern and Golovnin positions on the matter of the Bay of San Francisco and its future ownership. But they were pragmatists, and much had passed in North America since Kruzenshtern had spoken of the benefits that Russia might obtain in gaining San Francisco Bay. Regrettably, the bay was not, in fact, in Russian hands. "It is certainly," wrote Kotzebue, "*a great pity* that we were not beforehand with the Spaniards. The advantages of possessing this beautiful bay are incalculable."[73] But for all Mexico's weakness to the north of Monterey, the moment for aggressive action had already passed. Russia should have moved into the area in strength in 1812.

Zavalishin's attitude towards Fort Ross and Russia's future role in Upper California was very different. Not for him the calm acceptance of the view that Russia's chance had slipped away. He concerned himself with future possibilities, not with the past. No sooner had he reached Fort Ross than he was seized with the idea of its huge potential value. In his view, in its present narrow limits, Fort Ross would always be a small, marginal asset to the state, a pawn in time of war, a farm of modest productivity.[74] Schmidt had been correct to stretch its boundaries, for its development as a strategically desirable and economically successful colony depended on an area more suitable for naval and Imperial designs. The present colony was nothing but a beachhead. Shelikhov's plans were good, but far too small. Fort Ross should be the starting-point of swift Russian expansion up the coast and inland: pioneers were immediately wanted. Such expansion north would have enormous naval value; for (as Zavalishin emphasized again, two years later, in his cell in Peter-and-Paul Fortress, St. Petersburg, as he awaited death or exile for his part in the Decembrist insurrection of 1825), "the acquisition of its harbours and the low cost of upkeep would allow us to maintain an observation fleet there. That fleet would give Russia mastery of the Pacific and control of the China trade; would consolidate our possession of the other settlements; and would, besides, serve to contain the influence of the United States and England."[75]

Zavalishin's thoughts on the Pacific question took clear shape only in 1826 and later years. Even in 1824, however, when he was in California, he had argued that the settlement of Ross should be expanded with the Navy's active help north to the boundary of the United States as fixed in 1819, south to San Francisco, and eastward to the Sacramento River. Such expansion had of course been contemplated by Kuskov. The novelty of Zavalishin's plan lay in its advocacy of direct and sweeping means to reach that end. The whole of California, in Zavalishin's view, should be brought into the Empire, perhaps by means of pressure that could easily be placed on Spanish royalists based on the missions. There should certainly be no negotiations, for negotiation would perforce involve the Mexicans and that would lend *de facto* recognition to the Mexican authority.

The presence of a well-armed ship or two, claimed Zavalishin, would minimize the risk of an attack by sea on an enlarged and wealthy colony. And if the Navy had facilities in some of the excellent California ports, it might extend its zone of influence around the rim of the Pacific. The Amur River mouth and Sakhalin might both support new Russian bases, while the plans that had been bungled in Hawaii could in due course be revived.[76] (As Golovnin and Lazarev had stressed the maritime ability and economic strength of the Americans for their own purposes, so Zavalishin underplayed it now.) The large new colony or province of Russian California would provide the Russian Navy with resources as Fort Ross had not. Indeed, bolstering Russia's naval strength in the Pacific and provisioning the northern settlements should be regarded as the two essential purposes of Russian California. But the Navy's widened role in the Pacific would not end the Company's responsibility for protecting its interests: an armed company vessel, too, should always be on station in the area. Meanwhile, a group of naval engineers would have been brought to California by sea, "to fortify the north bank of the sound in the port of San Francisco . . . build lighthouses on both shores . . . dig canals and build locks for the loading of ships . . . raise a fortress in Bodega and set up a shipyard there."[77]

On his return to St. Petersburg from the Pacific, Zavalishin wrote at least two memoranda on these questions, advocating annexation of a part or all of Upper California to the Russian Empire. He sent them to the council of the Company, and they were read with some approval by Mordvinov.[78] The admiral, it seems, offered the youthful naval officer a permanent position with the Company and sought Imperial permission to dispatch him as the manager at Ross in place of Schmidt, whom Murav'ev had lately criticized as "rash, and not a brilliant reader or writer."[79] Alexander I would not consent, for he had learned of Zavalishin's grand designs and of his dealings in California with such royalists as José Altimira of the San Francisco mission.[80] Nonetheless, the Zavalishin memoranda were discussed by board and council and submitted to Count Nesselrode.[81] The matter went no further. Nesselrode had bitter memories of his negotiations with Sir Charles Bagot, then British ambassador, over Imperial pretentions on the fringes of the North Pacific. A convention on the twin issues of sovereignty and commerce on the Coast had been initialled by Nesselrode and Poletika for Russia and by Henry Middleton for the United States, but talks continued, as the Zavalishin projects were considered, with Sir Charles Bagot's replacement, Stratford Canning. Even Zavalishin's references to an "Order of the Restoration" (founded by himself) made Nesselrode uncomfortable.[82] Zavalishin's Californian hopes, in short, were doomed. He twice vainly sought meetings with the tsar to make his case for intervention in America and swift colonization of the hinterland of Ross.[83] He was refused even a discharge from the Navy. Alexander was not seeking confrontation on the far side of the world with any state. The time had yet to come when diplomatic and political considerations in the Balkans and in Western Europe would not hamper the development of Russian naval strength in the Pacific.

EDICTS AND TREATIES: RUSSIAN PROSPECTS IN DECLINE (1824-25)

It was company servants, not Americans, who chiefly suffered from the edicts of September 1821 and from the total ban on international trade in northern settlements including Novo-Arkhangel'sk. Year after year, they had depended more or less on grain from California, where the increasing competition from American and English traders forced the value of the Russian exports down, made grain more costly, and increased the risk attendant on a disappointing harvest, as in 1823.[84] The rye spoiled on *Elena*'s voyage and the generally unneeded goods that she conveyed to the Pacific for a half a million roubles worsened the position.[85] Murav'ev, his spirits lowered by a reading of the Russo-American convention, by which citizens of the United States had gained the right to hunt and trade in waters north of 54° 40', informed the Company of his opinion. The Americans were now at liberty to take their craft up Russian rivers to the source of furs. To Murav'ev, as to Mordvinov in the capital, it was deplorable.[86] Murav'ev boarded *Elena* on 4 November 1825 and left the Coast and its exigencies forever. Returning to the Baltic via California, he took a valuable mixed cargo of peltry, to which sugar was added in Brazil.[87]

Despite the adverse circumstances and residual affection for Baranov, Murav'ev had proved popular at Novo-Arkhangel'sk. He was a member of a highly educated family and liberal in outlook. There had also been achievements in the North since his arrival. Novo-Arkhangel'sk itself was much enlarged, and the treatment of the Company's least servants had improved. Under Khramchenko and A. Etolin, in the *Golovnin* and the *Baranov,* a survey was completed in 1822-24 of the coasts from Bristol Bay west to the mouth of the Kuskokwim River and of Norton Sound, as the Americans and British called those places. And the Russians of the settlements had, as a company, weathered the storm unleashed upon them by their countrymen in 1821.

For the first time, under provisions of the Anglo-Russian convention signed on 28 February 1825 by Stratford Canning and Nesselrode, Russian North America acquired an eastern limit. South of Novo-Arkhangel'sk, it was to stretch no more than thirty miles inland from tidewater, while in the south the Russian border was, again, 54° 40′N. Novo-Arkhangel'sk was to be opened for a ten-year term to shipping under British registration.

In this clear delimiting of Russian territory, Golovnin and Admiral Mordvinov saw a partial cancellation of the Company's best efforts on the Coast for the preceding twenty years. Nesselrode, conversely, saw precise delimitation as desirable: "for in a sense, this marks the *beginning* of the Pacific colonies' political existence, and of their freedom from danger, because now, for the first time, their relations with foreign Governments have been determined."[88] Article VI of the convention, treating navigation rights on rivers flowing into the Pacific, merits full quotation here:

> VI: It is understood that the subjects of His Britannic Majesty from whatever quarter they may arrive, whether from the ocean or from the interior of the continent, shall forever enjoy the right of navigating freely, and without any hindrance whatever, all rivers and streams which, in their course towards the Pacific Ocean, may cross the line of demarcation upon the line of coast described in Article III [the 141st parallel].[89]

It was the crucial article. By it, the British gained the right to seek their peltry at its source upriver. Slim as it already was, the Russian *lisière* was stripped of almost all its mercantile, though not of all political, potential. If foreigners could sail upriver undisturbed, under the guns of Russian ships and forts at river mouths, what was the point of building forts or keeping ships along the Coast? The darkest apprehensions of Mordvinov, Golovnin, and their associates in Company and Navy had been realized thanks to the emperor's determination to risk nothing far afield that might do damage close to home. The forward Navy party lost the game along the Coast as a result of having almost won, too grandly, in September 1821.

NAVAL ASPECTS OF POLITICAL REVERSE

The Company's own losses have been analyzed elsewhere. But, what did the Russian Navy lose in the Pacific and in North America as a result of the developments of 1824-25? As a consequence of the conventions signed in 1824-25, it may be said first, the expansionist or forward naval party in the capital lost the initiative for the first time in twenty years. The loss of self-assurance and of impetus was felt from Petropavlovsk to Fort Ross. The time of Russian aggrandizement in the North Pacific area was over; nor would Alexander listen to Mordvinov's urgings that some sections of the Anglo-Russian convention be revised and renegotiated. To be sure, Russian ships continued to make voyages from Kronstadt to the North Pacific Ocean both for trading and for scientific purposes. In 1826, Lütke and Staniukovich left for the North Pacific outposts in the sloops *Seniavin* and *Moller*.[90] By then any idea of dispatching Russian squadrons to patrol off North America was far removed from the official mind; and when Lazarev brought *Kreiser* back to Kronstadt, she was not replaced in the Pacific by another warship. Captain Chistiakov, indeed, needed the services of naval officers and twice as many pilots on the California-Sitka run: *Baikal* and *Kiakhta, Golovnin, Okhotsk* were in the South in 1825-27. But the chances of his suite being enlarged, or of more officers and men being sent out for active service, were remote.[91] Okhotsk and Petropavlovsk, too, were largely left alone. It was as though the two conventions numbed the Russian Navy's nerve and will where the Pacific was concerned.

Zavalishin's plans had probably not been more practical than the imperialist projects of Rezanov, Schaeffer, Ljungstedt, and the Yankee-Russian Irishman, Peter Dobell.[92] But what of plans for the strategically more tenable northerly areas of Russian domination and for further exploration and expansion on the mainland of America north-east of Novo-Arkhangel'sk? Here, the effect of the conventions was to freeze naval initiative in a politically important fashion. Illustrative of the process was the fate of the sub-Arctic naval plans developed by Lieutenant V. P. Romanov in the early weeks of 1823.

Romanov (1796-1864), geographer, proponent of free trade, and radical, worked in the Arctic with Vasil'ev in *Otkrytie* (1820). He thus took his place in the long line of Russian officers whose interest in Russian North America derived one from another: Billings and Sarychev, Kruzenshtern, Vasil'ev, Kotzebue. By the same token he participated in a process by which naval, scientific, and commercial interests in the far North and in the navigable passage gained emphatically imperialist overtones during the reign of Alexander I. Romanov's own Imperial-cum-naval plans had grown while he was serving with *Otkrytie* and on reflection at St. Petersburg in 1822 when he had made a study of the past, present conditions, and potential of the company possessions in America. Like Zavalishin's, his imagination had been fueled by a visit to the North Pacific area, but unlike Zavalishin, he believed that northern settlements, and not Fort Ross, should be the focal points of Russian enterprise in North America. He did, however, successfully petition A. V. Müller to instruct the Navy Hydrographic Department to chart and map Fort Ross and its dependencies.[93]

Romanov was a pragmatist. He recognized that Russia could maintain her weakened economic influence along the Coast only if rising British influence from the interior were stopped before it seeped over the mountains to the ocean. Russian factories, he argued, should be built without delay at certain points along the mainland, and new colonists and trappers should be taken in by sea with naval help.[94] There was no reason to abandon thoughts of pushing Russian influence north-east into the continent. A British party, led by Franklin, had recently traced the Coppermine River to its mouth, claiming the so-called Barren Ground for Britain, but the Coppermine was far from Mount St. Elias. In two memoirs, sent in January 1823 to the chief of naval staff, Romanov recommended that a Russian naval party should "describe" the vast interior "between the Copper River and the Hudson Strait," that is, to the northern tip of modern Quebec, and from the "Icy Promontory" eastward, possibly collaborating with the second expedition to be led by Captain Franklin.

For its part, the Naval Ministry was unimpressed by these immense designs, which were referred to the directors of the Company as being pertinent to company activity, present or future. At this juncture, the lieutenant made the friendship of a prominent director, I. Prokof'ev, and, like other naval officers with North Pacific plans and aspirations, he drew close to a new servant of the Company—a future leader of the insurrectionary movement in St. Petersburg, K. F. Ryleev.

Ryleev was in company employment as a manager, and he discharged his office duties conscientiously.[95] He had an interest in the Pacific and America. His heart, however, was in literary and political activity. He introduced Romanov to A. A. Bestuzhev (-Marlinskii), a fellow dissident, who in his turn placed two at least of Romanov's articles about the North Pacific colonies in almanacs or journals of the day.[96] Merely to think of Zavalishin, of Torson and Romanov in the North Pacific context, is to recognize a Company-Decembrist-Navy nexus. Understandably, the presence of these future "ne'er-do-wells" and "vagabonds" in Russian vessels in the North (and South) Pacific, in the last years of the reign of Alexander, predisposed his younger brother and successor, Nicholas I, against the naval enterprise in the Pacific and the Company.[97]

Ryleev had himself not seen America, but he was quite persuaded that the colonies should trade with anyone in the attempt to save morale and to restore their economic viability. In his opinion as in Simpson's, the 1821 ukases were "sweeping and absurd,"[98] and the "description" of an unknown area would be some basis for whatever territorial pretensions might in due course be advanced. He believed the lands in question were not a part of any state.[99] Ryleev was alive to the enormous economic and strategic implications of Romanov's plans and did his best to have the Company adopt them. But he lacked in influence, and Romanov was not destined to return to the Pacific. His peripheral involvement in the liberal Decembrist movement led to his imprisonment and professional disgrace. Ironically, both he and Zavalishin were enabled by their status as "state criminals" to bring their projects to the government's attention far more fully than before; and both delighted in *de facto* recognition by the Crown of their political existence and their personal opinions on these matters.

Meanwhile, at the company main office, a deplorable financial situation had emerged and been concealed with assistance from the council. It was basically a question of mismanagement and, hence, of unprofitability. Since 1820, sales of furs and other goods had not begun to meet the escalating costs of sending vessels round the world. Company debts had risen sharply since the ban on trade with foreigners at Novo-Arkhangel'sk. In 1822 and for a second time in 1823, company shareholders received no dividend; but ships continued to be bought, salaries paid, and in the company main building hospitality was offered to officials of importance as in other and more profitable times.[100]

At last, the board acknowledged that the overall financial situation of the Company was grave. At the behest of the Imperial State Council, a commission was established by the minister of finance, Kankrin, to investigate the issue. Golovnin was promptly named to the commission. At length, all but one of the directors were exonerated from the charge of fiscal irresponsibility, and all blame was imputed to a single individual, Benedict Cramer, an American, the representative in Russia of the bankers Cramer, Smith, and Company. Cramer went quietly, resigning from the board. For the directors who survived these trying days, disgrace had been averted. For the Navy, full control of the Pacific colonies was guaranteed. It was a hollow legacy.

Conclusion and Reflections

Russia's naval aims and operations in the North Pacific region differed basically from those in other waters, in the eighteenth and early nineteenth centuries. First, they reflected scientific and exploratory impulses which were, initially, almost as potent as the factors of political "necessity" with which they ultimately merged.[1] Nor were exploratory and scientific elements ever quite absent from political and mercantile designs for the remote North-East of Asia. Such elements were present in other Russian naval ventures: in the White, Black, Baltic, Caspian, and Aral Seas; but in the North Pacific venture, they were stronger from the outset and remained so. In their search for a navigable passage over Russia and Siberia, Bering and Chichagov and Krenitsyn and Billings undertook much valuable scientific work, by no means all of which was maritime in nature. Naval officers, indeed, made contributions to a range of sciences, including botany, astronomy, ethnology, and physics. Kotzebue and Vasil'ev merely developed the examples of their predecessors from the time of Bering on; and, in the main, the sailing orders of commanders of Pacific expeditions emphasized that exploration and the sciences should be pursued as far as possible. The scientific lustre of the Russian Navy's North Pacific venture was increased during the early nineteenth century by the distinguished work of Baltic German officers (Kruzenshtern, Kotzebue, Bellingshausen). These, in turn, lent a new aura of prestige to Pacific ventures, insofar as they were Baltic-based and rested upon voyages of circumnavigation, but they did nothing to enhance the service prospects of those officers based on the North Pacific region.

Russia's naval undertakings and objectives in that region differed, secondly, as a result of the essentially exploitative nature of the Russian-cossack enterprise in the remote North-East and East, in the Aleutians, and in North America. Not only was the Navy's very presence in the North Pacific area linked with the lure of furs and with the need to guard the fur supply from natives (hence the sea-route to Kamchatka) or from foreigners; from the beginning, it had cloudy international implications.

Finally, Russia's naval aims in the Pacific were distinctive as a consequence of weakness—local weakness, in the far North-East and East, where peculation and an element of maritime incompetence were institutional—but also, more significantly, on the international scale of naval capability. While Russian consciousness of the Pacific and eventually of American possessions both as threatened borderlands and as the sources of "soft gold" or precious peltry placed the Navy in an odd, supportive role, the fact of weakness on the high seas made it difficult even for autocrats to cast it in another, grander part. Always, the Russian Crown was pondering the possible reactions of the courts of Spain, England, or both to bolder moves in the Pacific. For this and other reasons, which included an awareness that Britain in particular might well retaliate in Europe, north or south, against a forward Russian policy in North Pacific waters or the Orient, and the enormous distance between European Russia and Okhotsk with the resultant bad communication lines, Pacific matters took a low priority. When danger grew in Europe, resources were withdrawn from the Pacific: hence, the cancellation of Mulovskii's expedition and the modest naval presence in the far North-East and East until the close of the Napoleonic Wars. The cautious Russian move onto the North-west Coast and southward merely emphasized what was peculiar and difficult about the Navy's Eastern function. For the move, which in itself led to no strengthening of Russia's naval presence in the area, was from a power vacuum into "a field of international rivalry, where Russian, Spanish, British, and American imperialism vied for territory and resources, with outright military conflict always a possibility."[2]

In short, a naval presence was required in the North Pacific area; yet for political rather than strictly naval reasons the Navy was restricted to an unheroic part in the Pacific, round the rim of which meanwhile cossack and foreign influence crept unabated. The situation was both paradoxical and, by its very nature, galling to the forward-looking servant of the Navy.

On the one hand, naval officers, seamen, and pilots had been playing an important part in the expansion of the Russian hunting-trading enterprise. Indeed, in 1803, with the departure of the Kruzenshtern-Lisianskii expedition to the North Pacific colonies, their role became major: first, assisting and supporting exploratory work; second, aiding commercial exploitation, but tempering human exploitation in Kamchatka, the Aleutian and Kurile Island chains, and on the Coast; thirdly, lending material support and moral aid to Russian settlers, cossack hunters, loyal Aleuts; fourth, provisioning outposts; fifth, furthering diplomatic ends. Nor had the coming of the Navy from the South, as opposed to Arctic Asia (to which parts it had been sent repeatedly, despite the oceanic impulses of officers like N. F. Golovin and Saunders), eased the rigours of the work of naval officers and men based at Okhotsk or in Kamchatka. Still, the Navy was connected with sub-Arctic exploration as in Vitus Bering's day. It was an ample programme, certainly. And yet it lacked the central warlike and assertive element of naval programmes everywhere. It left no room for guns at sea. Hardly surprisingly, some younger officers who had seen action in the west and served abroad as Volunteers (Iu.F. Lisianskii, M. P. Lazarev, V. M. Golovnin) found this position vexing. It was calculated to affront the naval patriot, ambitious for his service as for Russia as a whole: the mere thought of losing face in an unequal struggle with a foreign power off Kamchatka or the Coast, it seemed, was to ensure that Russian subjects hide their proper aspirations in the North Pacific area and, worse, use the convenient facade of a commercial company. V. M. Golovnin was especially provoked that a company directed by "civilians" and "merchants" should be recognized as the official agency of Russian jurisdiction in that area. Thus, in the early nineteenth century, arose that open lack of sympathy towards the Russian-American Company and all its local servants on the part of Navy men, which at the close of the Napoleonic Wars became a regular campaign, waged by a handful of young officers with powerful supporters in St. Petersburg, to oust that Company from its position of authority in the Pacific settlements. The naval interest successfully replaced the merchant as the main force in the council of the Company in 1816-17. Within four years, the naval party seemed victorious over the merchants of the company main board and in the settlements themselves, where Murav'ev then served as naval governor. But naval "victory" was self-defeating: no sooner had the two ukases of September 1821 been added to the bans on trade with foreigners in the Pacific Russian colonies, than foreign anger was provoked as it had never been in Catherine II's cautious times. The stage was set for the delimiting of Russian North America in 1824-25; "Russian Columbia" was not to be.

Had decisive steps been taken to assert the Russian presence on the Coast even as late as 1810, Russia would in fact have had no cause to fear a countermove by England or Spain. Nor, for that matter, was Madrid in a position to do much to harm the Russian national interest in Europe. But the point is not that neither Spain nor England acted, or were likely to take measures, to arrest Russian expansion in the North Pacific region. The point is that the Russian *apprehension* of a counter-move, by Britain in particular and not in the Pacific, had significant effects on Russian policy for the Pacific. Russia's lack of military and economic strength on the Pacific made a policy of circumspection prudent, even necessary. Whereas the Baltic and Black Sea fleets existed to control specific coastal seas, control of the Pacific to the south of the Aleutian chain was only a recognized objective of the Navy for a hapless three-year period from 1821 to 1824. Given these circumstances, it is easy to sympathize with officers like Lazarev and Golovnin who held that Russia's naval weakness in the North Pacific area was self-perpetuating and that Russia, through her Navy, could control the North Pacific if she would. Hypercaution, both perceived, had led to constant non-investment of resources in the far North-East and East and in the colonies, which might have strengthened Russia's hand in North America. There had been various lost opportunities; vessels, guns, and colonists had not been sent to the Aleutians and the Coast. Because the state was not committed to the North Pacific venture or, at least, was not committed to expansion of effective Russian power, semi-failures and the problems of provisioning the North Pacific outposts from the Baltic or Okhotsk became more likely to persist. Perhaps the Navy, like the Company, would find it difficult to feed the Russian settlements; but a half-hearted commitment to the task almost ensured failure. Naturally patriots in naval uniform deplored the Russian Naval Ministry's indolence where the Pacific was concerned. By 1803, Russia seemed poised to spread her influence along the Coast to the Columbia and even to New Albion. Grain did not ripen in the area of Sitka as it would in California; and whereas Californios met increasingly unfavourable conditions on the few occasions when they did press north, Russians met more balmy weather moving south. The Russian Navy might be Baltic-oriented still, but it had servants on the shores of Asia and America ready to undertake new ventures. Again, a growing number of ambitious, able officers based in the Baltic were aware of the enormous economic and strategic possibilities confronting Russia in the East. Since James Trevenen's presentation of his "North Pacific Project" (1787), Russian officers and merchants had anticipated the commercial-scientific venture undertaken by *Nadezhda* and *Neva* in 1803-6. More recently, the Company and Navy had been sending vessels out to the colonies most seasons. The Napoleonic Wars diverted French and British energies away from the Pacific, and the War of 1812 had stayed the hand of the "Bostonians." Viewed from Madrid or London, Russia's situation in the North Pacific area was highly promising.

And yet by 1825 even the possibility of Russian domination of the North Pacific basin, which the maritime and mercantile activity of Russians on the Coast and in the Kurile Islands, in Hawaii and at Ross had only lately seemed to render imminent, had vanished. It had vanished, in the first place, as a consequence of the conventions which the bans on trade with foreign subjects and the Navy's hollow triumph over Russian merchants had made probable if not inevitable. But, essentially, the hopes and aspirations of the forward naval party and the prospects of the North Pacific colonies themselves had all been dimmed by two large failures. The Navy had not managed to provision the Pacific settlements reliably and economically, nor had it lent material assistance or moral aid to servants of the Company, in whom the Russian national interest was vested, when it had been most urgently required and, politically at least, would have produced a high return. Essentially, the naval situation in the North Pacific region was the same in 1810 as it was half a century before. Because the Navy was so weak in the Pacific, the activities of its ambitious and far-sighted officers were largely hidden by an enterprise well calculated to increase the Navy's strength. It would certainly have done so in the first half of Catherine II's reign had she been willing to commit herself to the development of Russian economic and strategic influence in the remote North-East and East. Ever preoccupied with matters nearer home, however, the empress did not look upon commitment of that kind as either sensible or possible while, on an international plane, it had been possible (1764-68). The collapse of the Mulovskii expedition merely emphasized a pattern of Imperial priorities which, in their times, Chirikov, Miatlev, Krenitsyn, Sarychev, and Minitskii all tried and failed to readjust.

In 1808-10, and in the time of Murav'ev, the price was paid for a decision to restrain both naval growth and cash investment in Kamchatka and beyond. A. A. Baranov's efforts to give substance to Rezanov's southern projects in the absence of a solid underpinning of materiel, money and manpower were valiant. The absence of effective opposition by the European powers, whom Napoleon continued to preoccupy, enhanced his chances of success. By 1812, Russians were building on the coast of California, three years later, in Hawaii. Yet already, at the mouth of the Columbia, the cost to Russia of the lack of a sufficient naval presence and commitment had been great.

Compared with California or Oahu, the Columbia territory was close to Novo-Arkhangel'sk. It had a mild and pleasant climate. "I dare say," remarked N. P. Rezanov on 16 February 1806, "that we shall be in a position to attract our colonists to the Columbia from various places."[3] At the time, there was no European power in the region. As a company of traders, the Nor'westers were—in 1808 as later—an unstable group, with little influence in London. In the spring of 1810, even Simon McGillivray, politically the most significant Nor'wester there, failed totally to rouse Lord Wellesley to action where Gray's River was concerned, though he waxed eloquent on Astor, Clark, and Lewis, and the danger of American control of the Columbia and all surrounding countries.[4] The Americans themselves had slender claim to the reportedly rich lands around the river. J. J. Astor, whose Astoria was to be built some seven miles from open water in 1812, did not have captains in the area in 1808-10. Only a few days' sail from Sitka, the Russians might have built a fort unseen and unimpeded by Americans or Englishmen, if not by local Indians. Once built, a fort and farm would be strategically quite tenable and might provision both itself and its defenders in the North. The failure of the Nikolai Bulygin-Tarakanov expedition in 1808-9 was an overall misfortune for the Russian enterprise in the Pacific. That no second expedition was attempted with another, larger vessel and another, well-supplied and able company of seamen was an even greater one, for which no blame attached to servants of the Navy.

The Navy had been sent to the Pacific in the early eighteenth century not as an independent force but in a difficult, support capacity. Its role remained supportative and difficult. It had been sent, not round the globe as certain officers envisaged, but to Arctic latitudes in search of navigable seaways through the ice. Not till the early nineteenth century were southern routes approved of in St. Petersburg. Official thinking on the Navy's proper role in the Pacific area, in short, presented obstacles of two main sorts to those like Kruzenshtern, the Lazarevs, and V. M. Golovnin, who viewed that role as strategically important and politically, as well as scientifically extensive. First, there were obstacles connected with the Navy's long involvement with the search for open water in the Arctic as opposed to warmer waters in the East; then there were those to do with long association with the fur trade as a minor and, at times, a secret partner. Golovnin addressed himself to the solution of this latter set of problems; Kruzenshtern, to resolving the former. Both were partially successful. They contributed directly to the work of a Pacific "special service," expeditions from the Baltic to the North Pacific outposts connected with the Baltic Germans, science, and prestige. And by that token, both men placed their names and reputations in the brightest single column of the record of the Navy's early effort in the North and South Pacific; for the Navy's double failure in provisioning and as an adequate deterrent force off the Pacific settlements was counterbalanced by the sum of the achievements of its Kotzebues, Bergs, and Bellingshausens. Yet, paradoxically, Golovnin and Kruzenshtern were both contributing towards the ultimate defeat of their ambitions for the service and the state in the Pacific and in North America. They viewed success in terms of mastery of the Pacific settlements and of the Russian merchant interest. So, once again, one sees the sequence of apparent naval victory (over Buldakov and the board), the bans on trade with foreign subjects in the colonies, the period of hardship (1821-24), the conventions, and the bursting of Imperialist dreams. There is a poignancy about the blossoming of naval aspirations and Imperial ambitions in the 1820's: the Pacific and American designs of Zavalishin and Romanov among other youthful officers. Such aspirations were not new in naval circles; but at last, they fluttered temptingly within the bounds of practicality—or only just beyond its margin. In reality, all were impossible for the familiar and fundamental reason that the state had not committed its resources and its energies to North Pacific regions when it might have and was once again unwilling to embark upon adventures that might well have repercussions nearer home.

The Russian Navy learned two lessons from the sum of its experience in North Pacific waters in the eighteenth and the early nineteenth centuries. (The non-existence of a navigable seaway through the Arctic to the Orient and foreign opposition to the further growth of Russian North America were lessons for the Russian state.) The first was that the Navy was incapable of a "great power" role in the Pacific in the absence of a base of economic, agricultural, and military strength on the Pacific or, at least, in Transbaikalia. Supply lines were too long and too uncertain. Much depended on belated recognition of priorities advanced by V. A. Miatlev in 1753-54. Furs might fuel enterprise, but food must feed entrepreneurs and other servants of the state in inhospitable or distant areas. The second lesson was that Russia's Baltic Fleet or, for that matter, White Sea Fleet or Black Sea Fleet, could not maintain an economical or even constant presence in the North Pacific Ocean. Geographical reality impinged on naval policy. The naval force in the Pacific and the far North-East, it followed, should be largely self-sufficient with local yards and arsenals as well as seamen and, at no great distance, farms. It might be small by Baltic standards, but it should always be efficient and reliable enough to cope with North Pacific problems and/or threats of foreign provenance without the prospect of a rapid reinforcement.

The developments of 1824-25 caused loss of confidence and will in naval circles where the North Pacific Ocean was concerned. Naval decline, at all events, was quite perceptible in the Pacific in the period ensuing that here studied, that is, from 1825 to 1854. Nor did the wholly unsuccessful Anglo-French attack on Petropavlovsk-in-Kamchatka in the course of the Crimean War induce the government to reassess its military and maritime priorities. The North Pacific was in general neglected till the middle of the present century.

And yet, significantly, servants of the Navy strove at intervals throughout the nineteenth century to meet the challenge of the early disappointments in the North Pacific basin. The work of Captain G. A. Nevel'skoi and the Russian occupation of ''Amuria'' in the mid-century on one level was merely an extension of the effort to provision Russia's North Pacific settlements, both Asian and American. It was an effort to which many naval officers, notably commandants at Petropavlovsk and Okhotsk and in the colonies, had long contributed to the extent that they were able, introducing horticulture, cattle-breeding, husbandry. Such officers, from 1825 into the age of ironclads, which merely aggravated problems of provisionment, repair facilities and fueling in the Pacific, far from Russian mines and farms, had learned the first of the two lessons mentioned earlier. As to the second, that of building up a modern, self-sufficient naval force in the Pacific, neither they nor any other naval officers proved able to exert sufficient pressure where it counted to avert the needless tragedy of 1904. At least the triumph of Japan obliged the government at large to face that lesson, which has ever since been borne in mind at Kronstadt and in Moscow.

Abbreviations

ACLS	American Council of Learned Societies
AGO	Arkhiv Geograficheskogo Obshchestva SSSR (Leningrad)
AHR	American Historical Review
ASEER	American Slavic and East European Review
AVPR	Arkhiv Vneshnei Politiki Rossii (Moscow)
BCHQ	British Columbia Historical Quarterly
CHR	Canadian Historical Review
CHSQ	California Historical Society Quarterly
DNB	Dictionary of National Biography (London, 1885-1912)
ES	Entsiklopedicheskii slovar' (St.P., 1890-1907)
HAHR	Hispanic American Historical Review
IVGO	Izvestiia Vsesoiuznogo Geograficheskogo Obshchestva
JRAHS	Journal of the Royal Australian Historical Society
L.	Leningrad
M.	Moscow
M.M.	Mariner's Mirror
MSb	Morskoi sbornik
OHQ	Oregon Historical Quarterly
PAAS	Proceedings of the American Antiquarian Society
PHR	Pacific Historical Review
PSZRI	Polnoe Sobranie Zakonov Rossiiskoi Imperii
PNQ	Pacific Northwest Quarterly
RBS	Russki biograficheskii slovar'
SEER	Slavonic and East European Review
St. P.	St. Petersburg
TsGIAL	Central State Historical Archive in Leningrad
TsGADA	Central State Archive of Ancient Acts (Moscow)
TsGAVMF	Central State Archive of the Navy of the USSR (Leningrad)
ZAD	Zapiski Admiralteiskogo Departamenta (Morskogo Ministerstva)
ZGDMM	Zapiski Gidrograficheskogo Departamenta Morskogo Ministerstva
ZIRGO	Zapiski Imperatorskogo Russkogo Geograficheskogo Obshchestva
ZVTD	Zapiski Voenno-Topograficheskogo Departamenta.

Notes

NOTES TO CHAPTER ONE

1. John Perry, *The State of Russia under the Present Czar, in Relation to the Several Great and Remarkable Things He Has Done, as to His Naval Preparations, etc.* (London, 1716), p. 61; S. M. Solov'ev, *Istoriia Rossii s drevneishikh vremen*, 2d. ed. (St. P., n.d.), 4:641.
2. K. Trusevich, *Posol'skie i torgovye otnosheniia Rossii s Kitaem* (M., 1892), 155-88.
3. A. V. Efimov, *Iz istorii russkikh ekspeditsii na Tikhom okeane: pervaia polovina XVIII veka* (M., 1948), pp. 28-30.
4. V. N. Berkh, *Pervoe morskoe puteshestvie Rossiian, predpriniatoe dlia reshesniia geograficheskoi zadachi—soediniaetsia li Aziia s Amerikoi* (St. P., 1823), p. 4ff.; *PSZRI* (1830-1916): 8, doc. 4649.
5. V. Guerrier (Ger'e), *Leibnitz in seinem Beziehungen zu Russland und Peter dem Grossen: eine geschichtliche Darstellung* (St. P. and Leipzig, 1873), p. 187.
6. Efimov, *Iz istorii russkikh ekspeditsii*, pp. 58-60; V. A. Divin, *Russkie moreplavaniia na tikhom okeane v XVIII veke* (M., 1971), p. 56.
7. V. Iu. Vize, *Uspekhi russkikh v issledovanii Arktiki* (M., 1948), 1:109-10.
8. *Pis'ma i bumagi Imperatora Petra Velikogo* (St.P.-L., 1887-1952), 1:doc. 71.
9. M. M. Bogoslovskii, *Petr I: materialy dlia biografii* (M., 1941), 2:153ff.; I. I. Golikov, *Deianiia Petra Velikago, mudrago preobrazitelia Rossii*, 2d. ed. (M., 1837), pp. 120-25.
10. Further on early Russian knowledge of Japan, G. A. Lensen, *The Russian Push toward Japan: Russo-Japanese Relations, 1697-1875* (Princeton, 1959).
11. Reproduced by F. G. Kramp in *Remarkable Maps of the XV, XVI and XVII Centuries* (Amsterdam, 1897), 4: plate 1; see also G. Cahen, *Les cartes de la Sibérie au XVIII siècle* (Paris, 1911), p. 57.
12. D. M. Lebedev, *Geografiia v Rossii petrovskogo vremeni* (M.-L., 1950), pp. 19-29.
13. If the undertaking was committed to paper, it has yet to be discovered.
14. B. P. Polevoi, "Zabytyi nakaz A. A. Viniusa," *Priroda* (M., 1965): no. 5, pp. 4-12.
15. Guerrier, *Leibnitz in seinem Beziehungen*, p. 25; Bogoslovskii, *Petr I*, 2: pp. 113-18; O. Roy, *Leibnitz et la Chine* (Paris, 1972), pp. 66-86.
16. N. A. Ustrialov, *Istoriia tsarstvovaniia Petra Velikogo* (St. P., 1858), 6: 26-28; A. V. Efimov, *Iz istorii velikikh russkikh geograficheskikh otkrytii v severnom ledovitom i Tikhom okeane* (M., 1950), pp. 288-89.
17. Guerrier, *Leibnitz in seinem Beziehungen*, pp. 192-244.
18. Saint-Simon, *Mémoires*, ed. A. de Boislisle (Paris, 1920), 31:374-88.
19. Sven Waxell (Vaksel), *Vtoraia Kamchatskaia ekspeditsiia Vitusa Beringa* (M.-L., 1940), pp. 22-23.
20. George V. Lantzeff and Richard A. Pierce, *Eastward to Empire: Exploration and Conquest on the Russian Open Frontier, to 1750* (Montreal, 1973), pp. 204-8.
21. A. I. Timofeev, ed., *Pamiatniki sibirskoi istorii XVIII veka* (St. P., 1882-85), 2: docs. 117-19; S. P. Krasheninnikov, *Opisanie zemli Kamchatki, s prilozheniem raportov, donesenii i drugikh neopublikovannykh materialov* (M., 1949), pp. 476-88.
22. Timofeev, *Pamiatniki*, 1:441-64; 2:53-76; A. S. Sgibnev, "Istoricheskii ocherk glavneishikh sobytii v Kamchatke, 1650-1856 godov," *MSb*, 101 (1869): no. 4, pp. 84-100.

23. G. F. Müller, *Opisanie morskikh pute-shestvii po ledovitomu okeanu i po Vostochnomu moryu s Rossiiskoi storony uchinennykh* (St. P., 1758), pp. 314-16.
24. L. S. Berg, *Otkrytie Kamchatki i kamchatskie ekspeditsii Beringa*, 3d ed. (L., 1946), pp. 88-94; D. M. Lebedev, *Geografiia v Rossii*, pp. 58-68.
25. Müller, *Opisanie*, pp. 315-16; Timofeev, *Pamiatniki*, 2: doc. 1.
26. Frank A. Golder, *Russian Expansion on the Pacific, 1651-1850: An Account of the Earliest and Later Expeditions Made by the Russians along the Pacific Coast of Asia and North America* (Cleveland, 1914), pp. 100-103.
27. Timofeev, *Pamiatniki*, 2: docs. 11-12; Efimov, *Iz istorii russkikh ekspeditsii*, pp. 93-94.
28. Golder, *Russian Expansion*, pp. 105-8; Timofeev, *Pamiatniki*, 2:37-40.
29. Sgibnev, "Istoricheskii ocherk," pp. 95-97.
30. Berg, *Otkrytie Kamchatki*, pp. 93-94; Efimov, *Iz istorii russkikh ekspeditsii*, pp. 93-95 (on Müller's data); *Pis'ma i bumagi*, 1: doc. 71, and Ustrialov, *Istoriia tsarstvovaniia*, 3:91 (on Dutch shipwrights at Arkhangel'sk). Efimov contends that Bush had been captured while in Swedish naval service.
31. Divin, *Russkie moreplavaniia*, p. 37 and n (Bering's praise of Triaska).
32. *Dopolneniia k aktam istoricheskim* (St. P., 1846-72), 11:201; N. N. Ogloblin, *Obozrenie stolbtsov i knig Sibirskago prikaza, 1592-1768* (M., 1895-1900), 3:118ff. On early Okhotsk, A. S. Sgibnev, "Okhotskii port s 1649 po 1852 god," *MSb*, 105 (1869): no. 11, pp. 1-92; no. 12, pp. 1-63.
33. Timofeev, *Pamiatniki*, 2: doc. 60 (Kharitonov's report of 24 October 1719 on the Iakutsk-Okhotsk Tract); also J. R. Gibson, *Feeding the Russian Fur Trade: Provisionment of the Okhotsk Seaboard and the Kamchatka Peninsula, 1639-1856* (Madison and London, 1969), chs. 1-3.
34. Golder, *Russian Expansion*, pp. 119-21; S. Znamenskii, *V poiskakh Iaponii: iz istorii russkikh geograficheskikh otkrytii i morekhodstva v Tikhom okeane* (Vladivostok, 1929), pp. 47-54.
35. Sgibnev, "Okhotskii port," pp. 45-80;

36. Lantzeff, *Siberia in the Seventeenth Century*, p. 78.
37. P. N. Butsinskii, *Zaselenie Sibiri i byt eë pervykh nasel'nikov* (Kharkov, 1889), pp. 272ff.
38. Lebedev, *Geografiia v Rossii*, pp. 60-62; Efimov, *Iz istorii russkikh ekspeditsii*, p. 99.
39. Butsinskii, *Zaselenie*, p. 190.
40. Timofeev, *Pamiatniki*, 2: doc. 35; Lantzeff and Pierce, *Eastward to Empire*, pp. 206-7.
41. Timofeev, *Pamiatniki*, 2:53-58, 76-83.
42. Divin, *Russkie moreplavaniia*, pp. 27-30; Efimov, *Iz istorii russkikh ekspeditsii*, p. 87; Krasheninnikov, *Opisanie zemli Kamchatki*, pp. 486-87.
43. A. S. Sgibnev, "Bol'shoi Kamchatskii nariad: ekspeditsiia El'china," *MSb*, 100 (1868): no. 12; Timofeev, *Pamiatniki*, 2:109.
44. Efimov, *Iz istorii russkikh ekspeditsii*, p. 133.
45. Müller, *Opisanie morskikh puteshestvii*, pp. 318-20; L. S. Berg, *Otkrytie Kamchatki*, pp. 94ff; Golder, *Russian Expansion*, pp. 108-9.
46. A. S. Sgibnev, "Popytki russkikh k zavedeniiu torgovykh snoshenii s Iaponieiu v XVIII i nachale XIX stoletii," *MSb*, 105 (1869): no. 7, pp. 87-90; Lensen, *The Russian Push*, pp. 1-16.
47. N. Pavlov-Sil'vanskii, *Proekty reform v zapiskakh sovremennikov Petra Velikogo* (St. P., 1897), pp. 42-44; Znamenskii, *V poiskakh Iaponii*, pp. 74-75.
48. N. Pavlov-Sil'vanskii, *Propozitsii Fedora Saltykova: rukopis' iz sobraniia P. N. Tikhanova* (St. P., 1891), p. 88.
49. £300 per annum, 1698-1701; then irregular payment: Perry, *The State of Russia*, pp. iii, 80, on meetings with Saltykov.
50. Lebedev, *Geografiia v Rossii*, p. 83.
51. Perry, *The State of Russia*, p. 61.
52. See A. J. von Krusenstern, *A Voyage Round the World, in the Years 1803, 4, 5 & 6, . . . on Board the Ships Nadeshda and Neva*, trans. R. B. Hoppner (London, 1814), 1:57-58.
53. "Ekstrakt zhurnalov moreplavaniia i

George V. Lantzeff, *Siberia in the Seventeenth Century: A Study of the Colonial Administration* (New York, 1972), pp. 60, 69-71.

opisaniia Kaspiiskogo moria, kotoroe proiskhodilo v 1715-1720 i 1727 godakh,'' *ZGDMM*, 10 (1852): pp. 551-52; Znamenskii, *V poiskakh Iaponii*, p. 75.

54. Golikov, *Deianiia Petra Velikago*, 8:129; Lebedev, *Geografiia v Rossii*, p. 86; also *Sbornik Imperatorskago Russkago Istoricheskago Obshchestva* (St. P., 1884), 40: 422-23 for the text of Campredon's despatch to Paris concerning this expedition.

55. A. I. Andreev, "Rol' Russkogo Voenno-Morskogo Flota v geograficheskikh otkrytiiakh XVIII veka" *MSb*, (1947): no. 4, pp. 181-82.

56. *PSZRI*, 7: doc. 4649.

57. Efimov, *Iz istorii russkikh ekspeditsii*, pp. 28-30. I follow Efimov in distinguishing between "economic" (that is, financial) and "political" (that is, territorial and military) objectives. Also Divin, *Russkie moreplavaniia*, pp. 44-45.

58. Efimov, *Iz istorii velikikh russkikh geograficheskikh otkrytii*, p. 24.

59. V. N. Berkh, *Pervoe morskoe puteshestvie*, passim; A. P. Sokolov, "Severnaia ekspeditsiia, 1733-1743," *ZGDMM*, 9 (1851): 190-340; J. G. Gmelin, *Reise durch Sibirien, 1733-1743* (Göttingen, 1751), 1:3-8; E. G. Kushnarev, "Nereshennye voprosy pervoi kamchatskoi ekspeditsii," in *Russkie arkticheskie ekspeditsii XVII-XX vekov* (L., 1964), passim.

60. N. N. Ogloblin, "Pervyi iaponets v Rossii, 1701-1705," *Russkaia starina*, 72 (1891): no. 10, pp. 11-24; Berg, *Otkrytie Kamchatki*, pp. 68-69, 160-61; E. Ia. Fainberg, *Russko-iaponskie otnosheniia v 1697-1875 godakh* (M., 1960), pp. 20-21; Lensen, *The Russian Push*, pp. 27-29.

61. Timofeev, *Pamiatniki*, 1:478-79; Sgibnev, "Popytki russkikh k zavedeniiu," p. 88; also Krasheninnikov, *Opisanie zemli*, p. 475, and Berg, *Otkrytie Kamchatki*, p. 62 on a Japanese shipwreck by the River Tigil around 1695.

62. Krasheninnikov, *Opisanie zemli*, pp. 486-87; Sgibnev, "Istoricheskii ocherk," pp. 84-85; Berg, *Otkrytie Kamchatki*, p. 142.

63. Golder, *Russian Expansion*, pp. 119-21; Divin, *Russkie moreplavaniia*, pp. 27-30.

64. A. Pokrovskii, "Bering i ego ekspeditsiia," in *Ekspeditsiia Beringa* (M., 1941), p. 24; Efimov, *Iz istorii russkikh ekspeditsii*, p. 88; Znamenskii, *V poiskakh Iaponii*, pp. 55-60.

65. Sgibnev, "Bol'shoi Kamchatskii nariad," pp. 132ff; Efimov, *Iz istorii russkikh ekspeditsii*, pp. 133-34.

66. Timofeev, *Pamiatniki*, 2:109.

67. Bogoslovskii, *Petr I: materialy*, 4:288-91; Efimov, *Iz istorii russkikh ekspeditsii*, p. 136; S. Elagin, comp., *Materialy dlia istorii Russkogo Flota* (St. P., 1865-1904), 9:534-35; Lebedev, *Geografiia v Rossii*, p. 143.

68. *PSZRI*, 4: doc. 3266.

69. Timofeev, *Pamiatniki*, 2: doc. 73.

70. Znamenskii, *V poiskakh Iaponii*, pp. 61-69; V. I. Grekov, *Ocherki iz istorii russkikh geograficheskikh issledovanii v 1725-65 godakh* (M., 1960), pp. 6ff; map in Efimov, *Iz istorii russkikh ekspeditsii*, p. 137.

71. However, they did not pass beyond the sixth island, that is, Simushir: cf. Berg, *Otkrytie Kamchatki*, pp. 151-52; also P. N. Pekarskii, *Nauka i literatura pri Petre Velikom* (St. P., 1862), 1:347-48. Divin's slight of S. R. Tompkins (*Russkie moreplavaniia*, p. 38n) is regrettable.

72. Grekov, *Ocherki iz istorii*, for analysis of the map.

73. Golikov, *Deianiia Petra Velikago*, 9:129; Efimov, *Iz istorii russkikh ekspeditsii*, p. 88; Berg, *Otkrytie Kamchatki*, pp. 151-52.

74. Summary in Ian Grey, *Peter the Great* (London, 1962), p. 442.

75. L. N. Maikov, ed., *Rasskazy Nartova o Petre Velikom* (St. P., 1891), p. 99.

76. Frank A. Golder, *Bering's Voyages* (New York, 1922-25), 1:7-8.

77. *PSZRI*, 7: doc. 4649; "Doneseniia flota-kapitana Beringa ob ekspeditsii ego k vostochnym beregam Sibiri," *ZVTD*, 10 (St. P., 1847): pt. 1, suppl. 2, pp. 69-70.

78. TsGAVMF, *fond* kantseliarii Apraksina, "Zapisnaia knizhka," pt. 1, pp. 35-36.

NOTES TO CHAPTER TWO

1. P. Lauridsen, *Vitus Bering: The Discoverer of Bering Strait,* trans., J. E. Olsen, 2d. ed. (Freeport, N.Y., 1969), pp. 5-6.
2. C. R. Boxer, *The Dutch Seaborne Empire, 1600-1800* (New York, 1965), pp. 105-9.
3. Carl Thunberg, *Travels in Europe, Africa and Asia, performed between the Years 1770 and 1779* (London, 1795), 1:112-13; J. Stavorinus, *Voyages to the East Indies, by the late John Splinter Stavorinus, Esq., Rear-Admiral in the Service of the States-General* (London, 1798), 2:111-12; 3:465-66.
4. V. N. Berkh, *Zhizneopisaniia pervykh rossiiskikh admiralov, ili opyt istorii Rossiiskogo Flota* (St. P., 1831-34); RBS, 9:501-7.
5. [John Deane], *The Russian Fleet under Peter the Great, by a Contemporary Englishman, 1724,* ed. Sir Cyprian Bridge (London, 1899), index under Cruys.
6. Lauridsen, *Vitus Bering,* p. 10.
7. [Deane], *The Russian Fleet,* pp. 25, 41, 44-45.
8. Ibid., pp. 9, 56, 82, 89; John Charnock, *Biographia Navalis, or, Impartial Memoirs of the Lives and Characters of Officers of the Navy of Great Britain, from the Year 1660 to the Present Time* (London, 1794-98), 3:308-9 (on Admiral Gordon); J. Scheltema, *Rusland en de Nederlanden beschouwd in derzelver wederkeerige betrekkingen, door Mr. Jacobus Scheltema* (Amsterdam, 1817-19), 3:286-87 (on Sievers in Russia).
9. B. G. Ostrovskii, *Bering* (L., 1938), pp. 88-96; A. A. Pokrovskii, ed., *Ekspeditsii Beringa: sbornik dokumentov* (M., 1941), pp. 54ff.
10. "Doneseniia Beringa," p. 70.
11. Lantzeff, *Siberia in the Seventeenth Century,* p. 49n.
12. On Spanberg, *ZGDMM,* 9:215-16; on Chirikov, Divin, *Russkie moreplavaniia,* pp. 47-48.
13. H. H. Bancroft, *History of Alaska, 1730-1885* (San Francisco, 1886), pp. 48-49; Karl von Baer (Ber), "Zaslugi Petra Velikogo po chasti rasprostraneniia geograficheskikh poznanii o

Rossii," *ZIRGO* (St. P., 1849), bk. 3, pp. 217-53, bk. 4, pp. 260-83; A. P. Sokolov, "Bering i Chirikov," *Severnaia pchela* (St. P., 1849): nos. 98-99. V. A. Divin, *Velikii russkii moreplavatel' A. I. Chirikov* (M., 1953), passim.
14. Divin, *Russkie moreplavaniia,* p. 48.
15. TsGAVMF, *fond* 216 (Beringa), *delo* 52, p. 248.
16. TsGAVMF, *fond* 216, op. 1, *delo* 87, pp. 60-64.
17. "Doneseniia Beringa," p. 72.
18. Ibid., p. 74; on P. A. Chaplin, *Obshchii morskoi spisok* (St. P., 1885-1907), 2:469-70.
19. Timofeev, *Pamiatniki,* 2: doc. 60 on the Iakutsk-Okhotsk Tract; also J. R. Gibson, *Feeding the Russian Fur-Trade,* passim.
20. TsGAVMF, *fond* kantseliarii Apraksina, "Zapisnaia knizhka," pt. 1, pp. 35-37.
21. Butsinskii, *Zaselenie Sibiri,* pp. 272-77.
22. Lantzeff, *Siberia in the Seventeenth Century,* pp. 160-61.
23. Efimov, *Iz istorii russkikh ekspeditsii,* p. 99n.
24. A. S. Sgibnev, "Navigatskie shkoly v Sibiri," *MSb,* 87 (1866): no. 11, pp. 3-44.
25. Lantzeff, *Siberia in the Seventeenth Century,* pp. 59-60; Sgibnev, "Okhotskii port," no. 11.
26. "Doneseniia Beringa," p. 72.
27. Ibid., p. 73.
28. TsGAVMF, *fond* 216, op. 1, *delo* 87, pp. 226-33.
29. Ia. P. Al'kor and L. K. Drezen, *Kolonial'naia politika tsarizma na Kamchatke i Chukotke v XVIII veke: sbornik arkhivnykh materialov* (L., 1935), pp. 47-50.
30. "Doneseniia Beringa," p. 73; A. Polonskii, "Pervaia Kamchatskaia ekspeditsiia Beringa, 1725-29 godov," *ZGDMM,* 8:546.
31. "Doneseniia Beringa," p. 74.
32. Polonskii, "Pervaia Kamchatskaia ekspeditsiia," pp. 548ff.
33. Divin, *Russkie moreplavaniia,* pp. 54-55.
34. M. V. Lomonosov, *Polnoe sobranie sochinenii* (M., 1952), 6:451. Golder, in

Russian Expansion on the Pacific, pp. 140-47, summarizes the voyage on the basis of Chaplin's log, together with its shortcomings in all senses.

35. Lebedev, *Geografiia v Rossii,* p. 97; Divin, *Russkie moreplavaniia,* pp. 59-65.

36. Polonskii, "Pervaia Kamchatskaia ekspeditsiia," pp. 550-56.

37. Lebedev, *Geografiia v Rossii,* pp. 97-98.

38. *Materialy dlia istorii russkogo flota* (St. P., 1879), 8:520.

39. L. Beskrovnyi, "Armiia i flot," in *Ocherki istorii SSSR,* ed. N. Druzhinin (M., 1957), 4:306 (naval decline); V. O. Kliuchevskii, *A History of Russia,* trans. C. J. Hogarth (N.Y., 1960), 4:307-15 (on the Germans).

40. Grekov, *Ocherki iz istorii russkikh issledovanii,* pp. 342-43. The "petition" became Bering's *Predlozheniia* of April 1730.

41. J. G. Gmelin, *Voyage en Sibérie* (Paris, 1767), p. 188.

42. Efimov, *Iz istorii russkikh ekspeditsii,* pp. 130-31, 154; Lauridsen, *Vitus Bering,* p. 207; A. P. Sokolov, "Severnaia ekspeditsiia 1733-1743 godov," *ZGDMM,* 9 (1851).

43. See Efimov, *Iz istorii russkikh ekspeditsii,* p. 100 for Homann's (1725) map of "Das Land Kamtzadalie sonst Jedso."

44. Lebedev, *Geografiia v Rossii,* pp. 247-53; *RBS,* 8:666-67.

45. Lebedev, *Geografiia v Rossii,* pp. 309-14; further on Kirillov's role in the second Bering expedition, cf. Sokolov, "Severnaia ekspeditsiia," 9:202ff.

46. A. Sk-, "General-Admiral A. I. Osterman," *MSb,* 30 (1857): pp. 66-82.

47. Sokolov, "Severnaia ekspeditsiia," pp. 425ff.

48. Lensen, *The Russian Push,* pp. 85-86; Sgibnev, "Istoricheskii ocherk," pp. 129-30.

49. Sokolov, "Severnaia ekspeditsiia," p. 428.

50. *PSZRI,* 8: docs. 5753, 5813.

51. TsGADA, *fond* Senata, *delo* 664, p. 71.

52. As Efimov notes, *Iz istorii russkikh ekspeditsii,* p. 234n, the edict appointing Skorniakov-Pisarev commandant was followed by several others, all relating to the coming expedition.

53. Lantzeff and Pierce, *Eastward to Empire,* pp. 211-14.

54. See note 46.

55. TsGADA, *fond* Senata, *delo* 664, pp. 68-72.

56. *PSZRI,* 8: doc. 6023.

57. Vize, *Uspekhi russkikh v issledovanii Arktiki,* pp. 109-10; Lantzeff and Pierce, *Eastward to Empire,* pp. 179-80.

58. Berkh, *Zhizneopisaniia admiralov,* 2:368-70; [Deane], *The Russian Fleet,* pp. 87-90.

59. Divin, *Russkie moreplavaniia,* pp. 95-96.

60. First published in full by V. A. Divin in "O pervykh proektakh russkikh krugosvetnykh plavanii," *Trudy Instituta Istorii Estestvoznaniia i Tekhniki,* 32 (L., 1961).

61. TsGADA, *fond* Senata, *delo* 666, p. 104.

62. Divin, *Russkie moreplavaniia,* p. 94.

63. TsGADA, *fond* Gosarkhiva, *razriad* 31, *delo* 9, pp. 11-12.

64. Divin, *Russkie moreplavaniia,* p. 97.

65. Pokrovskii, *Ekspeditsii Beringa,* pp. 94-98.

66. Divin, *Russkie moreplavaniia,* p. 98.

67. Sokolov, "Severnaia ekspeditsiia," 9:435-36.

68. Bancroft, *History of Alaska,* pp. 53-54, on Steller, whose "Journal" for 1733-41 appears in Golder's *Bering's Voyages,* 2.

69. Sgibnev, "Istoricheskii ocherk," pp. 129-30; Efimov, *Iz istorii russkikh ekspeditsii,* pp. 156-59; Al'kor, *Kolonial'naia politika,* pp. 47-81, 158-60.

70. Golder, *Russian Expansion,* pp. 155-62; Efimov, *Iz istorii russkikh ekspeditsii,* pp. 158-60; Bancroft, *History of Alaska,* pp. 37-40.

71. Divin, *Russkie moreplavaniia,* pp. 99-105; Lauridsen, *Vitus Bering,* pp. 72-73.

72. Lantzeff and Pierce, *Eastward to Empire,* pp. 215-16; Divin, *Russkie moreplavaniia,* pp. 112-18; Sokolov, "Severnaia ekspeditsiia," 9:206-8.

73. *PSZRI,* 8: doc. 6041.

74. Divin, *Russkie moreplavaniia,* p. 107.

75. *Materialy dlia istorii russkogo flota,* 8:426-27.

76. Divin, *Russkie moreplavaniia,* p. 101n: Sokolov, "Severnaia ekspeditsiia," 9:216-20.

77. *PSZRI*, 8: doc. 6291.
78. Lantzeff and Pierce, *Eastward to Empire*, p. 214.
79. Sokolov, "Severnaia ekspeditsiia," 9:208-9.
80. Duque di Liria y Xerica, *Diario del viaje a Moscovia del Duque di Liria y Xerica, embajador del Rey . . . Phelipe V* (Madrid 1889).
81. A. M. Soler, *Die Spanisch-Russischen Beziehungen im 18-en Jahrhundert* (Wiesbaden, 1970), pp. 49-66.
82. Efimov, *Iz istorii russkikh ekspeditsii*, p. 101.
83. D. K. Reading, *The Anglo-Russian Commercial Treaty of 1734* (New Haven, 1938), pp. 239-43; Efimov, *Iz istorii russkikh ekspeditsii*, pp. 250-52.
84. Including America.
85. Reading, *The Anglo-Russian Commercial Treaty*, pp. 240-41; M. P. Alekseev, ed., *Sibir' v izvestiiakh zapadnoevropeiskikh puteshestvennikov i pisatelei* (Irkutsk, 1941), pp. 66-67.
86. Reading, *The Anglo-Russian Commercial Treaty*, p. 258; Elias Trapaud, ed., *Des Kapitan John Eltons Tagebuch über seine Reise von Moskau nach den nordlichen gegenden von Persien* (Hamburg, 1790).
87. On the promulgation of his final (amended) orders: *PSZRI*, 9: doc. 6351.
88. Sokolov, "Severnaia ekspeditsiia," pp. 252-54; Golder, *Bering's Voyages*, 1:32-34.
89. Sokolov, "Severnaia ekspeditsiia," p. 254; Pokrovskii, *Ekspeditsii Beringa*, pp. 240-41.
90. TsGAVMF, *fond* 1212, *delo* 237, p. 90.
91. Golder, *Russian Expansion*, pp. 177-78.
92. Pokrovskii, *Ekspeditsii Beringa*, pp. 302-3.
93. Golder, *Bering's Voyages*, 1:54ff.
94. Lantzeff, *Siberia in the Seventeenth Century*, pp. 159-60.
95. Golder, *Russian Expansion*, pp. 158-59.
96. P. A. Slovtsov, *Istoricheskoe obozrenie Sibiri* (St. P., 1886), pp. 83-85; *Akty istoricheskie* (St. P., 1841-42), 2:33-34.
97. TsGAVMF, *fond* 1212, *delo* 237, pp. 75-90.
98. A. S. Sgibnev, "Materialy dlia istorii

Kamchatki: ekspeditsiia Shestakova," *MSb*, 100 (1869): no. 2, pp. 25-26.
99. Efimov, *Iz istorii russkikh ekspeditsii*, pp. 160-61.
100. Sokolov, "Severnaia ekspeditsiia," pp. 363-65; Golder, *Russian Expansion*, pp. 226-27; Divin, *Russkie moreplavaniia*, pp. 129-30.
101. TsGADA, *fond* Senata, *delo* 1327, p. 79/obv.
102. Lensen, *The Russian Push*, pp. 48-50.
103. Pokrovskii, *Ekspeditsii Beringa*, pp. 234-35; Divin, *Russkie moreplavaniia*, pp. 121-22.
104. Lensen, *The Russian Push*, 50-54; Divin, *Russkie moreplavaniia*, p. 124.
105. Divin, *Russkie moreplavaniia*, p. 126.
106. Pokrovskii, *Ekspeditsii Beringa*, pp. 181-82.
107. Lensen, *The Russian Push*, p. 54.
108. A. S. Sgibnev, "Popytki russkikh k zavedeniiu torgovykh snoshenii s Iaponieiiu v XVIII i nachale XIX stoletii," *MSb*, 100 (1869): no. 7, pp. 55-60; E. Ia. Fainberg, *Russko-Iaponskie otnosheniia v 1697-1875 godakh* (M., 1960), chs. 1-2.
109. TsGADA, *fond* Senata, *delo* 1089, p. 828.
110. Pokrovskii, *Ekspeditsii Beringa*, pp. 262-63.
111. Divin, *Russkie moreplavaniia*, pp. 134-39.
112. Lensen, *The Russian Push*, p. 60.
113. Spanberg had in 1740 suppressed Walton's Japanese journal and chart: Divin, *Russkie moreplavaniia*, pp. 131-32.
114. TsGADA, *fond* Senata, *delo* 1327, p. 631.
115. Divin, *Russkie moreplavaniia*, p. 139.
116. Golder, *Russian Expansion*, p. 172n.
117. "Doneseniia Beringa," pp. 72-73.
118. Cited by Golder, *Bering's Voyages*, 1:36-37.
119. Pokrovskii, *Ekspeditsii Beringa*, pp. 274-76; Bancroft, *History of Alaska*, pp. 75-98; Grekov, *Ocherki iz istorii russkikh issledovanii*, pp. 109-30.
120. D. M. Lebedev, *Plavanie A. I. Chirikova na paketbote "Sv. Pavel" k poberezh'iam Ameriki* (M., 1951), pp. 204ff; Pokrovskii, *Ekspeditsii Beringa*, pp. 277-78; J. C. Beaglehole, ed., *The Journals of Captain*

James Cook: Volume III. The Voyage of the Resolution and Discovery, 1776-1780 (Cambridge, 1967), 1:1ix.

121. Waxell, *Vtoraia Kamchatskaia ekspeditsiia Vitusa Beringa*, pp. 70-106; Steller's "Journal" in Golder, *Bering's Voyages*, 2; G. F. Müller, *Sammlung russischer Geschichten* (St. P., 1758), 3:392-93; Bancroft, *History of Alaska*, pp. 88-92.

122. G. Williams, *The British Search for the Northwest Passage in the Eighteenth Century* (London, 1962), pp. 140-41; Steller's remarks in full in *IVGO*, 75 (L., 1943): 42ff.

123. Golder, *Russian Expansion*, pp. 212-13.

124. *Materialy dlia istorii russkogo flota*, 9:255-62; on Chirikov's own superior cartographic work, Efimov, *Iz istorii russkikh ekspeditsii*, pp. 174-75; Divin, *Russkie moreplavaniia*, pp. 169-73.

125. Gibson, *Feeding the Russian Fur Trade*, passim; F. F. Veselago, *Kratkaia istoriia russkogo flota* (M., 1939), p. 200.

126. Sgibnev, "Navigatskie shkoly," *MSb*, 89 (1866): no. 11, pp. 3-44; N. S. Iurtsovskii, *Ocherki po istorii prosveshcheniia v Sibiri* (Novo-Nikolaevsk, 1923), pp. 30-32.

NOTES TO CHAPTER THREE

1. L. G. Beskrovnyi, "Armiia i flot," *Ocherki istorii S.S.S.R.* (M., 1957), p. 307.

2. V. O. Kliuchevskii, *History of Russia*, trans. C. J. Hogarth (N.Y., 1960), 4:307-15.

3. V. A. Divin, "O pervykh proektakh russkikh krugosvetnykh plavanii," *Trudy Instituta Istorii Estestvoznaniia i Tekhniki*, 32 (M., 1961): 330-36.

4. Pokrovskii, *Ekspeditsii Beringa*, pp. 408-9; "Iz istorii osvoeniia Severnogo morskogo puti," *Krasnyi arkhiv* (M., 1935), 4:141-42.

5. Divin, *Russkie moreplavaniia*, p. 164.

6. S. Solov'ev, *Istoriia Rossii* (St. P., 1879), 23:8-9.

7. F. F. Veselago, ed., *Materialy dlia istorii russkogo flota*, 2d. ed. (St. P., 1896), 9:1.

8. Divin, *Russkie moreplavaniia*, p. 165.

9. Efimov, *Iz istorii velikikh russkikh geograficheskikh otkrytii*, pp. 198-200.

10. See bibliography.

11. S. E. Fel', "Kartografiia Rossii XVIII veka," *Trudy Instituta Istorii Estestvoznaniia i Tekhniki*, 37 (M., 1961): 249-50; Lomonosov, *Polnoe sobranie sochinenii*, 7:373-74.

12. TsGADA, *fond* Senata, *delo* 57, passim.

13. N. I. Pavlenko, *Razvitie metallurgicheskoi promyshlennosti Rossii v pervoi polovine XVIII veka* (M.-L., 1953), pp. 80-81.

14. TsGAVMF, *fond* N. F. Golovina, *delo* 1, p. 52.

15. Sgibnev, "Okhotskii port," no. 11, pp. 36ff.

16. S. B. Okun', *The Russian-American Company*, trans. C. Ginsburg (Cambridge, Mass., 1951), pp. 11-12 (Justi's mercantilist followers).

17. Sgibnev, "Okhotskii port," no. 12, passim.

18. Bancroft, *History of Alaska;* Sgibnev, "Okhotskii port," no. 11, pp. 31-33.

19. On *promyshlenniki*, cf. R. H. Fisher, *The Russian Fur Trade, 1550-1700* (Berkeley, 1943), pp. 30ff.; Okun', *Russian-American Company*, chs. 2-3.

20. Here and subsequently, *promyshlenniki* on the Aleutian Islands are included in the general term cossack.

21. Divin, *Russkie moreplavaniia*, p. 200.

22. R. V. Makarova, *Russkie na Tikhom okeane vo vtoroi polovine XVIII veka* (M., 1968), passim, esp. pp. 38-42.

23. J. C. Beaglehole, ed., *The Journals of Captain James Cook: Volume III*, 2:1355, 1449.

24. M. I. Belov, *Semen Dezhnev*, 2d.ed. (M., 1955), pp. 46-47.

25. I. Veniaminov, *Zapiski ob ostrovakh Unalashkinskago Otdela* (St. P., 1840), 1: passim; J. L. Schlözer, ed.,

Neue Nachrichten von denen neuen-deckten Inseln der See zwischen Asia und Amerika (Hamburg, 1776), pp. 31-57.

26. V. N. Berkh, *Khronologicheskaia istoriia otkrytiia Aleutskikh ostrovov, ili podvigi rossiiskogo kupechestva* (St. P., 1823), pp. 53-54.

27. Bancroft, *History of California* (San Francisco, 1885), 2:61.

28. D. M. Afanas'ev, "Rossiisko-Amerikanskie vladeniia," *MSb*, 71 (1864): no. 3, p. 14.

29. L. S. Berg, *Otkrytie Kamchatki*, p. 285; N. N. Zubov, *Otechestvennye moreplavateli—issledovateli morei i okeanov* (M., 1954), p. 101: S. R. Tompkins, *Alaska: Promyshlennik and Sourdough* (Oklahoma, 1945), p. 20.

30. Makarova, *Russkie na Tikhom okeane*, p. 43.

31. Divin, *Russkie moreplavaniia*, pp. 198-99.

32. P. S. Pallas, ed., *Neue Nordische Beyträge* (St. P., 1781), 2:302-7; Krasheninnikov, *Opisanie zemli Kamchatki*, pp. 499-501; Al'kor, *Kolonial'naia politika*, pp. 83-88.

33. V. A. Divin, "Vtoraia Sibirsko-Tikhookeanskaia ekspeditsiia i voprosy khoziaistvennogo osveshcheniia Dal'nego Vostoka," *Letopis' Severa* (M., 1957), 2:55-76; also Gibson, *Feeding the Russian Fur Trade*, chs. 1-3.

34. Divin, *Russkie moreplavaniia*, pp. 208-11.

35. *PSZRI*, 12:830.

36. TsGIAL, *fond* 1341, op. 303, *delo* 4856, pp. 54-55.

37. P. I. Kabanov, *Amurskii vopros* (Blagoveshchensk, 1959), pp. 27-30.

38. Details of merchants' origins and investments in P. Tikhmenev, *Istoricheskoe obozrenie obrazovaniia Rossiisko-Amerikanskoi Kompanii i deistvii eë do nastoiashchego vremeni* (St. P., 1861-63), pt. 1.

39. N. N. Ogloblin, *Obozrenie stolbtsov i knig Sibirskago prikaza, 1592-1768* (M., 1895-1900), 2:46-47.

40. TsGADA, *fond* 259, op. 22, *delo* 485, pp. 437-38.

41. TsGIAL, *fond* 1341, op. 303, *delo* 4856, p. 435.

42. TsGADA, *fond* 259, op. 22, *delo* 485, p. 436.

43. Schlözer, *Neue Nachrichten*, pp. 55-57; Berkh, *Khronologicheskaia istoriia*, pp. 44-45, 75-76; Veniaminov, *Zapiski ob ostrovakh*, 2:100-101.

44. Bancroft, *History of Alaska*, pp. 134ff.

45. TsGIAL, *fond* 1341, op. 303, *delo* 4856, pp. 54-56.

46. Berkh, *Khronologicheskaia istoriia*, pp. 52-53; Divin, *Russkie moreplavaniia*, pp. 212-13; Bancroft, *History of Alaska*, pp. 140-49 (Glotov in 1762-65).

47. Veselago, *Kratkaia istoriia russkogo flota* (M., 1939), p. 85.

48. Kliuchevskii, *History of Russia*, 5:28; M. S. Anderson, "Great Britain and the Growth of the Russian Navy in the 18th Century," *M. M.*, 42 (1956): 132-46.

49. Notably in London and The Hague.

50. Veselago, *Kratkaia istoriia*, p. 87.

51. W. Laird-Clowes, *A History of the Royal Navy* (London, 1899-1904), 3:326-27.

52. R. C. Anderson, "British and American Officers in the Russian Navy," *M. M.*, 23 (1947): 17-27; A. G. Cross, "Samuel Greig, Catherine the Great's Scottish Admiral," *ibid.*, 60 (1974): 251-54.

53. On personalia, O. F. Winter, *Repertorium der diplomatischen Vertreter aller Länder* (Graz, 1965), vol. 3 (1764-1815); also A. M. Soler, *Die Spanisch-Russischen Beziehungen im 18 Jahrhundert* (Wiesbaden, 1970).

54. W. L. Cook, *Flood Tide of Empire: Spain and the Pacific Northwest, 1543-1819* (New Haven and London, 1973), pp. 46-47.

55. Archivo General de Indias (Seville: Catalogues 442, 494). (Copies in the Bancroft Library, Berkeley, California.)

56. C. E. Chapman, *The Founding of Spanish California: The Northwestward Expansion of New Spain, 1687-1783* (N.Y., 1973: reprint of 1916 ed.), pp. 60-61.

57. Burriel, *Noticia*, 3:1-19.

58. Cook, *Flood Tide of Empire*, p. 45.

59. Williams, *The British Search for the Northwest Passage*, pp. 144-47.

60. Documents cited in extract by S. R. Tompkins and M. L. Moorehead, "Russia's Approach to America. Part

2: from Spanish Sources, 1761-1777,"
BCHQ, 12 (1949): 231-55.

61. Ibid., p. 235.

62. Lomonosov, *Polnoe sobranie sochinenii*, 7: p. 284.

63. Belov, *Istoriia otkrytiia i osvoeniia severnogo morskogo puti*, index under Chichagov, V.Ia.

64. "Petr Velikii," Canto I, lines 169-70, 173; see also A. Morozov, *Mikhail Vasil'evich Lomonosov* (L., 1952), pp. 765-78.

65. Archivo General de Indias, America en General, Legajo 1 (Herreria to Grimaldi, 30 March 1764); Bancroft, *History of Alaska*, 154-55.

66. TsGAVMF, *fond* Vysochaishikh ukazov, bk. 21, pp. 4-6.

67. TsGAVMF, *fond* 315, *delo* 381, p. 6.

68. P. V. Chichagov, "Zapiski," *Russkaia starina* (St. P., October 1886): 35-53.

69. On Nagaev, V. N. Berkh, *Zhizneopisanie Admirala A. I. Nagaeva* (St. P., 1831).

70. V. Zakharov, "M. V. Lomonosov i russkoe nauchnoe moreplavanie," *Morskoi flot* (L., 1948): nos. 7-8, pp. 66-81.

71. A. V. Efimov, *Atlas geograficheskikh otkrytii v Sibiri i Severo-Zapadnoi Amerike XVII-XVIII vekov* (M., 1964), pp. 87-89 and map no. 130.

72. Sgibnev, "Istoricheskii ocherk glavneishikh sobytii," 102, pp. 37-38; 105, pp. 39-40; Divin, *Russkie moreplavanii*, p. 216.

73. Efimov, *Iz istorii russkikh ekspeditsii*, p. 147.

74. TsGADA, *fond* 199 (Müller), *delo* 528, pt. 2, item 10 ("O moreplavanii rossiiskikh promyshlennikov").

75. A. P. Sokolov, "Ekspeditsii k Aleutskim ostrovam kapitanov Krenitsyna i Levasheva 1764-1769 godov," *ZGDMM*, 10 (1852): 42-54.

76. H. T. Fry, *Alexander Dalrymple and the Expansion of British Trade* (Toronto, 1970), pp. 100-101.

77. On couriers, V. N. Aleksandrenko, *Russkie diplomaticheskie agenty v Londone v XVIII veke* (Warsaw, 1897), 1:352-64.

78. Sokolov, "Ekspeditsii k Aleutskim ostrovam," pp. 55ff.

79. Golder, *Bering's Voyages*, 2:148, 244-

45; Efimov, *Iz istorii russkikh ekspeditsii*, p. 147.

80. TsGADA, *fond* 199 (Müller), *delo* 528, bk. 6, pp. 21-22 (voyage of 1761-63).

81. TsGADA, *fond* 290 (A. R. Vorontsova), *delo* 6, no. 29.

82. Jacob Stählin von Storcksburg, *An Account of the New Northern Archipelago Lately Discovered by the Russians in the Seas of Kamtschatka and Anadir*, trans. C. Heydinger (London, 1774), pp. 12-13.

83. A. I. Alekseev, *Gavriil Andreevich Sarychev* (M., 1966), pp. 157-58; also note 81.

84. Beaglehole, *Journals of Captain James Cook*, 1:lxiv.

85. Tompkins and Moorehead, "Russia's Approach to America," p. 231.

86. TsGAVMF, *fond* 315 (Razvitie morskoi torgovli), *delo* 381, pp. 3.

87. TsGAVMF, *fond* 216, *delo* 77, p. 1.

88. Bancroft, *History of Alaska*, p. 159n.

89. Okun', *Russian-American Company*, pp. 9-10.

90. TsGAVMF, *fond* Kabineta E. I. Velichestva po morskoi chasti: o morskikh ekspeditsiiakh, op. 1, *delo* 131, p. 276.

91. Divin, *Russkie moreplavaniia*, p. 229.

92. TsGADA, *fond* 199, *delo* 540, bk.2, pp. 16-19.

93. TsGAVMF, *fond* 216, *delo* 77, p. 25.

94. Cited by Divin, *Russkie moreplavaniia*, pp. 229-30.

95. Sokolov, "Ekspeditsii k Aleutskim ostrovam," pp. 77-80.

96. Sgibnev, "Okhotskii port," no. 11, pp. 49-50.

97. TsGAVMF, *fond* E. I. Velichestva po morskoi chasti . . ., op. 1, *delo* 131, pp. 274-75; Cook, *Flood Tide of Empire*, pp. 45-47.

98. TsGAVMF, *fond* 913, op. 1, *delo* 4, pp. 91-92.

99. Sokolov, "Ekspeditsii k Aleutskim ostrovam," p. 80.

100. TsGAVMF, *fond* 216, *delo* 77, pp. 56-58.

101. Sokolov, "Ekspeditsii k Aleutskim ostrovam," p. 81.

102. TsGADA, *fond* 199, *delo* 528, bk.20, p. 54.

103. TsGADA, *fond* 199, *delo* 539, item 2 ("Izvestie o galiote *Sv. Pavel*").

104. Divin, *Russkie moreplavaniia*, pp. 238-42.
105. Ibid., pp. 245-48.
106. Sokolov, "Ekspeditsii k Aleutskim ostrovam," pp. 93-94.
107. Divin, *Russkie moreplavaniia*, p. 248.
108. Ibid., p. 254.
109. A. N. Krishtofovich, "Geologiia," in *Tikhii Okean* (L., 1926), pp. 40-41.
110. Divin, *Russkie moreplavaniia*, pp. 246-47.
111. Berkh, *Khronologicheskaia istoriia*, p. 80.
112. Ibid., pp. 66-67.
113. TsGADA, *fond* 199, *delo* 546 (2), item 9.
114. TsGADA, *fond* 199, *delo* 528 (2), item 6; L. S. Berg, *Ocherki po istorii russkikh geograficheskikh otkrytii* (L., 1946), p. 292.
115. Efimov, *Atlas*, p. 101; Sokolov, "Ekspeditsii k Aleutskim ostrovam," pp. 97-100.
116. Pallas, *Neue Nordische Beyträge*, 3:274-76.
117. The essential work remains H. I. Priestly's *José de Galvez, Visitor-General of New Spain, 1765-1771* (Berkeley, 1916).
118. Chapman, *Founding of Spanish California*, pp. 87-90.
119. Cook, *Flood Tide of Empire*, p. 53.
120. H. R. Wagner, "The Memorial of Pedro Calderon y Henriquez Recommending Monterey as a Port for the Philippine Galleons, with a View to Preventing Russian Encroachment in California," *CHSQ*, 23 (1944): 219-25; also Chapman, *Founding of Spanish California*, p. 75.
121. Chapman, *Founding of Spanish California*, p. 221.
122. Ibid., p. 227.
123. Archivo General de Indias, Catalogue 2900.
124. Ibid., Catalogue 2901 (Lacy to Grimaldi, 1 May 1775, etc.).
125. Chapman, *Founding of Spanish California*, pp. 418-19.
126. Archivo General de Indias, Catalogue 2901 (Bancroft Library copy).
127. T. S. Farrelly, "A Lost Colony of Novgorod in Alaska," *SEER* (American Series), 3 (1944): 33-38.

128. I. Andreevskii, K. Arsen'ev, eds., *Entsiklopedicheskii slovar'* (St. P., 1890-1904), 79:199-202
129. V. I. Smirnov, ed., *Leonard Eiler: perepiska: annotirovannyi ukazatel'* (L., 1967), index under Bering, Steller, etc.
130. Fry, *Alexander Dalrymple*, pp. 100-128.
131. Williams, *The British Search for the Northwest Passage*, p. 141; M. S. Anderson, *Britain's Discovery of Russia, 1553-1815* (London, 1958), pp. 86-87.
132. Anderson, *Britain's Discovery of Russia, 1553-1815*, pp. 9, 71-72.
133. R. C. Anderson, "British and American Officers," pp. 17-27; Cross, "Samuel Greig," pp. 251-53; P. Bartenev, ed., *Arkhiv kniazia Vorontsova* (M., 1870-95), 10:325; V. A. Divin, "Zhurnal puteshestviia michmana Nikifora Poluboiarinova v Indiiu," *Trudy Instituta Istorii Estestvoznaniia i Tekhniki*, 27 (1959): pp. 44ff.
134. *DNB*, 2:667.
135. R. Rea, "John Blankett and the Russian Navy in 1774," *M.M.*, 41 (1955): 245-49.
136. On Blankett: *Gentleman's Magazine*, 72 (1802): 35-36.
137. P. H. Clendenning, "Admiral Sir Charles Knowles and Russia, 1771-74," *M.M.*, 61 (1974): 43.
138. Veselago, *Materialy dlia istorii russkogo flota*, 11:720-22.
139. PRO State Papers: 91/102 and 103 (Harris-Suffolk correspondence, nos. 5, 9, etc.) on Greig's political importance by 1778.
140. V. Fitzhardinge, "Russian Naval Visitors to Australia, 1862-88," *JRHAS*, 52 (1966): pt. 2, pp. 129-58.
141. S. P. Oliver, ed., *The Memoirs and Travels of Mauritius Augustus, Count Benyowsky* (London, 1904), pp. 218-19.
142. G. V. Blue, "A Rumor of an Anglo-Russian Raid on Japan, 1776," *PHR*, 8 (1939): 453-54.
143. For example, in his *Histoire du commerce de la Russie* (1788).

NOTES TO CHAPTER FOUR

1. Ia.M. Svet, "Cook and the Russians," trans. P. Putz, Beaglehole, *Journals of Captain James Cook: Volume III*, 2: appendix; 1:654, 2:1242, 1338-39.
2. Ibid., 1:714; 2:1550.
3. Ibid., 1:650-51.
4. Ibid., 1:clxiii-iv; W. Lenz, ed., *Deutsch-Baltisches Biographisches Lexikon, 1710-1960* (Köln-Wien, 1970), p. 37; Sgibnev, "Istoricheskii ocherk," 7:23-25.
5. Beaglehole, *Journals of Captain James Cook. Volume III*, 1:700-701, 703.
6. Ibid., 2: appendix, pp. 7-8.
7. Ibid., pp. 6-7.
8. Ibid., 2:1553.
9. Ibid., p. 1550.
10. Ibid., 1:714; Williams, *The British Search for the Northwest Passage*, pp. 210-11.
11. S. D. Watrous, ed., *John Ledyard: Journey through Russia and Siberia, 1787-88* (Madison, 1966), intro.; *Gentleman's Magazine*, 55 (1785): pt. 2, pp. 570-71; C. V. Penrose, *A Memoir of James Trevenen, 1760-1790*, ed. C. Lloyd, R. C. Anderson (London, 1959), pp. 88ff.
12. Cook, *Flood Tide of Empire*, p. 115.
13. M. B. Grenader, "Istoricheskaia obuslovlennost' vozniknoveniia Severovostochnoi ekspeditsii 1785-1795 godov," *Uchonnye Zapiski Petropavlovskogo Gosudarstvennogo Pedagogicheskogo Instituta* (Petropavlovsk, 1957), bk. 2, pp. 22-35.
14. TsGADA, *fond* Vorontsova, *delo* 754, passim; Okun', *Russian-American Company*, p. 51.
15. TsGAVMF, *fond* 172, *delo* 367, pp. 260-64.
16. See bibliography, Sauer, Martin. Ukase of 8 August 1785.
17. G. A. Sarychev, *Puteshestvie kapitana Billingsa cherez Chukotskuiu zemliu ot Beringsa proliva do Nizhnekolymskogo ostroga, i plavanie kapitana Galla na sudne 'Chornom Orle' po severovostochnomu okeanu v 1791 godu* (St. P., 1811), pp. 143-91.
18. P. A. Tikhmenev, *Istoricheskoe obozrenie*, 1:210ff. on these and related matters.

19. TsGAVMF, *fond* 1214, *delo* 1, pp. 9-37.
20. *Obshchii morskoi spisok* (St. P., 1890), 3:88.
21. G. A. Sarychev, *Puteshestvie po severo-vostochnoi chasti Sibiri, Ledovitomu moriu i Vostochnomu Okeanu* (M., 1952), pp. 36-37; Martin Sauer, *An Account of a Geographical and Astronomical Expedition to the Northern Parts of Russia, Performed in the Years 1785 to 1794, Narrated from the Original Papers* (London, 1802), pp. 12-13.
22. TsGAVMF, *fond* 1214, *delo* 1, pp. 39-40.
23. Ibid., p. 40/obv.; also L.Ia. Shternberg, "Etnografiia," in *Tikhii Okean: Russkie nauchnye issledovaniia* (L., 1926), pp. 151-53.
24. Sarychev, *Puteshestvie po severo-vostochnoi chasti Sibiri*, pp. 285-86.
25. TsGAVMF, *fond* 1214, *delo* 1, p. 41.
26. Divin, *Russkie moreplavaniia*, p. 258; Bancroft, *History of Alaska*, p. 284.
27. Cited by Divin, ibid., p. 259.
28. A. I. Alekseev, *Sarychev*, pp. 49-50.
29. Divin, *Russkie moreplavaniia*, p. 259.
30. M. I. Belov, *Istoriia otkrytiia i osvoeniia Severnogo morskogo puti* (M., 1956), 1:423.
31. TsGADA, *fond* Gosarkhiva, *razriad* 24, *delo* 62, pp. 29-30.
32. See A. I. Andreev, *Russkie otkrytiia v Tikhom okeane i Severnoi Amerike v XVIII i XIX vekakh* (M., 1944), pp. 98-102.
33. A. Savin, "Okhotsk," *ZGDMM*, (1851): 148-61; A. I. Alekseev, *Okhotsk-kolybel' russkogo tikhookeanskogo flota* (Khabarovsk, 1959), ch. 2.
34. Sauer, *An Account*, pp. 41-42; also pp. 275-76 (on Okhotsk galiots).
35. Ibid., p. 296.
36. TsGAVMF, *fond* 913, op. 1, *delo* 159, p. 338.
37. TsGAVMF, *fond* 1214, *delo* 21, pp. 428-30; Sauer, *An Account*, p. 212; George Mortimer, *Observations and Remarks Made during a Voyage to the Islands of Teneriffe . . . and the Fox Islands on the Northwest Coast of*

America in the Brig "Mercury," Commanded by John Henry Coxe (London, 1791).

38. Cited by Divin, *Russkie moreplavaniia*, p. 261.

39. Tikhmenev, *Istoricheskoe obozrenie*, 1:33-34.

40. Sarychev, *Puteshestvie po severo-vostochnoi chasti Sibiri*, pp. 144-46.

41. It is now in the Saltykov-Shchedrin Public Library, Leningrad, *Rukopisnyi otdel*, F. 4, no. 874.

42. Sauer, *An Account*, pp. 150-60.

43. Divin, *Russkie moreplavaniia*, p. 264.

44. Sarychev, *Puteshestvie po severo-vostochnoi chasti Sibiri*, p. 149.

45. Sauer, *An Account*, pp. 168-71.

46. *Materialy dlia istorii russkikh zaselenii po beregam Vostochnago okeana* (St. P., 1861), 1:51-55.

47. Cook, *Flood Tide of Empire*, p. 125, for the Spanish perspective.

48. Sauer, *An Account*, p. 188.

49. TsGAVMF, *fond* 1214, *delo* 20, p. 302 (council on Kayak Island); Divin, *Russkie moreplavaniia*, p. 273.

50. Sauer, *An Account*, pp. 245-47; Bancroft, *History of Alaska*, pp. 292-93.

51. Bancroft, *History of Alaska*, pp. 293-94.

52. Divin, *Russkie moreplavaniia*, p. 274.

53. Sauer, *An Account*, pp. 287-88; F. W. Howay, *A List of Trading Vessels in the Maritime Fur Trade, 1785-1825*, ed. R. A. Pierce (Kingston, Ont., 1973), p. 16.

54. von Krusenstern, *A Voyage Round the World*.

55. Sauer, *An Account*, p. 288; Bancroft, *History of Alaska*, p. 296.

56. Divin, *Russkie moreplavaniia*, pp. 274-75.

57. Sarychev, *Puteshestvie po severo-vostochnoi chasti Sibiri*, p. 25.

58. Efimov, *Atlas geograficheskikh otkrytii*, maps 171-72, 155, etc.; Alekseev, *Sarychev*, p. 158.

59. Further on this, Bancroft, *History of Alaska*, pp. 299-301.

60. Okun', *Russian-American Company*, p. 195; Andreev, *Russkie otkrytiia v Tikhom okeane*, pp. 98ff.

61. See Watrous, *John Ledyard's Journey*, intro., 10-24.

62. TsGADA, *fond* Gosarkhiva, *razriad* 24, *delo* 61, p. 3; *DNB*, 2:795-96.

63. Charles Vinicombe Penrose, *A Memoir of James Trevenen, 1760-1790*, ed. C. Lloyd, R. C. Anderson (London, 1959), pp. 87ff.

64. Ibid., p. 28.

65. Brief details in Andreev, *Russkie otkrytiia v Tikhom okeane* (1944), pp. 202-4.

66. Bancroft, *History of Alaska*, pp. 242-44; V. N. Berkh, "Izvestie o mekhovoi torgovle, proizvodimoi Rossiianami pri ostrovakh Kurilskikh, Aleutskikh, i severozapadnom beregu Ameriki," *Syn otechestva* (St. P., 1823), pt. 88:97-98.

67. Penrose, *Memoir of James Trevenen*, p. 94.

68. Ibid., p. 96.

69. TsGAVMF, *fond* 172, *delo* 367, pp. 1-13.

70. A. P. Sokolov, "Prigotovlenie krugosvetnoi ekspeditsii 1787 goda pod nachal'stvom kapitana Mulovskogo," *ZGDMM*, 6 (1848): 143-50.

71. TsGAVMF, *fond* I. G. Chernysheva, *delo* 376, pp. 20-40.

72. Sokolov, "Prigotovlenie krugosvetnoi ekspeditsii," pp. 148ff; E. P. Silin, *Kiakhta v XVIII veke* (Irkutsk, 1947), chs. 3-4; Okun', *Russian-American Company*, p. 11.

73. TsGAVMF, *fond* I. G. Chernysheva, *delo* 376, p. 322.

74. Divin, *Russkie moreplavaniia*, p. 289.

75. *PSZRI*, 22: doc. 16,530; Sokolov, "Prigotovlenie krugosvetnoi ekspeditsii," pp. 172-78.

76. H. R. Wagner, "The Creation of Rights of Sovereignty through Symbolic Acts," *PHR*, 7 (1938): 297-326; N. Frolov, *Sobranie starykh i novykh puteshestvii* (M., 1855), 4:529-41.

77. Andreev, *Russkie otkrytiia* (1948), pp. 278-80, 365-67; Gibson, *Imperial Russia in Frontier America* (N.Y., 1976), pp. 68-70.

78. TsGADA, *fond* Gosarkhiva, *razriad* 10, op. 3, *delo* 16, p. 132.

79. See Lantzeff, *Siberia in the Seventeenth Century*, p. 96.

80. TsGADA, *fond* Gosarkhiva, *razriad* 10, op. 3, *delo* 16, p. 133.

81. Foreseen by Peter I: see chapter 2 here.

82. Divin, *Russkie moreplavaniia*, p. 291.

83. TsGAVMF, *fond* 172, *delo* 376, p. 262.

84. Cited by Okun', *Russian-American Company*, p. 17.

85. G. A. Lensen, *The Russian Push,* p. 71; S. I. Novakovskii, *Iaponiia i Rossiia* (Tokyo, 1918), pp. 45ff.
86. Cited by Okun', *Russian-American Company,* p. 17.
87. Cook, *Flood Tide of Empire,* pp. 115-16.
88. Ibid., 116-17.
89. Priestly, *José de Galvez,* p. 300.
90. Cook, *Flood Tide of Empire,* pp. 146-99 for a survey; also H. I. Priestly, ed., "The Log of the 'Princesa' by Esteban José Martinez," *Revista Mexicana de la Historia,* 18 (1958): 232-33.
91. See note 76.
92. E. Vila Vilar, *Los Rusos en America* (Seville, 1966), pp. 75-80; Cook, *Flood Tide of Empire,* p. 125; Bancroft, *History of Alaska,* pp. 271-73.
93. Sauer, *An Account,* p. 197.
94. Cook, *Flood Tide of Empire,* p. 125.
95. K. T. Khlebnikov, "Zapiski o koloniiakh Rossiisko-Amerikanskoi Kom-

panii," AGO, *razriad* 99, op.1, no.112, pp. 8-9, 32-36: also, in this connection, R. A. Humphrey, "Richard Oswald's Plan for an English and Russian Attack on Spanish America, 1781-82," HAHR, 18 (1938): 95-101.
96. TsGAVMF, *fond* I. G. Chernysheva, *delo* 376, pp. 411-12; Penrose, *Memoir of James Trevenen,* pp. 98-99.
97. F. F. Veselago, *Kratkaia istoriia russkogo flota* (M., 1939), p. 136; also *Materialy dlia istorii russkogo flota,* 12:551-52 (Mulovskii's death).
98. Bancroft, *History of Alaska,* pp. 251-52; Gibson, *Imperial Russia,* pp. 9-10.
99. V. N. Berkh, *Khronologicheskaia istoriia,* pp. 168-69; *Ocherk iz istorii Amerikanskoi pravoslavnoi dukhovnoi missii (Kadiakskoi missii 1794-1837 godov)* (St. P., 1894), pp. 226-29; Sauer, *An Account,* p. 171.
100. Berkh, *Khronologicheskaia istoriia,* p. 169.

NOTES TO CHAPTER FIVE

1. Tikhmenev, *Istoricheskoe obozrenie,* 1:18ff; Divin, *Russkie moreplavaniia,* pp. 323-24; Andreev, *Russkie otkrytiia* (1948), pp. 208ff.
2. *Materialy dlia istorii russkikh zaselenii po beregam Vostochnago okeana* (St. P., 1861), 4:3ff; Efimov, *Iz istorii russkikh ekspeditsii,* pp. 304-6; Sauer, *An Account,* pp. 170-72.
3. G. I. Shelikhov, *Rossiiskogo kuptsa imenitogo rylskogo grazhdanina Grigor'ia Shelikhova pervoe stranstvovanie s 1783 po 1787 god* (St. P., 1791), pp. 28-41; see also notes by Okun', *Russian-American Company,* pp. 278-80; Tikhmenev, *Istoricheskoe obozrenie,* 1:9-13; 2: suppl. (instructions of 4 May 1786).
4. Tikhmenev, *Istoricheskoe obozrenie,* 1:15.
5. Cited by Andreev, *Russian Discoveries in the Pacific and in North America in the Eighteenth and Nineteenth Centuries,* trans. Carl Ginsburg (Ann Arbor, 1952), pp. 85-89 (translation of Andreev, *Russkie otkrytiia,* 1944).
6. Ibid., pp. 82-83 ("Memorandum on the Privileges . . .").

7. Okun', *Russian-American Company,* pp. 29-30.
8. AGO, *fond* G.IV.1, docs. 4-6; Tikhmenev, *Istoricheskoe obozrenie,* 1:20-22.
9. Veselago, *Kratkaia istoriia russkogo flota* (M., 1939), p. 200.
10. Gibson, *Imperial Russia,* pp. 62-64; Sauer, *An Account,* pp. 41-42.
11. AGO, *fond* G.IV.1, doc. 92.
12. See Andreev, *Russkie otkrytiia* (1944), pp. 98-102; Okun', *Russian-American Company,* p. 195.
13. Andreev, *Russian Discoveries,* pp. 82-83.
14. Tikhmenev, *Supplement of Some Historical Documents to the Historical Review of the Formation of the Russian-American Company,* trans. D. Krenov (Seattle, 1938), pp. 155-56; J. F. G. de La Pérouse, *A Voyage Round the World* (London, 1798), 3:40; Peter Dobell, *Travels in Kamtchatka and Siberia* (London, 1830), 1:297-98.
15. Divin, *Russkie moreplavaniia,* pp. 325-29; Andreev, *Russian Discoveries,* pp. 89-95.
16. Details in V. N. Berkh, "Izvestie o

mekhovoi torgovle, proizvodimoi Rossiianami pri ostrovakh Kurilskikh, Aleutskikh . . .," *Syn otechestva* (St. P., 1823): 89:97-99; Howay, *List of Trading Vessels*, pp. 6ff.

17. Andreev, *Russian Discoveries*, pp. 92-95 (cf. Articles VIII); supporting data in K. T. Khlebnikov, "Zapiski o koloniiakh Rossiisko-Amerikanskoi Kompanii," AGO, *razriad* 99, op. 1, no. 112, pp. 7-9, 35ff.

18. Andreev, *Russian Discoveries*, p. 12.

19. Shelikhov, *Rossiiskogo kuptsa . . . pervoe stranstvovanie*, pp. 38-44; Andreev, *Russkie otkrytiia* (1948), pp. 297-300.

20. Andreev, *Russkie otkrytiia* (1944), pp. 101-2.

21. Andreev, *Russkie otkrytiia* (1948), pp. 278-80, 365-67; also Gibson, *Imperial Russia*, pp. 69-70 (Early plans for the Uda).

22. Biographical data in K. T. Khlebnikov, *Baranov*, trans. C. Bearne (Kingston, Ont., 1973); also Bancroft, *History of Alaska*, pp. 315-17.

23. Okun', *Russian-American Company*, pp. 38-39; Tikhmenev, *Supplement*, p. 287, 156.

24. Okun', *Russian-American Company*, pp. 32-33; Gibson, *Imperial Russia*, pp. 6-7. Originally connected with a region further south, "Slavarossiia" was applied to the settlement at Iakutat Bay in 1795.

25. An adequate biography of Rezanov has yet to appear; but see G. Atherton, "Nikolai Petrovich Rezanov," *North American Review* (N.Y., 1909): no.189, pp. 651-61. H. Chevigny. *Russian America* (N.Y., 1965), pp. 67-69, must be treated no less gingerly.

26. Okun', *Russian-American Company*, pp. 32ff; see also August von Kotzebue, *Das Merkwürdigste Jahr meines Lebens* (Berlin, 1802), 2:148-49.

27. Pertinent materials in Alaska History Research Project, *Documents Relative to the History of Alaska*, trans. T. Lavrischeff (College, Alaska, 1936-38), vol. 1; see also M. E. Wheeler, "The Origins of the Russian-American Company," *Jahrbucher für Geschichte Osteuropas* (1966): pp. 485-94.

28. Okun', *Russian-American Company*, p. 39.

29. Ibid., pp. 46-48; also A. G. Mazour, "The Russian-American Company: Private or Government Enterprise?," *PHR*, 13 (1944): 168-73.

30. P. N. Pavlov, ed., *K istorii Rossiisko-Amerikanskoi Kompanii: sbornik dokumental'nykh materialov* (Krasnoiarsk, 1957), pp. 19-21.

31. Okun', *Russian-American Company*, pp. 95, 99.

32. G. I. Davydov, *Dvukratnoe puteshestvie v Ameriku morskikh ofitserov Khvostova i Davydova* (St. P., 1810), 1:4-10; Tikhmenev, *Supplement*, pp. 309-14.

33. Okun', *Russian-American Company*, pp. 99-100; S. Ikonnikov, *Graf N.S. Mordvinov* (St. P., 1873), ch. 6.

34. Hence an embarrassing interlude at Verona in 1822, when Wellington asked the tsar about Russian activities on the North-west Coast.

35. Gibson, *Imperial Russia*, pp. 64-65.

36. For biographia, W. Lenz, ed., *Deutsch-Baltisches Biographisches Lexikon, 1710-1960* (Köln-Wien, 1970), p. 421; also F. F. Veselago, *Admiral Ivan Fedorovich Kruzenshtern* (St. P., 1869); *ES*, 16:849.

37. G. R. V. Barratt, *The Rebel on the Bridge: A Life of the Decembrist Baron Andrey Rozen* (London, 1975), pp. 7-17, 27-32.

38. Veselago, *Admiral Kruzenshtern*, pp. 2-3. Relatives were simultaneously entering the Swedish naval service: W. James, *Naval History of Great Britain* (London, 1822-26), 5:19.

39. Veselago, *Admiral Kruzenshtern*, p. 3.

40. A. Aslanbegov, *Admiral Aleksei Samuilovich Greig: biograficheskii ocherk* (St. P., 1873), pp. 3-5.

41. PRO, Adm. 1/498, cap. 370; V. V. Nevskii, *Pervoe puteshestvie Rossiian vokrug sveta* (M., 1951), pp. 33-35.

42. PRO, Adm. 1/498, cap. 370 (Murray to Stephen, 16 August 1794); *DNB*, 1:342 (Murray in India).

43. von Krusenstern, *A Voyage Round the World*, 1:32-33: J. Marshall, *Royal Navy Biography* (London, 1824), 2:61 (on Hartwell, recently of *Thetis*, and John Elphinston's son-in-law).

44. J. Ralfe, *Naval Biography* (London, 1828), 3:212; 4:98-99; James, *Naval History*, 1:495; Urey Lisiansky, *A Voyage Round the World in the Years*

1803, 4, 5, & 6 (London, 1814), trans. by the author, p. xviii.

45. Details of actions against the French in Nevskii, *Pervoe puteshestvie*, pp. 34ff.

46. von Krusenstern, *A Voyage Round the World*, pp. xxiv-v.

47. PRO, Adm. 1/1516, cap. 404 (Boyles to Nepean, 16 March 1797).

48. W. Laird-Clowes, *A History of the Royal Navy* (London, 1899-1904), 4:279, 283, 296-97, 408, 411-12.

49. TsGIA, *fond* XVIII veka, doc. no. 5196 ("Zapiski leitenanta Iuriia Lisianskogo").

50. Sauer, *An Account*, p. 287.

51. L. Dermigny, *La Chine et l'Occident: le commerce à Canton au XVIIIe siècle* (Paris, 1964), 3:1240-42.

52. von Krusenstern, *A Voyage Round the World*, 2:289.

53. Dobell, *Travels*, 1:297-98; also Andreev, *Russkie otkrytiia* (1948), pp. 365-67.

54. Dobell, *Travels*, 2:24-25.

55. Andreev, *Russkie otkrytiia* (1948), pp. 365-67.

56. Tikhmenev, *Supplement*, pp. 206-7.

57. *Vneshniaia politika Rossii XIX i nachala XX veka* (M., 1961-70), 2:297-98.

58. Howay, *List of Trading Vessels*, pp. 33, 35.

59. A copy had been sent ahead from London (September 1799).

60. von Krusenstern, *A Voyage Round the World*, 1:pp. xxv-xxvi; Nevskii, *Pervoe puteshestvie*, p. 35n.

61. von Krusenstern, *A Voyage Round the World*, 1:xxx; N. I. Turgenev, *Rossiia i russkie*, 3d. ed. (M., 1915), pp. 90-92, on Mordvinov's liberalism.

62. Lavrischeff, *Documents*, 3:270.

63. *Vneshniaia politika Rossii*, 2:297-98.

64. F. I. Shemelin, "Istoricheskoe izvestie o pervom puteshestvii Rossiian krugom sveta," *Russkii invalid* (St. P., 1823): nos. 23, 28, 31.

NOTES TO CHAPTER SIX

1. P. Tikhmenev, *Historical Review of the Formation of the Russian-American Company*, trans. D. Krenov (Seattle, 1939), 1:121-23; K. Voenskii, "Russkoe posol'stvo v Iaponiiu v nachale XIX veka," *Russkaia starina*, 84 (St. P., 1895): bk. 7, 125-28; V. G. Sirotkin, "Dokumenty o politike Rossii na Dal'nem Vostoke v nachale XIX veka," *Istoricheskie zapiski* (M., November-December 1962): 87-88.

2. von Krusenstern, *A Voyage Round the World*, 1:9-11; Shemelin, "Istoricheskoe izvestie," no. 23.

3. S. Novakovskii, *Iaponiia i Rossiia* (Tokyo, 1918), pp. 77-78; also *Russkaia starina*, 84, bk. 7, pp. 125-26 (the price paid).

4. Tikhmenev, *Historical Review*, 1:123.

5. Nevskii, *Pervoe puteshestvie*, pp. 29-30; F. I. Shemelin, *Zhurnal pervogo puteshestviia Rossiian vokrug zemnogo shara* (St. P., 1816), 1:4-8. Also V. N. Basnin, "O posol'stve v Kitai grafa Golovkina," *Chteniia v Obshchestve Istorii i Drevnostei Rossii* (M., 1875), 4:1-103 (political implications of the sailing of *Nadezhda* and *Neva*).

6. Lensen, *The Russian Push*, pp. 126-27.

7. M. I. Ratmanov, "Vyderzhki iz dnevnika krugosvetnogo puteshestviia na korable "Neva," *Iakhta*, 22 (St. P., 1876): 30ff.

8. von Krusenstern, *A Voyage Round the World*, 1:2.

9. Veselago, *Kratkaia istoriia russkogo flota*, pp. 178-90 (operations of 1798-1800).

10. von Krusenstern, *A Voyage Round the World*, 1:1-2.

11. Tikhmenev, *Historical Review*, 1:122ff; *Protokol Konferentsii Imp. Akademii Nauk* (St. P., for 13 April 1803: Kruzenshtern named corresponding member of the Academy).

12. Novakovskii, *Iaponiia i Rossiia*, pp. 74-77; Lensen, *The Russian Push*, p. 145. Andreev, *Russian Discoveries*, pp.13-16, 131 (on the clerks' orders from M. M. Buldakov, 10 July 1803).

13. von Krusenstern, *A Voyage Round the World*, 7-8.

14. Ibid., 1:13.

15. Ibid., 1:56. For the outward voyage, the Kruzenshtern, Lisianskii, and Langsdorf accounts complement each other.

16. Andreev, *Russian Discoveries*, p. 138.
17. G. H. von Langsdorf, *Voyages and Travels in Various Parts of the World, during the Years 1803-1807* (London, 1813-14), 1:28-76.
18. TsGAVMF, *fond* 14, *delo* 898 ("O gnilosti macht . . .").
19. Lisiansky, *Voyage*.
20. Langsdorf, *Voyages and Travels*, 1:100.
21. TsGIA, *fond* 853 (Buldakova), *delo* 1, item 74 ("Zhurnal prikazov kapitana Kruzenshterna komande sudov 'Nadezhda' i 'Neva' "); on these orders, see N. A. Gvozdetskii, "Pervoe morskoe puteshestvie Rossiian vokrug sveta," *Priroda* (M., 1947): no. 1, pp. 85-88.
22. Lisiansky, *Voyage*, pp. 88-89.
23. Ibid., pp. 89-90.
24. On whom see G. M. Dening, ed., *The Marquesan Journals of Edward Robarts, 1797-1824* (Canberra, 1974).
25. N. I. Korobitsyn, "Journal," in Andreev, *Russian Discoveries*, p. 214.
26. On 16 April 1826, Russians were killed on Nuku Hiva: *Zapiski Uchongo Komiteta Morskogo Shtaba* (St. P., 1828), 1:144-49 (*Krotkii*'s visit).
27. L. G. Rozina, "Kollektsiia M. A. E. po Markizskim ostrovam," *Sbornik Muzeia Antropologii i Etnografii*, 21 (L., 1963): pp. 110-19.
28. Lisiansky, *Voyage*, p. 105.
29. See Porter's *Journal of a Cruise made to the Pacific Ocean in the United States Frigate "Essex," in 1812-1814* (Boston, 1815), and note 26.
30. Ratmanov (see note 7) is as biased against Rezanov as Shemelin against Kruzenshtern in his (1816) Zhurnal (see note 5).
31. Survey in Lensen, *The Russian Push*, p. 136.
32. von Krusenstern, *A Voyage Round the World*, 1:102-3, 192.
33. Ibid., 1:183; also Lisiansky, *Voyage*, pp. 67, 70-71, 88-89.
34. S. B. Okun', ed., "Tsarskaia Rossiia i Gavaiskie ostrova," *Krasnyi arkhiv* (M., 1936): no. 6, pp. 181-86; R. A. Pierce, *Russia's Hawaiian Adventure, 1815-1817* (Berkeley, 1965).
35. Lisiansky, *Voyage*, pp. 99-104.
36. Ibid., pp.112-13; Andreev, *Russian Discoveries*, pp. 165-66; also Klaus Mehnert, *The Russians in Hawaii,*

1804-1819 (Honolulu, 1939), ch. 1.
37. Lisiansky, *Voyage*, p. 120.
38. Korobitsyn in Andreev, *Russian Discoveries*, pp. 166-67. Contemporary illustration of St. Paul's Harbour, chief settlement until 1808, in S. F. Fedorova, *Russkoe naselenie Aliaski i Kalifornii* (M., 1971), pl. 6.
39. Andreev, *Russian Discoveries*, p. 167; Lisiansky, *Voyage*, pp. 141-42.
40. See Bancroft, *History of Alaska*, p. 348.
41. Lisiansky, *Voyage*, p. 143; Khlebnikov, *Baranov*, pp. 33-34 (the value of Sitka to the Company); Gibson, *Imperial Russia*, pp. 10-12.
42. On *Unicorn*'s (and Barber's) movements about the Coast in the 1790's and 1802-4, see Howay, *List of Trading Vessels*, esp. p. 169.
43. S. E. Morison, *The Maritime History of Massachusetts, 1783-1860*, 4th ed. (Cambridge, Mass., 1961), pp. 52-55.
44. Lisiansky, *Voyage*, pp. 145-49; Alaska History Research Project, *Documents*, 3:202-3 (O'Cain and other Nor'westmen on the Coast in 1799-1804); Gibson, *Imperial Russia*, pp. 154-58.
45. Okun', *Russian-American Company*, p. 99; also Tikhmenev, *Supplement*, p. 156.
46. Tikhmenev, *Historical Review*, 283-84; *Materialy dlia istorii russkikh zaselenii*, 4:63.
47. Lisiansky, *Voyage*, pp. 156-58.
48. Ibid., pp. 162-64; K. T. Khlebnikov, "Zapiski o koloniiakh v Amerike Rossiisko-Amerikanskoi Kompanii," AGO, *razriad* 99, op. 1, no. 111 (pt. 1, pp. 6ff).
49. Ratmanov, "Zhurnal," nos. 18, 22; Shemelin, "Istoricheskoe izvestie," nos. 8-9, 23, 28, 31.
50. von Krusenstern, *A Voyage Round the World*, 1:210.
51. Voenskii, "Russkoe posol'stvo v Laponiiu," p. 127.
52. Ibid., p. 204.
53. von Krusenstern, *A Voyage Round the World*, 1:212.
54. V. Nabokov, ed. and trans., *Eugene Onegin* (N.Y., 1964), 2:428-30 (the subsequent life of "Tolstoi-amerikanets").
55. von Krusenstern, *A Voyage Round the World*, 1:215-16.

56. E. Ia. Fainberg, *Russko-Iaponskie otno-sheniia v 1697-1875 godakh* (M., 1960), pp. 52-66; Divin, *Russkie more-plavaniia,* pp. 304-23.
57. Lensen, *The Russian Push,* pp. 142-43.
58. Ibid., p. 152.
59. A. S. Polonskii, "Kurily," *ZIRGO,* 4 (1871): 554-55.
60. von Krusenstern, *A Voyage Round the World,* 1:286.
61. Alaska History Research Project, *Documents,* 3:179-80 (Rezanov's hope to force Japan to export rice); Davydov, *Dvukratnoe puteshestvie,* 1:26-36; V. A. Bilbasov, ed., *Arkhiv grafov Mordvinovykh* (St. P., 1902), 3:570-72.
62. von Krusenstern, *A Voyage Round the World,* 2:5-6.
63. Ibid., 2:67-68.
64. V. Lagus, *Erik Laksman; ego zhizn', puteshestviia, issledovaniia i perepiska* (St. P., 1890); A. S. Sgibnev, "Popytki russkikh k zavedeniiu torgovykh snoshenii s Iaponieiu," *MSb,* 100 (1869): no. 1, pp. 52-54.
65. See Novakovskii, *Iaponiia i Rossiia,* pp. 100-104; Lensen, *The Russian Push,* pp.154-55.
66. von Krusenstern, *A Voyage Round the World,* 2:46-52.
67. Langsdorf, *Voyages and Travels,* 1:322-23.
68. Ibid., 1:345-47; von Krusenstern, *A Voyage Round the World,* 2:94-101.
69. Lisiansky, *Voyage,* p. 190.
80. Ibid., p. 218; *Materialy dlia istorii,* 3:126-27.
71. Andreev, *Russian Discoveries,* pp. 176-78. Compare with Golovnin's 1818 description of the same scene: Gibson, *Imperial Russia,* pp. 10-11. *Materialy dlia istorii,* 3:6-10 (shipping at Novo-Arkhangel'sk).
72. Lisiansky, *Voyage,* p. 220; Khlebnikov, *Baranov,* pp. 49-50; Aleksei Lazarev, *Zapiski o plavanii voennogo shliupa "Blagonamerennyi" v Beringov proliv i vokrug sveta . . .* (M., 1950), p. 239 (the kitchen-gardens in 1820).
73. Lisiansky, *Voyage,* pp. 251-54; also R. G. Ward, ed., *American Activities in the Central Pacific, 1790-1870* (Ridgewood, N.J., 1967), 4:31-67.
74. Dermigny, *La Chine et l'Occident,* 3:1242.
75. von Krusenstern, *A Voyage Round the World,* 2:289.
76. Andreev, *Russian Discoveries,* pp. 187-88.
77. Novakovskii, *Iaponiia i Rossiia,* pp. 90-91.
78. Lisiansky, *Voyage,* pp. 271-76; von Krusenstern, *A Voyage Round the World,* 2:289-90.
79. Sirotkin, "Dokumenty o politike," p. 87 (Sarychev on provisioning costs); Tikhmenev, *Supplement,* pp. 206-7.
80. Alaska History Research Project, *Documents,* 3:163; *Vneshniaia politika Rossii,* 4:241; Bancroft, *History of Alaska,* p. 348.
81. von Krusenstern, *A Voyage Round the World,* 2:248.
82. J. P. Faivre, *L'Expansion française dans le Pacifique, 1800-1842* (Paris, 1960), pp. 104, 107.
83. See J. G. Kohl, *Russia and the Russians in 1842* (London, 1843), 2:200-202; Barratt, *Rebel on the Bridge,* pp. 17-37.
84. Lenz, *Deutsch-Baltisches Lexikon,* pp. 40-41, 468.
85. See bibliography here. Lenz, *Deutsch-Baltisches Lexikon,* p. 52 on a cousin, Moritz Anton Berg, in *Neva* (1806-8: to the Pacific colonies).
86. von Krusenstern, *A Voyage Round the World,* 1:11; Lenz, *Deutsch-Baltisches Lexikon,* p. 410.
87. Kohl, *Russia and the Russians,* pp. 201-2.
88. Lisiansky, *Voyage,* pp. 318-19.
89. Career details in E. L. Shteinberg, *Zhizneopisanie russkogo moreplavatelia Iu. Lisianskogo* (M., 1948); also V. G. Belinskii, *Sobranie sochinenii v 3 tomakh* (M., 1948), 3:112 (success of 1814 *Voyage*).
90. Lenz, *Deutsch-Baltisches Lexikon,* p. 284-85; *Zapiski Uchonogo Komiteta Morskogo Shtaba* (St. P., 1835), 2:355-57; N. A. Ivashintsev, *Russkie krugosvetnye puteshestviia s 1803 po 1849 god* (St. P., 1872), pp. 16-17, 35-38.
91. Langsdorf, *Voyages and Travels,* 2:12. Tikhmenev, *Supplement,* p. 287 on company ships.
92. *Slava Rossii,* foundered in 1794.
93. von Krusenstern, *A Voyage Round the World,* 2:194-96, 217-19.
94. Ibid., 2:220.

NOTES TO CHAPTER SEVEN

1. Voenskii, "Russkoe posol'stvo v Iapon-iiu," pp. 212-14; Tikhmenev, *Istoricheskoe obozrenie*, 1:111-12.
2. Novakovskii, *Iaponiia i Rossiia*, pp. 110-11.
3. Langsdorf, *Voyages and Travels*, 2:12; Alaska History Research Project, *Documents*, 3:178.
4. von Krusenstern, *A Voyage Round the World*, 2:108-9, 112.
5. V. M. Golovnin, *Memoirs of a Captivity in Japan During the Years 1811-1813* (London, 1824), 3:280-84 (delightfully hostile treatment of Rezanov). Tikhmenev, *Historical Review*, 1:197-98.
6. Golovnin, *Memoirs*, 3:281-82; Tikhmenev, *Istoricheskoe obozrenie*, 1:153-54.
7. See Sgibnev, "Popytki russkikh," pp. 58-60; Lensen, *The Russian Push*, pp. 167-76.
8. Sgibnev, "Popytki russkikh," p. 59.
9. Golovnin, *Memoirs*, 3:282-83.
10. Further on the raids, see Lensen, *The Russian Push*, pp. 170-76; and Davydov, *Dvukratnoe puteshestvie*, 2: passim.
11. Sgibnev, "Popytki russkikh," pp. 65-66; Novakovskii, *Iaponiia i Rossiia*, pp. 121-23.
12. Langsdorf, *Voyages and Travels*, 2:296-300; John D'Wolf, *A Voyage to the North Pacific and a Journey through Siberia* (Cambridge, Mass., 1861), pp. 39-40; Lensen, *The Russian Push*, p. 175.
13. Langsdorf, *Voyages and Travels*, 2:96-100; Nikolai Rezanov, *The Rezanov Voyage to Nueva California in 1806*, trans. T. C. Russell (San Francisco, 1926), pp. 4-5; Valaam Monastery, *Ocherk iz istorii Amerikanskoi pravoslavnoi dukhovnoi missii (Kadiakskoi missii, 1794-1837 godov)* (St. P., 1894), pp. 139-40, etc. (lack of meat and initiative).
14. Details in Khlebnikov, *Baranov*, 32ff; Andreev, *Russian Discoveries*, pp. 176-78; Lisiansky, *Voyage*, p. 218.
15. Description in Washington Irving's *Astoria* (Portland, n.d.), p. 420.
16. Gibson, *Imperial Russia*, p. 13.
17. Davydov. *Dvukratnoe puteshestvie*, 1:195.
18. Tikhmenev, *Historical Review*, 1:178, 184; *Materialy dlia istorii*, 3:136-37.
19. Pavlov, *K istorii Rossiisko-Amerikanskoi Kompanii*, p. 158; Tikhmenev, *Historical Review*, 1:145.
20. Tikhmenev, *Istoricheskoe obozrenie*, 2 (suppl.): 210; see also *Supplement*, p. 287.
21. F. W. Howay, "An Outline Sketch of the Maritime Fur Trade," Canadian Historical Association *Annual Report* (1932), p. 7; Gibson, *Imperial Russia*, pp. 154-56.
22. As required by Article II of the Company's original charter: United States, Congress, Senate, *Proceedings of the Alaskan Boundary Tribunal* (Washington, D.C., 1904), 2:23.
23. *Materialy dlia istorii*, 3:4, 13; *Vneshniaia politika Rossii*, 6:279; Gibson, *Imperial Russia*, pp. 156-60.
24. Khlebnikov, *Baranov*, p. 34.
25. Tikhmenev, *Historical Review*, 1:45, 285.
26. Arkhiv Vneshnei Politiki Rossii (M): *fond* 1, Otdela E.Imp. Velich. Sobstvennoi kantseliarii: 1802, *delo* 152, p. 4.
27. Rather superficial surveys in Atherton, "Nikolai Petrovich Rezanov," pp. 654-60, and A. Yarmolinsky, "A Rambling Note on 'The Russian Columbus,' " *Bulletin of the New York Public Library*, 31 (1927): 707-13. February 1806 trade plans in Alaska History Research Project, *Documents*, 3:179-80; Tikhmenev, *Supplement*, pp. 334-35.
28. Tikhmenev, *Historical Review*, 1:197-98; *Supplement*, p. 427; Langsdorf, *Voyages and Travels*, 2:94, 99, 136.
29. Rezanov, *Voyage*, pp. 5-6.
30. D'Wolf, *A Voyage to the North Pacific*, pp.39-40; Langsdorf, *Voyages and Travels*, 2:89.
31. Tikhmenev, *Istoricheskoe obozrenie*, 1:146.
32. Tikhmenev, *Supplement*, p. 427; *Materialy dlia istorii*, 3:137.
33. Langsdorf, *Voyages and Travels*, 2:135ff.

34. Tikhmenev, *Istoricheskoe obozrenie,* 2:233 (Rezanov on a Russian colony on the Columbia); Rezanov, *Voyage,* pp. 28-30.
35. Langsdorf, *Voyages and Travels,* 2:146.
36. Rezanov, *Voyage,* pp. 30-31; Bancroft, *History of California,* 2:66-67 (dramatic survey).
37. Tikhmenev, *Supplement,* p. 395-96; Gibson, *Imperial Russia,* pp. 176-77.
38. Bancroft, *History of California,* 2:72-73.
39. Langsdorf, *Voyages and Travels,* 2:183.
40. Khlebnikov, *Baranov,* p. 59; Tikhmenev, *Supplement,* p. 407.
41. Sir George Simpson, *Narrative of a Journey Round the World* (London, 1847), 1:377-79.
42. Tikhmenev, *Istoricheskoe obozrenie,* 1:162 (the death).
43. Atherton, "Nikolai Petrovich Rezanov," pp. 660-61; for an amusingly hostile treatment of Rezanov the Imperialist, R. Greenhow, *History of Oregon . . .* (London, 1844), pp. 273-74.
44. Golovnin, in *Materialy dlia istorii,* 2:86.
45. Khlebnikov, *Baranov,* p. 53.
46. His provisioning problems and solutions to them echoed those of the Portuguese, of another age: see C. R. Boxer, *The Portuguese Seaborne Empire, 1415-1825,* 2d.ed. (London, 1973), pp. 213-17.
47. Tikhmenev, *Istoricheskoe obozrenie,* 2:233 (despatch of 16 February).
48. Khlebnikov, *Baranov,* p. 71.
49. This account rests on Tarakanov's statement to V. M. Golovnin of 1810, printed in the latter's *Sochineniia i perevody* (St.P., 1864), 4:406-28.
50. Tikhmenev, *Istoricheskoe obozrenie,* 1:207-8; *Vneshniaia politika Rossii,* 4: 163-64.
51. "Predstavlenie Soveta Rossiisko-Amerikanskoi Kompanii Aleksandru I o tseli soobraznosti zakliucheniia torgovogo dogovora s Ispanskoi Kalifornieiu . . .," TsGADA, *fond* 796, op. 1, *delo* 163.
52. The proclamation, "Obrashchenie glavnogo pravleniia R.-A. Kompanii k blagorodnym gospodam gishpantsam, zhivushchim v Kalifornii," is now in the Manuscript Division of the Saltykov-Shchedrin Public Library, Leningrad: *fond* 204, carton 32, doc. 36.
53. Bancroft, *History of California,* 2:297-98; see also Khlebnikov, *Baranov,* p. 83.
54. Khlebnikov, *Baranov,* p. 84; M. E. Wheeler, "Empires in Conflict and Coöperation: The Bostonians and the Russian-American Company," *PHR,* 40 (1971): 419-41; Gibson, *Imperial Russia,* pp. 157-59, 169, 180-81.
55. Khlebnikov, *Baranov,* p. 84.
56. Lenz, *Deutsch-Baltisches Lexikon,* pp. 284-85.
57. PRO Adm.1/1927, cap.9-10 (Hallowell from St. Thomas); H. H. Breen, *St. Lucia, Historical, Statistical, and Descriptive* (London, 1844), pp. 110-12 (actions of June 1803).
58. See Sir N. Nicolas, *The Despatches and Letters of Vice-Admiral Lord Nelson* (London, 1844) 5:448-49; 6:42-43 (Russians with Nelson); also C. Oman, *Nelson* (London, 1947), p. 108 (thoughts of Russian service).
59. Ivashintsev, *Russkie krugosvetnye puteshestviia,* p. 17; G. R. V. Barratt, *The Russian Navy and Australia to 1825: The Days Before Suspicion* (Melbourne, 1979) Ch.2.
60. Khlebnikov, *Baranov,* p. 74.
61. Cited by R. A. Pierce, *Russia's Hawaiian Adventure,* pp. 37-39.
62. See bibliography here under Golder (1930), Mazour (1937), Mehnert (1939), Bradley (1968).
63. A. Campbell, *A Voyage Round the World from 1806 to 1812, in which Japan, Kamchatka, the Aleutian Islands and the Sandwich Islands Were Visited,* 2d. ed. (New York, 1819). See also Bancroft, *History of Alaska,* p. 491n.
64. Campbell, *Voyage* p. 81.
65. Rossiisko-Amerikanskaia Kompaniia: *Sheffer Papers,* trans. Lantzeff: Bancroft Library, Berkeley, MS. P-N 4, pp.11-12; Tikhmenev, *Istoricheskoe obozrenie,* 1:166 (alleged British naval response to *Neva*).
66. V. N. Berkh, "Nechto o Sandvichevykh ostrovakh," *Syn otechestva* (St. P., 1818), no. 2, p. 162.
67. Khlebnikov, *Zhisneopisanie Aleksandra Andreevicha Baranova* (St. P., 1835), pp.161-62; Campbell, *Voyage,* p. 81.

68. Andreev, *Russian Discoveries*, pp.165-66; Pierce, *Russia's Hawaiian Adventure*, pp. 37-39.

69. Okun', *Russian-American Company*, p. 153; *Sheffer Papers*, MS. P-N 4, pp. 126-27.

70. Pierce, *Russia's Hawaiian Adventure*, p. 39.

71. H. W. Bradley, *The American Frontier in Hawaii: The Pioneers (1789-1843)* (Gloucester, Mass., 1968), p. 48.

72. Ibid., p. 34.

73. Bibliography under Mazour (1937); Gibson, *Imperial Russia*, pp. 143-49.

74. Khlebnikov, *Baranov*, pp. 75, 117.

75. Ibid., pp. 72-73.

76. See ch. 9 below.

NOTES TO CHAPTER EIGHT

1. V. M. Golovnin, *Puteshestvie na shliupe "Diana" iz Kronshtadta v Kamchatku* (M. 1961), introduction, iii-vi.

2. TsGAVMF, *fond* 7, op. 1, *delo* 2 ("Zapisnaia knizhka"), pp. 240-43

3. Port of Spain. See Laird-Clowes, *History of the Royal Navy*, 4:395 and note 49 to ch. 5 here, on Russian Volunteers in the West Indies.

4. TsGAVMF, *fond* 7, op. 1, *delo* 2, pp. 251-52 (action against Greek privateer in Bay of Servera, February 1805).

5. Ibid., p. 256; also N. Nozikov, *Russian Voyages Round the World*, trans. E. and M. Lesser (London, 1944), p. 76.

6. TsGAVMF, *fond* 7, op. 1, *delo* 2, p. 257.

7. See P. Mel'nitskii, *Admiral Rikord i ego sovremenniki* (St. P., 1856); L. I. Rikord, *Admiral P. I. Rikord: biograficheskii ocherk* (St. P., 1875).

8. Golovnin, *Puteshestvie*, p.v; Laird-Clowes, *History of the Royal Navy*, 4:408-12.

9. Ivashintsev, *Russkie krugosvetnye puteshestviia*, p. 223.

10. Bilbasov, *Arkhiv grafov Mordvinovykh*, 3:574-77; Tikhmenev, *Supplement*, pp. 286-87; von Krusenstern, *A Voyage Round the World*, 2:194-96, 217-19.

11. Golovnin, *Puteshestvie*, p. 147.

12. Golovnin's account is supplemented by his reports, in *Materialy dlia istorii*, 1:70-72 ("Zapiska . . . o nyneshnem sostoianii Rossiisko-Amerikanskoi Kompanii"); 2:10ff, ("Zamechaniia o Kamchatke . . .").

13. Ibid., 1:71.

14. Ibid., pp. 76-77; Gibson, *Imperial Russia*, pp. 159-60 (U.S. Government unwilling to intervene on North-west Coast).

15. Gibson, *Imperial Russia*, 157, 169.

16. V. M. Golovnin, ed., *Zapiski Vasiliia Mikhailovicha Golovnina v plenu u Iapontsev v 1811, 1812 i 1813 godakh . . .*, ed. N. Grech (St. P., 1851: enlarged from 1816 ed.), 1:6-10.

17. See Lensen, *The Russian Push*, pp. 197-98 (based on archival work by Masahide Hiraoka and Iichiro Tokutomi).

18. Golovnin, *Zapiski*, 1:16, 22.

19. Ibid., p. 12.

20. Ibid., pp. 15-17.

21. Lensen, *The Russian Push*, p. 200.

22. Ibid., pp. 205-78.

23. Golovnin, *Zapiski*, 1:101-5.

24. Ibid., pp. 106-7.

25. Lensen, *The Russian Push*, pp. 212-13.

26. P. I. Rikord, *Zapiski flota-kapitana Rikorda o plavanii ego k iaponskim beregam v 1812 i 1813 godakh* (St. P., 1875), pp.3-6; Lensen, *The Russian Push*, p. 222.

27. Golovnin, *Zapiski*, 1:97.

28. *Materialy dlia istorii*, 1:6-16 (report from Minitskii of 24 September 1815); Dobell, *Travels in Kamtschatka*, 1:297-98; Tikhmenev, *Supplement*, p. 287; Minitskii, "Opisanie Okhotskogo porta," *Syn otechestva*, 21 (St. P., 1829): pp. 136-53.

29. Rikord, *Zapiski*, pp. 7-13.

30. Cited by Lensen, *The Russian Push*, pp. 228-29.

31. Golovnin, *Zapiski*, 2:135-47; Lensen, *The Russian Push*, pp. 240-41.

32. Golovnin, *Zapiski*, 2:67-73.

33. Novakovskii, *Iaponiia i Rossiia*, pp. 124-26.

34. Lensen, *The Russian Push*, p. 248. In the Stalinist period, his observations were distorted, e.g., in Iu. Zhukov, *Russkie i Iaponiia* (M., 1945).
35. Golovnin, *Zapiski*, 3:45-46.

36. Ibid., pp. 52-53.
37. A. S. Polonskii, "Kurily," pp. 565-69.
38. Lensen, *The Russian Push*, p. 261.
39. Golovnin, *Zapiski*, 3:93-108.

NOTES TO CHAPTER NINE

1. Nevskii, *Pervoe puteshestvie Rossiian*, pp. 192-93.
2. Khlebnikov, *Baranov*, pp. 86-87; Gibson, *Imperial Russia*, pp. 161-62.
3. Ivashintsev, *Russkie krugosvetnye puteshestviia*, pp. 23-24; A. A. Samarov, ed., *Russkie flotovodtsy: M. P. Lazarev* (M., 1952), 1:22-24, 63-64.
4. Irving, *Astoria*, p. 420.
5. Bancroft, *History of California*, 2:305.
6. Okun', *Russian-American Company*, p. 100; Tikhmenev, *Supplement*, pp. 309-16.
7. Pierce, *Russia's Hawaiian Adventure*, passim; Gibson, *Imperial Russia*, p. 143n.
8. A. D. Dobrovol'skii, *Otto fon Kotsebue: russkie moreplavateli* (M., 1953); O. von Kotzebue, *A Voyage of Discovery into the South Sea and Beering's Straits undertaken in the Years 1815 to 1818* (London, 1821).
9. Kotzebue, *Voyage*, 1:29-30.
10. A. D. Ivanovskii, *Gosudarstvennyi kantsler graf Nikolai Petrovich Rumiantsev: biograficheskii ocherk* (St. P., 1871), pp. 96ff.
11. Ibid., pp. 7, 10-11.
12. Veselago, *Kratkaia istoriia russkogo flota*, pp. 230-32.
13. Ibid., pp. 246-47. My translation.
14. M. A. Bestuzhev, cited in G. R. V. Barratt, ed. and trans., *Voices in Exile: The Decembrist Memoirs* (Montreal, 1974), pp. 42-43.
15. Veselago, *Kratkaia istoriia russkogo flota*, pp. 290-91.
16. Kotzebue, *Voyage*, 1:12-16.
17. Ibid., pp. 29-30; see also A. von Chamisso, *Werke* (Berlin, 1856), 2: passim.
18. Kotzebue, *Voyage*, 1:93; Ivashintsev, *Russkie krugosvetnye puteshestviia*, p. 27.
19. Kotzebue, *Voyage*, 1:273-74; Louis

Choris, *Voyage pittoresque autour du monde* (Paris, 1822) (plates of Unalaska Island).
20. Kotzebue, *Voyage*, 1:272; von Chamisso, *Werke*, 2:10-60.
21. Bancroft, *History of California*, 2:270-71, 310.
22. Ibid., pp. 279-80, 309-10; Tikhmenev, *Istoricheskoe obozrenie*, 1:214.
23. Kotzebue, *Voyage*, 1:279-86; 3:38-51.
24. Bancroft, *History of California*, 2:311-13.
25. Gibson, *Imperial Russia*, pp. 143-49 for summary.
26. Ibid., pp. 144-45; Pierce, *Russia's Hawaiian Adventure*, pp. 191-97.
27. Kotzebue, *Voyage*, 1:328.
28. G. Vancouver, *A Voyage of Discovery* (London, 1798), 3:65-66; G. F. Mathison, *A Visit to Brazil, Chile, Peru, and the Sandwich Islands* (London, 1825), pp. 426-27; R. Cox, *Adventures on the Columbia River* (N.Y., 1832), pp. 38-39 (on Young, Marini, Holmes and Adams).
29. Gibson, *Imperial Russia*, p. 148.
30. Ivashintsev, *Russkie krugosvetnye puteshestviia*, pp. 28-34; Kotzebue, *Voyage*, 2:291ff; A. Sharp, *The Discovery of the Pacific Islands* (Oxford, 1960).
31. Ivashintsev, *Russkie krugosvetnye puteshestviia*, p. 34.
32. Kotzebue, *Voyage*, 1:305; also Tikhmenev, *Historical Review*, 1:232-33.
33. K. T. Khlebnikov, "Zapiski o Kalifornii," *Syn otechestva* (St. P., 1829): no. 2, pp. 401-3; D. I. Zavalishin, "Delo o kolonii Ross," *Russkii vestnik* (St. P., 1866): 61-62.
34. Further on these matters, Okun', *Russian-American Company*, p. 67.
35. Published in his 1826 *Atlas*.
36. AVPR, *fond* Rossiisko-Amerikanskoi Kompanii, *dela* 284, 285, Golovnin's

memoranda of 1815-17 (to Kozodavlev, minister of internal affairs, Traversay, et. al.: TsGAVMF, *fond* 7, op. 1) were reworked and incorporated in his "Zapiska o sostoianii Rossiisko-Amerikanskoi Kompanii v 1818 godu." *Materialy dlia istorii*, 1:48-115.

37. Okun', *Russian-American Company*, pp. 95-98.
38. Ibid., p. 105; Mazour, "The Russian-American Company," pp. 168-73.
39. Sgibnev, "Okhotskii port," no. 12; *Zapiski Uchonogo Komiteta Morskogo Shtaba* (St. P., 1833), 2:335-57; Lenz, *Deutsch-Baltisches Lexikon*, pp. 284-85.
40. M. Raeff, *Siberia and the Reforms of 1822* (Washington, 1955), pp. 22-23.
41. Rikord, *Zapiski*, pp. 3-11; Polonskii, "Kurily," pp. 562-63.
42. See *Materialy dlia istorii*, 3:16ff.
43. Ibid., pp. 18-19.
44. Ivashintsev *Russkie krugosvetnye puteshestviia*, pp. 225-26.

45. R. A. Pierce, intro. to Khlebnikov, *Baranov*, pp. ix-x; Bancroft, *History of Alaska*, pp. 555-56; Ivashintsev, *Russkie krugosvetnye puteshestviia*, pp. 68-69.
46. Choris, *Voyage*, p. 7; Golovnin, *Puteshestvie na shliupe "Diana,"* 1:280-82; Gibson, *Imperial Russia*, pp. 114-15, 182-83.
47. Tikhmenev, *Historical Review*, 1:264-65; *Materialy dlia istorii*, 3:78.
48. Zavalishin, "Delo o kolonii Ross," pp. 60-61; L. A. Shur, *K beregam Novogo Sveta* (M., 1971), pp. 140-41.
49. Khlebnikov, *Baranov*, p. 96.
50. Ibid., p. 97; Tikhmenev, *Istoricheskoe obozrenie*, 1:242-45; Bancroft, *History of Alaska*, pp. 510-12.
51. Khlebnikov, *Baranov*, p. 97.
52. Ivashintsev, *Russkie krugosvetnye puteshestviia*, p. 37; Shur, *K beregam*, index under "Gagemeister."

NOTES TO CHAPTER TEN

1. G. A. Sarychev, *Puteshestvie flota kapitana Sarycheva po severo-vostochnoi chasti Sibiri, Ledovitomu moriu, i Vostochnomu okeanu . . . s 1785 po 1793 god* (St. P., 1802), 2:122-26; also ch. 4 above.
2. I. Veniaminov, *Zapiski ob ostrovakh Unalashkinskago otdela* (St. P., 1840), 1:passim; Berkh, *Khronologicheskaia istoriia*, pp. 45-52.
3. Berkh, *Khronolog. istoriia*, p. 47 (edict issued at Okhotsk by S. Zubov, 29 August 1770).
4. Details in Fedorova, *Russkoe naselenie Aliaski*, ch. 1.
5. See R. V. Makarova, *Russkie na Tikhom okeane vo vtoroi polovine XVIII veka* (M., 1968), pp. 64-68.
6. *Materialy dlia istorii*, 3:7-9.
7. Edict issued at Okhotsk by G. Kozlov-Ugrenin, 15 June 1787: text in Bancroft, *History of Alaska*, pp. 311-12n.
8. *Materialy dlia istorii*, 3:7-16 (report no. 1931).
9. United States, National Archives, Washington, D.C., "Records of the Russian-American Company, 1802-

1867: Correspondence of Governors General," vol. 3 (Zelenskii correspondence).
10. Ivashintsev, *Russkie krugosvetnye puteshestviia*, p. 227; F. Debenham, ed. and trans., *The Voyage of Captain Bellingshausen to the Antarctic Seas, 1819-1821* (London, 1945), 1:6-7.
11. Okun', *Russian-American Company*.
12. *Materialy dlia istorii*, 3:3-5.
13. Institut Istorii Akademii Nauk SSSR: "Materialy po istorii Rossiisko-Amerikanskoi Kompanii: doc. nos. 44 & 49" (entertainment for Arakcheev).
14. Okun', "Tsarskaia Rossiia i Gavaiskie ostrova," no. 5, pp. 165-66; "Zapiski grafa K. V. Nesselrod," *Russkii vestnik* (M. October 1865): 519-25.
15. *Materialy dlia istorii*, 3:2 (doc. no. 1510).
16. D. Perkins, "Russia and the Spanish Colonies, 1817-1818," *AHR*, 28 (1923): pp. 656-73; Okun', *Russian-American Company*.
17. V. Bezobrazov, *Graf F. P. Litke* (St. P., 1888), chs. 2-3; Lenz, *Deutsch-Baltisches Lexikon*, pp. 478,

886; Lütke's and F. F. Matiushkin's *Kamchatka* journals given in Shur, *K beregam.*

18. Ivashintsev, *Russkie krugosvetnye puteshestviia*, p. 41.
19. But see anonymous article in *The Friend* (Honolulu, July 1894), p. 51, "Golovnin's Visit to Hawaii in 1818."
20. *Materialy dlia istorii*, 3:92-93.
21. Ibid., pp. 48-49, 86, 93-94, 109-13, 126.
22. [Archimandrite Bolotov], "Kratkoe opisanie ob Amerikanskom ostrove Kad'iake," *Drug prosveshcheniia* (St. P., October 1805): 89-106.
23. Valaam Monastery, *Ocherk iz istorii Amerikanskoi missii*, pp. 25ff.; see also Bancroft, *History of Alaska*, pp. 304, 459.
24. Khlebnikov, *Baranov*, p. 98.
25. Khlebnikov, *Zhizneopisanie Baranova*, pp. 174-75.
26. Khlebnikov, *Baranov*, p. 98.
27. Ibid., pp. 99-100; Ivashintsev, *Russkie krugosvetnye puteshestviia*, p. 37.
28. B. M. Gough, ed., *To the Pacific and Arctic with Beechey* (Cambridge, 1973), p. 4.
29. Kotzebue, *Voyage*, 1:325-26.
30. *Historical Records of Australia: Series 1*, 7:474-76; 8:626 Barratt, "Russian Navy and Australia," sec. 5.
31. H. W. Bradley, *The American Frontier in Hawaii: The Pioneers* (Gloucester, Mass., 1968), pp. 48-49.
32. Ibid., pp. 96-97; also B. M. Gough, *The Royal Navy and the Northwest Coast of North America, 1810-1914* (Vancouver, 1971), ch. 1.
33. Bradley, *American Frontier in Hawaii*, p. 103.
34. Cited by L. P. Kirwan, *A History of Polar Exploration* (New York, 1960), p.77.
35. Cited by A. Day, *The Admiralty Hydrographic Service, 1795-1919* (London, 1967), pp. 27-38.
36. Details in F. F. Bellingsgauzen, *Dvukratnye izyskaniia v Iuzhnom ledovitom okeane i plavanie vokrug sveta v prodolzhenie 1819, 1820 i 1821 gg . . .*, ed. E. E. Shvede (M., 1960), pp. 9-12.
37. A. P. Lazarev, *Zapiski o plavanii voennogo shliupa "Blagonamerennyi" v Beringov Proliv i vokrug sveta dlia otkrytii v 1819-1822 godakh* (M., 1950), pp. 5-6, 21-30; see also V. V. Kuznetsova, "Novye dokumenty o russkoi ekspeditsii k Severnomu poliusu," *IVGO, 3* (L., 1968): 237-45, and bibliography here under Ostrovskii, B.

38. Bellingsgauzen, *Dvukratnye izyskaniia*, pp. 11-12.
39. The author is currently preparing a short work on Russian ethnological activity in New South Wales, 1814-1822. On the "northern division's" voyage, see K. Gillesem (Gilsen), "Puteshestvie na shliupe 'Blagonamerennyi' dlia issledovaniia beregov Azii i Ameriki za Beringovym prolivom s 1819 po 1822 god," *Otechestvennye zapiski*, 66 (St. P., 1849), sec 8; and Aleksei Lazarev's *Zapiski* (note 37).
40. See Gough's introduction, *To the Pacific and Arctic with Beechey* (orders of 10 February 1825, suggesting use of Kotzebue Sound).
41. E. W. Hunter Christie, *The Antarctic Problem: An Historical and Political Study* (London, 1951), p. 109.
42. Bellingsgauzen, *Dvukratnye izyskaniia*, pp. 20-21.
43. See Barratt, *Bellingshausen: A Visit to New Zealand (1820)* (Palmerston North, N.Z. 1979), ch. 1.
44. Bellingsgauzen, *Dvukratnye izyskaniia*, pp. 192-93.
45. Ibid., p. 195; further on this visit to Sydney, see G. R. V. Barratt, *The Russian Navy and Australia to 1825* (Melbourne, 1979), ch. 4.
46. Mitchell Library, Sydney: *Lachlan Macquarie Journals*: CY A771, pp. 215-17.
47. V. M. Golovnin, *Puteshestvie na shliupe Diana iz Kronshtadta v Kamchatku* (M., 1961), p. 126.
48. See note 43.
49. Golovnin, *Puteshestvie na shliupe Diana*, pp. 140-42, (meeting with Matara, Bay of Plenty chief's son); Barratt, *Bellingshausen: A Visit to New Zealand*, ch. 1.
50. A. Sharp, *The Discovery of the Pacific Islands* (Oxford, 1960), pp. 198-99.
51. Bellingsgauzen, *Dvukratnye izyskaniia*, pp. 329-31; V. N. Sementovskii, ed., *Russkie otkrytiia v Antarktike v 1819-1821 godakh* (M. 1951), pp. 168-69, 258.

52. V. Fitzhardinge, "Russian Ships in Australian Waters, 1807-1835," *JRAHS*, 51 (1965): 140-42.

53. Bellingsgauzen, *Dvukratnye izyskaniia,* pp. 385-89.

54. F. Debenham, *Antarctica* (London, 1959), p. 47.

55. It appeared in R. McNab's *Murihiku and the Southern Islands* (Invercargill, N.Z., 1907), pp. 190-98.

56. Debenham, *Antarctica,* p. 48.

57. Details in A. I. Andreev's preface to the 1949 ed. of Bellingsgauzen, *Dvukratnye izyskaniia*; see also Sementovskii, *Russkie otkrytiia v Antarktike,* p. 284.

NOTES TO CHAPTER ELEVEN

1. I.e., the triumvirate replacing Rezanov.
2. Okun', *Russian-American Company,* p. 96.
3. M. Dovnar-Zapol'skii, *Memuary dekabristov* (St. P., 1906), pp. 130-31; K. F. Ryleev, *Polnoe sobranie sochinenii* (L., 1934), pp. 490-91.
4. See Okun', *Russian-American Company,* pp. 97-98, 101-2.
5. *Materialy dlia istorii,* 3:48.
6. Okun', "Tsarskaia Rossiia i Gavaiskie ostrova," no. 6, pp. 180-86.
7. Cited by Okun', *Russian-American Company,* p. 80.
8. Tikhmenev, *Historical Review,* 1:244-45; Ivashintsev, *Russkie krugosvetnye puteshestviia,* p. 64; Gibson, *Imperial Russia,* p. 164.
9. Bancroft, *History of Alaska,* pp. 526-27n; Pierce, *Russia's Hawaiian Adventure,* pp. 141-42; Ivashintsev, *Russkie krugosvetnye puteshestviia,* pp. 60-63.
10. At Monterey, 28 August 1821.
11. Okun', *Russian-American Company,* p. 52.
12. Gibson, *Imperial Russia,* pp. 12-13; Gillesem, "Puteshestvie na shliupe 'Blagonamerennyi,' " sec. 8, pp. 3-6; Bancroft, *History of Alaska,* p. 535.
13. K. T. Khlebnikov, "Zapiski o koloniiakh Rossiisko-Amerikanskoi Kompanii," AGO, *razriad* 99, op. 1, no. 112, pp. 28-42.
14. Bancroft, *History of California,* 2:636 (Khlebnikov's data).
15. Gibson, *Imperial Russia,* pp. 12, 18.
16. *Materialy dlia istorii,* 2:149-50.
17. Ibid., pp. 30ff.
18. Ibid., 2:61 (order no. 105, 15 December 1820).
19. Anon., "Kratkaia istoricheskaia zapiska o sostoianii Rossiisko-Amerikanskoi Kompanii," AGO, *razriad* 99, op. 1, no. 29, pp. 4-6.

20. Gibson, *Imperial Russia,* pp. 181-82.
21. Okun', *Russian-American Company,* p. 127.
22. AVPR, fond Kantseliarii Ministerstva Vneshnikh Del: 1823, *delo* 3646, pp. 23-24.
23. Okun', *Russian-American Company,* pp. 127-28.
24. U.S., Congress, Senate, *Proceedings of the Alaskan Boundary Tribunal* (Washington, D.C., 1904), 2:23.
25. See note 22; also Tikhmenev, *Historical Review,* 1:264-65, and *Materialy dlia istorii,* 2:78 (the 1817 visit).
26. *Vneshniaia politika Rossii,* 6:280; Gibson, *Imperial Russia,* pp. 113-16.
27. Otto von Kotzebue, *A New Voyage Round the World, in the Years 1823, 24, 25 & 26* (London, 1830), 2:122-23; Golovnin, *Puteshestvie,* 1:274.
28. M. Huculak, *When Russia Was in America: The Alaska Boundary Treaty Negotiations, 1824-25* (Vancouver, 1971), on Poletika's career.
29. AVPR, *fond* Kantseliarii Ministerstva Vneshnikh Del: 1823, *delo* 8735, pp. 5-6.
30. Tikhmenev, *Istoricheskoe obozrenie,* 1:222.
31. AVPR, *fond* Kantseliarii Ministerstva Vneshnikh Del: 1823, *delo* 8735, p. 6.
32. Okun', *Russian-American Company,* p. 131.
33. United States National Archives, "Records of the Russian-American Company, 1802-1867," 3:83 (company main office to Governor Murav'ev).
34. See note 16 to ch. 10.
35. Cited by Okun', *Russian-American Company,* p. 132.
36. *Materialy dlia istorii,* 2:99.
37. AVPR, *fond* Rossiisko-Amerikanskoi Kompanii, *delo* 284, passim.

38. Anon., "Kratkaia istoricheskaia zapiska," pp. 4-5.
39. Choris, *Voyage pittoresque,* p. 9; Gibson, *Imperial Russia,* p. 162.
40. Text given in full by Huculak, *When Russia Was in America,* pp. 127-31.
41. A. de Nesselrode, ed., *Lettres et papiers du chancelier comte de Nesselrode* (Paris, 1904), 2:38ff (autobiographical fragment).
42. P. Kennedy Grimsted, *The Foreign Ministers of Alexander I* (Berkeley and Los Angeles, 1969), pp. 196, 210.
43. Hudson's Bay Company Archives (Ottawa), A/6/20 (27 February 1822).
44. AVPR, *fond* Kantseliarii Ministerstva Vneshnikh Del: 1822, *delo* 3645, pp. 30-33.
45. Okun', *Russian-American Company,* pp. 224-26.
46. Ivashintsev, *Russkie krugosvetnye puteshestviia,* 69-70; A. P. Shabel'skii, *Voyage aux colonies russes de l'Amérique, fait au bord du sloop de guerre "l'Apollon" pendant les années 1821, 22 et 23* (St. P., 1826), ch. 1; S. P. Khrushchev, "Plavanie shliupa Apollona . . . v 1821-1824 godakh," *ZAD,* 10 (St. P., 1826): 200-216.
47. AVPR, *fond* Kantseliarii Ministerstva Vneshnikh Del: 1822, *delo* 3645, pp. 32-33.
48. Samarov, *Russkie flotovodtsy: M. P. Lazarev,* vol. 1 (documents relating to 1822-25 voyage); Andrei P. Lazarev, *Plavanie vokrug sveta na shliupe Ladoge v 1822, 23 i 24 godakh* (St. P., 1832), pp. 4-16.
49. Ivashintsev, *Russkie krugosvetnye puteshestviia,* pp. 229, 233.
50. Zavalishin's account of this voyage, "Krugosvetnoe plavanie fregata 'Kreiser' v 1822-1825 godakh, pod komandoiu Mikhaila Petrovicha Lazareva," ultimately appeared (M., 1877) in *Drevniaia i novaia Rossiia,* no. 5, pp. 54-67; no. 6, pp. 115-25; no. 7, pp. 199-214; and no. 10, pp. 143-58; see also bibliography here, under Zavalishin, Chentsov.
51. TsGAVMF, *fond* 1166, *delo* 666, pp. 383-85.
52. Details in G. R. V. Barratt, "Russian Warships in Van Diemen's Land: *Kreyser* and *Ladoga* by Hobart Town, 1823," *SEER,* 53 (1975): pp. 566-78.
53. *Historical Records of Australia: Series*

3, 4:73 (Sorell to Bathurst); Ivashintsev, *Russkie krugosvetnye puteshestviia,* pp. 233-34.
54. TsGAVMF, *fond* 212, *delo* 4093, pp. 126-27 (Lazarev to A. V. Müller, 23 July 1823); on Müller, Veselago, *Kratkaia istoriia russkogo flota,* pp. 295-96.
55. D. I. Zavalishin, *Zapiski dekabrista* (München, 1904), 1:118-20.
56. TsGAVMF, *fond* 203, *delo* 1123, pp. 7-10.
57. See Tikhmenev, *Istoricheskoe obozrenie,* 1:335-50 on this.
58. Okun', *Russian-American Company,* p. 68; Gibson, *Imperial Russia,* p. 164.
59. Ivashintsev, *Russkie krugosvetnye puteshestviia,* pp. 67-68; Tikhmenev, *Istoricheskoe obozrenie,* 1:336.
60. Gibson, *Imperial Russia,* p. 164.
61. Okun', *Russian-American Company,* pp. 71-72.
62. Khlebnikov, *Zhizneopisanie Baranova,* p. 64.
63. TsGAVMF, *fond* 1166, *delo* 9, p. 5.
64. U.S. National Archives; "Records of the Russian-American Company," 4:6.
65. Tikhmenev, *Istoricheskoe obozrenie,* 1:339-40; Gibson, *Imperial Russia,* pp. 164-65 and n.
66. José Fernandez, "Cosas de California": MS in Bancroft Library, C-D 10: pp. 25-27 (sea-otter-wheat trade agreements); *Materialy dlia istorii,* 3:N 148-49.
67. Khlebnikov, "Zapiski o Kalifornii," *Syn otechestva* (St. P., 1829): no. 2, pp. 400-410; *Materialy dlia istorii,* 3:78, 148.
68. Bancroft, *History of California,* 2:483-84, 494.
69. Fernandez, "Cosas de California," pp. 25-27.
70. Kotzebue, *A New Voyage,* 2:71-150.
71. Sharp, *Discovery of the Pacific Islands,* pp. 206-7; E. S. Dodge, *Beyond the Capes: Pacific Exploration from Captain Cook to the Challenger, 1776-1877* (Boston, 1971), pp. 251-54.
72. Choris, *Voyage pittoresque,* p. 7.
73. Kotzebue, *A New Voyage,* 2:123.
74. Gibson, *Imperial Russia,* pp. 116-18.
75. Cited by Okun', *Russian-American Company,* p. 136.
76. Zavalishin, "Delo o kolonii Ross,"

Russkii vestnik, 62 (St. P., 1866): 55-58.
77. Cited by Okun', *Russian-American Company*, p. 138.
78. Zavalishin, *Zapiski*, 1:151-55.
79. U.S. National Archives, "Records of the Russian-American Company," 28:290-91.
80. Zavalishin, "Kaliforniia v 1824 godu," *Russkii vestnik* (St. P., 1865): 322-68; Okun', *Russian-American Company*, pp. 137-40.
81. Zavalishin, *Zapiski*, 1:148-49.
82. See Okun', *Russian-American Company*, p. 133.
83. M. N. Pokrovskii, ed., *Vosstanie dekabristov: materialy po istorii vosstaniia dekabristov: Dela Verkhovnogo Ugolovnogo Suda i Sledstvennoi Kommissii* (M., 1925), 3:147-48, 250-52.
84. U.S. National Archives, "Records of the Russian-American Company," 28:418, 201-2; 3:85, 163.
85. Anon., "Kratkaia istoricheskaia zapiska," pp. 10-11.
86. AVPR, fond Kantseliarii Ministerstva Vneshnikh Del: 1823, *delo* 3646, pp. 19-22 (Murav'ev to the board); 1827, *delo* 7316, pp. 7-9 (Mordvinov to Nesselrode, 3 February 1824); Bilbasov, *Arkhiv grafov Mordvinovykh*, 6:643.
87. Tikhmenev, *Istoricheskoe obozrenie*, 1:340; Ivashintsev, *Russkie krugosvetnye puteshestviia*, pp. 86-87.
88. AVPR, fond Kantseliarii Ministerstva Vneshnikh Del: 1824, *delo* 3717, pp. 27-28.
89. Text from Huculak, *When Russia Was in America*, p. 77. Full text and supporting documents in U.S. Congress, Senate, *Proceedings of the Alaskan Boundary Tribunal*, vol. 1.
90. Ivashintsev, *Russkie krugosvetnye puteshestviia*, pp. 92, 99.
91. *Materialy dlia istorii*, 4:133-41 (Lütke on Novo-Arkhangel'sk).
92. See bibliography under Dobell, Golder (1930), Mazour (1936); also Bilbasov, *Arkhiv grafov Mordvinovykh*, 6:615-16.
93. Okun', *Russian-American Company*, p. 108.
94. Further on this, see G.R.V. Barratt, "The Russian Interest in Arctic North America: The Kruzenshtern-Romanov Projects, 1819-23," *SEER*, 53 (1975): 38-40: also V. Semenov, *Siberia: Its Conquest and Development*, trans. J. R. Foster (Baltimore, 1963), pp. 229-31.
95. Okun', *Russian-American Company*, pp. 109-12.
96. Ibid., pp. 107-8 (N. A. Bestuzev's interest in the colonies); Chentsov, for further bibliographical aides.
97. M. K. Azadovskii, "14 dekabria v pis'makh A. E. Izmailova," *Pamiati dekabristov* (L., 1926), 1:242; Barratt, *Voices in Exile*, pp. 22-23, 36, 139.
98. George Simpson, *Fur Trade and Empire: George Simpson's Journal, 1824-25*, ed. F. Merk (Cambridge, Mass., 1931), p. 71; Okun', *Russian-American Company*, pp. 113-14.
99. Okun', *Russian-American Company*, p. 112; but see J. Galbraith, *The Hudson's Bay Company as an Imperial Factor, 1821-1869* (Toronto, 1957), ch. 1, on J. H. Pelly's view on this question.
100. TsGIAL, *fond* 48, op. 1, *delo* 78, pp. 6-8.; Khlebnikov, "Zapiski o koloniiakh v Amerike Rossiisko-Amerikanskoi Kompanii," AGO, *razriad* 99, op. 1, no. 111, pt. 3; K. F. Ryleev, *Polnoe sobranie sochinenii* (L., 1934), pp. 490-91; Akademiia Nauk SSR: Institut Istorii (Leningrad): Materialy po istorii Rosiisko-Amerikanskoi Kompanii, docs. 44 and 49; Okun', *Russian-American Company*, p. 70.

CONCLUSION AND REFLECTIONS

1. Efimov, *Iz istorii russkikh ekspeditsii*, pp. 18-30.
2. Gibson, *Imperial Russia*, p. viii.
3. Tikhmenev, *Istoricheskoe obozrenie*, 2:233.
4. Public Archives of Canada, Ottawa, Q/113, pp. 228-30; *CHR*, 17 (1936): 305-12.

Bibliography

It would be wrong for the potential Western student of the Russian Navy's earlier activity in the Pacific to suppose that TsGAVMF (Tsentral'nyi Gosudarstvennyi Arkhiv Voenno-Morskogo Flota SSSR) is the only source of relevant original material and hence the key to all his chances. In reality, a wealth of such material, basically of three kinds—articles, letters, and despatches or reports—may be examined in a number of the main Soviet archives. Both because the present book raises questions it does not answer and because it seems that access to at least *some* more central Soviet repositories of original material is growing easier than was the case earlier, it seemed useful to include here observations that might spare others time and effort. The following remarks concern the larger Leningrad and Moscow archives holding documents which bear directly on Pacific naval matters of the eighteenth and early nineteenth centuries; with bibliographies to serve as starting points; and with facilities. All students contemplating working visits to the institutions mentioned are advised first to acquaint themselves with P. Kennedy Grimsted's first-rate guide, *Archives and Manuscript Repositories in the USSR: Leningrad and Moscow* (Princeton, 1972).

Tsentral'nyi Gosudarstvennyi Arkhiv Voenno-Morskogo Flota SSSR

Among the best-organized ministerial archives of the nineteenth century, and a direct descendant of the Admiralty College Archive formed in 1718, TsGAVMF remains officially closed to foreign scholars. Increasingly, however, the administration of the archive shows itself prepared, if foreign visitors have ample time and excellent credentials, to make documents from earlier historical collections (*fonds*) available to them in the main reading-room of the Tsentral'nyi Gosudarstvennyi Istoricheskii Arkhiv SSSR, known as TsGIAL. Armed with a pass or reader's ticket, the researcher has his own archival worker or *sotrudnik* help him place specific orders for materials, which are in due course sent out to the reading-room of TsGIA, (where materials from other local archives are consulted by the foreigner.) Of special value to the student of Pacific naval matters of the age of sail are those of the 3,000 *fonds* of TsGAVMF that relate to chancelleries of the naval chiefs-of-staff and of the Admiralty College (ministry from 1802). Still more valuable are the *fonds* relating to distinguished individuals who played a major part in the Pacific undertaking: I. F. Kruzenshtern (14), Joseph Billings (1214), Vitus Bering (216). Always assuming that no Soviet researcher is at work on them when the request is made, hundreds of documents that bear upon that undertaking may be made accessible to the accepted foreigner in TsGIA. Other fonds of special relevance to the Pacific context include: 203 (Voennaya po flotu kantseliariia); 432 (Morskoi Kadetskii Korpus); and 1166 (M. F. Reineke.) While waiting for the delivery of materials, the visitor may avail himself of TsGAVMF's own library of 15,000 volumes.

Major inconveniences for the would-be user of documents held in TsGAVMF are the unavailability (to him) of detailed *opisi* of various constituent collections and the non-existence of a modern and comprehensive published description of the archive's holdings. The secrecy with which the *opisi* are still surrounded can only be taken fatalistically; there is, however, something to lessen the inherent inconvenience of having no contemporary guide at hand. One can consult beforehand the now widely scattered work, *Arkhivy SSSR.: Leningradskoe otdelenie Tsentral'nogo Istoricheskogo Arkhiva: putevoditel' po fondam* (Leningrad: Lenoblizdat, 1933). Compiled by M. Akhun, V. Lukomskii and others, and edited by A. K. Drezen, the guide covered the archive in question as then constituted. A good sixth of its holdings were naval (described on pp. 197-248 of the guide). Although shortly afterwards moved and administered as TsGAVMF, these naval holdings were nowhere else described; nor has another, more comprehensive list yet been published—though work is said to be progressing steadily on one—to make the 1933 guide obsolete for the purposes of naval research. One or two of the ten volumes of *Opisaniia del arkhiva Morskogo Ministerstva za vremia s poloviny XVII do nachala XIX stoletiia* (St. P., 1877-1906), have similarly retained their usefulness. A high proportion of the documents inventoried are from the eighteenth century. Again, the fact that the archive housing the materials concerned has had several names during the present century does not basically affect the value of these volumes: the organization of naval *fonds* has been maintained over the generations to a noteworthy extent.

Tsentral'nyi Gosudarstvennyi Arkhiv Drevnikh Aktov (TsGADA)

For the naval specialist, the documents of greatest value that are kept in TsGADA are of later eighteenth-century origin. (In theory, indeed, pre-Revolutionary papers that postdate 1801 are kept in TsGIA, but in fact some nineteenth-century materials are to be found in TsGADA, and among them are such documents as those—*fond* 30, *delo* 67—that best suggest conditions under which a Russian officer became a Volunteer in the Dutch or British navies of the time of Kruzenshtern.) Of special interest to all naval historians are papers in the subdivision known as Gosarkhiv, that is, the Gosudarstvennyi Arkhiv Rossiiskoi Imperii founded in 1834, that have to do with naval progress. They comprise a special section, or *razriad* (now no. 21), of the large subdivision that is Gosarkhiv. Likewise of interest to the historian of Russia's naval progress on the Black and Baltic Seas, as well as half way round the globe, are certain portions of the records of the Senate's Chancery, First, Second, Third and Fourth Departments for the period 1711-96. Many of these, which were originally housed in the enormous Moscow Archive of the Ministry of Justice, where for decades they remained uncatalogued, bear upon expeditionary, maritime, and naval matters. For the student of the Navy in the East, however, TsGADA has no single more invaluable bundle of materials than those connected with the eighteenth-century historian G. Müller, who participated personally in the Second Bering Expedition and had access to Siberian archives during the 1730's and 40's. Müller's great portfolios, held under reference *fond* 199, once formed a part of the main Moscow Archive which now comprises part of TsGADA (although still administered as a half-independent section) and which had itself in 1852 swallowed the records of the earlier Siberian *Prikaz* for 1564-1768. Needless to say, the Müller papers and the holdings of the old *Prikaz* are full of references to Okhotsk and the Pacific littoral. The best starting-point is Mikhail Putsillo's *Ukazatel' delam i rukopisiam, otnosiashchimsia do Sibiri i prinadlezhashchim Moskovskomu Glavnomu arkhivu Ministerstva Inostrannykh Del* (Moscow, 1879), (for records of that ministry also formed a part of the post-revolutionary TsGADA, although those post-dating 1719 were later moved to the Arkhiv Vneshnei Politiki Rossii). Although ancient in its own right, the Putsillo guide remains of value, since, again, the documents referred to have retained their former ordering regardless of the renaming and removals of the institution that still held them in Putsillo's day. The same applies to the essential but now venerable *Opisanie dokumentov i bumag, khraniashchikhsia v Moskovskom arkhive Ministerstva Iustitsii* (St. P.-M., 1869-1921: 21 vols.), still used by archival assistants of TsGADA: though the current *fond* numbers are allocated to materials comparatively recently, the nineteenth-century enumeration system has been kept. Among the naval-cum-Pacific topics on which light is shed by documents in TsGADA are: civilian-service relations at Okhotsk and the position of the Admiralty Office there in the Siberian administrative system; the assistance given to the Admiralty College, in its expeditionary ventures, by officials in Siberia; and the preparing and despatching of those naval expeditions to the East.

Tsentral'nyi Gosudarstvennyi Istoricheskii Arkhiv SSSR

Here, as in TsGAVMF, the foreigner is hampered by an absence of recent and comprehensive guides to holdings and is thoroughly dependent on the efforts of *sotrudniki* who do have access to such typed inventories as are at hand. He can, however, make good use of *Arkhivy SSSR: Leningradskoe otdelenie Tsentral'nogo Istoricheskogo Arkhiva: putevoditel' po fondam,* ed. A. K. Drezen (Leningrad, 1933), pages 197-248 of which list naval items which were then in *TsGIAL* but were later moved to *TsGAVMF.* Among the former ministerial records now preserved in TsGIA which bear on naval and Pacific issues are those of the nineteenth-century Ministries of Commerce, Trade, and Justice (branches not situated in Moscow), as well as of the Imperial Chancery. (In the *fond* of the First Section of this last and mighty chancery, for instance, is N. P. Rezanov's correspondence from the North Pacific area of 1804-7, bearing on A. A. Baranov, the Khvostov-Davydov maritime adventure, and Russia's future role in California.) Also useful as a starting-point for the historian who realizes that a quantity of documents relating to the Navy in the East are to be found among the records of non-naval ministries, for instance, those of Justice and of Commerce, is the guide to *TsGIAL*—as it then was— by S. Valk and V. V. Bedin: *Tsentral'nyi Gosudarstvennyi Istoricheskii Arkhiv SSSR v Leningrade: putevoditel'* (Leningrad, 1956).

Undoubtedly, however, the most precious records for the student of the Russian naval venture in Pacific waters that are *now* preserved in TsGIA are those (many) records that relate to the relationship between the Russian-American Company and naval officers. *Fond* 853 is that of Mikhail Buldakov, long the chairman of the Company's embattled board: it is replete with papers that cast light on the beginnings of the Kruzenshtern-Lisianskii voyages. TsGIA contains the holdings of the former archive of the Department of Manufacture and Domestic Commerce, under the jurisdiction of which the Company's governing board was placed in 1811 and remained for many years (see Okun', *Russian-American Company,* pp. 97-98). It is thus in TsGIA that one finds materials related to the 1816 ''Company-and-Navy crisis'' with which V. M. Golovnin and M. P. Lazarev were deeply implicated, as to company and naval attitudes towards such crises as were brought about by Schaeffer (in the Sandwich Islands) and by anti-Spanish activists (at Ross).

Arkhiv Vneshnei Politiki Rossii SSSR (AVPR)

Since Russia's navy, like all other major navies, has repeatedly had dealings with the representatives of foreign governments, and since its officers have often served as agents or apologists for Russia overseas, this is an archive that should not be overlooked by the historian of the pre-Revolutionary Russian Navy. One might say, indeed, that in such places as Japan and California, Russian maritime and diplomatic interests and objects were so interwoven, in the age of sail, as to be almost inextricable. AVPR contains the diplomatic record of the Russian Crown and Empire from the time of Peter until 1917. For students of the Russian naval venture in the East, its most important sections are those holding records of the chancellery of the Ministry of Foreign Affairs which, until 1923, had been retained in the old archive of the ministry itself in Petrograd. These chancellery papers are now arranged by year, with subdivisions for outgoing and incoming correspondence and for embassies and missions overseas. Under such years as 1817-23, a wealth of information may be found about the Navy's changing role in North Pacific waters and about the early phases of that international crisis brought about by the Imperial ukases of September 1821. Among the files for 1802 and 1803 are documents indicative of Count Rumiantsev's and of A. R. Vorontsov's increasing readiness to back a naval effort in the East, lest Russia's portion of the fur-trade in the Orient at large be further shrunk by competition from the English-speaking world.

Also of interest to the historian of Russia's progress in the North Pacific area and of relations with authorities in North and South America, in which perforce the Navy played no minor part, are documents in two of the *razriady* (II and V) which, before 1923, had been retained not by the chancellery of the foreign ministry, but in that ministry's St. Petersburg Main Archive. (The *razriady* are of early nineteenth-century, not recent, origin.) *Razriad* II contains the records of relations with the governments of Asia and of North and South America, so touch on naval-diplomatic matters; *razriad* V contains the records of the Russian mission in Japan and China.

As usual, the unavailability of a modern general description of holdings is compounded by the inaccessability, to Western scholars, of the archive's own card-catalogues and *opisi*. In view of this, and of the AVPR policy of showing visitors only those papers which have been specifically requested through the staff assistants (sometimes, parts of files are made available), it is the more important to examine every guide that does exist. On this, one may consult the splendid work by P. K. Grimsted (pp. 254-56).

Arkhiv Akademii Nauk SSSR: Leningradskoe Otdelenie

This, the oldest archival institution of the Academy (established in July 1728), contains more than a thousand *fonds*. They are divided into three main groups. The first is of the records of the actual Academy, with subdivisions for the records of its chanceries and numerous dependent institutes. The second is of *fonds* of individuals—scholars and scientists, many of whom played leading parts in the Siberian and North Pacific ventures of the eighteenth century. The last holds, *inter alia*, maps, sketches, and materials from expeditions sponsored by, and of especial interest to, leading members of the eighteenth-century Academy. The archive is accustomed to receiving scholars from abroad, many of whom also avail themselves of the Academy's fine library, familiarly known as BAN. There are, moreover, good inventories for almost all the *fonds* still kept in Leningrad (nos. 1-350, 701-1,510), and visitors may use them under loose surveillance by the staff.

Ironically, three of the guides that are of greatest value now to the non-Soviet researcher into Russia's early naval undertakings in the far North-East and East, and who has come to the Academy in Leningrad, were published at a time when not one Western visitor had leave to study Russian naval history of *any* period—at least from Russian manuscripts. They are respectively concerned with academic correspondence, expeditions, and the Geographical Department of the eighteenth-century Academy: *Uchonaia korrespondentsiia Akademii Nauk XVIII veka: nauchnoe opisanie, 1766-1782*, compiled by I. I. Liubimenko, edited by G. A. Kniazev and L. B. Modzalevskii: *Trudy arkhiva AN SSSR*, vol. 2 (M.-L., 1937; 606 p.); *Materialy dlia istorii ekspeditsii Akademii nauk v XVIII i XIX vekakh: khronologicheskie obzory i opisanie arkhivnykh materialov*, compiled by V. F. Gnucheva, edited by V. L. Komarov, L. S. Berg: *Trudy arkhiva AN SSSR*, vol. 4 (m.-L., 1940; 310 pp.); and *Geograficheskii departament Akademii nauk XVIII veka*, compiled by V. F. Gnucheva, edited by A. I. Andreev, L. B. Modzalevskii: *Trudy arkhiva AN SSSR*, vol. 6 (M.-L., 1946; 446 pp.).

Arkhiv Leningradskogo Otdeleniia Instituta Istorii AN SSSR (LOII)

A large proportion of the holdings of this archive are the *fonds* of prominent and noble Russian families. Among these are the Vorontsovs; and it was on the Vorontsov family papers now in LOII that P. I. Bartenev based his forty-tome *Arkhiv kniazia Vorontsova* (M., 1870-97). Other family collections are as yet unpublished; and of these, a dozen offer naval students much of interest, the families in question having boasted admirals, for example, the Menshikovs and Golovins. Also in LOII are a number of materials relating to the fortunes of the Russian-American Company. Taken together with the relevant materials in the extensive Vorontsov collection, these throw light on A. R. Vorontsov's role in the launching of the Kruzenshtern-Lisianskii venture; on the ever-strained relations between Company and Navy in the West, as in the East; and on the Billings expedition that foreshadowed their uncomfortable partnership.

Published works describing holdings of LOII are available in the Institute's own library. Moreover, photocopying facilities are now available: all is arranged through the Academy of Sciences' Leningrad Archive and through BAN. Finally, the visiting researcher has an annotated guide, which mentions other, not yet superseded guides to local holdings: *Putevoditel' po arkhivu Leningradskogo otdeleniia Instituta Istorii*, compiled by I. V. Valkina and others, edited by A. I. Andreev and others (M.-L., 1958; 603 pp.).

Arkhiv Geograficheskogo Obshchestva Akademii Nauk SSSR (AGO)

This archive's holdings were described in a comparatively recent guide, *Russkie geografy i puteshest-venniki: fondy arkhiva Geograficheskogo Obshchestva,* compiled by T. P. Matveeva et al. (L., 1971). Among materials of interest to the historian of Russia's naval venture in the East are the Veselago Collection; the invaluable papers that relate to G. Shelikhov's efforts to involve the central Government in his Pacific enterprise—correspondence with Irkutsk (*razriad* 99, op.1 and G.IV.1.). Also filed under *razriad* 99, op.1 are essays on Pacific matters, for example, the company settlements, the condition and prospects of Kodiak and Ross, by K. T. Khlebnikov.

ARCHIVAL MATERIALS
(Contents of items in Russian repositories are briefly described.)

1. Central State Archives

a) Tsentral'nyi Gosudarstvennyi Arkhiv Voenno-Morskogo Flota SSSR (TsGAVMF: Leningrad)

fond 7, op. 1, *delo* 2 (V. M. Golovin's notebook, 1802-5; service as a Volunteer, early actions); *delo* 5 (his early distinction as signals officer, interpreter).

fond 14 (I. F. Kruzenshterna), *dela* 12-13 (Kruzenshtern's earlier service); *delo* 898 (Lisianskii in Brazil, 1803). This *fond* contains 529 items, dating from 1787. Many bear on Pacific issues.

fond 172, op. 1, *delo* 376 (administrative preparations for Mulovskii's expedition, chart collecting); *delo* 589 (would-be members of that expedition).

fond 203, *delo* 1123 (M. P. Lazarev to A. V. Müller from San Francisco, 10 December 1823: survey of *Kreiser*'s voyage).

fond 212, *delo* 4093 (further on *Kreiser* and *Ladoga* in 1823).

fond 216 (Beringa), op.1, *delo* 52 (Spanberg's character); delo 87 (Spanberg's activities, 1725-27).

fond 315, *delo* 381 (M. V. Lomonosov and instructions for V. Ia. Chichagov in 1764; objectives of the expedition).

fond 913, op. 1, *delo* 4 (the activities of M. Levashev in 1786-88); delo 159 (building *Slava Rossii* at Okhotsk; Hall and his people).

fond 972, op. 1, *delo* 414 (the staffing of the Billings expedition).

fond 1166, *delo* 9 (P. S. Nakhimov on Novo-Arkhangel'sk and California, 5 January 1824); *delo* 666 (officers with *Kreiser* and *Ladoga* in 1823-24).

fond 1212, *delo* 237 (Bering's relations with Skorniakov-Pisarev and other Siberian officials).

fond 1214 (Billingsa), *delo* 1 (Billings' final instructions); *delo* 21 (regarding the *Mercury,* privateer, and Coxe); *delo* 20 (the officers' council on Kayak Island).

fond Admiralteistv-Kollegii, *delo* 44 (A. I. Chirikov, his naming to Bering's expedition in 1725).

fond Kantseliarii F. M. Apraksina: "Zapisnaia knizhka" (orders on transport and provisioning of Bering's first expedition, 1725).

fond grafa I. G. Chernysheva, *delo* 376 (origins and collapse of the Mulovskii expedition, 1786-87); *delo* 408 (P. S. Pallas and his floating namesake).

fond admirala N. F. Golovina, *delo* 1 (Chirikov's efforts to maintain a naval presence in the Aleutians, 1741).

fond E. Imp. Velichestva po morskoi chasti, op. 1, *delo* 131 (the need to circumnavigate Kodiak; its political separateness from Spanish America, 1764).

fond Vysochaishikh ukazov: bk. 21.

b) Tsentral'nyi Gosudarstvennyi Arkhiv Drevnikh Aktov (TsGADA: Moscow)

fond 30, *delo* 67 (concerning Russian Volunteers with foreign navies, 1802-11).

fond 183, *delo* 89 (merchant V. N. Bosnin's paper on the *Nadezhda-Neva* expedition and its readying).

fond 199 (the G. F. Müller portfolios), port. 528, pt. 1, item 1 (G. Skorniakov-Pisarev's orders of 1 April 1732); pt. 2, item 10 (early *promyshlenniki* in the Aleutians); port. 511, pt. 1, item 1 (horrors of the Iakutsk-Okhotsk Tract, by Jacob Lindenau); port. 540, pt. 1, item 2 (preparations for Krenitsyn-Levashev expedition, 1765-66); port. 546, item 9 (Levashev's journal made available to Robertson).

fond 214 (*Sibirskii Prikaz*), op. 18, *delo* 2039 (Ivan Eniseiskii on Atlasov's Kamchatkan campaigns).

fond 259, op. 22, *delo* 485 (Governor-General Miatlev's assistance of Bechevin and Shalaurov).

fond 290 (A. R. Vorontsova), *delo* 6 (account of Russian voyages of exploration in North Pacific waters, to 1785, written circa 1788); *delo* 754 (Vorontsov's awareness of British and Spanish threats to Russia's Pacific interests).

fond 796, op. 1, *delo* 163 (company efforts to gain Imperial support in the endeavour to conclude a trade pact with Spanish California); *delo* 290 (material sent to St. Petersburg by N. P. Rezanov; notes on Commandant Bukharin, transports from Okhotsk).

fond Senata, *delo* 57 (impracticality of agriculture in the North-East); *delo* 664 (Skorniakov-Pisarev's orders of 10 May 1731; his hypothetical collaboration with Bering); *delo* 666 (Vice-Admiral Wilster joins Russian service, 1721; his projects); *delo* 1089 (Spanberg to replace Bering as commander in North-East); *delo* 1327 (debate on Walton-Spanberg routes, presence in Japan).

fond Gosarkhiva, *razriad* 10, op. 3, *delo* 16 (qualifications for membership of Mulovskii's expedition; procedures in the Pacific, use of serving men); *razriad* 21, *delo* 9 (skills expected of his seamen); *razriad* 24, *dela* 61, 62 (Pil' criticizes Billings; Bolts offers his services to Ostermann: various correspondence relating to the Pacific, 1780's).

c) Tsentral'nyi Gosudarstvennyi Istoricheskii Arkhiv (TsGIA: Leningrad Division)

fond 48, op. 1, *delo* 78 (V. P. Romanov's Arctic and American plans, 1826).

fond 853 (M. M. Buldakova), *delo* 1, item 74 (Kruzenshtern's orders to his people in the Pacific, 1804-5).

fond 1341, op. 303, *delo* 4856 (Miatlev's plans to have warships in the East, to build a base on Amur River, 1753-54).

d) Tsentral'nyi Gosudarstvennyi Voenno-Istoricheskii Arkhiv (TsGVIA)

fond Voenno-Uchonogo Arkhiva Glavnogo Shtaba (Upravleniia General'nogo Shtaba), *delo* 18,085 (J.-B. Scherer's assessment of Russian prospects in the far North-East and in America).

2. Other Archives in Leningrad and Moscow

e) Arkhiv Vneshnei Politiki Rossii (AVPR: Moscow)

fond Pervogo Otdela E. Imp. Velichestva Sobstvennoi Kantseliarii: 1802, *delo* 152 (Rezanov to Baranov, 18 April 1802, on the need to push south from Sitka).

fond Kantseliarii Ministerstva Vneshnikh Del: 1822, *delo* 3645 (*Apollon* to patrol the Northwest Coast, 1822); 1823, *delo* 3646 (Gagemeister on the Pomos Indians of Fort Ross and its prospects); 1823, *delo* 8735 (Poletika to Nesselrode on the closeness of Ross to Monterey, the dubiousness of company claims to it); 1824, *delo* 3717 (Nesselrode's defence of the delimitation of Russian America on the south and east); 1827, *delo* 7316 (Mordvinov's dissatisfaction with these new limits; his fears for the future).

fond Rossiisko-Amerikanskoi Kompanii, *dela* 284, 285 (Golovnin and Lazarev influence the company council, 1816-17; the ban on fur sales to foreign vessels of January 1818; Company-Navy relations, 1817-18); *delo* 291 (main office to tsar, 1819, on the advantages of oceanic supply, difficulties of shipment via Okhotsk).

f) Arkhiv Geograficheskogo Obshchestva SSSR (AGO: Leningrad)

razriad 99, op. 1, nos. 2-4 (Shelikhov-Iakobi correspondence; the activity of hunters in the Aleutians, to 1788); op. 1, no.29 (anonymous paper, "Brief Historical Note on the State of the Russian-American Company"); op. 1, no. 60 (Khlebnikov on the island and district of Kodiak); op. 1, no. 111 (Khlebnikov on the company colonies in America); op. 1, no. 112 (Khlebnikov on the company settlements in general). *Razriad* 119, *delo* 361 (essay by Kruzenshtern on the projected French invasion of Ireland, 1796).
fond G.IV.1, Nos. 4-6 (Shelikhov's dealings with Iakobi, the latter's approval of the dispatching of a naval squadron to the Pacific in 1787-88); no. 92 (merchant recognition of the need for imported naval expertise).

g) Arkhiv Leningradskogo Otdeleniia Instituta Istorii Akademii Nauk SSSR (Institut Istorii AN SSSR, also known as LOII)

Materialy po istorii Rossiisko-Amerikanskoi Kompanii: nos. 44, 49 (company directors entertain high functionaries, 1816-17; board resists encroachments on its prerogatives by council members); no. 181 (Baranov-Shelikhov correspondence, 1791; Billings spoils Aleuts). *Fond* 44 (N. P. Likhachev collection), nos. 22-25 (S. K. Greig as Anglo-Russian figure; his influence); *fond* 238, nos. 1-3 (papers relating to N. F. Golovin; the 1732 Pacific proposal).

h) Saltykov-Shchedrin Public Library, Leningrad: Rukopisnyi Otdel

F.IV. no. 874 (Joseph Billings' journal, 1786-88). F.IV. no. 59 (F. I. Shemelin's journal aboard *Nadezhda*, 1803-6); F.IV. no. 68 (M. I. Ratmanov's journal of the same period: the Kruzenshtern-Rezanov clashes); Sobranie Titova, no. 2272 (letter from Lt. Romberg to friends from Petropavlovsk, 16 August 1804).

i) Lenin Library, Moscow: Rukopisnyi Otdel

fond 204, carton 32, no. 36 (the 1810 company proclamation to "noble Spaniards living in California").

3. *Archives in the Estonian SSR*

j) Eesti NSV Riikliik Ajaloomuuseum (Estonian State Museum of History, Tallin)

Collections in the Museum Archive relating to families of Russian naval officers with local connections, and to those officers' early lives: Bellingshausen, V. N. Berkh, Otto and Moritz von Kotzebue, Hermann Löwenstern. Complementary materials and illustrations in the archive and library of the nearby Academy of Sciences of the Estonian SSR.

k) Tsentral'nyi Gosudarstvennyi Istoricheskii Arkhiv Estonskoi SSR (Tartu)

fond 1414: 482 items relating to I. F. Kruzenshtern, his family, sons, career successes, the earliest from 1793.

4. *Archives in English-Speaking States*

l) United States of America: National Archives, Washington, D.C.

"Records of the Russian-American Company, 1802-1867: Correspondence of Governors General."

m) The Bancroft Library, Berkeley, California. (Manuscripts Room)

C-D 10. Captain José Fernandez, "Cosas de California".
P-K 29. Anon. "Early Commerce in the North Pacific".
P-N 4. "Sheffer Papers," trans. G. Lantzeff. Copies of Catalogues in the Archivo General de Indias,
Seville, Spain: nos. 442, 494, 2901.

n) Hudson's Bay Company Archives, Ottawa

A. 6/20.
A. 8/1.

o) Public Archives of Canada, Ottawa

Q/113.

p) Public Record Office, London

Admiralty Records: Adm. 1, Adm. 7, Adm. 55/112. (James Cook), 55/120 (Gore), 55/122 (King),
Adm. 55/17, 55/27.
State Papers: 91/9, 91/102, 91/103.

q) The British Library: Manuscript Room (London)

Add. MSS 28,143 and 28,144. MSS. 2185-86A, 2591A, MSS 9256.

r) The Mitchell Library, Sydney (and Archives Authority of N.S.W.)

CY A. 771, (Lachlan Macquarie Journals); CY A. 774 (Macquarie Diary).
Banks Papers, vol. 22.
Archives Office, micro. reel no. 47, (Allan Cunningham Journal).

BIOGRAPHICAL AND BIBLIOGRAPHICAL AIDS: A SELECT LIST

Chapman, C. E.   *Catalogue of Materials in the Archivo General de Indias For the History of the Pacific Coast.* Berkeley, 1919.
Chentsov, N. M.   *Vosstanie dekabristov: bibliografiia.* M., 1929.
Chernevskii, P. O.   *Ukazatel' materialam dlia istorii torgovli, promyshlennosti i finansov v predelakh Rossiiskoi Imperii: ot drevneishikh vremen do kontsa XVIII veka.* St. P., 1883.
Eberstadt, E., and sons.   *The Northwest Coast: A Century of Personal Narratives of Discovery, Conquest, and Exploration: 1741-1841.* N.Y., 1941.
Entsiklopedicheskii slovar'.   Ed. I. Andreevskii, K. Arsen'ev. St. P., 1890-1904.
Entsiklopediia voennykh i morskikh nauk.   St. P., 1893.
Essig, A.   "A Bibliography Relating to the Russians in California." *CHSQ,* 12 (1933): 210-16.
Golder, F. A.   *A Guide to Materials for American History in Russian Archives.* 2 vols. Washington, D.C., 1917-37.
Golitsyn, N. N.   *Portfeli G. F. Millera.* M., 1899.
Grachev, V. A.   "Obzor istochnikov po istorii Priamur'ia i Okhotsko-Kamchatskogo kraia." *Trudy Gosudarstvennogo Dal'nevostochnogo Universiteta,* ser. 3, no. 5. Vladivostok, 1927.
Horecky, P. L.   *Russia and the Soviet Union: A Bibliographical Guide to Western Language Publications.* Chicago, 1965.
Kaidanov, N. P.   *Sistematicheskii katalog delam Sibirskogo Prikaza.* St. P., 1888.
Kerner, R. J.   "Russian Expansion to America: Its Bibliographical Foundations." *Papers of the Bibliographical Society of America,* 25 (1931): 111-29.
Lenz., W., ed.   *Deutsch-Baltisches Biographisches Lexikon, 1710-1960.* Köln-Wien, 1970.

Mezhov, V. I. *Sibirskaia bibliografiia: ukazatel' knig i statei o Sibiri na russkom iazyke i odnykh tol'ko knig na inostrannykh iazykakh za ves' period knigopechataniia.* St. P., 1903.
Russkii biograficheskii slovar'. 25 vols. Ed. A. A. Polovtsov, B. L. Modzalevskii. St. P., 1896-1918.

PACIFIC NAVAL HISTORY: SELECTED REFERENCE WORKS

Berkh, V. N. *Khronologicheskaia istoriia otkrytiia Aleutskikh ostrovov, ili podvigi rossiiskago kupechestva.* St. P., 1823.
Beskrovnyi, L. G. "Armiia i flot." *Ocherki istorii S.S.S.R.* M., 1957.
Boxer, C. R. *The Dutch Seaborne Empire, 1600-1800.* N.Y., 1965.
Burney, James. *A Chronological History of North-Eastern Voyages of Discovery, and of the Early Navigations of the Russians.* London, 1819.
Charnock, J. *Biographia Navalis; or, Impartial Memoirs of the Lives and Characters of Officers of the Navy of Great Britain, from the Year 1660 to the Present Time.* 6 vols. London, 1794-98.
Diccionario maritimo Espagnol. Madrid, 1864.
Dumont D'Urville, J. *Histoire universelle des voyages.* Paris, 1860.
Harris, John. *Navigantium atque itinerantium biblioteca; or, A Complete Collection of Voyages and Travels.* London, 1744-48.
Faivre, J. P. *L'Expansion française dans le Pacifique, 1800-1842.* Paris, 1960.
Ivashintsev, N. A. *Russkie krugosvetnye puteshestviia s 1803 po 1849 god.* St. P., 1872.
James. W. *Naval History of Great Britain from the Declaration of War by France.* London, 1822-26.
Laird-Clowes, W. *A History of the Royal Navy.* London, 1899-1904.
Mitchell, D. W. *A History of Russian and Soviet Seapower.* London, 1974.
Morison, S. E. *The Maritime History of Massachusetts, 1783-1860.* Boston, 1941.
Makarova, R. V. *Russkie na Tikhom okeane vo vtoroi polovine XVIII veka.* M., 1968.
Nozikov, N. *Russkie krugosvetnye moreplavaniia.* M., 1941.
Obshchii Morskoi Spisok. 14 vols. St. P., 1885-1907.
Ralfe, J. *Naval Biography.* 5 vols. London, 1828.
Rich, O. *Bibliotheca Americana Nova: A Catalogue of Books Relating to America in Various Languages, Including Voyages to the Pacific.* London, 1846.
Sharp, A. *The Discovery of the Pacific Islands,* Oxford, 1960.
Sokolov, M. S. *Letopis' krushenii i pozharov sudov Russkogo Flota ot nachala eio do 1854 goda.* St. P., 1855.
Veselago, F. F. *Materialy dlia istorii Russkogo Flota.* 18 vols. St. P., 1880-1904.
Ward, R. G., ed. *American Activities in the Central Pacific, 1790-1870.* Ridgewood, N. J., 1967.
Zubov, N. N. *Otechestvennye moreplavateli-issledovateli morei i okeanov.* M., 1954.

PRIMARY PRINTED MATERIAL

Alaska History Research Project. *Documents Relative to the History of Alaska.* Vols. 3 and 4. College, Alaska, 1936-38.
Al'kor, Ia.P., Drezen, L. K., comps. *Kolonial'naia politika tsarizma na Kamchatke i Chukotke v XVIII veke: sbornik arkhivnykh dokumentov.* L., 1935-36.
Anon. [Bolotov]. "Kratkoe opisanie ob Amerikanskom ostrove Kadiake." *Drug prosveshcheniia* (St. P., October 1805): 89-106.
Arkheograficheskaia Kommissiia: Dopolneniia k aktam istoricheskim. 12 vols. St. P., 1846-72. Index, 1875.

Arkhiv admirala P. V. Chichagova.   St. P., 1885.

[Atlasov. V.].   "Dve 'Skaski' VI. Atlasova ob otkrytii Kamchatki." Ed. N. N. Ogloblin. *Chteniia v Imperatorskom Obshchestve Istorii i Drevnostei Rossiiskikh pri Moskovskom Universite,* 3 (1891), 1:1-18.

Bartenev, P., ed.   *Arkhiv kniazia Vorontsova.* 40 vols. M., 1870-95.

Bell, John.   *Travels From St. Petersburg in Russia to Diverse Parts of Asia.* Glasgow, 1763.

Bellingsgauzen, F. F.   *Dvukratnye izyskaniia v Iuzhnom Ledovitom okeane i plavanie vokrug sveta, v prodolzhenie 1819, 20 i 21 godov, sovershennye na shliupakh "Vostok" i "Mirnyi."* St. P., 1831; 2d ed., 1949, ed. A. I. Andreev; 3d ed., 1960, ed. E. E. Shvede. Translated by F. Debenham as *The Voyage of Captain Bellingshausen to the Antarctic Seas, 1819-1821.* 2 vols. London, 1945.

————.   *Atlas k puteshestviiu kapitana Bellingsgauzena v Iuzhnom Ledovitom okeane i vokrug sveta v prodolzhenie 1819, 20 i 21 godov.* St. P., 1831.

————.   "Donesenie kapitana Bellingsgauzena iz Porta Zhaksona o svoem plavanii." *ZAD* (St. P., 1823), 5:201-19.

Belov, M. I., comp.   *Russkie morekhody v Ledovitom i Tikhom okeanakh: sbornik dokumentov o velikikh russkikh geograficheskikh otkrytiiakh na Severo-vostoke Azii v XVII veke.* L., 1952.

Benyowsky, M. A.   *Voyages et mémoires de Maurice Augustus, Comte de Benyowsky, contenant ses opérations militaires en Pologne, son exil au Kamtschatka. . . .* Paris, 1791.

Bering, Vitus.   "Donesenie flota-kapitana Beringa ob ekspeditsii ego k vostochnym beregam Sibiri. *ZVTD,* 10 (1847): pt. 1, suppl. 2:69-79.

————.   "Dokumenty po ekspeditsii kapitan-komandora Beringa v Ameriku v 1741 godu." Ed. V. Andreev, *MSb,* 5 (1893), pp. 1-16. Cf. also Pokrovskii below.

Berkh, V. N.   *Karta rossiiskikh vladenii v Severnoi Amerike.* St. P., 1812.

————.   "Nechto o Sandvichevykh ostrovakh." *Syn otechestva* (1818): pt.7, pp. 158-65.

————.   "Izvestie o mekhovoi torgovle, proizvodimoi Rossiianami pri ostrovakh Kurilskikh, Aleutskikh, i severozapadnom beregu Ameriki." *Syn otechestva* (1823): pt. 88, pp. 243-64; pt. 89, pp. 97-106.

Bezborodko, A. A. *Pis'ma A. A. Bezborodko k grafu P. A. Rumiantsevu, 1775-1793.* Ed. P. M. Maikov. St. P., 1900.

Bilbasov, V. A., ed.   *Arkhiv grafov Mordvinovykh.* St. P., 1902.

Bodega y Quadra, J. F. de la.   "Primer Viaje hasta la altura de 58°N., 1775." *Anuario de la Direccion de Hidrografia,* 3 (1865): pp. 279-93; "Segunda salida hasta los 61 grados en la fragata 'Nuestra Senora de los Remedios de la Favorita', 1779." Ibid., pp. 294-331.

Buache, P.   *Considerations géographiques et physiques sur les nouvelles découvertes au nord de la Grande Mer, appelée vulgairement la Mer du Sud, avec des cartes qui i sont relatives.* Paris, 1753.

Burriel, Andres.   *Noticia de la California, y de su conquista temporal, y espiritual, hasta el tiempo presente: sacada de la historia manuscrita formada en Mexico ano de 1739 por el Padre Miguel Venegas, de la Compania de Jesus.* Madrid, 1757.

Calderon y Henriquez, Pedro.   "The Memorial of Pedro Calderon y Henriquez Recommending Monterey as a Port for the Philippine Galleons, with a View to Preventing Russian Encroachment in California." Ed. and trans. H. Wagner. *CHSQ,* 23 (1944): 219-25.

Campbell, Archibald.   *A Voyage Round the World, from 1806 to 1812, in which Japan, Kamchatka, the Aleutian Islands and the Sandwich Islands were Visited.* Edinburgh, 1816.

Catherine II, Empress. *Sochineniia.* Ed. A. N. Pypin. St. P., 1901-7.

Chamisso, A. von.   *A Sojourn at San Francisco Bay, 1816.* San Francisco, 1936.

————.   *Werke.* 2 vols. Berlin, 1856.

Chaplin, P.   Logbook, 1725-31: given in abridged form by V. N. Berkh in *Pervoe morskoe puteshestvie Rossiian, predpriniatoe dlia resheniia geograficheskoi zadachi, soediniaetsia li Aziia s Amerikoiu?* St. P., 1823.

Choris, M. Louis.   *Voyage pittoresque autour du monde* Paris, 1822.

Cook, James, and King, James.   *A Voyage to the Pacific Ocean, undertaken by the Command of His Majesty, for making Discoveries in the Northern Hemisphere. To determine the Position and Extent of the West Side of North America; Its Distance from Asia; and the Practicability of a Northern Passage to Europe.* 3 vols. London, 1784.

————. *The Journals of Captain James Cook.* 3 vols. Ed. J. C. Beaglehole. Cambridge, 1955-67.

Corney, Peter. *Voyages in the Northern Pacific: A Narrative of Several Trading Voyages, from 1813 to 1818 . . . with a Description of the Russian Establishments on the Northwest Coast.* Honolulu, 1896.

Dalrymple, A. *A Plan for Promoting the Fur-Trade and Securing It to This Country, by Uniting the Operations of the East-India and Hudson's Bay Companies.* London, 1789.

[Deane, John]. *The Russian Fleet under Peter the Great, by a Contemporary Englishman.* Ed. Sir C. Bridge. London, 1899.

Davydov, G. I. *Dvukratnoe puteshestvie v Ameriku morskikh ofitserov Khvostova i Davydova.* St. P., 1810.

Defoe, Daniel. *The Consolidator, or Memoirs of Sundry Transactions from the World in the Moon.* London, 1705.

————. *An Impartial History of the Life and Actions of Peter Alexowitz.* London, 1723.

Delisle, J. N. *Explication de la Carte des nouvelles découvertes au nord de la Mer du Sud.* Paris, 1752.

————. *Nouvelles Cartes des découvertes de l'amiral de Fonte et autres navigateurs . . . dans les mers septentrionales.* Paris, 1753.

Dobell, Peter. *Travels in Kamtschatka and Siberia.* 2 vols. London, 1830.

D'Wolf, John. *A Voyage to the North Pacific and a Journey through Siberia.* Cambridge, Mass., 1861.

Efimov, A. V., comp. *Atlas geograficheskikh otkrytii XVIII veka.* M., 1964.

————. *Iz istorii velikikh russkikh geograficheskikh otkrytii v severnom ledovitom i Tikhom okeane.* M., 1950.

Elagin, S., comp. *Materialy dlia istorii russkogo flota.* St. P., 1865-67.

Elton, John. *Des Kapitan John Eltons Tagebuch über seine Reise von Moskau nach den nordlichen gegenden von Persien.* Ed. E. Trapaud. Hamburg, 1790.

————. 1732 Project given by A. V. Efimov in *Iz istorii russkikh ekspeditsii na Tikhom okeane; pervaia polovina XVIII veka.* M., 1948, pp. 251-52.

Franklin, Benjamin. *Writings.* Ed. A. H. Smythe. New York, 1905-7.

Galkin, N. "Pis'ma g. Galkina o plavanii shliupov 'Vostoka' i 'Mirnogo' v Tikhom okeane." *Syn otechestva,* (1822): pt. 49, pp. 97ff.

Gillesem (Gilsen), K. "Puteshestvie na shliupe 'Blagonamerennyi' dlia issledovaniia beregov Azii i Ameriki za Beringovym prolivom s 1819 po 1822 god." *Otechestvennye zapiski,* 66. (1849), sec. 8.

Gmelin, J. G. *Reise durch Sibirien, von dem Jahr 1733 bis 1743.* 2 vols. Göttingen, 1751-52; *Voyage en Sibérie.* Paris, 1767.

Golikov, I. I. *Deianiia Petra Velikogo.* 10 vols. M., 1788-97.

Golovin, N. F. and Saunders, T. 1732 Project given by V. A. Divin, in "O pervykh proektakh russkikh krugosvetnykh plavanii." *Trudy Instituta Istorii Estestvoznaniia i Tekhniki,* 32 (1961).

Golovnin, V. M. *Zapiski Vasiliia Mikhailovicha Golovnina v plenu u Iapontsev v 1811, 1812 i 1813 godakh, i zhizneopisanie avtora.* St. P., 1851.

————. "Zapiska Kapitana 2-ogo ranga Golovnina o sostoianii Rossiisko-Amerikanskoi Kompanii v 1818 godu." In *Materialy dlia istorii russkikh zaselenii po beregam Vostochnago okeana.* St. P., 1861. Also in this collection is Golovnin's "Puteshestvie na shliupe 'Kamchatka.'"

————. *Sochineniia i perevody.* St. P., 1864-65.

————. *Puteshestvie na shliupe "Diana" iz Kronshtadta v Kamchatku.* M., 1961.

Greig, Samuel. "Sobstvennoruchnyi zhurnal kapitan-komandora S. K. Greiga v Chesmenskii pokhod." *MSb,* 2 (1849): 649-52.

Hagemeister, L. A. *Despatches from the Hawaiian Islands, 1809,* given by R. A. Pierce, *Russia's Hawaiian Adventure, 1815-1817.* Berkeley, 1965.

Ides, E. Y. *Three Years Travel from Moscow Overland to China.* London, 1706, anon. translation from Dutch.

Khlebnikov, K. T. "Zapiski o Amerike." in *Materialy dlia istorii,* pt. III, pp. 88ff.

_____. "Zapiski o Kalifornii." *Syn otechestva*, (1829): no. 2, pp. 208-27, 276-88, 336-47, 400-410.

_____. *Zhizneopisanie Aleksandra Andreevicha Baranova*. St. P., 1835. Translated by Colin Bearne, in abridged form, as *Baranov*. Kingston, Ont., 1973.

Khrapovitskii, A. V.   *Dnevnik (s 18 ianvaria 1782 po 17 sentiabria 1793 goda)*. M., 1901)

Khrushchev, S. P.   "Plavanie shliupa *Apollona* v 1821-1824 godakh." *ZAD*, 10 (1826): 200-72.

Klochkov, E. A.   "Puteshestvie vokrug sveta v kolonii Rossiisko-Amerikanskoi Kompanii."*Severnyi arkhiv*, 24 (1826): 202-19.

Kohl, J. G.   *Russia and the Russians in 1842*. London, 1843.

Korobitsyn, N. I.   "Zhurnal." In A. I. Andreev, *Russian Discoveries in the Pacific and in North America in the 18th and 19th Centuries*. Translated by Carl Ginsburg. Ann Arbor, 1952.

Kotzebue, M. von.   "Pis'mo otsu iz Iaponii." *Vestnik Evropy* (1806): no. 12, pp. 44-46.

Kotzebue, Otto von.   *A Voyage of Discovery into the South Sea and Beering's Straits, undertaken in the Years 1815 to 1818*. 3 vols. London, 1821.

_____. *A New Voyage Round the World, in the Years 1823, 24, 25 & 26*. 2 vols. London, 1830.

Krasheninnikov, S. P.   *Opisanie zemli Kamchatki, s prilozheniem raportov, donesenii i drugikh neopublikovannykh materialov*. St. P., 1755. Translated by James Grieve, M.D., as *The History of Kamtschatka, and the Kurilski Islands, with the Countries Adjacent*. London, 1764.

Krusenstern, A. J. von.   *A Voyage Round the World, in the Years 1803, 4, 5 & 6, by Order of His Imperial Majesty Alexander 1, on Board the Ships Nadeshda and Neva*. Translated by R. B. Hoppner. 2 vols. London, 1814. (From the Russian text, *Puteshestvie vokrug sveta v 1803, 4, 5 i 6 godakh*. St. P., 1809-13.)

Langsdorf, G. H. von.   *Bemerkungen auf einer Reise um die Welt in den Jahren 1803 bis 1807*. Frankfurt, 1812. Translated as *Voyages and Travels in Various Parts of the World, during the Years 1803-1807*. London, 1813-14.

La Pérouse, J. F. G. de.   *Voyage autour du monde*. 4 vols. Paris, 1797.

Lavrischeff, T., trans.   See Alaska History Research Project.

Lazarev, Aleksei P.   *Zapiski o plavanii voennogo shliupa "Blagonamerennyi" v Beringov proliv i vokrug sveta v 1819-1822 godakh*. M., 1950.

Lazarev, Andrei P.   *Plavanie vokrug sveta na shliupe "Ladoga" v 1822, 1823, i 1824 godakh*. St. P., 1832.

Lazarev, Mikhail P.   "Izvlechenie iz zhurnala puteshestvuiushogo krugom sveta Rossiiskogo leitenanta Lazareva." *Syn otechestva* (1815): no. 26, pp. 255ff.

_____. "Pis'mo A. A. Shestakovu." *MSb* (1918): no. 1, pp. 53-63.

_____. Various despatches given by A. A. Samarov, ed., in *Russkie flotovodtsy: M. P. Lazarev*. 2 vols. M., 1952.

Ledyard, John.   *John Ledyard's Journal of Captain Cook's Last Voyage*. Ed. J. K. Munford. Corvallis, 1963.

_____. *John Ledyard: Journey through Russia and Siberia in 1787-1788*. Ed. S. D. Watrous. Madison, 1966.

Leibnitz, G. W. von.   *Sbornik pisem i memorialov Leibnitsa, otnosiashchikhsia k Rossii i Petru Velikomu*. Ed. V. Ger'e. St. P., 1873; simultaneous German ed., Leipzig.

Liria, Xerica y, Duque di.   *Diario del viaje a Moscovia del Duque di Liria y Xerica, embajador del Rey Phelipe V*. Madrid, 1889.

Lisiansky, Urey.   *A Voyage Round the World in the Years 1803, 4, 5 & 6, Performed in the Ship "Neva."* London, 1814.

Lomonosov, M. V.   "Kratkoe opisanie raznykh puteshestvii po Severnym moriam, i pokazanie vozmozhnogo prokhodu Sibirskim okeanom v Vostochnuiu Indiiu." In *Sochineniia* (L., 1934), v. 7.

_____. *M. V. Lomonosov: materialy dlia biografii, sobrannye akademikom P. S. Biliarskim*. St. P., 1865.

Lütke, F. P.   "Dnevnik" (1817-18). Given in extract by L. A. Shur in *K beregam Novogo Sveta*. M., 1971.

Marchand, Etienne.   *Voyage autour du monde, 1790-1792*. Paris, n.d.

Martos, A.   *Pis'ma o vostochnoi Sibiri*. M., 1827.

Materialy dlia istorii russkikh zaselenii po beregam Vostochnogo okeana. St. P., 1861; supplement to *MSb* (1861): no. 1.

Meares, J. *Voyages made in the years 1788 and 1789 from China to the North West Coast of America.* London, 1790.

Minitskii, M. I. "Nekotorye izvestiia ob Okhotskom porte i uezde onogo, dostavlennye kapitan-leitenantom Minitskim v 1809 godu." ZAD, (1815): 87-103

―――. "Opisanie Okhotskogo porta." *Syn otechestva* (1829): no. 21, pp. 136-53, 206-21.

M'Konochie, A. *Considerations on the Propriety of Establishing a Colony on One of the Sandwich Islands.* Edinburgh, 1816.

Mortimer, George. *Observations and Remarks made during a Voyage to the Islands of Teneriffe . . . and the Fox Islands on the Northwest Coast of North America in the Brig "Mercury," Commanded by John Henry Coxe.* London, 1791.

Müller (Miller), G. F. "Opisanie morskikh puteshestvii po Ledovitomu i po Vostochnomu moriu so rossiiskoi storony uchinnykh." In *Sochineniia i perevody k pol'ze i uveseleniiu sluzhashchie.* St. P., 1758.

―――. *Sammlung Russischer Geschichte.* 9 vols. St. P., 1732-64. Vol. 3, 1758, has the original German text of the above.

―――. *Opisanie Sibirskago tsarstva i vsekh proisshedshikh v nem del ot nachala a osoblivo ot pokoreniia ego Rossiiskoi derzhave po sii vremena.* St. P., 1787. 2d. ed.; slight variations from that of 1750.

―――. *Istoriia Sibiri.* 2 vols. M.-L., 1937-41.

N., A.N., comp. *Sibirskie goroda: materialy dlia ikh istorii: Nerchinsk, Selenginsk, Iakutsk.* M., 1886.

Nartov, A. K. *Rasskazy Nartova o Petre Velikom.* Ed. L. N. Maikov. St. P., 1891.

Nelson, Horatio. *The Despatches and Letters of Vice-Admiral Lord Viscount Nelson.* Ed. N. H. Nicolas. London, 1844.

Nesselrode, Karl. *Lettres et papiers du chancelier comte de Nesselrode.* 2 vols. Ed. A. de Nesselrode. Paris, 1904.

―――. "Zapiski grafa K. V. Nesselroda. *Russkii vestnik,* 186 (1865): 519ff.

Novosil'skii, P. M. *Iuzhnyi polius: iz zapisok byvshego morskogo ofitsera.* St. P., 1853.

Obshchii morskoi spisok. 14 vols. St. P., 1885-1907.

Ogloblin, N. N., ed. *Obozrenie stolbtsov i knig Sibirskogo Prikaza 1592-1768 godov.* 4 vols. M., 1895-1900.

Olearius, Adam. *Vermehrte Newe Beschreibung der Muscowitischen und Persischen Reyse.* Schleswig, 1656; 2d ed. Facsimile reprint, Tübingen, 1971.

Oswald, Richard. "Richard Oswald's Plan for an English and Russian Attack on Spanish America, 1781." Ed. R. A. Humphrey, *HAHR,* 18 (1938): 95-101.

Pacific Voyages: Selections from Scots Magazine, 1771-1808. Ed. J. S. Marshall. Portland, Ore., 1960.

Pallas, P. S. "Nachrichten von den russischen Entdeckungen zwischen Asia und Europa." *Buschings Magazin für die neue Historie und Geographie,* 16 (1782); 235-86.

―――. *Reise durch verschiedene Provinzen des Russischen Reichs.* 3 vols. St. P., 1771-76.

―――. *Nordische Beyträge.* 7 vols. St. P., 1781-96.

Pavlov, P. N., ed. *K istorii Rossiisko-Amerikanskoi Kompanii: sbornik dokumental'nykh materialov.* Krasnoiarsk, 1957.

Penrose, C. V. *A Memoir of James Trevenen, 1760-1790.* Ed. R. C. Anderson, C. Lloyd. London, 1959.

Perry, John. *The State of Russia under the Present Czar, in Relation to the Several Great and Remarkable Things He Has Done, as to His Naval Preparations, Etc.* London, 1716.

Peter Alekseevich, Tsar. *Pis'ma i bumagi Imperatora Petra Velikogo.* 9 vols. St. P.-L., 1887-1952.

Pokrovskii, A., ed. *Ekspeditsii Beringa: sbornik dokumentov.* M., 1941.

Poletika, P. I. Despatches given the anonymous article, "The Correspondence of Russian Ministers in Washington, 1818-1825." *AHR,* 18 (1913): 309-45.

Polnoe sobranie zakonov Rossiiskoi Imperii s 1649 goda. 240 vols. St. P., 1830-1916.

Poluboiarinov, N. "Indian Journal, 1763-64." Given by V. A. Divin. "Zhurnal puteshestviia michmana Nikifora Poluboiarinova v Indiiu." *Trudy Instituta Istorii Estestvoznaniia i Tekhniki,* 27 (1959).

Polunin, F. *Geograficheskii leksikon Rossiiskogo Gosudarstva, sobranyi Fedorom Poluninym, s ispravleniiami i dopolneniiami G. F. Millera.* M., 1773.

Ratmanov, M. I. "Vyderzhki iz dnevnika krugosvetnogo puteshestviia na korable 'Neva,'" *Iakhta* (1876): no. 32.

Rezanov, N. P. "Pis'mo k I. I. Dmitrievu" (April 1803). *Russkii arkhiv,* 4 (1866): 1331-32.

————. "Pervoe puteshestvie Rossiian vokrug sveta, opisannoe N. Rezanovym, Polnomochnym Poslannikom ko Dvoru Iaponskomu." *Otechestvennye zapiski,* 10 (1822): 194-219; 11, pp. 90-144; 12, pp. 196-211; 14 (1823): 25-37, 328-50; 15, pp. 248-74; 20 (1824); 131-63, 204-23; 23 (1825): 173-88, 366-96; 24, pp. 73-96.

————. Cited by G. H. Langsdorf, in *Langsdorff's Narrative of the Rezanov Voyage to Nueva California in 1806 . . . .* Translated by T. C. Russell. San Francisco, 1926.

Rikord, P. I. *Zapiski flota-kapitana Rikorda o plavanii ego k iaponskim beregam v 1812 i 1813 godakh.* t. P., 1875.

Rossiiskii, A. "Vypiska iz zhurnala shturmana Alekseia Rossiiskogo." *Sorevnovatel' prosveshcheniia* (1820): no. 11, pp. 125-46; no. 12, pp. 246-56.

Russko-Kitaiskie otnosheniia, 1689-1916: ofitsial'nye dokumenty. M., 1958.

Saint-Simon, Duc de. *Mémoires.* Vol. 31. Ed. A. de Boislisle. Paris, 1920.

Saltykov, Fedor. *Propozitsii Fedora Saltykova: rukopis' iz sobraniia P. N. Tikhanova.* Ed. N. Pavlov-Sil'vanskii. St. P., 1891.

Sandwich, John, Earl of. *The Private Papers of John, Earl of Sandwich, 1771-1782.* London, 1938.

Sarychev, G. A. *Puteshestvie flota kapitana Sarycheva po severovostochnoi chasti Sibiri, Ledovitomu moriu, i Vostochnomu okeanu, v prodolzhenie os'mi let, pri Geograficheskoi i Astronomicheskoi ekspeditsii pod nachal'stvom flota kapitana Billingsa s 1785 po 1793 god.* 2 vols. St. P., 1802.

————. *Puteshestvie kapitana Billingsa cherez Chukotskuiu zemliu ot Beringovo proliva do Nizhnekolymskogo ostroga, i plavanie kapitana Galla na sudne "Chornom Orle" po severo-vostochnomu okeanu v 1791 godu.* St. P., 1811.

Sauer, Martin. *An Account of a Geographical and Astronomical Expedition to the Northern Parts of Russia, Performed in the Years 1785 to 1794. Narrated from the Original Papers.* London, 1802.

Scherer, J. B. *Recherches historiques et géographiques sur le Nouveau Monde.* Paris, 1777.

[Schözer, J.?]. *Neue Nachrichten von den neuendeckten Inseln in der See zwischen Asia und Amerika.* Hamburg, 1776.

Shabel'skii, A. P. *Voyage aux colonies russes de l'Amérique, fait au bord du sloop de guerre "L'Apollon" pendant les années 1821, 1822 et 1823.* St. P., 1826.

————. "Prebyvanie g. Shabel'skogo v Novoi Gollandii." *Severnyi arkhiv* (1826): pt. 23, pp. 43-61.

Shelikhov, G. I. *Rossiiskogo kuptsa Grigoriia Shelikhova pervoe stranstvovanie s 1783 po 1787 god iz Okhotska po Vostochnomu okeanu k Amerikanskim beregam.* St. P., 1791.

————. *Rossiiskogo kuptsa Grigoriia Shelikhova prodolzhenie stranstvovanie po Vostochnomu okeanu k Amerikanskim beregam v 1788 godu.* St. P., 1792. The former was translated in part by William Tooke as "The Voyage of Gregory Shelekhof." In *Varieties of Literature.* London, 1795, pp. 1-42.

Shemelin, F. I. *Zhurnal pervogo puteshestviia Rossiian vokrug zemnogo shara.* St. P., 1816.

————. "Istoricheskoe izvestie o pervom puteshestvii Rossiian vokrug sveta." *Russkii invalid,* 146 (1823): nos. 23-28, 31-36, 49.

Sibirskie goroda: materialy dlia ikh istorii XVII i XVIII stoletii: Selenginsk, Nerchinsk, Iakutsk. Comp. N.A.N. M., 1886.

Sierra, B. de la "Fray Benito de la Sierra's Account of the Hezeta Expedition to the Northwest Coast in 1775." Ed. H. R. Wagner. *CHSQ,* 9 (1930): 201-8.

Simonov, I. M. "Plavanie shliupa 'Vostok' v Iuzhnom Ledovitom okeane." *Kazanskii vestnik* (Kazan', 1822): no. 3.

———. "Izvestie o puteshestvii kapitana Bellingsgauzena v 1819-1821 godakh." *Severnyi arkhiv* (1824): pt. 7.

———. "Shliupy 'Vostok' i 'Mirnyi,' ili plavanie Rossiian v Iuzhnom Ledovitom okeane i okolo sveta." In *Russkie otkrytiia v Antarktike v 1819-1821 godakh,* ed. V. Sementovskii. M., 1951, pp. 49-175.

Simpson, Sir George. *Narrative of a Journey Round the World.* London, 1847.

———. *Fur Trade and Empire: George Simpson's Journal, 1824-1825.* Ed. F. Merk. Cambridge, Mass., 1931.

Sirotkin, V. G., comp. "Dokumenty o politike Rossii na Dal'nem Vostoke v nachale XIX veka." *Istoricheskie zapiski* (1962): 85-99.

Sokolov, A. P., ed. "Prigotovlenie krugosvetnoi ekspeditsii 1787 goda pod nachal'stvom Mulovs-kogo." *ZGDMM,* 6 (1848): 142-91.

———. "Ekspeditsii k Aleutskim ostrovam kapitanov Krenitsyna i Levasheva, 1764-1769 godov." *ZGDMM,* 10 (1850): pp. 17-99. Both articles contain much original material.

Spanberg, Morten. Documents in A. Pokrovskii, ed., *Ekspeditsii Beringa: sbornik dokumentov.* M., 1941.

Staehlin, J. von. *An Account of the New Northern Archipelago, Lately Discovered by the Russians in the Seas of Kamtschatka and Anadir.* Translated by C. Heydinger. London, 1774.

Stavorinus, J. *Voyages to the East Indies, by the late John Splinter Stavorinus, esq., Rear-Admiral in the Service of the States-General.* 3 vols. London, 1798.

Steller, G. W. *Beschreibung von dem Lande Kamtschatka, dessen Einwohnern, deren Sitten, Nahmen, Lebensart und verschiedenen Gewohnheiten.* Frankfurt, Leipzig, 1774.

———. "Reise von Kamtschatka nach Amerika mit dem Commandeur-Capitan Bering." In P. S. Pallas. *Neue Nordische Beyträge,* vol. 5. St. P., Leipzig, 1793, pp. 129-236; 6:1-26. Also in *Nordische Beyträge,* for 1793, is Steller's "Tagenbuch seiner Seereise aus dem Petripauls-Hafen in Kamtschatka bis an die westlichen Küsten von America. . . ." Translated by Frank Golder in vol. 2 of his *Bering's Voyages.* (New York, 1925), pp. 9-187.

Strahlenberg, P. J. von. *An Historico-geographical Description of the North and Eastern parts of Europe and Asia, but More Particularly of Russia, Siberia, and Great Tartary.* London, 1738. Translated from original Stockholm ed., 1730.

Strange, James. *James Strange's Journal and Narrative of the Commercial Expedition from Bombay to the North-West Coast of America.* Madras, 1928.

Tarakanoff, V. P. *A Statement of My Captivity Among the Californians.* Los Angeles, 1953.

Tikhmenev, P., comp. *Istoricheskoe obozrenie obrazovaniia Rossiisko-Amerikanskoi Kompanii i deistvii eio do nastoiashchego vremeni.* St. P., 1861-63. Translated by D. Krenov as *The Historical Review of the Formation of the Russian-American Company.* Seattle, 1939-40.

———. *Supplement of Some Historical Documents to the Historical Review of the Formation of the Russian-American Company.* Translated by D. Krenov. Seattle, 1938.

Timofeev, A. I., ed. *Pamiatniki Sibirskoi istorii XVIII veka.* 2 vols. St. P., 1882-85.

Tompkins, S. R., and Moorehead, M. L. "Russia's Approach to America: Part II, From Spanish Sources: 1761-1775," *BCHQ,* 13 (1949): 231-55.

Torrubia, José. *I Moscoviti nella California, o sia dimostrazione della verita del passo all'America Settentrionale nuovamente scoperto dai Russi.* Roma, 1759.

Tumanskii, F., comp. *Sobranie raznykh zapisok i sochinenii, sluzhashchikh k sostavleniiu polnogo svedeniia o zhizni Petra Velikogo.* St. P., 1788.

United States, Congress, Senate. *Proceedings of the Alaskan Boundary Tribunal.* Washington, 1904.

Valaam Monastery. *Ocherk iz istorii Amerikanskoi pravoslavnoi dukhovnoi missii (Kadiakskoi missii 1794-1837 godov).* St. P., 1894.

Veniaminov, I. *Zapiski ob ostrovakh Unalashkinskago otdela.* St. P., 1840.

Veselago, F. F., comp. *Materialy dlia istorii russkogo flota.* 18 vols. St. P., 1880-1904.

Vinius, A. A. 1697 instructions given by B. P. Polevoi, ed., in "Zabytyi nakaz A. A. Viniusa." *Priroda* (1965): no. 5, pp. 4-12.

Vneshniaia politika Rossii XIX veka: dokumenty Rossiiskogo Ministerstva Inostrannykh Del: Seriia I, 1801-1815. Vol. 1. M., 1961.

Vosstanie dekabristov: materialy po istorii vosstaniia dekabristov: dela verkhovnogo ugolovnogo suda i sledstvennoi kommissii. Ed. M. N. Pokrovskii. M.-L., 1925-71.
Vrangel', F. P. Puteshestvie po beregam Sibiri i po Ledovitomu moriu, sovershennoe v 1820-1824 godakh. St. P., 1841.
Waxell, Sven. Vtoraia Kamchatskaia ekspeditsiia Vitusa Beringa. M.-L., 1940.
Witsen, N. Noord en oost Tartarye, behelzende eene beschryving van verscheidene Tartersche en nabuurige gewesten. . . . 2d. ed. Amsterdam, 1705.
Zavalishin, D. I. "Kaliforniia v 1824 godu." Russkii vestnik (1865): 322-68. "Delo o kolonii Ross." Russkii vestnik (1866): 36-65. "Krugosvetnoe plavanie fregata 'Kreiser' v 1822-25 godakh, pod komandoiu Mikhaila Petrovicha Lazareva." Drevniaia i novaia Rossiia (1877): nos. 6, 7, 10, 11.
―――. Zapiski dekabrista. München, 1904.

SECONDARY SOURCES

Adrianov, S. A. "K voprosu o pokorenii Sibiri." ZMNP, 286 (1893): sec. 4, pp. 522-50.
Afanas'ev, D. M. "Rossiisko-Amerikanskie vladeniia." MSb, 71 (1864): no. 3, pp. 5ff.
Aleksandrenko, V. N. Reliatsii kniazia A. P. Kantemira iz Londona, 1732-1733 godov. M., 1892.
―――. Russkie diplomaticheskie agenty v Londone v XVIII veke. Vol. 1. Warsaw, 1797.
Alekseev, A. I. Brat'ia Shmalevy. Magadan, 1958.
―――. Okhotsk-kolybel' russkogo tikhookeanskogo flota. Khabarovsk, 1958.
―――. Gavriil Andreevich Sarychev. M., 1966.
Alekseev, M. P., ed. Sibir' v izvestiiakh puteshestvennikov i pisatelei. 2 vols. Irkutsk, 1932-36.
Anderson, M. S. "Great Britain and the Growth of the Russian Navy in the Eighteenth Century." M.M., 42 (1956): no. 1, pp. 132-46.
―――. Britain's Discovery of Russia, 1553-1815. London, 1958.
Anderson, R. C. "British and American Officers in the Russian Navy." M.M., 32 (1947): 17-27. Incomplete, flawed list.
Andreev, A. I. Russkie otkrytiia v Tikhom okeane v pervoi polovine XVIII veka. M., 1943.
―――. Russkie otkrytiia v Tikhom okeane i Severnoi Amerike v XVIII-XIX vekakh. M., 1944; modified ed. in 1948. Translated by Carl Ginsburg as Russian Discoveries in the Pacific and in North America in the Eighteenth and Nineteenth Centuries. Ann Arbor, 1952.
―――. "Rol' russkogo voenno-morskogo flota v geograficheskikh otkrytiiakh XVIII veka." MSb (1947): no. 4, pp. 34ff.
―――. Ocherki po istochnikovedeniiu Sibiri: vypusk 1, XVII vek. 2d ed. M.-L., 1960.
Andreev, V. A., ed. "Dokumenty po ekspeditsii kapitana-komandora Beringa v Ameriku v 1741 godu." MSb (1893): no. 5, pp. 1-16.
Aslanbegov, A. Admiral Aleksei Samuilovich Greig: biograficheskii ocherk. St. P., 1873.
Azadovskii, M. K. "14 dekabria v pis'makh A. E. Izmailova." Pamiati dekabristov. Vol. 1. L., 1926.
Baer (Ber), K. von. "Zaslugi Petra Velikogo po chasti rasprostraneniia geograficheskikh poznanii o Rossii i pogranichnykh s neiu zemliakh Azii." ZIRGO, 3 (1849): 217-53; 4:260-83.
Bakhrushin, S. V. S. V. Bakhrushin: nauchnye trudy, III. Izbrannye raboty po istorii Sibiri XVI-XVII vekov. M., 1955.
Bancroft, H. H. History of California. San Francisco, 1885.
―――. History of Alaska, 1730-1885. San Francisco, 1886.
Barbashev, N. A. K istorii morekhodnogo obrazovaniia v Rossii. M., 1959.
Barratt, G. R. V. Voices in Exile: The Decembrist Memoirs. Montreal, 1974.
―――. The Rebel on the Bridge: The Life and Times of Baron Andrey Rozen. London, 1975.
―――. "The Russian Interest in Arctic North America: The Kruzenshtern-Romanov Projects, 1819-23." SEER, 53 (1975): no. 130.

————. "Russian Warships in Van Diemen's Land: *Kreyser* and *Ladoga* by Hobart Town, 1823." *SEER,* 53 (1975): no. 133, pp. 566-78.

————. "The Russian Navy and New Holland: Part 1." *JRAHS,* 64 (1979), pt. 4.

————. *Bellingshausen: A Visit to New Zealand, 1820.* Palmerston North, N.Z. 1979.

————. *The Russian Navy and Australia to 1825: The Days Before Suspicion.* Melbourne, 1979.

Basnin, V. N. "O posol'stve v Kitai grafa Golovkina." *Chteniia v Obshchestve Istorii i Drevnostei Rossii* (1875): no. 4, pp. 1-103.

Beaglehole, J. C. *The Exploration of the Pacific.* London, 1947.

Belov, M. I. *Istoriia otkrytiia i osvoeniia Severnogo morskogo puti.* 3 vols. M.-L., 1956-59.

————. *Semen Dezhnev.* 2d ed. M., 1955.

Benton, T. H., comp. *An Abridgement of Debates in the Congress of the United States, 1759-1856.* 16 vols. New York, 1857-63.

Berg, L. S. *Otkrytie Kamchatki i kamchatskie ekspeditsii Beringa.* Petrograd, 1924.

————. "Pervye karty Kamchatki," *IVGO,* 85 (1943): no. 4, pp. 3-67.

————. *Ocherki po istorii russkikh geograficheskikh otkrytii.* 2d ed. M.-L., 1949.

Berkh, V. N. "Poslednee pis'mo o Billingsovoi ekspeditsii k izdateliu Syna Otechestva." *Otechestvennye zapiski,* 62 (1820): no. 10.

————. "Pobeg grafa Ben'evskogo iz Kamchatki vo Frantsiiu." *Syn otechestva,* 71 (1821): nos. 27-28.

————. *Pervoe morskoe puteshestvie Rossiian, predpriniatoe dlia resheniia zadachi, soediniaetsia li Aziia s Amerikoiu* St. P., 1823.

————. "Biograficheskie svedeniia o kapitan-komandore Vituse Beringe." *Severnyi arkhiv,* 6 (1823): no. 8, pp. 11-35.

————. *Khronologicheskaia istoriia otkrytiia Aleutskikh ostrovov, ili podvigi rossiiskogo kupechestva.* St. P., 1823.

————. *Zhizneopisaniia pervykh rossiiskikh admiralov, ili opyt istorii Rossiiskogo Flota.* St. P., 1831-34.

Beskrovnyi, L. G. "Armiia i flot." In *Ocherki istorii S.S.S.R.* M., 1957.

Bezobrazov, V. *Graf F. P. Litke.* St. P., 1888.

Blue, G. V. "French Interest in Pacific America in the Eighteenth Century." *PHR,* 4 (1935): 246-66.

————. "A Rumor of an Anglo-Russian Raid on Japan, 1776." *PHR,* 8 (1939): 453-54.

Bobb, B. *The Viceregency of Antonio Maria Bucareli in New Spain, 1771-1779.* Austin, 1962.

Bogoslovskii, M. M. *Petr pervyi: materialy dlia biografii.* L., 1940-48.

Bolkhovitinov, N. *Stanovlenie russko-amerikanskikh otnoshenii, 1775-1815.* M., 1966.

Boxer, C. R. *The Dutch Seaborne Empire, 1600-1800.* New York, 1965.

————. *The Portuguese Seaborne Empire, 1415-1825.* 3d ed. London, 1973.

Bradley, H. W. "The Hawaiian Islands and the Pacific Fur Trade, 1785-1813." *PNQ,* 30 (1939): 275-99.

————. *The American Frontier in Hawaii: The Pioneers, 1789-1843.* Gloucester, Mass, 1968.

Breitfuss, L. "Early Maps of North-Eastern Asia and of the Lands Around the North Pacific." *Imago mundi,* 3 (1939): 87-99.

Brückner (Brikner), A. *Istoriia Ekateriny II.* St. P., 1885.

————. "Vtoraia polovina XVIII veka v pis'makh brat'ev S. i A. Vorontsovykh." *Vestnik Evropy* (August 1888), bk. 8.

Buache, J. N. *Mémoire sur les pays de l'Asie et de l'Amérique, situés au nord de la Mer du Sud.* Paris, 1775.

Butsinskii, P. *Zaselenie Sibiri, i byt eio pervykh nasel'nikov.* Kharkov, 1889.

Chapman, C. E. *The Founding of Spanish California: The Northwestward Expansion of New Spain, 1687-1773.* New York, 1916.

————. *A History of California: The Spanish Period.* New York, 1921.

Chechulin, N. D. *Vneshniaia politika Rossii v nachale tsarstvovaniia Ekateriny II, 1764-1772.* St. P., 1896.

Chinard, G. *Voyage de Lapérouse sur les côtes de l'Alaska et de la Californie, 1786.* Baltimore, 1937.

Clendenning, P. H. "Admiral Sir Charles Knowles and Russia, 1771-74." *M.M.*, 61 (1975): no. 1, pp. 39-49.

Cook, W. L. *Flood Tide of Empire: Spain and the Pacific Northwest, 1543-1819.* New Haven and London, 1973.

Coxe, William. *An Account of the Russian Discoveries Between Asia and America, to Which Are Added, the Conquest of Siberia and the History of the Transactions and Commerce Between Russia and China.* London, 1780.

Cross, A. G. "Samuel Greig, Catherine the Great's Scottish Admiral." *M.M.*, 60 (1974): no. 3, pp. 251-65.

Davidson, G. C. "The Tracks and Landfalls of Bering and Chirikof on the Northwest Coast of America." *Transactions and Proceedings of the Geographical Society of the Pacific*, 2nd series, 1 (1901): 1-44.

Day, Sir A. *The Admiralty Hydrographic Service, 1795-1919.* London, 1967.

Dening, G. M., ed. *The Marquesan Journals of Edward Robarts, 1797-1824.* Canberra, 1974.

Dermigny, L. *La Chine et l'Occident: le commerce à Canton au XVIIIe siècle.* Paris, 1964.

Dik, N. E. *Deiatel'nost' i trudy M. V. Lomonosova v oblasti geografii.* M., 1961.

Divin, V. A. *Velikii russkii moreplavatel' A. I. Chirikov.* M., 1953.

―――. *K beregam Ameriki.* M., 1956.

―――. "Vtoraia Sibirsko-Tikhookeanskaia ekspeditsiia i voprosy khoziaistvennogo osveshcheniia Dal'nego Vostoka." *Letopis' Severa*, bk. 2. M., 1957.

―――. "O pervykh proektakh russkikh krugosvetnykh plavanii." *Trudy Instituta Istorii Estestvoznaniia i Tekhniki*, 32 (1961): 330ff.

―――. *Russkie moreplavaniia na Tikhom okeane v XVIII veke.* M., 1971.

Dobbs, Arthur. *Observations on the Russian Discoveries . . . by Governor Dobbs.* London, 1754.

Dobrovol'skii, A. D. *Otto fon Kotzebue: russkie moreplavateli.* M., 1953.

Dumitrashko, N. V. "Iu.F. Lisianskii i russkie krugosvetnye puteshestviia." In the 1947 M. ed. of Lisianskii's *Puteshestvie vokrug sveta na korable "Neva."* St. P., 1812.

Engel, Samuel. *Mémoires et observations géographiques et critiques sur la situation des pays septentrionales de l'Asie et de l'Amérique.* Lausanne, 1765.

Essig, E. O. "The Russian Settlement at Ross." *CHSQ*, 12 (1933): 191-209.

Efimov, A. V. "Rossiia i kolonizatsiia Ameriki v pervoi polovine XVIII veka." *Izvestiia AN SSSR: Seriia istorii i filosofii*, 4 (1947): no. 2.

―――. *Iz istorii russkikh ekspeditsii na Tikhom okeane: pervaia polovina XVIII veka.* M., 1948.

Evteev, O. A. *Pervye russkie geodezisty na Tikhom okeane.* M., 1950.

Fainberg, E. Ia. *Russko-Iaponskie otnosheniia v 1697-1875 godakh.* M., 1960.

Faivre, J. P. *L'Expansion française dans le Pacifique, 1800-1842.* Paris, 1960.

Fedorova, S. F. *Russkoe naselenie Aliaski i Kalifornii.* M., 1971.

Fel', S. E. Kartografiia Rossii XVIII veka." *Trudy Instituta Istorii Estestvoznaniia i Tekhniki*, 37 (1961): 248ff.

Fischer, J. E. *Sibirische Geschichte von der Entdeckung Sibiriens bis auf die Eroberung dieses Landes durch die russischen Waffen.* 2 vols. St. P., 1768.

Fisher, R. H. *The Russian Fur Trade, 1550-1700.* Berkeley, 1943.

―――. "Semen Dezhnev and Professor Golder." *PHR*, 25 (1956): 286-94.

Fitzhardinge, V. "Russian Ships in Australian Waters, 1807-1835." *JRAHS*, 51 (1965).

―――. "Russian Naval Visitors to Australia, 1862-1888." *JRAHS*, 52 (1966): pt. 2, pp. 129-58.

Fry, H. T. *Alexander Dalrymple and the Expansion of British Trade.* Toronto, 1970.

Gibson, J. R. "Sables to Sea Otters: Russia Enters the Pacific." *Alaska Review* (1968-69): 203-17.

―――. *Feeding the Russian Fur Trade: Provisionment of the Okhotsk Seaboard and the Kamchatka Peninsula, 1639-1856.* Madison and London, 1969.

―――. *Imperial Russia in Frontier America: The Changing Geography of Supply of Russian America, 1784-1867.* New York, 1976.

Gnucheva, V. F. "Lomonosov i Geograficheskii Departament Akademii Nauk." In *Lomonosov: sbornik statei i materialov.* M.-L., 1940.

_____. *Geograficheskii Departament Akademii Nauk XVIII veka*. M.-L., 1946.
Golder, F. A. "Proposals for Russian Occupation of the Hawaiian Islands." In *Hawaii: Early Relations With England-Russia-France*, ed. A. P. Taylor, R. J. Kuykendall. Honolulu, 1930.
_____. *Russian Expansion on the Pacific, 1641-1850: An Account of the Earliest and Later Expeditions Made by the Russians along the Pacific Coast*. Cleveland, 1914.
_____. *Bering's Voyages: An Account of the Efforts of the Russians to Determine the Relation of Asia and America*. 2 vols. New York, 1922-25.
Goldenberg, L. *Fedor Ivanovich Soimonov, 1692-1780*. M., 1966.
Gordeev, A. A. *Istoriia kazakov*. 4 vols. Paris, 1968-71.
Greely, A. W. "The Cartography and Observations of Bering's First Voyage." *National Geographical Magazine*, 3 (1892): 205-30.
Grekov, V. I. *Ocherki iz istorii russkikh geograficheskikh issledovanii v 1725-1765 godakh*. M., 1960.
Grenader, M. B. "Istoricheskaia obuslovlennost' vozniknoveniia severovostochnoi geograficheskoi ekspeditsii 1785-1795 godov." *Uchonye zapiski Petropavlovskogo Gos. Pedagogicheskogo Instituta* (1957): bk. 2, pp. 55-72.
_____. "Poslednie gody deiatel 'nosti T. I. Shmaleva." *Letopis' Severa*, 7 (1975): 93-113.
Guerrier (Ger'e), V. *Leibnitz in seinem Beziehungen zu Russland und Peter dem Grossen: eine geschichtliche Darstellung*. Leipzig, 1873.
Gvozdetskii, N. A. "Pervoe morskoe puteshestvie Rossiian vokrug sveta." *Priroda* (1947): no.1, pp. 85-88.
Hernandez y Sanchez-Barba, M. "Espagnoles, Rusos e Ingleses en el Pacifico Norte, durante el Siglo XVIII." *Informacion juridica*, 121 (1953): 549-66.
_____. *La ultima Expansion Espagnola en America*. Madrid, 1957.
Howay, F. W. "An Outline Sketch of the Maritime Fur Trade." Canadian Historical Association, *Annual Report* (1932): 5-14.
_____. "Letters Concerning Voyages of British Vessels to the Northwest Coast of America, 1787-1809." *OHQ*, 39 (1938): 307-13.
_____. *A List of Trading Vessels in the Maritime Fur Trade, 1785-1825*. Ed. with an introduction by R. A. Pierce. Kingston, Ont., 1973.
Huculak, M. *When Russia Was in America: The Alaska Boundary Treaty Negotiations, 1824-25, and the Rôle of Pierre de Poletica*. Vancouver, Mitchell Press, 1971. Ukrainian nationalist emphasis, but contains useful data.
Ikonnikov, S. *Graf N. S. Mordvinov*. St. P., 1873.
Iurtsovskii, N. S. *Ocherki po istorii prosveshcheniia Sibiri*. Novo-Nikolaevsk, 1923.
Ivanovskii, A. D. *Gosudarstvennyi kantsler graf Nikolai Petrovich Rumiantsev: biograficheskii ocherk*. St. P., 1871.
Ivashintsev, N. A. *Russkie krugosvetnye puteshestviia s 1803 po 1849 god*. St. P., 1872. Translated by G. R. V. Barratt, *Russian Voyages of Circumnavigation*. Kingston, Ont., 1980.
Kabanov, P. I. *Amurskii vopros*. Blagoveshchensk, 1959.
Kaempfer, E. *The History of Japan, Giving an Account of the Antient and Present State and Government of that Empire, translated by J. C. Scheuchzer*. London, 1728.
Kanagev, S. "Okhotsk." *Severnoe obozrenie*, 3 (1850): 363-84.
Kerner, R. J. *The Urge to the Sea: The Course of Russian History. The Role of Rivers, Portages, Ostrogs, Monasteries and Furs*. Berkeley, 1942.
Kliuchevskii, V. O. *A History of Russia*. Translated by C. J. Hogarth. New York, 1960.
Kramp, F. G., ed. *Remarkable Maps of the XV, XVI and XVII Centuries*. Amsterdam, 1897.
Krause, Aurel. *The Tlingit Indians*. Translated by E. Gunther. Seattle, 1956.
Kurts, B. *Russko-kitaiskie snosheniia v 16, 17 i 18 stoletiiakh*. Kharkov, 1929.
Kushnarev, E. G. "Nereshennye voprosy pervoi kamchatskoi ekspeditsii." In *Russkie arkticheskie ekspeditsii XVII-XX vekov*. L., 1964.
Kuykendall, R. *The Hawaiian Kingdom, 1778-1854*. Honolulu, 1938.
Kuznetsova, V. V. "Novye dokumenty o russkoi ekspeditsii k Severnomu poliusu," *IVGO* (1968): no. 3, pp. 237-45.
Lagus, V. *Erik Laksman: ego zhizn', puteshestviia, issledovaniia i perepiska*. St. P., 1890. Translated from Swedish ed.

Lantzeff, G. V. *Siberia in the Seventeenth Century: A Study of the Colonial Administration*. Berkeley, 1943. Reprinted 1972.

———, and Pierce, R. A. *Eastward to Empire: Exploration and Conquest on the Russian Open Frontier, to 1750*. Montreal, 1973.

Lauridsen, P. *Vitus Bering: The Discoverer of Bering Strait*. Translated by J. E. Olsen. Chicago, 1889. Apologetic work.

Lebedev, D. M. *Geografiia v Rossii petrovskogo vremeni*. M.-L., 1950.

———. *Plavanie A. I. Chirikova na paketbote "Sv. Pavel" k poberezh'iam Ameriki*. M., 1951.

Lensen, G. A. *The Russian Push toward Japan: Russo-Japanese Relations, 1697-1875*. Princeton, 1959.

Levin, M. G., and Potapov, L. P., eds. *Narody Sibiri*. M., 1956. English translation, *The Peoples of Siberia*. Chicago, 1964.

Longstaff, F. V. "Spanish Naval Bases and Ports on the Pacific Coast of Mexico, 1513-1833." *BCHQ*, 16 (1952): 181-89.

Mahan, A. T. *The Influence of Sea Power Upon History, 1660-1783*. London, 1890.

Mahr, A. C. *The Visit of the "Rurik" to San Francisco in 1816*. Stanford, 1932, pp. 267-460.

Makarova, R. V. *Russkie na Tikhom okeane vo vtoroi polovine XVIII veka*. M., 1968. Translated by R. A. Pierce and A. S. Donnelly as *Russians on the Pacific, 1743-1799*. Kingston, Ont., 1975.

Maltebriun, V. "O plavanii vokrug sveta korablei 'Nadezhda' i 'Neva' 1803-1806 godov." *Vestnik Evropy*, 121 (1822): no. 1.

Marshall, J. *Royal Navy Biography*. 5 vols. London, 1824.

Masterton, J. R. "Bering's Successors, 1745-80: Contributions of Peter Simon Pallas to the History of Russian Exploration Toward Alaska." *PNQ*, 38 (1947): 35-83, 109-55.

Mazour, A. G. "Dr. Yegor Scheffer: Dreamer of a Russian Empire in the Pacific." *PHR*, 6 (1937): 15-20.

———. "The Russian-American Company: Private or Government Enterprise?" *PHR*, 13 (1944): 168-73.

———. "The Russian-American and Anglo-Russian Conventions, 1824-1825: An Interpretation." *PHR*, 16 (1945): 303-10.

Mehnert, K. *The Russians in Hawaii, 1804-1819*. Honolulu, 1939.

Mel'nitskii, P. *Admiral Rikord i ego sovremenniki*. St. P., 1856.

Miliukov, P. *Gosudarstvennoe khoziaistvo Rossii v pervoi chertverti XVIII veka*. St. P., 1892.

Mitchell, D. W. *A History of Russian and Soviet Seapower*. London, 1974.

Mitchell, M. *The Maritime History of Russia, 1848-1948*. New York, 1949.

Morison, S. E. *The Maritime History of Massachusetts, 1783-1860*. 4th ed. Boston, 1961.

Morse, H. B., ed. *Chronicles of the East India Company Trading to China, 1635-1834*. 5 vols. Cambridge, 1926-29.

Nebol'sin, P. I. *Pokorenie Sibiri*. St. P., 1849.

Nevskii, V. V. *Pervoe puteshestvie Rossiian vokrug sveta*. M., 1951.

Nichols, I. C. "The Russian Ukase and the Monroe Doctrine: A Re-evaluation." *PHR*, 36 (1967): 13-26.

Novakovskii, S. I. *Iaponiia i Rossiia*. Tokyo, 1918.

Ogloblin, N. N. "Pervyi iaponets v Rossii, 1701-1705." *Russkaia starina*, 72 (1891): no. 10, pp. 11-24.

Ogorodnikov, V. I. *Ocherki istorii Sibiri do nachala XIX veka*. Vladivostok, 1924.

Okladnikov, A. P., ed. *Istoriia Sibiri: tom vtoroi: Sibir' v sostave feodal'noi Rossii*. M., 1968.

Okun', S. B., ed., "Tsarskaia Rossiia i Gavaiskie ostrova." *Krasnyi arkhiv*, nos. 5, 6. M., 1936.

———. *Rossiisko-Amerikanskaia Kompaniia*. M., 1939. Translated by Carl Ginsburg as *The Russian-American Company*. Cambridge, Mass., 1951.

Pavlenko, N. I. *Razvitie metallurgicheskoi promyshlennosti Rossii v pervoi polovine XVIII veka*. M.-L., 1953.

Pavlov-Sil'vanskii, N. *Proekty reform v zapiskakh sovremennikov Petra I*. St. P., 1897.

Pekarskii, P. N. *Nauka i literatura pri Petre Velikom*. St. P., 1862.

———. *Istoriia Imperatorskoi Akademii Nauk*. St. P., 1870.

Perkins, D.   "Russia and the Spanish Colonies, 1817-1818." *AHR*, 28 (1923): 656-73.
Platonov, S. F.   *Proshloe russkogo severa*. Berlin, 1924.
Polonskii, A. S.   "Pervaia Kamchatskaia ekspeditsiia Beringa, 1725-29 godov." *ZGDMM*, 8 (1850); slightly revised version in *Otechestvennye zapiski*, 75 (1851): pt. 8, pp. 1-24.
_____.   "Kurily." *ZIRGO*, po otdeleniiu etnografii, 4 (1871): pp. 367-576.
Priestly, H. I.   *José de Galvez, Visitor-General of New Spain, 1765-71*. Berkeley, 1916.
Porter, K. W.   "The Cruise of Astor's Brig 'Pedler,' 1813-1816.' *OHQ*, 31 (1930): 223-30.
Raeff, M.   *Siberia and the Reforms of 1822*. Washington, 1955.
Ramming, M.   "Uber den Anteil der Russen an der Eröffnung Japans für den Verkehr mit den Westlichen Mächten." *Mitteilungen der Deutschen Gesellschaft für Natur- und Völkerkunde Ostasiens*, 21 (1926): pt. B.
Ratto, H.   *La Expedicion de Malaspina*. Buenos Aires, 1945.
Rea, R.   "John Blankett and the Russian Navy, 1774." *M.M.*, 41 (1955): 245-49.
Reading, D. K.   *The Anglo-Russian Commercial Treaty of 1734*. New Haven, 1938.
Rikord, L. I.   *Admiral P. I. Rikord: biograficheskii ocherk*. St. P., 1875.
Rozina, L. G.   "Kollektsiia Muzeia Antropologii i Etnografii po Markizskim ostrovam." *Sbornik Muzeia Antropologii i Etnografii*, 21 (1963): 110-19.
_____.   "Kollektsiia Dzhemsa Kuka v sobraniiakh Muzeia Antropologii i Etnografii," *Sbornik Muzeia Antropologii i Etnografii*, 23 (1966).
Savin, A. S.   "Okhotsk." *ZGDMM*, 9 (1851): 148-61.
Scheltema, J.   *Rusland en de Nederlanden beschouwd in derzelver wederkeerige betrekkingen, door Mr. Jacobus Scheltema*. 3 vols. Amsterdam, 1817-19.
Semenov, V.   *Siberia: Its Conquest and Development*. Translated by J. R. Foster. Baltimore, 1963.
Sergeev, M. A.   *Kuril'skie ostrova*. M., 1947.
Sgibnev, A. S.   "Navigatskie shkoly v Sibiri." *MSb*, 87 (1866): no. 11, pp. 3-44.
_____.   "Bol'shoi Kamchatskii Nariad: ekspeditsiia El'china." *MSb*, 95 (1868): no. 12.
_____.   "Popytki russkikh k zavedeniiu torgovykh snoshenii s Iaponieiu v XVIII i nachale XIX stoletii." *MSb*, 100 (1869): no. 7.
_____.   "Okhotskii port s 1649 po 1852 god." *MSb*, 105 (1869): no. 11, pp. 1-92; no. 12, pp. 1-63.
_____.   "Istoricheskii ocherk glavneishikh sobytii v Kamchatke, 1650-1856 godov." *MSb*, 105 (1869): nos. 4-8.
_____.   "Bunt Ben'evskogo v Kamchatke v 1771 godu." *Russkaia starina*, 15 (1876): 526-42, 757-69.
Shakhovskoi, A.   "Izvestiia o Gizhiginskoi kreposti." *Severnyi arkhiv*, 4 (1822): 283-312.
Shashkov, S. S.   "Rossiisko-Amerikanskaia Kompaniia." In *Sobranie sochinenii S. S. Shashkova*. St. P., 1898, 2:632-52.
Shunkov, V. I.   *Ocherki po istorii kolonizatsii Sibiri v XVII-nachale XVIII vekov*. M.-L., 1946.
Shur, L. A.   *K beregam Novogo Sveta*. M., 1971.
Shternberg, L.Ia.   "Etnografiia." In *Tikhii okean: russkie nauchnye issledovaniia*. L., 1926, pp. 148ff.
Shteinberg, E. L.   *Zhizneopisanie russkogo moreplavatelia Iu.F. Lisianskogo*. M., 1948.
Silin, E. P.   *Kiakhta v XVIII veke*. Irkutsk, 1947.
Slovtsov, P. A.   *Istoricheskoe obozrenie Sibiri*. St. P., 1886.
Smirnov, V., ed.   *Leonard Eiler: perepiska: annotirovannyi ukazatel'*. L., 1967.
Sokol, A. E.   "Russian Expansion and Exploration in the Pacific." *SEER*, 11 (1952): 85-105.
Sokolov, A.   *Proekt Lomonosova i ekspeditsiia Chichagova 1765 goda*. St. P., 1854.
Soler, A. M.   *Die Spanisch-Russischen Beziehungen im 18-em Jahrhundert*. Wiesbaden, 1970.
Solov'ev, S. M.   *Istoriia Rossii s drevneishikh vremen*. 29 vols. in 7. St. P., 1895?
Steuart, A. F.   *Scottish Influences in Russian History*. Glasgow, 1913.
Svet, Ia.M., ed.   *Tret'e plavanie kapitana Dzhemsa Kuka: plavanie v Tikhom okeane v 1776-1780 godakh*. M., 1971.
Taylor, G. P.   "Spanish-Russian Rivalry in the Pacific, 1769-1820." *The Americas*, 25 (1958): 109-27.
Tompkins, S. R.   *Alaska, Promyshlennik and Sourdough*. Norman, Okla., 1945.

Trusevich, K.   *Posol'skie i torgovye otnosheniia Rossii s Kitaiem.* M., 1882.

Ustrialov, N.   *Istoriia tsarstvovaniia Petra Velikogo.* St. P., 1858.

Veselago, F. F.   *Ocherk russkoi morskoi istorii.* St. P., 1875.

————.   *Admiral Ivan Fedorovich Kruzenshtern.* St. P., 1869.

————.   *Spisok russkikh voennykh sudov, s 1668 po 1860 god.* St. P., 1852.

————.   *Kratkaia istoriia russkogo flota.* M., 1939.

Vila Vilar, E.   *Los rusos en America.* Seville, 1966.

Vishnevskii, B. N.   *Puteshestvennik Kirill Khlebnikov.* Perm, 1957.

Vize, V.Iu.   *Moria Sovetskoi Arktiki: ocherki po istorii issledovaniia.* 2d. ed. L., 1939.

————.   *Uspekhi russkikh v issledovanii Arktiki.* M., 1948.

Voenskii, K.   "Russkoe posol'stvo v Iaponiiu v nachale XIX veka." *Russkaia starina,* 84 (1895): 123-41, 201-35.

Volkl, E.   *Russland und Lateinamerika, 1741-1841.* Wiesbaden, 1968.

Wagner, H. R.   "Apocryphal Voyages to the Northwest Coast of America." *PAAS,* n.s., 41 (1931): 179-234.

————.   *The Cartography of the Northwest Coast of America to the Year 1800.* 2 vols. Berkeley, 1937.

————.   "The Creation of Rights of Sovereignty through Symbolic Acts." *PHR,* 7 (1938): 297-326.

Wheeler, M. E.   "Empires in Conflict and Co-operation: The Bostonians and the Russian-American Company." *PHR,* 40 (1971): 419-41.

Williams, G.   *The British Search for the Northwest Passage in the Eighteenth Century.* London, 1962.

Winter, O. F.   *Repertorium der diplomatischen Vertreter aller Länder, 1764-1815.* Graz, 1965.

Zagoskin, N. P.   *Russkie vodnye puti i sudovoe delo v dopetrovskoi Rossii.* Kazan', 1909.

Zakharov, V. A.   "M. V. Lomonosov i russkoe nauchnoe moreplavanie." *Morskoi Flot* (1948): nos. 7-8, 66-71.

Znamenskii, S.   *V poiskakh Iaponii: iz istorii russkikh geograficheskikh otkrytii i morekhodstva v Tikhom okeane.* Vladivostok, 1929.

Index

1. People

3. Ships and Vessels